EXPLORING THE HEART

Discoveries in Heart Disease and High Blood Pressure

Exploring the Heart

Discoveries in Heart Disease and High Blood Pressure

JULIUS H. COMROE, JR., M.D.

W. W. NORTON & COMPANY
New York   *London*

The text of this book is composed in Caledonia,
with display type set in Tiffany.
Composition and manufacturing by
The Maple-Vail Book Manufacturing Group
Book design by Winston Potter

First Edition

Library of Congress Cataloging in Publication Data

Comroe, Julius Hiram, 1911–
    Exploring the Heart: Discoveries in Heart Disease and High Blood Pressure
    Includes index.
    1. Medical research—History.   2. Medical in-
novations—History.   I. Title.
R852.C55 1983   610′.9   83-2145

ISBN 0-393-01708-7

W. W. Norton & Company, Inc., 500 Fifth Avenue, New York, N.Y. 10110
W. W. Norton & Company Ltd., 37 Great Russell Street, London WC1B 3NU

1 2 3 4 5 6 7 8 9 0

To Robert Dunning Dripps,
my colleague in our "research on
research" until his sudden death
in October 1973.

Contents

Acknowledgments

I express my appreciation to the Barra Foundation (Robert McNeil, president, and Regina Ryan, consulting editor) both for a grant and for critical advice; to Aida Cordano for invaluable library search and research; to Marilee Fisher for her expert typing and seemingly endless correcting and retyping—cheerfully, even without the luxury of a word processor; to my wife for her unrelenting search for and elimination of biomedical jargon, for critical readings of each draft, and for correcting galleys (as "galley slave"); and to my associates in the University of California, San Francisco's Cardiovascular Research Institute and colleagues in many countries for suggestions and for making original or hard–to–find material available to me.

J.H.C.

EXPLORING THE HEART

Discoveries in Heart Disease and High Blood Pressure

1

Introduction

This is a book about discovery in medicine and surgery and how some important discoveries have come about. I have written it in English stripped clean of all scientific language and jargon, because I intend it for mainly the lay public and only for those physicians and medical scientists who understand lay language and are what I call "bilingual." Despite the increasing number of television programs and newspaper columns that deal with human health and disease, most of the public is unaware of *how* discoveries in medicine and surgery actually occur. Yet the story of how living bodies work and how these workings were discovered is one of the most exciting and fascinating on earth; no science fiction writer at his very best would have had the imagination and ingenuity to invent a whole functioning living human body.

Why this unawareness? Partly because of medical scientists. Although collectively they are prolific writers and turn out about 250,000 articles a year in more than 4,000 scientific journals published in more than 100 countries, their articles are presented in a specially prescribed sequence, IMRAD (introduction, methods, results, and discussion), and in a special, highly compressed language of jargon and abbreviations ("alphabet soup"). Strictly verboten by editors of almost all medical journals is the scientist telling his readers what stimulated him to do his research or make his observations, or admitting his failures, wrong starts, and disappointments, or recounting how he finally got on the right track. Editors frown upon speculating on the significance of an author's work to those in closely related fields, attempting to interest an even wider audience, and promoting public understanding of science. Why these restrictions? Partly to reduce the lengths of articles and costs of publication, and partly because of scientific ethics, the scientist's modesty, and the widely accepted maxim "A good scientist never goes beyond his facts."

Also responsible for public unawareness of paths to discovery are physicians and surgeons themselves. For example, on December 24, 1967, Christiaan Barnard of South Africa and two eminent American cardiac surgeons "faced the nation" on Martin Agronsky's special one-hour television program "Transplantation of the Human Heart." The four of them spoke for one hour to what must have been the largest American audience ever to watch a program dealing with health and disease. Yet not once did any of the three surgeons, or the moderator, neither on the program nor in the transcript, reveal to this huge audience a single fragment of prior research essential to successful cardiac surgery, or pay even a five-second tribute to the decades of basic research by thousands of scientists in many countries that made it possible for a surgeon to even consider transplanting a human heart.

Part of the blame for the public's unawareness must also go to those writers for television and newspapers who are specially trained to enlighten the public. This seems paradoxical because both media devote many hours or columns to human health and disease. Perhaps the scriptwriter or science reporter believes that he knows best what his mass audience wants to know, that he can interest the public only in "breakthroughs," and that to maintain his ratings he must feed his public one a day. Furthermore, it appears that the breakthrough must be the work of no more than one or two heroes so as not to befuddle his audience. And so the public believes that one man, Edison, invented motion pictures (though he really did not), that Marconi invented the wireless (though he really did not), that Fleming discovered penicillin (though he really did not), and that Salk discovered polio vaccine (though he really did not). As a result, we are kept ignorant of the tremendous effort on the part of many earlier workers—in many disciplines, countries, and decades—who produced the knowledge necessary to make the discovery inevitable. Lord Ritchie-Calder distinguished between those who "made it *possible*" and those who "made it *happen*." The public knows only the one who "made it happen" and it is *he* who becomes forevermore the *discoverer*. Yet for polio vaccine the Nobel Prize went to three (of many) who "made it possible"; their names are not household words. I am sure that many a television scriptwriter or science reporter did have his story right, but the constraints of time or space and the autocrats of the cutting room, by deleting mention of those who made the discovery *possible*, helped to create a single hero.

The public is well aware of the tremendous advances in surgical operations on the heart and blood vessels (including open heart surgery, cardiac transplantation, and replacing damaged valves and clogged coronary arteries with new ones); the cardiac surgeon is at the very top of the mountain. But the public does not know how he got there: Did he suddenly cry, "Eureka!" and, in one mighty Superman leap, jump from sea level to the top of the highest peak? (Fig. 1.1). Or did he go up the steps at the back of the mountain laboriously carved over centuries by hundreds of scientists working in many countries and in a dozen or more disciplines? (Fig. 1.2). He did, in fact, go up the back of the mountain.

Let's emphasize a few of these steps on the long road up. When general anesthesia was discovered in 1842 and then rediscovered and put into widespread use in 1846, the practice of surgery exploded in many directions, except for surgery on the heart and lungs—organs wholly within the chest. Cardiac surgery did not take off until almost 100 years later, and the first successful operation on an open heart, with an outside-the-body artificial heart–lung completely taking over the function of the patient's own heart, did not occur until 107 years after ether anesthesia was widely available. What held back cardiac surgery? What was required before a surgeon could predictably and successfully repair defects in the heart or coronary arteries? Most surgeons would answer that the laboratory was an absolute requirement; but they do not mean a "discovery" laboratory but, rather, the surgical animal laboratory, where surgeons practice and perfect their technical skills. Surgical techniques are, of course, important, but what the public really needs to know is what *knowledge* had to be acquired before open heart surgery could become a routinely successful procedure.

First, of course, was learning how to bypass the heart and lungs with an outside-the-body artificial heart–lung. This was essential because intricate operations required that the surgeon work on a completely motionless, nonbeating heart. As we shall see, a young surgeon, John Gibbon, took fifteen years out of his life to build and test such a device— between 1933 and 1952 (that's nineteen years; the army took four of the nineteen). So our question now becomes, Why Gibbon? Why did he begin work in 1933? What did he need to know (knowledge already accumulated by others before him) to build his machine? He needed the following:

A pump whose design and material would not damage red blood cells

A completely safe way of keeping blood from clotting in his artificial outside-the-body heart–lung

The basic discovery of the existence of human blood groups that led to blood typing, which for the first time permitted a physician to transfuse blood safely from donor to recipient and provided the surgeon with safe blood to use in pump–oxygenators

Basic knowledge of red blood cells, their life-span in the body, and how to preserve their life outside the body—knowledge that led to the storage of blood for emergencies and then to blood banks

Basic knowledge of the processes of diffusion and exchange of oxygen and carbon dioxide across the lungs

But even after Gibbon devised a machine that worked like a charm in an anesthetized animal, he needed to know a lot more before he could operate on a patient whose heart needed repair. He needed the following:

New diagnostic techniques, to supplement clinical judgment, to tell him exactly where and what the damage was. These required the previous discovery of X rays, the electrocardiograph, and the technique of cardiac catheterization (passing a long, slender tube along a vein into a cardiac chamber to withdraw samples of blood for chemical analysis and to inject liquids that stopped X rays and permitted visualization of a cardiac defect).

General anesthesia and knowledge of how to administer this to a patient with an open thorax (chest).

Knowledge of how to stop the heartbeat long enough to complete even a very long operation on an open heart, with the certain knowledge that at the end of the operation, he could start the heart again and be sure that it would continue to beat normally.

The new sciences of bacteriology and knowledge of bacterial infections, chemotherapy, and antibiotics.

Knowledge of techniques of tissue preservation, tissues ready to serve when needed as patches or substitutes for diseased parts.

Figure 1.1. Did the cardiac surgeon make one giant leap to the pinnacle?

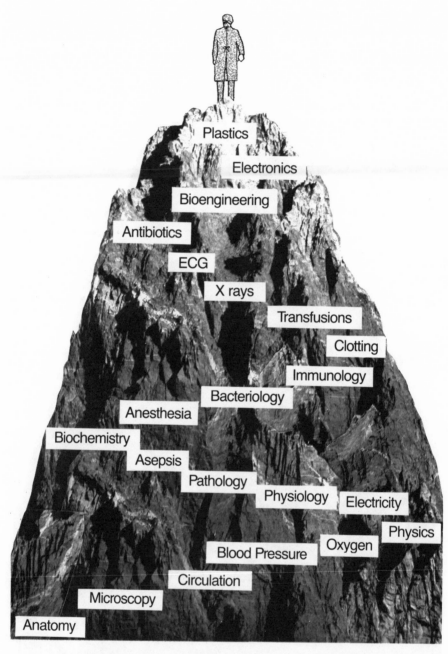

Figure 1.2.   Or did he climb the steps up the back of the mountain?

Knowledge of how to construct artificial heart valves and use them to replace irreparably damaged human valves.

Knowledge of how to suture large and small blood vessels, joining them end to end or side to end.

How many patients who have undergone open heart surgery know of the tremendous efforts of many scientists through the years that provided the basic and practical knowledge which was essential for their successful operation? Not many, if any, and I doubt if any hospital staff has taken time to educate their captive patients recovering from an operation on their coronary arteries.

In 1970, Dr. Robert Dripps, Vice-President for Medical Affairs at the University of Pennsylvania, and I began what we thought was a useful way of spending a sabbatical year: studying systematically how the great modern discoveries in medicine and surgery had in fact come about—the events and forces that promoted progress and those that held it back. We soon learned that it was not a one-year job, but at least a ten-year one. So we decided to limit our study largely to discoveries in heart and lung disease. After Dr. Dripps' untimely death in 1973, I continued for four more years the study of more than 6,000 scientific reports that contributed eventually to modern advances in medicine and surgery.

This book deals only with the development of knowledge essential for modern advances in the diagnosis and treatment of diseases of the heart and arteries and of high blood pressure, but diseases of the heart and blood vessels (including many types of heart disease, narrowing of the coronary and cerebral arteries, arteriosclerosis, and high blood pressure) are our number 1 killers. In 1980 they accounted for 1,020,150 deaths in the United States, as many as *all other causes combined:* A total of 51% of all peacetime deaths were due to cardiovascular disorders; deaths from cancer were way behind (25%) and deaths from accidents (5%) and from hundreds of other causes (19%) added together made up the other 24%. Because more than 50% of the population will eventually die from one of the disorders discussed in the eight chapters in this book, readers should have a direct interest in learning how medicine and surgery have progressed this far and what remains to be discovered in future years.

I have told you a bit about what this book *is.* I think it equally important to tell you what it is *not:*

It is not a "how-to" or "what-to-do" book.

It is not a book on "health maintenance," the "delivery of health care," or the "costs of health care."

It is not a complete textbook of medicine for the layman.

It is not even a complete textbook of cardiology for the layman.

It is not a complete account of all the new knowledge in cardiac surgery, blood vessel surgery, and high blood pressure that led to better diagnosis and treatment. (If it were, you wouldn't be able to lift this book, let alone pay for it.) Nor is it a collection of anecdotes selected to "prove" a point of view.

It is not a preaching book, but I do have convictions, based on my study, on what is important for progress in medicine and surgery.

In this introductory chapter I will mention only two of my convictions. The first is that neither the government nor voluntary health agencies can order up specific medical discoveries on a specific schedule as one would order a McDonald's hamburger or even as one would plan for the takeoff of a space shuttle. In 1964, the National Heart Institute, with the encouragement of a distinguished Nobel laureate, did draw up a crash program for construction of an artificial heart with an energy source to be completely implantable *within* a patient's chest. The schedule called for contracts to be signed by July 1, 1965, and the first artificial heart to be implanted in a needy patient on Saint Valentine's Day, February 14 (not February 13 or 15), 1970 (not 1971 or 1972). It is now 1983, and a totally implantable artificial heart (all inside the body, including the source of energy) is still not in sight. True, a first step was taken in Salt Lake City on December 2, 1982, when surgeons removed Barney Clark's dying heart and replaced it with an inside-the-chest plastic heart; however, the compressed air power source remained completely outside Clark's body, connected to his plastic heart by tubes. Dr. Clark suffered from a variety of complications and died six weeks after the operation. This was a dramatic operation and may someday be successful for a longer period; however, the experience emphasizes that the ideal solution is to learn the basic causes and prevention of heart disease so we no longer have need for a totally implantable artificial heart.

Not to be outdone by the National Heart Institute, Congress resolved on July 15, 1970, "that it is the sense of the Congress that the conquest of cancer is a national crusade to be accomplished by 1976 as an appropriate commemoration of the two-hundredth anniversary of our country." Six years for the cure of cancer! The year 1976 is past, many billions of dollars have come and gone, and cancer is still here. A story that may be apocryphal is appropriate here. At a party, an aristocratic young Englishwoman informed George Bernard Shaw that she was planning an evening of entertainment for a charity, and loftily suggested that as his contribution to the festivities he "dash off a little play" for her. Shaw replied, "I should be delighted. But you must do me a favor in return. As you know, I am childless. Would you dash off a little baby for me?"

My second conviction is that although we've come a long way, areas of ignorance of how cells, tissues, and organs of the body function in health and disease greatly outnumber our areas of full knowledge. Benjamin Franklin wrote, "The doorstep to the temple of wisdom is knowledge of our own ignorance," and much later, Ronald Duncan and Miranda Weston-Smith in their 1978 *Encyclopedia of Ignorance* wrote, "Compared to the pond of knowledge, our ignorance is atlantic." We still have a long way to go.

For the rest, I prefer that you read, do some thinking, draw your own conclusions, and raise some questions of your own. George Santayana said, "Those who do not remember the past are condemned to repeat it"; here is some of the past—what can we learn from it? I do not believe that study of the past enables us to predict the future, but it does put a spotlight on mistakes and missed opportunities to help us avoid them in the years ahead.

2

The Need for an Artificial Heart

The story of modern open heart surgery began with the heart–lung machine, and the story of the heart–lung machine began on October 3, 1930, at Massachusetts General Hospital in Boston. A patient there, Edith S., was recovering nicely from a fairly routine gallbladder operation when she suddenly had a queer feeling in her right chest followed almost immediately by a sharp pain there. Within minutes she became pale and apprehensive and labored for each breath; her pulse became weak and rapid and her blood pressure dropped 50 points. All of these signs pointed to a dreaded complication: A blood clot, formed in a vein in her leg or abdomen during the operation on her gallbladder or while she was confined to complete bed rest afterward, had broken loose and traveled with venous blood flowing upward into the right side of her heart; it was then propelled by the right ventricle into the pulmonary artery, where it had lodged, blocking free flow of blood from the right heart to the lungs (Fig. 2.1).

When a clot forms in a leg or abdominal vein, it does little or no harm if it remains permanently anchored to the wall of the vein. If, however, it breaks loose and is free, it moves upward with the venous blood, entering larger and larger veins, until it reaches the right atrium, the reservoir for the right ventricle. From there it passes through the tricuspid valve (the opening between the atrium and the ventricle) into the right ventricle. Contraction of the right ventricle closes the tricuspid valve, opens the pulmonic valve, and pushes blood into the main pulmonary artery or trunk that conducts blood to all parts of the lungs.

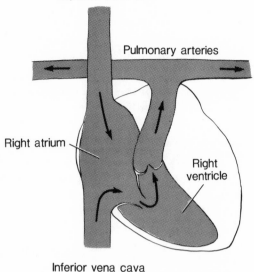

Figure 2.1. **The right side of the heart. The arrows show the direction of the flow of venous blood (shaded area) in the upper and lower large veins (venae cavae) that bring blood from tissues to the right atrium and right ventricle. They then show the course of this blood after it is propelled by contraction of the right ventricle into the main pulmonary arteries to the lungs. The contours of the entire heart, including the left atrium and left ventricle, are shown by the unshaded area. Edith S.'s blood clot blocked the main pulmonary trunk and both the right and left pulmonary arteries.**

Until it enters the pulmonary trunk, the free-floating clot moves in ever-widening channels; however, once in the pulmonary trunk, it must enter ever-*narrowing* channels and sooner or later partially or completely block a vessel. Clots blocking both pulmonary arteries or the main pulmonary trunk cause death in a few minutes because blood flow comes to a standstill everywhere. Clots blocking the pulmonary trunk only partly, or lodged only in the right or left pulmonary artery, still permit blood to circulate.

"Well," you will say, "off to the operating room, open the patient's chest, slit the pulmonary trunk, and remove the clot." In 1960 and beyond, yes; but the year was 1930 and for the previous 2,000 years the heart had been forbidden territory for surgeons. In 350 B.C., Aristotle, the great Greek scholar whose influence dominated Western science and philosophy for more than 1,000 years, stated solemnly, "The heart alone of all viscera cannot withstand injury." Even in 1883, Europe's most renowned surgeon, Christian Albert Theodor Billroth, pronounced, "A surgeon who tries to suture a wound in the heart deserves to lose the esteem of his colleagues."* So surgeons for many centuries believed in the absolute vulnerability of the heart to surgical procedures and even to touching. No one dared to challenge the Greek philoso-

---

*Every great man is entitled to a mistake or two. Billroth made two. He was also a vigorous opponent of Lord Lister's surgical asepsis.

pher–scientist or the eminent European surgeon until 1897, when a German surgeon, Ludwig Rehn, sewed up a wound in a man's heart and the patient survived, and in 1902, when Dr. Luther L. Hill of Alabama, whose son, Lister Hill, was later to become U.S. Senator from Alabama and a founder of the National Heart Institute, again challenged authority and successfully closed a stab wound in the heart of a 13-year-old boy. But neither operation led to a flood of surgical procedures on the heart. Considering that ether was discovered in the 1840s, this is surprising at first thought, because general anesthesia for the first time in history freed patients from surgeon-induced pain and gave all surgeons a new and priceless tool: time—time for slow, careful work, time to permit more challenging operations, and time to perform longer procedures. Before the advent and use of ether, the surgeon's most precious asset was speed; amputations, for example, had been clocked, from start to finish, in as little as 29 seconds!

But even after the discovery of anesthesia, time did not solve the problems of the surgeon who elected to operate on the heart, because the heart pumps about 10 pints of blood each minute and every cell in the body depends on the continuous flow of this blood. If the surgeon deliberately stops the flow of blood, the patient's brain will die in about 6 minutes, and 6 minutes is rarely long enough for even the simplest of operations on the heart. But if the surgeon cannot stop the flow of blood for fear of killing the patient, neither can he cut into the heart while it is still pumping blood; he would then have the almost impossible task of operating in a sea of blood, with more spurting into the chest with each heartbeat.

Nevertheless, surgeons had been trying since the early 1900s to remove blood clots that block or almost block the pulmonary arteries. Paul Trendelenburg, a famous German surgeon, wrote in 1912, "Twelve times we have done it at the clinic, my assistants oftener than myself, and not once with success. And yet, I would continue trying." There was, at last, a single success in 1924, but by 1930 only 8 of 141 patients operated upon by European surgeons had survived Trendelenburg's type of operation, and none of 14 patients had survived such operations at Boston's Massachusetts General Hospital and Peter Bent Brigham Hospital, among the best in the United States. Even as late as 1944, Albert Ochsner, a leading American surgeon, stated, "I hope we will not have any more reports on the removal of pulmonary emboli—an operation which should be of historic interest only."

Let us now go back to October 3, 1930, to Edith S. with a known pulmonary embolus and to Dr. Edward Churchill, surgeon at Massachusetts General Hospital. Churchill had a life or death decision to make. He knew from the dismal surgical history of this operation that there was little or no chance of saving the patient's life by operating at once, but a better chance if he waited and watched, hoping that with time a large clot in the pulmonary artery might spontaneously fragment into smaller bits. You may question the wisdom of this: How can twenty fragments be better for the patient than one larger clot? Because of the tremendous reserve of arteries within the lung, if twenty fragments float into and block twenty small pulmonary arteries, blood can again flow freely through the now open main artery, its two main branches, and hundreds of *un*obstructed smaller pulmonary arteries. The lungs have more small arteries than their owner needs (Fig. 2.2); indeed one func-

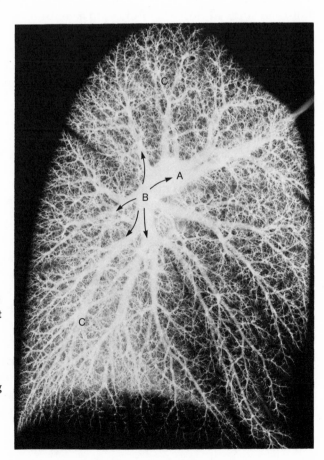

Figure 2.2.   X ray of the arterial tree of a human lung at autopsy, its vessels filled with a radio-opaque fluid. For each lung there are one pulmonary artery, about 1,000 small arterioles 0.04 inch wide, and about 600 million capillaries 0.0003 inch in diameter. A human lung has enough vessels to permit loss of a lobe or of a whole lung without disabling the patient.

tion of some of these small pulmonary arteries is to protect the rest of the body by trapping and then disposing of small clots or clusters of cells that should not, but do, enter the venous bloodstream. If it were not for this protective mechanism, blood clots from veins could pass through the lungs and block small arteries in the heart, brain, or other organs, with a fatal or disabling outcome.

On the other hand, Churchill knew that if he waited too long to see if the clot would break up spontaneously, even minutes too long, the patient might die or suffer brain damage. He weighed the risks and decided not to perform an operation until he was certain that the patient had no chance of recovering without surgical intervention. But to minimize the danger of waiting even a moment too long, he moved her into the operating room and put his surgical team on instant alert; surgery could begin literally within seconds if necessary. He also assigned his full-time surgical Research Fellow to a continuous watch by her bedside and to report any change in her condition.

Physicians and surgeons are often pictured nowadays as cold, unfeeling, egocentric individuals, with little or no concern for the patient as a human being. I am sure that a few seem to the patient to fall into this category, but medical history is, as you will see, replete with instances of research-initiated and important lifesaving discoveries eventually made because of a physician's sense of complete helplessness and anguish in caring for a dying patient, and his determination to replace ignorance with knowledge.

This was one such instance. In this case, the surgical Research Fellow assigned to watch Edith was John Gibbon, who had just finished an internship in Philadelphia. He sat by Edith's bed all afternoon and all through the night. For seventeen hours he worried about the possible operation, telling himself that there must be a way to save his patient's life and trying to think of how. He knew the history of the operation, that it had to be completed in about 6 minutes or less or the brain would die; he knew too that only rarely had the operation been done in less time, and then only by the speediest of surgeons. It would be virtually impossible to hurry the operation. It required a minimal number of surgical procedures: anesthesia, opening the thorax, temporary closure of the pulmonary trunk, opening the pulmonary artery, flushing out the blood clots, and sewing the artery together again. But, Gibbon reasoned, if you can't lower the water, you can raise the bridge. What the surgeon needed was not greater speed, but more time in which to work. All night long, Gibbon thought of solution after solution and finally came up with the answer: an artificial, outside-the-body heart–lung machine that would take over the vital pumping function of the natural heart and the oxygenating function of the natural lungs.

Gibbon's seventeen hours of visualizing, designing, and planning were interrupted abruptly at 8:05 A.M., when he could no longer obtain Edith's blood pressure, and the surgical team sprang into action. They knew exactly what they had to do. Working with precision and speed gained from long experience together, they opened the young woman's chest and tightened a rubber tube slipped around the pulmonary artery to stop any blood that might still be flowing past the clot through the artery. Then they made an opening in the main artery and removed the blood clots from it and from both of its main branches. As they closed the opening in the artery, the clock recorded 8:12 A.M.: The operation had taken 7 minutes. It was too slow. The patient died, despite all their efforts and skill. That particular operation failed, but it became one of the most important in surgical history, for it led directly to the great lifesaving advance of open heart surgery. John Gibbon's planning did not stop with Edith's death; it was interrupted, but at that time, he made an irrevocable decision to pursue a research career that he hoped would permit him to develop the artificial heart–lung he visualized that night. He did, and he became the first to use it to perform successful open heart surgery 23 years later.

To appreciate the scope and complexity of the plan that ran through Gibbon's mind that long October night, it is essential to know the design of our natural heart, lungs, and circulation. The heart is too complex to understand by studying a single photograph, so we will use a series of simple diagrams. We already started by picturing only the right side of the heart (Fig. 2.1) as though it were a separate reservoir and pump connected only to the pulmonary circulation. Now we shall look at the design of the left side, again as though it were a separate reservoir and pump. Finally we will slide the right and left sides together and see the wonderfully compact design of this dual pump and understand better why its design and purpose baffled all anatomists until the time of William Harvey (1628).

First, let us review some similarities between the right and left pumps. Each has a collecting system (veins) that fills a thin-walled, muscular reservoir (atrium) that in turn periodically fills the pump (ventricle) which rhythmically spurts blood into a distributing system (arteries and arterioles) delivering blood into an exchange system (extremely thin-walled capillaries) where substances pass back and forth between tissues and blood (or in the lungs, between air and blood).

The functions of the right side of the heart are to receive venous blood and pump it into a distributing system that divides, subdivides, and further subdivides until there are more than 600 million pulmonary capillaries (give or take a few million) that are in intimate contact with 300 million thin-walled pulmonary air sacs (again, give or take a few million) (Fig. 2.3). Here gas exchange occurs. It involves both oxygen and carbon dioxide: Oxygen (O_2) enters the blood and carbon dioxide (CO_2) leaves it, and so efficiently that within a second venous blood has become arterial blood. At that moment the right pump has fulfilled its function. The right ventricle doesn't have to think about supplying some capillaries with a larger blood flow each minute and others with little or none. It does no work to take up oxygen or give up carbon dioxide; this occurs by diffusion in the air sacs of the lungs. All the right ventricle must do is develop a pumping pressure just high enough to push blood, against the force of gravity, to and through all of the pulmonary capillar-

Figure 2.3.   The pulmonary circulation. The arrows show the venous (dark gray) blood pumped by the right ventricle into the pulmonary trunk and then into the right and left pulmonary arteries, entering the pulmonary circulation. The poorly oxygenated blood flows into hundreds of millions of capillaries surrounding air sacs where it eliminates excess carbon dioxide and becomes loaded with oxygen. It then passes as arterial (light gray) blood into the collecting pulmonary veins, headed for the left side of the heart.

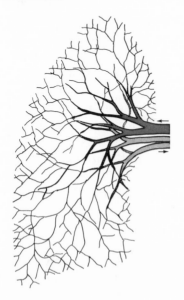
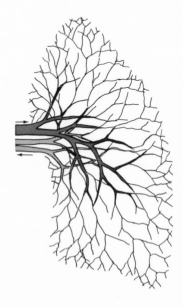

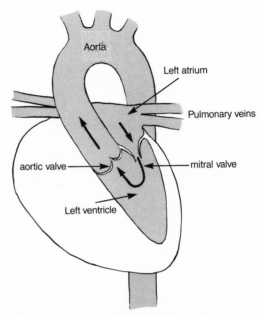

Figure 2.4. The left heart. Oxygenated blood (shaded area) coming from the lungs in the pulmonary veins fills the left atrium, then, during relaxation of the left ventricle, flows through the open mitral valve into the ventricle. When the left ventricle contracts, its high pressure shuts the mitral valve, opens the aortic valve (between the left ventricle and the aorta), and propels arterial blood into the aorta, which distributes it to all of the main arteries of the head, neck, thorax (chest), abdomen, and limbs.

ies, including those at the top of the lungs, of a standing or sitting man.

The left ventricle, however, must generate a much higher pressure in the aorta and its main branches (Fig. 2.4). It must pump oxygenated blood, against the force of gravity, to the top of the brain (or to the tip of the toes if the person decides to stand on his head). It must also produce a high enough pressure in the arteries within the kidneys to deliberately filter water from blood—water that eventually reaches the urinary bladder as modified water, or urine (see p. 276); and the aortic pressure must be high enough to distribute arterial blood through numerous branches to the head, arms, chest, abdomen, and lower limbs and to the heart muscle itself (through its coronary arteries) (Fig. 2.5)— organs whose tissues are much "tighter" than the diaphanous membranes in the lungs. These branches feed into hundreds of millions of thin-walled capillaries where the blood pressure is just high enough at the beginning of the capillary and just low enough at the end to allow exchange of many substances between blood and tissues: Everything in blood needed by body tissues for their function, growth, repair, and regulation leaves the first part of the capillaries, and everything that tissue cells want to eliminate or distribute enters at the far end of the capillaries—magic, indeed, considering that a human capillary is less than 1 millimeter long.

Between the right and left sides of the heart are the lungs, a miraculous piece of biological engineering that brings fresh air through an

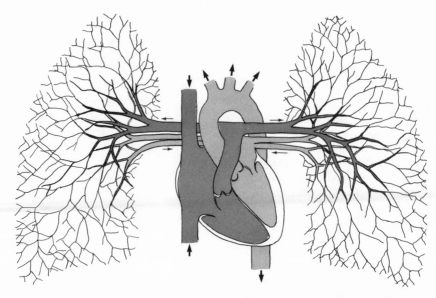

Figure 2.5.   Figures 2.1, 2.3, and 2.4 are joined together here to form a schematic representation of both the right and left sides of the heart and the pulmonary and systemic circulations. Note that the "circulation" is not a geometric circle; it consists of multiple circuits but, if one starts with blood in the right ventricle, all of it passes through these circuits and returns to the right ventricle. A complete block of the pulmonary trunk, therefore, prevents blood from moving in any vessel.

intricate system of branching tubes into 300 million air sacs, in which air is separated from blood in the 600 million pulmonary capillaries by a membrane only 4 millionths of an inch thick. This permits the inward diffusion of O_2 and the outward diffusion of CO_2.

And finally throughout the whole system of blood tubes flows what Goethe called a "superextraordinary juice," blood—a fluid that grabs onto O_2 and CO_2 when and where it should and lets go when and where it should, blood that ideally stays liquid when it should and clots when it should.

Now we can picture the immensity of Gibbon's plan. First was its audacity. It involved constructing an outside-the-body system that could for a number of hours supply all of the body with an adequate flow of well-oxygenated, liquid blood and eliminate the body's excess CO_2. Second, his apparatus had to be sterile, in constant readiness, and completely dependable. Third, he had to develop the surgical skills needed to plug the inlet tubes of his heart–lung machine into the collecting system for the right ventricle, reroute all of the venous blood through a substitute lung, and then pump this newly oxygenated blood, using a high-pressure artificial heart, into the aorta (Fig. 2.6) for distribution to all of the tissues and organs of the body. Fourth, he had to acquire the techniques for surgical correction of cardiac and vascular disorders. And fifth, he had to learn how to disconnect his apparatus and put the patient's circulation together again.

For the future of cardiac surgery beyond 1930, it was indeed fortunate that Massachusetts General Hospital surgeon Churchill believed

Figure 2.6. The heart and circulation with a pump–oxygenator in place. The venous blood of the patient is collected from the upper and lower great veins (A), flows, by gravity or through a pump, into one of a number of types of oxygenators (B) (see Figs. 2.26 and 2.28), then through a pump (C), and back into a large systemic artery at a convenient site such as the aorta or a major branch of it (D). The distribution of arterial blood in this case begins at D and supplies all major arterial branches. (Circulation to the head, arms, chest, abdomen, and legs are omitted from this diagram.)

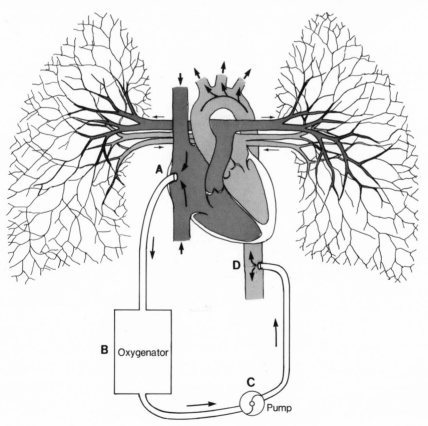

in research and had a Research Fellow, that he assigned this Fellow to the long, lonely vigil in 1930, and that the Fellow was John Gibbon, one with imagination, persistence, and an indomitable will. It took Gibbon fifteen years (excluding four years for wartime service), but, with the continuous help of his wife, Maly, he built his dream machine, and it worked.

Who was John Gibbon? After four years at Jefferson Medical College in Philadelphia (1923–1927), he became an intern at Pennsylvania Hospital there. It was during those two years that he developed his initial interest in research. He wrote in 1970 that he had by then forgotten the details of his 1928 investigation, but he did recall being stimulated by the realization that he could add to the store of human knowledge by controlled experimentation. There were three crucial circumstances that directed Gibbon into a research career. The first was this taste of research at an early age in his medical training. The second was that his chief of surgery did not discourage him; Gibbon consulted him about the possibility of being *both* a surgeon and a researcher and was assured that it was indeed possible. The third crucial point was that by 1930 at least a few surgical departments in the United States had active research divisions. So, in February 1930, he went off to one of these to work as a Research Fellow in surgery with Dr. Edward Churchill in Boston. It was during that long vigil, October 3, 1930, that Research Fellow Gibbon decided on his life's work—the substitute heart–lung. Without the early taste for research and the availability of advanced training in research, Gibbon would have gone on to the next operation and the next and the next. I am sure he would have been much richer, but the world much poorer.

In February of 1931, Gibbon's year at Massachusetts General Hospital came to an end and he moved back to Philadelphia, not alone, but with a newly acquired, lifetime research partner, Dr. Churchill's research assistant, Mary ("Maly") Hopkinson, who had just become his wife. He spent three and a half years in Philadelphia, partly in the practice of surgery and, another turning point in his career, partly in research on blood vessels in the laboratory of Dr. Eugene Landis, at the University of Pennsylvania. Landis was renowned for his precise studies on blood flow through capillaries and on the exchange of essential materials between capillaries and tissue cells, a field critical for Gibbon's later work.

At the end of that time, Gibbon and Maly returned to Boston for a year to begin at last actual work in Churchill's laboratory on the heart–lung apparatus. His plans aroused no real enthusiasm, even among his surgical colleagues, and he received no positive encouragement except from Landis. But even Landis had crossed his fingers behind his back and thought, "What a long, hard, impossible road to choose." But that year in Boston was decisive because it was then that the Gibbons achieved the first step of their "mission impossible," and after that there was no turning back. Though the experiments were not published until 1937, it was in 1935 that their apparatus was good enough to take over completely for 3 hours and 50 minutes the functions of the heart and lungs of a cat whose pulmonary artery was completely clamped to be sure that all natural circulation in the body had stopped. Gibbon in 1970 recalled that occasion:

I shall never forget the day in 1935 in the surgical research laboratory at the top of the Bulfinch Building of the Massachusetts General Hospital when for the first time we were able to take over the entire cardiorespiratory functions of a cat with an extracorporeal [outside-the-body] circulation. Although we had never quite expressed it to ourselves, I am sure that we were subconsciously working towards that end. When the final turns of the clamp completely shut off the pulmonary artery, with the blood pressure and the respirations remaining normal, we thought something incredible had happened. We fairly exploded with joy and danced around the laboratory. That was really the highlight not only of the first year, 1934–35, but of all the subsequent years of work until the first successful use of the apparatus on a human patient in 1953.

I have listened to some of my colleagues talk of the sheer joy, ecstasy, and great fun of their career in research. I'm skeptical, because times such as these are rare. Gibbon's description of two great moments of elation, exultation, and jubilation—one in 1935 and the second in 1953, with eighteen years in between—is much closer to the truth. Those eighteen years were filled with very long days of hard dogged work, hours of wakefulness at night, months of exploring one blind alley followed by another and then another, more disappointments than successes, unexpected technical difficulties, facing the indifference of surgical colleagues and, worse, their skepticism and thinly disguised scoffing and rejection. Even the best of scientists see few rainbows in the sky or pots of gold at the end of that rare rainbow. They do research because they are compulsive, driven to find the answer to a question, to solve a problem, and constitutionally built to tolerate long periods of frustration and then, once having solved the problem to *their own* satisfaction, to face the necessity of devoting even longer periods of time to amass enough experimental evidence to convince severe critics, judges, or congenital disbelievers.

After Gibbon's 1935 explosion of joy, there remained the huge job of scaling his apparatus upward in capacity from one suitable for a cat to one twenty times larger for man. He wasn't overwhelmed with financial support; the records show that over a crucial 2½-year period (1937 to mid-1939), he received two grants ($2,500 and $1,500), both from the Josiah Macy Foundation.

Then came World War II; Gibbon served in the U.S. Armed Services for four years. At the end of the war, Congress established the National Heart Institute; it awarded its first research grants in 1949. Among these was a grant of $26,827 to Gibbon, a grant that was renewed regularly until 1962, usually in the $20,000–$30,000 per year range.

Of equal importance to Gibbon was the valuable engineering help he received from International Business Machines between 1945 and 1961. At the end of World War II, when Gibbon became Professor of Surgery at Jefferson Medical College, one of Gibbon's freshman medical students opened a door for him to Thomas J. Watson, president of IBM. Gibbon recalled,

Through a freshman medical student at Jefferson, I learned that the research department of the International Business Machines Corporation might be interested in a project such as ours. Then followed a very fruitful association for six years with I.B.M. and Mr. Thomas J. Watson, then chairman of the board. I shall never forget the first time I met Mr. Watson at his office in New York City. He came into the anteroom where I sat, carrying reprints of my publications. He shook my hand and sat down beside me. He said the idea was interesting and asked what he could do to help. I remember replying rather bluntly that I did not want him to make any money from the idea, nor did I wish to make any money from it. He brushed my comments aside with a wave of his hand and said, "Don't worry about that." I then explained that what I needed was engineering help in the design and construction of a heart–lung machine large enough and efficient enough to be used on human patients. He replied, "Certainly. You name the place and time and I will have engineers there to discuss the matter with you." From that time on we not only had engineering help always available, but I.B.M. paid the entire cost of constructing the various machines with which we carried on the work for the next seven years.

The first machine that I.B.M. built for us was a very much enlarged air-conditioned apparatus with elaborate controls. There was no change in the artificial lung which was still a vertical revolving cylinder. The pumps used were the roller type, the rollers successively compressing a section of rubber tubing and thus did not require any valves.

IBM transformed a laboratory model for cats into one that could be used on full-sized patients, under sterile operating room conditions (Fig. 2.7). Industry does not usually offer its engineering know-how to medical scientists until a successful outcome is certain and profits are assured; Watson, fortunately, was an exception.

Ritchie-Calder observed that in science there are those who made it *happen* and those who made it *possible*. Almost invariably, time erases the memory of multiple contributions to a single discovery by attaching

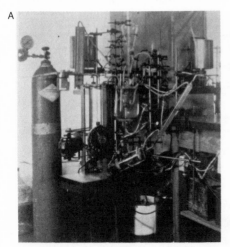

Figure 2.7.   (A) Gibbon's homemade heart–lung "machine" used in his laboratory in 1937 for keeping animals alive even after their main pulmonary artery was closed with a clamp. (B) Gibbon's compact, portable heart–lung machine as developed by IBM engineers for use in the operating room in his first successful open heart operation on a patient in 1953. A screen-type oxygenator (SO) projects from the upper left. The machine contains essentially the same elements as that in (A), but as a result of the years of development, all are now contained in one unit. The rotary blood pumps are incorporated into the rear of the apparatus, and the recording and control instruments are on the front of the cabinet.

to it the name of one man—the one who made it *happen* (e.g., circulation and Harvey, oxygen and Lavoisier). But again, almost invariably, many others deserve equal credit for making it *possible*. Sir Isaac Newton, the great English mathematician, physicist, and astronomer, wrote, "If I have been able to see a little farther than others, it is because I have stood on the shoulders of giants." Some of the giants who made discovery possible are still remembered; for Newton these were Copernicus, Brahe, Kepler, and Galileo.

Gibbon made the heart–lung machine happen. But before Gibbon could even visualize an outside-the-body pump–oxygenator, he needed to draw on a vast store of previous discoveries in many fields that made it possible. He needed to know the correct anatomy and functions of the heart and circulation. He needed to have a pump that would not damage blood or render it useless. He needed to know how to transfer blood safely from a donor to the pump and then to the patient. He needed to know the main functions of the lung and how to create an artificial lung that would duplicate the capabilities of the natural lung. If Gibbon had lived in the seventeenth, eighteenth, or nineteenth century, he would have failed, because what he needed to know just to get started had not yet been discovered. Indeed, one component crucial to the successful use of blood did not become available until 1934, the year that Gibbon began full-time work on his heart–lung machine. That component was heparin, the first safe anticoagulant, absolutely essential to keep blood liquid in an artificial system of pumps, tubes, and gas exchangers.

William Harvey's Circle

Before William Harvey, no one really knew what purpose the blood served in the body. Aristotle (384–322 B.C.) believed, for example, that the lungs were the seat of intelligence and that arteries normally contain air. Galen (130–200 A.D.), the great Greek physician–scientist who worked in Rome, believed that blood was formed in the liver from food absorbed through the intestines. This blood then flowed into the right heart (Fig. 2.8). From there most of it went to the pulmonary artery to nourish the lungs, but the rest passed through "invisible pores" in the muscle of the right ventricle to enter the left ventricle, where it mixed with "pneuma" coming from the lungs and became charged with "vital spirit." Galen also believed that waste products were regurgitated

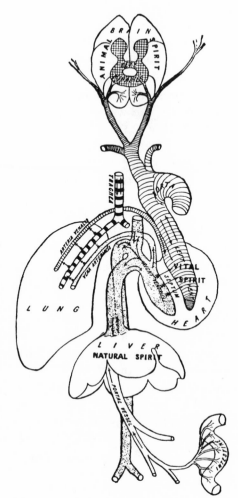

Figure 2.8. An artist's representation of Galen's written description of body function. Essential to Galen's thought was the concept of three "pneuma" or "spirits." The liver combined its own *natural* spirit with nutritive material coming to it from the intestines, and so formed venous blood. The left ventricle formed *vital* spirit by combining air brought to it from the trachea and drops of blood that seeped through pores in the ventricular wall (the septum). Blood in the brain became charged with a third, *animal* spirit, which reached all parts of the body by flowing through hollow nerves (not shown in the diagram).

through the valve into the right atrium and then into a pulmonary vein and the lung for excretion.

And such remained the accepted doctrine until 1628, when Harvey showed unequivocally that the heart was a pump and that its sole function was to pump blood to all the tissues of the body through a series of circles—in a circulation—back to the right heart, then through the lungs, and back to the left heart for a second circulation.

Harvey's discovery is still generally regarded as the most important event in the history of biology—not only because it established the true nature of the heart and circulation, but also because his discovery was the beginning of modern biological science in which actual experiments

on living humans and animals and evidence from them replaced speculation and abstract philosophical formulation.

Harvey rejected the ancient concept that blood "sweated" through
invisible pores in the muscular wall separating the right and left heart.
"But Damme," he wrote, "*there are no pores* and it is not possible to
show such" (Fig. 2.9). He proposed instead (with good arguments) that
blood flowed from the right heart through small openings in the pulmonary circulation to the left heart, so completing the circle. Harvey
got the anatomy straight, deduced the correct function, and in 1628
published *De Motu Cordis*, only 74 pages long.

Its publication was a risky business and Harvey knew it. Seventy-
five years earlier, Michael Servetus, a Spanish theologian, had been
burned at the stake for challenging the authority of the church. His last
heresy was a book, *Christianisma Restitutio*, published in 1553; in a
very small section of the book he tucked away his proposal that venous
blood actually flowed through small openings in the pulmonary circulation and not across the wall between the right and left ventricles. Also,
as late as 1600, Bruno had been burned at the stake in Rome for heret-
ical views on astronomy. And so Harvey wrote in 1628, "I not only fear
injury to myself from the envy of the few but I tremble lest I have
mankind at large for my enemies." Although Harvey did not have all of
mankind for his enemies, full acceptance of *De Motu Cordis* was slow.
The faculty of the University of Paris opposed his conclusions for more
than fifty years. Then, as resistance crumbled, Harvey met another fate
of discoverers. William Cruickshank in 1790 described the sequence:

When Harvey discovered the circulation of the blood, his opponents first
attempted to prove that he was mistaken; but finding this ground untenable,
they then asserted that it was known long before; Servetus, Colombo, and Cesalpinus, all knew it: and when they were informed, that if these gentlemen did
know anything of the matter, the world at large were totally ignorant of the
fact, and likely to have continued so, except for Harvey, they once more shifted
their ground, and said the discovery was of no use.

Unqualified universal recognition of Harvey as *the* discoverer came in
1957, when the Soviet Union issued a special commemorative stamp on
the tercentenary of Harvey's death (Fig. 2.10).

One reason for slow acceptance of his views may have been that
Harvey in 1628 had never *seen* the pulmonary capillaries; they were
invisible to the naked eye, or even to an eye aided by a hand lens. But

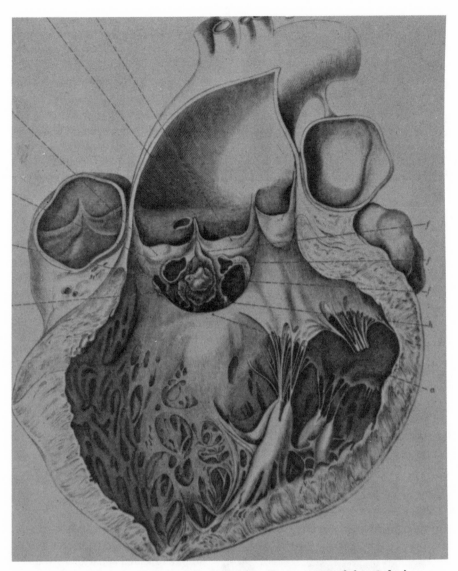

Figure 2.9. The inner surface of the ventricles. Harvey insisted that Galen's pores did not exist and that blood had to pass out of the right side of the heart and then through the circulation of the lungs in order to reach the left ventricle. Note that the internal walls of the ventricles are a jungle of muscular tubes and tendonlike cords whose function is to keep the valves from everting (like an umbrella blown inside-out) from the pressure in the ventricles. Without proper magnification or experiments, Galen could easily believe that blood passed through this jungle. This drawing is by Carl Rokitansky (1804–1878), pioneer pathologist–anatomist, who is said to have performed more than 3,000 autopsies himself.

he *knew* they must be there and presented convincing arguments for their existence. The compound microscope had been invented in the late 1500s, but no one used it to look at slices of lung until 1661, when Marcello Malpighi used one to observe the lung and found that there indeed were the "invisible" channels that connected the right heart to the left and closed the circle (Fig. 2.11). Fraser Harris, a physiologist-historian, put it neatly in the early 1900s: "Harvey made the existence of capillaries a logical necessity; Malpighi made it a histological [microscopic] certainty."

When I first read Harvey's *De Motu Cordis*, I wondered why no one in the thirteen centuries between Galen and Harvey, or Harvey himself, had ever tested experimentally the concept that invisible pores existed in the wall between the right and left ventricles. It turns out that six years before his death in 1657 (and ten years before Malpighi's work) Harvey did indeed obtain experimental proof that there were no pores in the muscle partition between the right and left ventricles, but a great abundance of them in the pulmonary circulation. In a letter to a friend, Harvey wrote in 1651,

In a strangled human body, the pulmonary artery and aorta are ligated [tied], the left ventricle opened, and a cannula placed in the vena cava, and water

Figure 2.10.   Postage stamp commemorating the 300th anniversary of Harvey's death. There was no British stamp to mark the occasion, despite repeated applications and entreaties. The USSR was the only country to issue a "Harvey stamp." A translation of the top two lines on the stamp is "The distinguished English doctor who discovered the circulation of the blood." The third line reads "William Harvey." The stamp was issued in June 1957, price 40 kopecks.

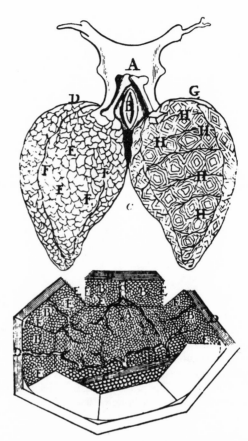

Figure 2.11.   Malpighi's illustration of a section of a frog's larynx and lungs, seen through his microscope, showing the "invisible capillary network" that conducts blood from the right ventricle through the pulmonary circulation to the left side of the heart. (D) the capillary network on the outer surface of the right lung and (G) the other lung with its front half sliced away to reveal the midsection of the lung.

forced in. The right ventricle is vehemently tumefied [swollen]. Through the opening in the left ventricle, however, not a drop of water or blood escapes [Fig. 2.12].

So now (the solution having been predicted), the syringe is introduced into the pulmonary artery, with a ligature around it lest water regurgitate into the right ventricle. We force the water in the syringe against the lungs and immediately water with copious amounts of blood leaps out of the cleft in the left ventricle, so that, as much water as is expressed into the lungs, so much flows out of the hiatus mentioned. You can experiment as often as you like, and know for certain that this is so. By this one experiment, I have easily butchered all the arguments of Riolan on this question.

Unchallenged authority is potentially one of the most serious deterrents to the advance of knowledge. Galen's authority went unquestioned for thirteen centuries. Although Andreas Vesalius, a sixteenth century anatomist, was certain that there were no pores in the wall sep-

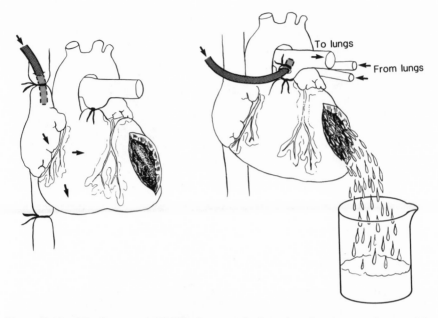

Figure 2.12. Harvey never published an article describing his 1651 perfusion of the pulmonary circulation, but he described his experiment in a letter to a friend. The lungs are not shown here, but in the diagram on the right, blood, when poured into pulmonary arteries, must have flowed quickly through the pulmonary circulation and then to the left side of the heart, in order to gush out of the slit in the wall of the left ventricle (artist's conception, 1980).

arating the right and left ventricles, he wrote, "We are compelled to wonder at the industry of the Creator of all things by which the blood sweats from the right ventricle to the left through invisible passages."

Why was it Harvey who discovered the circle? Possibly the time was about ripe. Sixteenth and early seventeenth century anatomists—not only Vesalius, but also Colombo, Servetus, Cesalpinus, and Fabricius of Padua—knew that Galen was wrong in one or more of his beliefs and began to raise questions, but they either could not grasp the concept of a full circle of blood or would not express it. Fabricius (Fig. 2.13) had even demonstrated that valves in the arm veins permitted blood to flow in only one direction—from the hand to the heart—but he never realized that he was looking at one part of a circle. Harvey had four things working for him: First, he was a student at the University of Padua for four years and the faculty there was fairly strongly anticlerical; second, he studied the heart at the time of Newton, who had developed the laws of motion and stimulated interest in mechanics, including that of water pumps, pumps with valves to ensure that water would flow in only one direction and not back and forth (Fig. 2.14); third, he believed strongly in direct proof obtained by experiments; and fourth, he became familiar with the work of Fabricius on valves in arm veins that made it mandatory that blood flow through them in only one direction.

Figure 2.13.   (A) Fabricius, Harvey's teacher at Padua, demonstrated in 1603 the presence of valves (each swollen segment identified by a small open circle) in the arm veins by fastening a band around the arm above the elbow just tightly enough to collapse the veins under the bands and prevent blood flow in veins toward the heart, but not tightly enough to prevent flow through the high-pressure arteries toward the hand. The veins became distended with blood only below the tourniquet. (B) Harvey's *De Motu Cordis* (1628) had only one illustration, with four parts. Here is his Fig. 1A, which is essentially the same as Fabricius's. Harvey carried the experiment a step further. Harvey pushed all the blood in the veins from the wrist to the elbow upward until the veins were flat, and then demonstrated that the veins refilled only starting at the hand, and then segment after segment distended closer to the body. Harvey's experiment proved that blood in arm veins flows only from the fingertips to the body and cannot flow in the opposite direction because of valves in the veins.

A

B

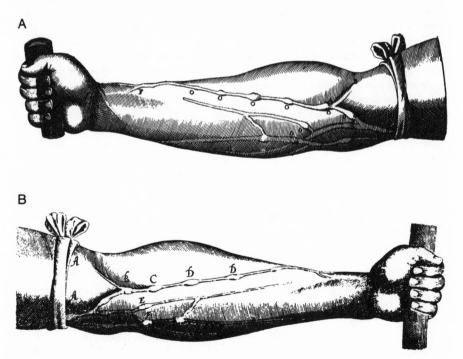

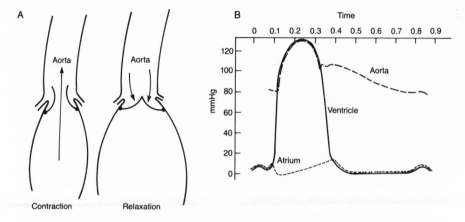

Figure 2.14. The opening and closing of the aortic valve between the left ventricle and the aorta. Key observations in Harvey's discovery of the circulation of the blood were the presence of valves in veins (see Fig. 2.13B) and a system of valves in the heart that convinced him that blood must traverse circles. The sketch of the aortic valve (A) shows that contraction of the left ventricle opens the aortic valve and forces blood into the aorta; the only other opening to or from the left ventricle is the mitral valve (not shown here) between the left atrium and the left ventricle, and it closes at the very beginning of left ventricular contraction. When the left ventricle relaxes, pressure in it falls to zero (atmospheric), the aortic valve closes, and blood refills the ventricle through the now open mitral valve. A modern, simultaneous recording of blood pressure in the left ventricle, aorta, and left atrium (B) shows that when the contracting left ventricle builds up a pressure in excess of that in the aorta, the aortic valve opens; when the left ventricle relaxes and pressure in it falls abruptly well below aortic pressure, back pressure in the aorta closes the aortic valve. The vertical scale is blood pressure measured in millimeters of mercury; the horizontal scale is time in seconds. In this case one complete heartbeat takes place between 0 and 0.75 second. The vessels leaving the aorta at its very beginning, just beyond the aortic valve, are the right and left coronary arteries that supply the heart muscle with blood.

Shortly before Harvey died in 1657 Robert Boyle, one of the founders of the Royal Society, asked him what first led him to suspect that blood flowed around a circle, away from the left ventricle and back to the right. Boyle wrote,

He answer'd me, that when he took notice that the valves in the veins of so many several parts of the body, were so plac'd that they gave free passage to the blood *towards* the heart, but oppos'd the passage of the venal blood the *contrary* way: that. . . . Nature had not plac'd so many valves without design: and no design seem'd more probable, than that, since the blood could not well, because of the interposing valves, be sent by the veins to the limbs; it should be sent through the arteries, and return through the veins, whose valves did not oppose its course that way.

So, the first essential knowledge that Gibbon needed for constructing an outside-the-body heart was the correct anatomy and function of the living heart; he got this from the work of an English physician (Harvey in 1628), two Dutch spectacle makers—H. and Z. Janssen, who in 1590 devised the first compound microscope—and an Italian microscopist, Malpighi, who used one in 1661 to confirm and complete Harvey's work. Malpighi acknowledged the aid of another essential collaborator: He wrote that whatever addition he had made to man's knowledge, he owed that addition to the *frog*, an animal with an almost transparent lung that lent itself admirably to microscopic observations. Harvey also owed something to the frog, for he succeeded in learning the sequence of contractions of the atrium and the ventricle by observing its slowly beating heart. "Slow-motion" movies were still centuries in the future and others were baffled or misled by looking at the rapidly beating hearts of other creatures; Fracastoro believed that "the movement of the heart was to be comprehended only by God!" Anatomy, optics, physiology, comparative anatomy, physics, microscopy, and the frog all came to the aid of Harvey and Malpighi.

So Harvey and Malpighi and hundreds more before Gibbon provided him with accurate maps of the heart and circulation. Had anyone before Gibbon made use of Harvey's research to create an artificial heart and circulation? In 1812, Julien LeGallois, a French physiologist, wrote, "If one could substitute for a heart, a kind of injection . . . of arterial blood, either natural or artificial, . . . one would succeed easily in maintaining alive indefinitely any part of the body whatsoever." LeGallois never did so, but he did get many scientists interested in perfusing organs (from the Latin *perfundere*, "to flow through")—not for the purpose of devising new surgical techniques, but simply to learn the function of each organ. For example, they let a solution of known composition flow, by gravity, into an artery to an organ and collected and analyzed what came out in the venous outflow, or they determined how long an organ could survive or even function normally when various nutrients were perfused through its circulation. In 1828 Kay used artificial circulation to restore the contraction of dying muscles, C. E. Lobell perfused a kidney in 1849, and in 1858 Edouard Brown-Séquard circulated blood through the head of an animal separated from its body and managed to revive some cerebral functions.

The heart, of course, came in for its share of perfusing, and numerous physiologists (the first, Newell Martin in 1881, at Johns Hopkins in Baltimore) learned the trick of running perfusion fluids backward in the aorta—toward the left ventricle—after tying off all side branches of the aorta except the coronary arteries. The pressure of fluid in the ascending aorta slammed shut the valves between the aorta and the left ventricle so that fluid could go only into the two coronary arteries that supply the heart muscle itself (see the right side of Fig. 2.14A). As can be seen by looking at the schema of a heart–lung machine (see Fig. 2.6), this technique was used by Gibbon, who pumped oxygenated blood both backward (toward the heart) and forward through a tube in the aorta. Perfusion of the coronary arteries also provided valuable information for twentieth-century surgeons on how to stop a heart and restart it simply by perfusing different salts (potassium or calcium) through the coronary circulation.

Initially the pressure used for organ perfusion was supplied by gravity flow, with the fluid reservoir raised as high as the ceiling if necessary. Later, when higher pressures were needed, pumps replaced the simple gravity system. Simple pumps fitted with valves to propel a strong stream of water in one direction had been designed and used for firefighting early in the seventeenth century, but the industrial revolution of the 1800s required and produced a far greater variety of pumps to create pressures above or below atmospheric. Physiologists and then physicians modified these for studies on animals or for giving blood transfusions to man. The latter required special designs: They had to be made of materials that could be sterilized and did not interact chemically with blood, and they had to be constructed so that they did not mash or fragment red blood cells. Gibbon did not have to devise a pump from scratch; he had a wide choice to use or modify. Indeed, one pump, now a component of several heart–lung machines, had been invented, reinvented, or improved at least nine times between 1855 and 1944, for nine versions of it are registered in the U.S. Patent Office. This is the roller pump, first patented in April 1855 by Porter and Bradley (U.S. Patent no. #12,753) (Fig. 2.15); Porter and Bradley even suggested that their pump could be used to pump the stomach and give injections. In 1935, 2,006,246 patents later, it turned up again as the DeBakey pump. It sometimes pays off to come in last.

Figure 2.15. The roller or rotary pump (A) was patented in the United States as early as 1855 by Porter and Bradley. One roller (46 at bottom of B) compresses the tube by its clockwise motion, squeezing, or "milking," the fluid ahead of it; the empty tube refills in time for the second roller (46 at top of B) to reach the bottom and so continue to push the contents through the circuit. Although Porter and Bradley designed the device to pump water and commercial fluids, they noted in the last sentence of their patent application, "We have also contemplated its application to the purposes of stomach pumps, and apparatus for injections." The pump in (B) is the DeBakey roller pump (patented in 1935; U.S. Patent no. 2,018,999). It operates on the Porter–Bradley principle and is also "an apparatus for injections."

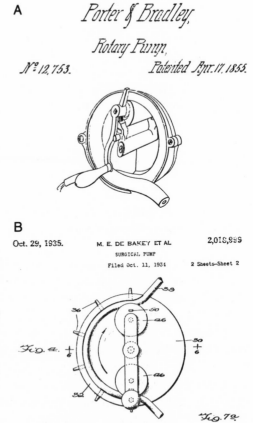

Intravenous Injections and Transfusions

Before Gibbon's outside-the-body heart–lung machine can be connected to the patient's circulation, it must be filled ("primed") with about 2 liters* of a suitable fluid. Nature, in its wisdom, decided millennia ago that the best inside-the-body circulating fluid to meet the needs of the body's organs, tissues, and cells is blood, with about half of it plasma and the other half red blood cells packed with a unique chemical, hemoglobin.

Is it safe to use balanced "physiological" salt solutions instead, as physiologists have done for 100 years in their laboratory research? The answer is that it is *possible* to use them when circumstances demand

*In these years of transition between the old measure of quarts and "fifths" and the newer metric system, remember that 1 quart is approximately 1 liter and 1 "fifth" (of a gallon) is about ⅘ of a quart, or 750 milliliters or cubic centimeters.

it,* but it is not ideal. Gibbon initially used a solution of gum acacia (a water-soluble gum) in his first experiments on cats, but his animals became acutely anemic because of dilution of their blood with non-blood, and he gave this practice up as soon as he could afford to buy blood. Furthermore, the cardiac function of patients operated upon by cardiac surgeons is usually abnormal to begin with and decreases during and for a while after an operation. Such hearts require a good supply of oxygen and nutrients during the operation and not a supply that is barely marginal. A demonstration of how little red blood a patient can have and still survive should be a fascinating entry in *Ripley's Believe It or Not,* but ideally the patient's blood should be kept as close to normal as possible throughout the operation, and the pump should be "primed" with safe blood.

The search for safe blood began in 1667, when the first transfusions known to Western medicine were performed in France and England. Thereafter, off and on, transfusions were part of medical practice, but they ran a stormy course for more than 250 years. The idea of injecting anything into a vein seems to have originated with Sir Christopher Wren—yes, the same Wren who was a great architect and built St. Paul's Cathedral in London and the same Wren who was a celebrated mathematician and professor of astronomy at Oxford, a town planner, and an artist who illustrated Thomas Willis's book on the brain and its circulation. There were more "Renaissance men" then than now, men with

---

*Occasionally a surgeon has no choice, such as one who must perform an open heart operation on a Jehovah's Witness, whose laws forbid "the eating of blood." In Leviticus 17:10–14, God forbade the Israelites to eat blood. The actual passage is

I have said to the people of Israel, You shall not eat the blood of any creature, for the life of every creature is its blood; whoever eats it shall be cut off.

The Israelites and present-day Orthodox Jews interpret this, as part of their kosher dietary laws, to mean that animal meat must be drained of blood before it is cooked and eaten. Jehovah's Witnesses interpret this passage far more literally, that no animal's blood may enter the human body by any route; as a result a Jehovah's Witness will refuse even a lifesaving transfusion of blood. Open heart surgery performed to save the life of a Jehovah's Witness thus requires that the cardiac surgeon fill the outside-the-body circulation with a "physiological" sugar or salt solution or some hemoglobin-free blood substitute and, in addition, avoid giving blood transfusions during or after the operation. By taking unusual precautions to prevent loss of the patient's blood during the operation, the surgeon can keep an adult alive during an open heart operation. Knowledge comes in strange ways. No committee on human experimentation would have approved a proposal by a surgeon to perform an open heart operation without blood on hand, ready to be transfused, but religious laws showed what the human body can take when pushed to the limit.

amazing talents in widely separate fields. Wren was one of these and in 1656 he suggested and directed the first recorded injection of fluid directly into the vein of a living animal. His tools were an animal bladder with a quill attached; using these, he injected wine and opium into a dog. He never wrote a report on it because he performed his injection nine years before the *Proceedings of the Royal Society* began publication, but he described it in a letter to Sir William Perry:

The most considerable experiment I have made of late is this: *I injected wine and ale into the mass of blood in a living dog,* by a vein, in good quantities, till he became extremely drunk; but soon after voided it by urine. It will be too long to tell you the effects of opium, scammony and other things which I have tried in this way. I am in further pursuit of the experiment, which I take to be of great concernment, and what will give great light to the theory and practice of physic.

A great architect and astronomer such as Wren was probably interested in intravenous injections because he was a student of Sir Charles Scarsburgh, who had learned firsthand of the circulation of the blood from William Harvey. It seems likely that Wren thought that he might well make use of Harvey's discovery and "give great light to the theory and practice of physic [medicine]." Once Harvey had discovered that blood *circulates* and Wren had found that he could inject fluids into it, transfusions of *blood* were inevitable.

One would have guessed that the first blood transfusions were done to replace blood lost by hemorrhages. This was not so; instead, their use was based on strong beliefs that the blood of a man or animal held the key to vigor, personality, and character. It was natural, therefore, that the early transfusions were of blood from the wild to the tame, the fierce to the timid, the healthy to the sick, the sane to the insane, and the young to the old. There were even attempts to resolve marital incompatibility by cross-transfusions of blood between man and wife.

Today it seems incredible that so many unlikely qualities could be attributed to blood, including a concern by some that a person receiving sheep blood might grow wool and sprout horns, or that transfusion of blood from a Scot might make a wastrel become thrifty! But remember that although Harvey had discovered that blood circulates, he had not discovered the *function* of blood and its reason for circulating. We know now that blood carries oxygen, glucose, amino acids, hormones, and many other essential substances *to* tissues, and carries *away* from tissues substances such as carbon dioxide, acids and excess heat, and materials formed in some cells to be used by others. But how could seventeenth century experimenters or physicians know this? Black had not yet discovered CO_2, and Priestley, Scheele, and Lavoisier had not yet discovered O_2; these were eighteenth century discoveries. Glucose, amino acids and the first hormone were nineteenth century discoveries.

Initially the sources of blood were sheep, oxen, calves, and dogs; its destination was any of these animals or man. There were no hollow needles, but there were quills, hollow bones, and silver tubes; there was no rubber or plastic flexible tubing for connections, but there were the windpipe of a duck and arteries and ureters of oxen, lambs, and calves; there were no syringes or plastic bags, but there were urinary bladders and pouches made from the skin of animals.

Richard Lower, an English physiologist, the first to demonstrate the function of the lungs, was also the first to transfuse blood to animals. In an experiment early in 1667, he drew off almost half of a dog's blood and replaced it with an equal amount of beer mixed with a little wine, injected intravenously. He repeated the sequence of removing blood and replacing it with his concoction until fluid drawn from the dog's vein "had less color than claret, several times diluted." He then went on to transfuse *blood* into dogs. He predicted that "this discovery will be employed with great profit for the human race if it is practised with due consideration and care."

The first recorded transfusion of blood to *man* was performed in mid-June 1667 in Paris. Jean Baptiste Denis, physician to Louis XIV, had experimented first by bleeding dogs almost to the point of death and then restoring life with a transfusion of blood from a calf. Denis was asked to treat a boy of 15 who had an obscure fever that had been treated by the then-favorite remedy for all obscure diseases—bloodletting, followed by more bloodletting. Defying established medical belief, that *bleeding* was the treatment of choice, a belief that persisted until the mid-1880s, Denis put his medical career on the line and *transfused* 9 ounces of blood from a sheep to the boy. His patient improved; this success encouraged Denis to continue his work, even though it set the medical profession against him. He gave a second transfusion to a healthy paid volunteer, who was none the worse for it, and a third to a dying patient whose condition also did not change for better or worse.

The fourth, fifth, and sixth transfusions he performed were historic because they eventually led to the banning of transfusions in medical practice. These three were not given to replace lost blood, as in his first patient, but to dampen the vigor of a newlywed male house servant who intermittently ran off for weekends of debauchery in Paris. For treating him, Denis selected a gentle animal, a calf, and transfused its blood into his patient twice within a few days. The second transfusion led to a severe but not fatal reaction. A few months later the servant became maniacal and his wife insisted on a third transfusion. The patient died the next day. Though there is some doubt that any blood actually entered the patient's veins during the third "transfusion," the Faculté de Médecine (the French predecessor of today's U.S. Food and Drug Administration) insisted that the transfusion caused the death, bitterly opposed further blood transfusions, and refused to give permission for them. A few years later, the Parlement of Paris banned them, the Royal Society of England announced its strong disapproval of the procedure, and the Pope forbade it in Rome and most European countries. As a result, for the next 150 years there were few blood transfusions, and none that were recorded.

It is fortunate that transfusions were banned until more knowledge accumulated, even though this did not occur until the early 1800s, and it is also fortunate that, when finally rediscovered, it was by someone trained in the scientific method and evaluation of experimental data. James Blundell, a London obstetrician and physiologist, was moved by the death of mothers from sudden massive hemorrhage during and after childbirth and decided to do something about it. This was another example of a major discovery initiated by a caring physician whose concern for his patients' well-being changed the course of his life. He spent the next ten years learning all that he could by studying the effects of transfusions in several species. He then at last performed his first successful transfusion in a patient. His experiments led him to two important recommendations: First, blood transfusions should be used to counteract serious hemorrhage that endangered the life of the patient (remember that this was only a decade after the death of Benjamin Rush, America's foremost physician, who was an almost fanatical advocate of treating patients with widely differing illnesses with frequent and generous bloodlettings); and second, blood from one species should never be transfused to a member of another species (Fig. 2.16).

Figure 2.16. Direct blood transfusion from a lamb to a patient by joining an artery in the lamb's neck to an arm vein of the patient, performed by Oscar Hesse in 1873. Hesse transfused sheep blood (about 5 ounces) into each of 15 men, some of whom suffered severe reactions. He continued to promote the use of such transfusions fifty years after Blundell's warning.

The Search for Safe Blood

Blundell's second recommendation should have been all that Gibbon needed to decide on a priming fluid for his pump–oxygenator—*human blood.* But, unfortunately, with the return of transfusions to medical practice, some serious reactions still occurred and transfusion of human blood to human patients again fell into disfavor. Two courses of action were possible: (1) Ban all transfusions and (2) go back to the laboratory and find out why patients had serious reactions to human blood.

To help Gibbon, someone had to take the second course, but because no one really had any inkling of the cause of reactions that occurred when sheep or dog blood was transfused to man, scientists first had to tackle the question of what actually happened when blood from any species was injected into the veins of another. In 1842 the French physiologist François Magendie discovered that the red blood cells of some species (birds and frogs) (Fig. 2.17) were unusual in either size or shape and that, using a microscope, he could easily tell them apart from mammalian red cells. Why care about the shape of the red cells in a crow or a frog? This may have been considered a useless activity when people were dying of transfusion reactions; but "useless" knowledge often turns out to be of great value. What Magendie did was to use "useless" red cells as markers to see what happened to such "foreign" red cells after they had been injected into the circulation of mammals. Though he had injected them for certain and they *had* to be there, these easy-to-recognize red cells could not be found in the circulating blood of mammals. What happened to them? Were they trapped in mammalian capillaries so that they could no longer circulate? Or did something in mammalian blood destroy nonmammalian red cells? The answers to these questions soon followed.

In 1869 Von Creite placed human red blood cells into serum from animals of other species and found that the red cells clumped together, or agglutinated. This was the forerunner of agglutination tests used today that permit us to avoid reactions by identifying incompatible blood before transfusing it. Five years later, Emil Ponfick, a pathologist in Rostock, Germany, examined a woman who died after receiving a direct artery-to-vein transfusion of sheep blood; he found bits of broken blood cells

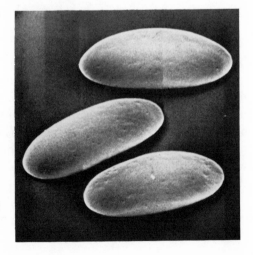

Figure 2.17.   Not all species of animals have red blood cells in the shape of biconcave discs, as does man (see Fig. 2.21). These elongated, oval biconvex cells are red cells from a fowl, easy to distinguish from human red cells when injected into man's circulating blood. This is another example when knowledge of animal physiology has been helpful to man (see text).

in her plasma. He tried to reproduce this experimentally by giving sheep blood to dogs and found that a severe transfusion reaction occurred, that sheep hemoglobin (that could have come only from destroyed red blood cells) was present in the urine of the dogs, and that some hemoglobin blocked the fine tubes of the kidney and led to failure of the kidney and death. Ponfick concluded that substances normally locked up in individual red cells become toxic when free in the plasma—free to damage and block the fine tubes in the kidneys that are the only paths by which newly formed urine can reach the bladder and be excreted. It thus became clear that as soon as the red cells of animals entered the bloodstream of man, something in human blood either directly destroyed (hemolyzed) the membranes of the foreign red cells or clumped whole cells into collections large enough to block capillaries.

Until this time, the process of immunity had been studied almost entirely as the response of a body to the injection of living viruses or to bacteria and their toxins—the formation of antibodies and antitoxins. In 1898 Jules Bordet, later to become director of the Pasteur Institute in Brussels, showed that injection of *body cells*—in this case, red blood cells—from one species to another led to the production of specific antibodies to the injected cells in the latter species. This was a discovery of great importance to the new science of immunology (it won the 1919 Nobel Prize for Bordet) because it proved that the reaction of an animal to a foreign protein is a *general biological* phenomenon and not limited to reactions to bacteria. It *explains*, rather than merely describes, the effects of infusing incompatible blood and of transplanting incompatible tissue cells, such as skin, kidneys, or heart.

So the *cause* of transfusion reactions was understood at last. But it did not explain reactions that occurred following transfusions of *human* blood to patients, reactions that were quite like those following transfusion of sheep blood. It seemed inconceivable that blood from a *human* donor could be incompatible with *human* blood in a patient. The explanation of these reactions came from one of the new breed of immunologists, Karl Landsteiner, in Vienna, who was conducting basic studies on the mechanism of immunity and the nature of antibodies and who was not in any way concerned with blood transfusions or reactions to them. In 1900 Landsteiner observed that when he added the normal blood serum of a human to the normal blood of another human, the red cells clumped—not in all cases, but in some. This meant to Landsteiner that *even within one species* (man), the plasma of some individuals contains substances capable of agglutinating the red blood cells of certain other individuals. He proved that this was not an accident due to disease, since it occurred in the blood of completely healthy men. He then went on to identify three blood groups in man; a fourth group was discovered a few years later. In the late 1930s, Landsteiner collaborated with Alexander Weiner and Philip Levine in the United States in the discovery of still another immunological difference in blood of humans: Some have and some do not have an Rh factor (more about this will be said later).

Landsteiner received the Nobel Prize in medicine and physiology in 1930, thirty years after his remarkable discovery. In addition to finding out why some transfusions lead to reactions and why some do not and laying the basis for safe blood transfusions, his observation became important in fields other than medicine. Usually we think of spin-offs always going in one direction: from physics (as in the case of X rays), chemistry, and engineering to medicine. However, in many cases an initial discovery in *medicine* has led to important advances in other fields. Landsteiner's discovery advanced the science of genetics when von Dungern and Hirszfeld (1910) showed that blood groups were inherited characteristics handed down in accordance with Mendel's law. It became important in law in two cases: It permitted identification of blood stains and often settled paternity disputes. It also had an impact on the science of anthropology, in tracing the movements of races over centuries. Now it has gone full circle—back to cardiac surgery—and has profoundly influenced the field of tissue and organ transplantation. Christiaan Barnard's dramatic transplant of a human heart into another man was technically well done, but his patient died days later because the *tissue* cells of the transplanted heart were attacked by the patient's antibodies. We now know that the *tissue* cells of one human usually differ from those of another and that transplantation of tissues or organs fails when the tissue cells of the donor and those of the patient are incompatible. In fact, it was the great experimental surgeon Alexis Carrel who first called attention to this in 1910.

In 1900 Landsteiner was immersed in studies of basic immunology and did not connect his discovery of subspecies of blood within man with the clinical problem of transfusion reactions. Seven years later, Ludwig Hektoen in Chicago, concerned because the famous Cleveland surgeon George Crile was performing large numbers of transfusions by stitching a donor's artery to a patient's vein without any consideration of blood types, suggested that transfusion reactions could be avoided by selecting a donor whose red cells are not clumped by the serum of the recipient and whose serum does not clump the red cells of the recipient. Hektoen diagrammed a simple test for selecting the proper donor, but did not follow up on it. Neither did Crile. Crile's response, two years later, was, "As they [the agglutinins] have not been found in the sera of suitable animals, it has not been possible to conduct experiments tending to prove this theory." But Crile really did not have to do experiments on animals to prove whether Hektoen was right or wrong. He could have assumed that Hektoen was right and determined whether he could eliminate transfusion reactions completely by dismissing volunteer donors whose red cells were clumped by his patient's serum.

In 1908 Reuben Ottenberg, then a surgical intern at German Hospital in New York City, actually did test the compatibility of the bloods of a husband and his wife before performing a Crile-type direct artery-to-vein transfusion between them. In the last paragraph of a 29-page paper on direct blood transfusions published in a surgical journal, Ottenberg mentioned his test casually: "It is possible now to determine beforehand whether hemolysis [dissolution of red cells] is likely to occur when any two bloods are to be mixed. Such an examination was made before the second transfusion described in this paper. A thing much to be desired is that a convenient clinical test for this purpose be devised." I doubt that many physicians got as far as p. 29, and when Ottenberg took a research position the next year at Columbia University's biochemical laboratory, it looked at first as though even he would not follow up on his clinical test; but he did. In 1911 he described a simple but effective cross-matching agglutination test. So it was not in the department of surgery, but in Columbia's basic science division, engaged in the most esoteric type of research "on the composition of protoplasm as well as the structural and dynamic relationships of all constituents and products," that Ottenberg devised his practical test—the direct cross-matching of bloods to see if the recipient's serum agglutinated the donor's red cells (Fig. 2.18). It took a while before the test won acceptance, even from those who specialized in giving transfusions, but eventually it was used routinely before every transfusion, and most reactions were avoided—most, but not all, because the Rh factor still had to be discovered.

Landsteiner, Wiener, Levine, Diamond, and others in the early 1940s (when Gibbon was still working on animals and had not yet used

Figure 2.18. Blood groups. Typing of blood according to groups is done by mixing serially blood of an unknown type with anti-A and then anti-B serum. The blood group is identified by noting those mixtures containing uniformly suspended cells and those containing clumped cells. The solid gray areas here, if seen under a microscope, would show individual red cells uniformly distributed; wherever there is an antigen–antibody reaction, there are clumps of cells separated by clear spaces, showing agglutination.

The letters A, B, AB, and O refer to the types of antigen naturally occurring in the red blood cells of each group. For example, blood in group O (bottom) shows no reaction to either anti-A or anti-B serum (no clumping of red cells), and therefore contains no antigens. Group O individuals are known as "universal donors" because their cells, transfused into patients of any of the other three groups, will not clump in the recipient's bloodstream. Blood in group AB (second from the bottom) clumps in the presence of both anti-A and anti-B sera, and therefore contains both A and B antigens.

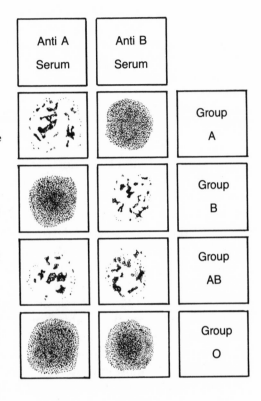

his pump on patients) noted severe reactions to second and third transfusions of blood from a single donor to a single patient, even though both the donor and recipient belonged to what everyone agreed was the same blood group. This led to the likelihood that the blood of some patients contained still another factor that could lead to agglutination of red cells; they named this the Rh factor (Rh being an abbreviation for the *rh*esus monkey whose blood contained the same factor or antigen). Research soon showed that red cells in about 85% of humans contained this factor; they were labeled Rh positive; in the other 15%, the Rh factor was missing, and these persons were labeled Rh negative. Usually the latter contained no *antibodies* against the Rh factor, and so the first transfusion of blood from an Rh-positive donor to an Rh-negative patient produced no reaction. However, these Rh-positive cells stimulated the formation of anti-Rh bodies in the patient; depending on the concentration of these antibodies, a transfusion reaction was now possible with a *second* transfusion of Rh-positive blood from the same or another donor into the now-sensitized patient. The best-known instance of such immunization is the case of an Rh-positive father and an Rh-negative mother who produce an Rh-positive fetus. Near or at birth Rh-positive cells from the fetus cross the placenta into the mother's circulation; the mother, whose red blood cells are Rh negative, regards these Rh-positive cells as foreign bodies and develops antibodies to Rh-positive cells. Nothing happens at the time of the birth of the first baby. However, between the birth of the first baby and the second pregnancy, the mother has formed antibodies against Rh-positive red cells. If these antibodies now cross the placenta and enter the second fetus' circulation before or during birth, they can clump or destroy fetal red cells, and if they destroy enough, undetected by the obstetrician, the baby may die.

An addition to the standard "cross-matching test" soon permitted physicians to know whether incompatibility to Rh factor was likely and allowed physicians to avoid transfusion reactions caused by use of Rh-incompatible blood. But nothing in medicine ever seems to be solved completely. The three factors found by Landsteiner in 1900 have now grown to more than 100 specific differences in the blood of *Homo sapiens;* fortunately, most of these cause no clinical problems.

The story of safe blood is a very long one. It began when a seventeenth century architect–astronomer–mathematician tried his hand at administering wine and opium intravenously and stimulated others to transfer blood first from animal to animal, then animal to man, and, finally, from man to man. Its long trail led to a whole new science of immunology, to the study of man's defenses against foreign materials (viruses, bacteria, tissue cells, proteins) that enter his bloodstream, and to lifesaving procedures such as transfusions, open heart surgery, and a start at predictably safe organ transplantation.

Gibbon's patients, by the time he was ready to perform his first open heart operation in man, were protected from reactions due to incompatible blood used to prime his pump–oxygenator. Many workers in many different fields and countries had identified the symptoms, determined the events that caused the reactions and finally the basic mechanism involved, and learned how to predict and prevent reactions.

But Gibbon needed still more. The safest blood in the world would have been useless if it clotted once removed from the circulation of a donor and placed in a heart–lung machine. Someone had to learn how to keep blood liquid outside the body.

Fortunately, the ideal nontoxic, naturally occurring anticoagulant, heparin, became available the very year, 1934, that Gibbon began his experimental work on his heart–lung machine; without it Gibbon would have had to spend years doing research on how to keep blood liquid outside the body. The work of many earlier scientists gave him what he needed, and just when he needed it.

The Story of Liquid Blood

We mentioned earlier some "superextraordinary" properties of blood. One of these is its property of staying liquid within the circulation but turning into a solid clot once it escapes from cut or torn blood vessels. In everyday life, clotting is a protective mechanism that may be lifesaving, but clotting in a heart–lung machine is a disaster.

The Greeks explained this liquid-to-solid phenomenon to their satisfaction by stating that blood was a living fluid and, when shed, died and became rigid as muscles do when they develop rigor mortis. Not until the end of the nineteenth century was there any real scientific explanation of clotting, and there were only a few crude ways to try to prevent it.

In the seventeenth century, Marcello Malpighi, who had discovered the pulmonary capillaries, isolated one of the essential components of a blood clot. He observed that white fibers (later called fibrin) could be separated from clotted blood, after which the blood became and stayed liquid. In 1821 Jean Prévost and Jean Dumas in France whipped freshly shed liquid blood with a wire eggbeater, a remarkable device found in any French kitchen! The fibrin threads stuck to it and what was left of the blood (defibrinated blood) remained liquid. Because this blood was obviously a good candidate to replace sheep blood in transfusions, Prévost and Dumas experimented with it and found to their satisfaction that it retained the qualities of fresh blood and that it could revive dogs bled almost to the point of death. Shortly thereafter, many physicians transfused defibrinated blood obtained from either humans or animals. Defibrination certainly permitted transfusion of blood without clogging tubes, arteries, and veins, but it was far from the ideal liquid. Whipping did nothing to eliminate immunological reactions, because the red cells were still there and some types were still "foreign."

Physicians learned two other ways to keep blood liquid during the time required for transfusion. One was to withdraw the donor's blood into a syringe and then inject it at once into the recipient's vein before it could clot. But the surface of a glass or metal syringe was unlike the lining of a natural artery or vein and Joseph Lister, of antisepsis fame, had shown in 1863 that unnatural or "foreign" surfaces promote blood clotting. Lister demonstrated that blood remained liquid for 24–48 hours in a horse's jugular vein that was tied off at both ends and removed from the body, but clotted in a few minutes when the same blood was transferred to a glass vessel. Clotting could be delayed a while by coating all foreign surfaces with paraffin, which to a certain extent mimicked the inside surface of blood vessels, but it was not a final answer.

The other way was to transfer blood without any contact with a foreign surface. As mentioned previously, Crile, in the early 1900s, had perfected a method for sewing the radial (wrist) artery of a donor to an arm vein of a recipient so that the donor's blood flowed directly into the patient without touching anything except the inner lining of an artery and of a vein. This overcame the problem of blood clotting and permitted skilled vascular surgeons, after they finally learned and made use of Landsteiner's and Ottenberg's discoveries, to perform reaction-free transfusions. And so a new specialty was born, the "transfusionist." However, direct artery-to-vein transfusions had many disadvantages. Being surgical procedures, they were expensive. They sacrificed a wrist artery of the donor, which was usually tied off at the end of the transfusion rather than repaired; this severely limited the possibility of repeated transfusions. Direct transfusions also prevented accurate knowledge of the volume of blood transfused, unless the surgeon had a means of weighing the donor or recipient with great precision before and during the transfusion. For these reasons, the technique had a short life, though it was revived briefly by a cardiac surgeon in the early 1950s, just before Gibbon's artificial heart–lung machine was ready for patients.

A far better and less expensive way had to be found to keep blood liquid. As is often the case, the best way was to discover the fundamental chemical mechanisms responsible for blood clotting and to learn from these how to prevent clotting. We learned earlier that blood remains liquid after white fibers, "fibrin," are mechanically separated from blood by whipping it. Obviously, fibrin had to come from something or some things present in blood. One of these was found to be a chemical, pro-thrombin, formed in the liver; under certain circumstances *pro*thrombin becomes transformed into *thrombin*. Thrombin then acts on another substance in blood, a normal plasma protein, *fibrinogen*, and converts it into fibrin threads. The knowledge summarized in the last fifty or so words did not magically appear during a coffee break; it required the work of many scientists, some right and some wrong, over many decades. But at last the knowledge was at hand.

The first naturally occurring anticoagulant discovered was a substance that prevented the action of thrombin on fibrinogen. It was named *hirudin* because it was isolated from the leech, a worm of the class Hirudinea. I suspect that many would regard a study of worms by medical scientists as an inane use of their time and of public or private money. But leeches are remarkable creatures. They are bloodsucking worms that physicians (or barber surgeons) at one time applied to the skin of patients for whom bleeding was recommended. Each leech can suck more than a teaspoon of blood from the patient and then store in pouches in its digestive tract enough blood to serve as its food for several months. Physicians often noted that after an engorged leech was removed from the patient's skin, bleeding from the skin continued. This observation suggested that the leech first pumped an anticoagulant into the skin before sucking blood. This proved to be correct, for in 1884 the anticoagulant was extracted from glands near the leech's suckers.

Landois used this substance as an anticoagulant in 1892, and Abel, Rowntree, and Turner, who built the first artificial kidney (for dogs) in 1914, used hirudin to keep blood from clotting as it flowed through thin cellophane-like tubes that permitted certain waste products to leave the blood (see Fig. 2.27). Abel and his group, appalled at the high cost of hirudin ($27.50 a gram in 1913), decided to buy their own leeches from "cupping barbers" of France and extract their own. Abel found that his own extract of leeches produced no changes in the blood pressure or respiration of rabbits, even when injected intravenously in large amounts, and was in no way harmful to his animals.

No one used hirudin after Abel, and physicians had no purified, naturally occurring anticoagulant until 1935, when heparin became available commercially. Few today have ever heard of hirudin, so why include this bit about the 1914 story? Because research doesn't always march straight ahead on an ideal schedule; often there are blind alleys and missed opportunities, and hirudin and the 1914 artificial kidney are among these. The fact is that a drug manufacturer did try to market hirudin, but despite *Abel's* success in purifying it, the *manufacturer* had none. I suspect that if physicians had been clamoring for hirudin to use in artificial kidneys, hirudin would have been purified right then and there. So the question is really, Why were physicians not ready for Abel's artificial kidney in 1914? Possibly this was because its clinical use would first require clinical research, and clinical investigation would require measurements of various chemical compounds in blood. But clinical biochemistry was just in its infancy.

At about the same time, citrated blood came on the scene. In 1890 two French physiologists, Nicholas Arthus and Colixte Pagès, studying the basic mechanism of blood coagulation, made an observation that was destined to be of tremendous importance to medicine and surgery. They found that calcium was essential for blood coagulation. If there is no free calcium, no clotting takes place. When they made blood calcium completely insoluble by adding chemicals such as oxalate or fluoride, blood remained liquid, in or out of the body. Physiologists who were studying the function of isolated organs of animals immediately made use of this finding, because it permitted them to use liquid blood as a perfusion fluid. But these chemicals were too toxic; on the other hand, citrate, which merely bound calcium to it so that there were relatively few free calcium ions in the plasma, seemed to be satisfactory for physiological studies.

One might have guessed that there would have been a rush in the 1890s to use citrated blood transfusions but there wasn't. We don't know why twenty-four years passed between the use of citrated blood in animal experiments and its use as an anticoagulant in human blood transfusions. Possibly it was the fear of causing harm; citrate can lower blood calcium to dangerously low levels when too much is given intravenously to humans. Sir Almroth Wright, the British pathologist who twenty-five years later was to do all he could to discourage Alexander Fleming from studying penicillin, knew of the effect of citrate on blood coagulation, and in 1894 he cautioned against injecting it into venous blood because it would bind all of the calcium salts in blood, make the blood completely incoagulable, and depress the function of heart muscle. This warning was appropriate for anyone who might have considered administering large amounts of citrate intravenously, and Gibbon and others have always been careful not to use large amounts of citrated blood to prime pump–oxygenators. But, strangely enough, Wright was also convinced that lemon and lime juices, which contain citrates, would be harmful if given to patients with scurvy, because such patients typically have spontaneous hemorrhages; he implicitly believed this, even though citrus juices had been used since 1748 with great success to cure and prevent scurvy. He seemed always to be partly right and partly wrong, and this over so many years that he earned the nickname Sir Almost Right. As Sir *Almost*, he did delay the use of citrated blood transfusions.

Wright, however, did not deter Albert Hustin in Brussels from performing the first successful indirect blood transfusion in man using citrate. In 1960, recalling his 1914 transfusion, Hustin emphasized that he was not looking for a new method of blood transfusion. He stated, "If this had been my intention I probably would have followed the usual tracks and would have succeeded at best in improving on some procedure or apparatus already known." Instead, Hustin, faced with a patient dying of carbon monoxide poisoning, suddenly realized that he might have saved this man's life if he could have withdrawn the blood that was loaded with carbon monoxide, eliminated the toxic gas from it, saturated the blood with oxygen, and reinjected it. This is another example of discovery initiated by the helplessness of a physician to care for his patient and his resolve to go to the research laboratory and find an answer to a specific problem. To accomplish his plan, Hustin needed a way of keeping blood fluid for an hour or so. While acting as the surgeon in his hospital, he had also done research in the physiological laboratory that required the use of liquid blood. He realized that defibrinated blood had been used as liquid blood but was probably unsafe for man; however, he believed that it might well be safe to use citrate, an anticoagulant that he had occasionally used in his animal experiments. This combination of his physiological background and knowledge and his concern about an immediate clinical problem led to his use of citrate for blood transfusion.

Hustin could not carry out his plan on the patient whose carbon monoxide poisoning had inspired the project. Being trained as an experimental scientist as well as a clinician, he first had to convince himself that there was a safe concentration of citrate that was also effective, one that would keep blood liquid without harming animals or humans. To decrease the concentration of calcium in blood, he decided to dilute blood with a glucose solution, known to be safe, and at the same time to add citrate. He then transfused this blood from rabbit to rabbit, dog to dog, man to dog and, finally, man to man. As a result of his work, blood could at last be removed from a donor and injected inexpensively and safely to a recipient without the risk and expense of a surgical operation. Equally important, the solution of glucose and citrate also happened to provide nutrition for blood cells and turned out to be a pretty good preservative for liquid blood. His work laid the foundation for blood banks, which provided liquid blood that could be given anywhere and at anytime (even on a battlefield, and World War I was just about to begin) without fear of severe reactions, if human error did not intervene. Citrate made transfusions easily available throughout the world and brought an abrupt end to the elite and expensive specialty of the blood transfusionist. It also provided another elegant demonstration of the principle that once a basic mechanism is understood and a rational approach developed, problems disappear and the practice of medicine becomes at once both less complex and less costly.

However, citrated blood would not be safe for priming Gibbon's pump oxygenator, because this would necessitate the use of several liters of blood, low or lacking in calcium ions, and free calcium is essential for optimal cardiac function. Nevertheless, the discovery of citrated blood was important to Gibbon's work in several ways. First, it revived interest in blood transfusions, which had fallen into disrepute in the 1890s. There were no blood transfusions during the Spanish–American war and only a few during World War I, and these toward the end. Second, it permitted indirect transfusions, which were simple for any physician to perform, and eliminated the surgical stitching of an artery to a vein; it also allowed storage of blood so that it could always be available, already typed and ready for emergency use. Third, any long surgical operation involves some blood loss; Hustin's discovery allowed Gibbon to use citrated blood at the end of an open heart operation, when needed to maintain blood pressure.

Gibbon still needed a completely harmless anticoagulant to keep fluid the large amounts of blood needed to prime the outside-the-body machine. His problem was solved by the discovery of heparin. Heparin did not result from a goal-directed effort to find a safe anticoagulant to use in an artificial kidney; it came from studying the basic mechanisms involved in blood clotting.

In 1915 Jay McLean, a young medical student from San Francisco, traveled to Baltimore to fulfill his dream of studying medicine at Johns Hopkins and to prepare for a career in academic surgery. On arrival he went to the medical school and introduced himself to the dean. The latter was surprised to see him, since McLean's application for admission had previously been turned down, but the next day he informed him of an unexpected vacancy. Because courses taken previously at the University of California in Berkeley satisfied Johns Hopkins' requirements in anatomy, biochemistry, and physiology, McLean was allowed to devote virtually the entire first year to research in physiology. This was a forerunner of today's deliberate program to encourage bright medical students to spend a full year in a research laboratory; how fortunate it was that McLean had taken his first year at a school (mirabile dictu, one in the Wild West) whose courses satisfied Hopkins' rigid requirements!

William Howell, chairman of the physiology department, gave McLean the task of studying a crude brain extract known to contain a powerful blood-clotting agent. McLean's task was to separate this substance from the rest of the extract, purify it, and test its blood-clotting activity and other properties. After months of hard work, he demonstrated that he could extract and purify a potent clotting agent. Some would have stopped there. But McLean had an invaluable characteristic for a scientist—*curiosity*. So quite on his own, to see whether the same material was present in other organs, he prepared similar extracts from both heart and liver. Since he was also measuring how long his clotting factor remained potent, he saved his crude extracts and measured their clotting activity at various time intervals. Luckily, the factor that *produced* clotting lost its activity so rapidly that McLean was able to find something else in the extract that still kept *its* activity. Remarkably, this second substance had precisely the opposite effect: It *prevented* coagulation. It was the first time that a naturally occurring anticoagulant had ever been found in mammals.

McLean told his professor that he had discovered a powerful anticoagulant. Howell was skeptical. So they allowed a small amount of blood to run from a cat's vein into a beaker, and McLean stirred all of his batch of anticoagulant into it. He placed it on Dr. Howell's table and asked his professor to call him when it clotted. It never did clot! They named McLean's anticoagulant heparin because they had extracted it from the hepar (Greek for liver); the name stuck, even though later heparin was found in much higher concentrations in other organs and tissues.

Considering the essential role of heparin today in cardiac and vascular surgery, it took a long time to purify heparin for clinical use. Animal experiments performed during the 1920s had demonstrated its effectiveness as an anticoagulant and in preventing the formation of clots inside and outside vessels; however, at that time it was costly to extract, difficult to prepare and purify, and low in potency. Its impurities frequently caused reactions. Because of these problems, it had been used only as a tool in laboratory work and, there, only by a few who had sufficient funds to afford it. Drug companies must now regret that they did not have the foresight to put some of their resources into purification and production of heparin. None did—possibly no one's crystal ball showed that vascular and cardiac surgery were only fifteen to twenty years away. Not even Howell suggested heparin's use in Abel's artificial kidney, even though Abel had devised it at Howell's own school four years earlier!

It was only because of Charles Best, codiscoverer of insulin, that the University of Toronto's Connaught Laboratories purified heparin. Why did Best need pure heparin? Because in 1926, when he was working with Sir Henry Dale in London on a basic problem related to the circulation, experiment after experiment was ruined by blood clotting in their blood pressure recorder. So on his return to Toronto in 1928, Best interested Arthur Charles and David Scott in purifying heparin and preparing it inexpensively. This they accomplished in 1933, and it was no accident that Gibbon's first successful use of his heart–lung machine, in a cat, came in 1934, the same year that heparin became available. Heparin enabled Gibbon to continue his experiments on the heart–lung machine and eventually perform the first successful operation in man.

Whenever a new drug comes into clinical use, it's a good idea to have ways of modifying or controlling its actions. There were several aspects of the action of heparin that presented challenges to scientists. One was that its effects, once in the body, wore off in 1–2 hours. In general, this is a pretty short time for drug effects to disappear, but cardiac surgeons would be happier if blood could regain its ability to clot as soon as all the skin stitches were in place. On the other hand, physicians or surgeons, fearful of clots forming within the veins of inactive patients confined to bed, would like an anticoagulant with a longer action. Because heparin is not absorbed when administered orally and must be given by injection, physicians and surgeons also needed a more slowly destroyed anticoagulant, effective when swallowed as pills, that could be used over days or weeks to prevent clotting within blood vessels.

Finding a drug to *shorten* the anticoagulant action of heparin, once it was no longer needed, came as unexpectedly as finding heparin itself.

Recall that McLean found a powerful *anti*coagulant when looking for a *coagulant*. In 1937 Erwin Chargaff and Kenneth Olson found an instant *antagonist* to the action of heparin while looking for a way to *prolong* its anticoagulant effect. Although some insulin substitutes are effective when taken orally, regular insulin, like heparin, is ineffective when taken orally. A few years earlier, scientists, mindful of the fact that diabetic patients had to inject insulin into one of their muscles several times a day, combined insulin with a chemical called protamine. This combination of protamine and insulin, once injected intramuscularly, released insulin slowly so that a larger dose of protamine–insulin lasts as long as four to six smaller doses of regular insulin. Chargaff and Olson reasoned that if protamine–insulin released insulin slowly, then protamine–heparin should release heparin slowly. To their surprise, they found that the combination of protamine with heparin completely and abruptly counteracted the anticoagulant action of heparin! Moral: Don't ignore things you've discovered but weren't looking for. Protamine is now used whenever the physician wants to terminate heparin action at once.

And so the discovery by McLean, a medical student, proved to be of tremendous value when the heart–lung machine was used in open cardiac surgery. It was effective, nontoxic, had a short life, and its action could be ended promptly by injecting protamine alone.

The solution to the other problem, that of finding an anticoagulant that could work for days or weeks without having to be injected continuously, came from a wholly unexpected source—veterinary medicine. In 1922–1924, Frank Schofield, a Canadian veterinarian in America, described "sweet clover" disease of cattle that occurred in North Dakota and Alberta, Canada. Cattle eating improperly cured sweet clover hay developed a tendency to bleed spontaneously, presumably because of a substance in the hay that interfered with blood coagulation. Schofield (1929), and later Lee Roderick (1931), found that the bleeding was due to a lack in blood plasma of one specific clotting factor, prothrombin, and that the substance responsible for this was a chemical formed when sweet clover had decomposed. Whatever it was, it was absorbed when eaten by cattle. In 1934 Karl Link and Harold Campbell, working at the University of Wisconsin's Agricultural Station, isolated, identified, and synthesized the active agent, now called dicumarol. The first clinical trials were in 1941 and 1942. Fortunately, a new test had been developed in 1934 by Kenneth Brinkhous, a physiologist interested in blood coagulation. This test was put to use clinically to measure prothrombin in blood so that physicians using dicumarol could control the dose and avoid in each patient the spontaneous hemorrhages suffered by cattle with sweet clover disease.

Dicumarol has no effect on the clotting of blood in a test tube; heparin or citrate must be used for this. Dicumarol acts specifically to inhibit just one of the body's thousands of functions, namely, the production of prothrombin by the liver, and the action of dicumarol can, when necessary, be antagonized by large doses of vitamin K, which probably acts on the same cells or receptors in the liver, but to *promote* the formation of prothrombin.

Citrate was used clinically from 1916 on; heparin became commercially available in pure and potent form in the mid 1930s, and dicumarol in the 1940s. The cardiac surgeon could now manage blood. He had three anticoagulants to serve three different needs, and he had ways of testing their effects in the body and ways of terminating anticoagulant action promptly.

Blood Banks

Were these discoveries enough for Gibbon and his project? Not quite. The surgeon also needed large amounts of the right kind of blood at the right moment. Blood preservation, storage, and banking at last met this need in the late 1930s and early 1940s. Again, as in learning about the function of the heart and lungs, blood transfusions, blood groups, rejection of "foreign" cells and tissues, and anticoagulants, many scientists had to make earlier discoveries. The story of preservation of cells may have begun in 1902 with Alexis Carrel. In the course of his studies of the total energy requirements of isolated perfused organs, he found that he could remove arteries from animals, store them in the refrigerator for days, and then sew them back in place, and they survived. But blood could not be stored in 1902, because no one had found an anticoagulant to keep it liquid. It was not until Hustin performed his first transfusion with citrated blood in Belgium in 1914 that physicians were freed from the urgent need to obtain and use donated blood immediately.

The first systematic effort to test a number of possible preservatives and compare their effectiveness was that of Rous and Turner, at the Rockefeller Institute in 1916, who worked on "kept cells." They found that a combination of dextrose and citrate (the same chemicals used by Hustin in 1914 to keep blood liquid) was most effective and could keep cells alive for 3–4 weeks.

Innovations in the use of blood for transfusions usually came just before or during wartime. The next war was the Spanish Civil War in the 1930s. Russian physicians developed large-scale storage systems for blood at the Sklyfavofsky Emergency Hospital in Moscow in 1936, and stored blood was first used on a massive scale during the Spanish Civil War, when more than 9,000 liters of blood were stored in and drawn out of the Barcelona blood bank between 1936 and 1939. Bernard Fantus established the first blood bank in the United States at Cook County Hospital in Chicago in 1937, so stored blood was available to Gibbon early in his research. The analogy to a "money bank" holds in that a depositor puts bills into his bank and gets bills back, though rarely the same bills, and a depositor puts his blood in a bank but rarely gets back the same blood.

Not all problems of blood storage and transfusion are solved, even today. Sometimes a patient needs a transfusion of platelets more than one of red cells, and platelets have a short life in storage. Platelets are the smallest cells in blood and they are twenty-five times less numerous than red cells, but they have important functions in plugging holes in capillaries and in aiding blood coagulation (Fig. 2.19). Also, the problem of transmission of disease by transfusion still remains; it has been greatly reduced by careful screening of donors and by tests before the collection and storage of blood, but viral hepatitis still occurs. However, the car-

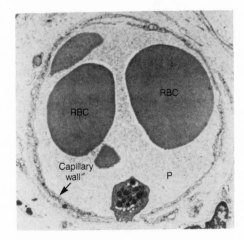

Figure 2.19.   Electron micrograph of a cross section of a capillary (×13,000). The capillary was deliberately dilated until a break occurred in its inner lining (at the bottom of the illustration). Note that a platelet (P), which normally will not stick to an intact lining, has attached itself to the tear in the vessel and plugged the hole. In larger vessels, platelets can plug much larger holes by first aggregating into a mass.

diac surgeon no longer has to worry that his technique and skill is limited by the supply of blood immediately available.

The Artificial Lung

The most difficult problem Gibbon had to overcome was building an artificial lung to oxygenate blood. In his very first year of full-time research, 1935, he was able to keep a cat alive for 2 to 3 hours using a heart–lung machine, without any help from the cat's own heart and lungs. So it was possible. But a 6-pound cat is $\frac{1}{30}$ the weight of a large man, and it would be impossible to fit an oxygenator 30 times as large as Gibbon's 1935 model inside a surgical operating room. One way of designing a compact oxygenator would be to learn how the human lung accomplishes its job. After all, the lungs of a man are pretty small, yet during his maximum muscular exercise, they can fully oxygenate 20–30 liters of blood per minute; all that Gibbon required to circulate in an immobile, anesthetized adult was 3–5 liters per minute.

If Gibbon, to learn how best to oxygenate blood, had sought help from the great men in art, literature, and learning of the Renaissance period, he would have been badly confused; that great surge of learning did not extend to studying the functions of a living human body. The authoritative teaching was then still that of Aristotle, that man breathed air in and out of his lungs to cool his blood. Aristotle taught that all mammals (including whales, which live in water) breathed air and all fishes breathed water, and that air or water served to cool them, "to temper the innate heat." He noted that warmer animals breathed more frequently; this he believed was because they had greater need to cool their bodies. He also stated that animals in closed vessels died because they continued to warm their environment and so could not cool themselves by breathing. It seems not to have occurred to Aristotle that air-breathing animals, including man, can live in tropical climates where the inspired air, being much greater than 100°F, cannot cool the body. Or perhaps he thought that the insides of the body were *very* hot. Aristotle was not an ignorant man; his was one of the greatest minds in ancient Greece. But his authority dampened the curiosity of some who might have found in the succeeding 1,800 years, by direct measurements, that he was wrong.

Not even Harvey in 1628 knew the function of the lung, and Gibbon would have obtained no help from studying Harvey's book. But Harvey started a new wave of experimental science in biology that resulted in more widespread study of living organs and tissues. It led to Malpighi's discovery of open channels (capillaries) throughout the pulmonary circulation (1661) and to learning the function of the lung (1667–1669). Robert Hooke and Richard Lower, in consecutive experiments, proved for the first time that the sacs in the lungs contained only air and that it was air passing into these sacs that was essential for changing blue venous blood into bright red arterial blood. They knew nothing about O_2. Air in the 1600s was believed unquestionably to be a single substance and not, as we know now, a mixture of oxygen, nitrogen, carbon dioxide, and some rare gases; the discovery of O_2 was still more than 100 years away. Essentially, Hooke and Lower proved that the rise and fall of the chest wall and the movements of the lungs were not essential (as then believed) for life as long as *air* moved into and out of the air sacs. Their experiments were simple. First, they removed the bony thorax of an animal, connected a tube to its windpipe, and blew air into the lungs until they were distended to their normal volume. Then, to obtain a flow of fresh air into and through the air sacs, they pricked many tiny holes in the outer surface of the inflated lung and blew fresh air into the trachea at the same rate that the air leaked out of their man-made pinholes. Although the thorax was gone and the lungs never moved or changed in size, the animal survived. Lower found that under these circumstances the venous blood became arterial in color, and so proved that the change from blue to red occurred entirely within aerated lungs and not in the heart. Hooke remarked in 1667, "I shall shortly further try, whether suffering the blood to circulate through a basin so as it may be openly exposed to the fresh air, will not suffice for the life of the animal." This promissory note, never enlarged upon by Hooke, was probably the first written speculation on devising an artificial lung, an essential part of a heart–lung machine.

The next essential step that made Gibbon's work possible was the discovery of the nature of the marvelous substance in air that maintains life in most species on earth. It is difficult to believe that oxygen was still unknown at the beginning of the American Revolution. Yet it was in 1776 that a Frenchman, Antoine Laurent Lavoisier, first demonstrated unequivocally that oxygen was a separable and very special component of air. He dispelled previous confusion caused by the use of meaningless labels (such as "dephlogisticated" air) and named the vital component "oxygen." But, as in the discovery of the circulation of the blood, others played important roles: With oxygen, it was John Mayow and Joseph Priestley, two Englishmen, and Carl Scheele, a Swede. Priestley was a chemist who discovered nitrous oxide, ammonia, sulfur dioxide, and carbon monoxide. He was also the first man to breathe pure oxygen and the first to note the "beauty and vivacity of a flame" in it. In 1775 he enclosed a mouse in a jar filled with a gas that he had released, chemically, from mercuric oxide and found that the gas "was much better than common air." Priestley also recognized nonmedical uses for his new gas: adding it to a flame to melt platinum and using it to explode gunpowder. However, Priestley never realized that he had discovered oxygen, because he could not disentangle himself from existing terminology and dogma; but his experiments *did* put Lavoisier on the right track.

What honors were heaped upon Lavoisier and Priestley for their discoveries? Lavoisier, the genius who began the Chemical Revolution of the late 1700s, was guillotined in 1794 by the French Revolution, because, as the president of the tribunal put it, "the Republic has no need for savants." The next day, Joseph Lagrange, France's great mathematician, observed, "It required only a moment to sever that head, and perhaps a century will not be sufficient to produce another like it." Priestley, who was both a scientist and a theologian, had dared to oppose England's slave trade and, even worse, expressed sympathy for the aims of the French Revolution—in an England fearful of its spread across the Channel. He escaped beheading, but in 1791 a mob burned his chapel, house, library, and laboratory in Birmingham, England, and he and his family fled for their lives, eventually settling in Pennsylvania. He became a friend of two leaders of the American Revolution, John Adams and Thomas Jefferson, who shared his Unitarian views. He was offered the professorship of chemistry at the University of Pennsylvania, but he refused to accept any public positions. He continued his work as a chemist until he died in 1804.

Several other important discoveries were needed for Gibbon to understand how relatively small natural lungs could do the job of a roomful of laboratory equipment. One of these was the discovery of hemoglobin, the remarkable chemical substance in red blood cells that grabs O_2 in the air sacs and carries it to organs and tissues, where it frees it for O_2-hungry cells.

Richard Lower, in 1667, knew that blue blood exposed to air became red, but he did not know why. Lavoisier isolated, identified, and labeled O_2 in 1776, but he knew nothing of hemoglobin. In the middle of the eighteenth century, Nicolas Lémery, a chemist, evaporated all the water from blood by heating it and found that the remaining dry ash contained iron; for identifying iron he used a method known today to every child— he separated the iron from dry powder by using a magnet! But he didn't know its function. At about the same time, physicians learned that feeding iron compounds to anemic patients caused their pale blood to become a healthy red color. Finally, chemists found that it was the red cells in blood that contained the iron and that iron was an essential part of the red pigment. In 1862 the great chemist Hoppe-Seyler purified and crystallized the red material in red blood cells, found that it was the substance responsible for accepting and releasing O_2, and named it hemoglobin.

Hemoglobin not only has the amazing ability to combine with O_2 in the lungs, but it is also remarkably generous in relinquishing it quickly to active tissues and cells when oxygenated blood flows through capillary beds (Fig. 2.20). How do we explain these unique chemical properties? Chemicals can react with other chemicals in a variety of ways. They can combine chemically to form fixed compounds (as a sodium ion combines with a chloride ion to form a fixed salt, sodium chloride) or they can simply dissolve in liquids, with no chemical reaction at all, as nitrogen gas dissolves in water or plasma, the amount going into solution depending directly on the pressure of the nitrogen molecules and the temperature. Hemoglobin, however, has an additional, special property of *associating* itself with O_2 to the point of saturation at the O_2 pressure normally present in the lungs and in the pulmonary capillaries. Then, when arterial blood, fully oxygenated, flows through the capillaries of active tissues that need O_2, oxyhemoglobin in the red cells releases its oxygen (oxyhemoglobin dissociates into hemoglobin and O_2), and the O_2 becomes readily available for tissue use. So as each liter of blood flows around Harvey's circle, it can, in just 1 or 2 seconds in the lung capillaries, load to the limit with O_2 (about 200 milliliters of O_2 per liter of blood); it then holds onto this O_2 as blood goes through the left side of the heart, into the aorta and its branches, and into the tissue capillaries; there, within a second or two, each liter can unload 50, 150, or even all 200 milliliters of O_2, depending on the needs of the tissues.

For those of you who like numbers, blood is about half straw-col-

Figure 2.20. The uptake and release of oxygen by hemoglobin. To demonstrate some unique properties of hemoglobin, put the same amount of blood in each of ten flasks, fill each flask with gas containing increasing amounts of O_2 (going from an oxygen pressure of 10 mmHg to one of 100 mmHg), and then stopper the flasks and shake them briefly. (See p. 214 in Chapter 6 for an explanation of mmHg, millimeters of mercury; 1 milliliter = $\frac{1}{1000}$ of a liter and 1 liter is about 1 quart.) Now measure the amount of O_2 in the blood in each flask. You will find that it increases very steeply in the low to middle range of pressures (10–40 mmHg), and then very little in the mid to high range (60–100 mmHg; see the curve). This is because hemoglobin has the unique property of becoming almost fully saturated with oxygen (it can combine with almost 200 milliliters of O_2 per liter of blood) at the oxygen pressure that normally exists in the lungs of a person breathing air, yet yields large amounts of its oxygen when the blood reaches active tissues, where the O_2 pressure is low. At point A (in the lungs), if the oxygen pressure decreases by 20 points (from 100 to 80 mmHg), the volume of oxygen combined with hemoglobin decreases very little. At point B (in the tissues), a decrease of 20 points (from 40 to 20 mmHg) releases 85 milliliters of oxygen, thereby making much of the oxygen present in the blood available to active cells. If a person's blood consisted only of plasma, its ability to take up and deliver oxygen would be indicated by a straight line starting at zero on the left and ending at 3 milliliters on the right (see the arrow).

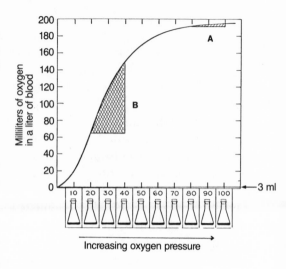

ored plasma and about half cells. Practically all the cells in blood are red blood cells (Fig. 2.21). An adult's blood contains about 25 thousand trillion red blood cells: Visualize that each red cell in the body flows past you once, in single file, and you are able to count ten of these per second, 24 hours a day, 365 days a year, with no time out to eat or sleep; it would take you 75,000 years to finish your count!

Each red cell contains about 280 million molecules of hemoglobin and each molecule of hemoglobin contains four atoms of iron, each of which can combine with one molecule of O_2. If you like, you can calculate the maximal volume of O_2 that your red cells can carry. If you don't like calculations, here is the approximate answer: When each liter (about 2 pints) of your blood passes through your pulmonary capillaries, its

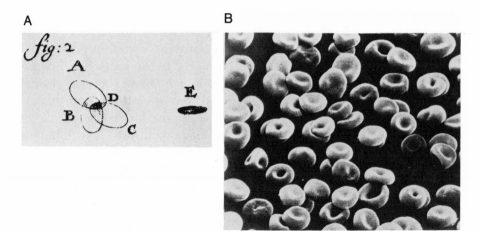

A　　　　　　　　　　　　B

Figure 2.21.　Red blood cells as (A) Leeuwenhoek saw them in 1696 and (B) seen through a scanning electron microscope. Leeuwenhoek confirmed Malpighi's discovery of the capillary system. In addition, he recognized the part the heart played in the circulation. Leeuwenhoek said, "I have never looked upon the Heart as the maker of the Blood, but only as an Engine that caused the Blood to circulate, driving it forcibly in to the Arteries, and by its opening, giving way for the Blood to come in again out of the Veins." Malpighi was the first to demonstrate the presence of blood corpuscles, but he mistook them for fat cells; Leeuwenhoek was the first to describe them accurately. We can see from the scanning electron micrograph that the cells are not spherical, but biconcave disks. This shape provides three remarkable advantages: It provides more surface area per unit of hemoglobin and a short distance for diffusion of oxygen to mid-cell; like a plastic bag half filled with water, it permits enough flexibility for the cell to squeeze through narrow capillaries (as Alan Burton put it, "like a raw oyster going down an esophagus"); and it permits the red blood cell to accept more fluid within its membranes without bursting. (Photograph (B) courtesy of Edi Ermes.)

hemoglobin can combine with 200 milliliters of O_2. This may not seem like a remarkable quantity, but it is sixty-seven times the maximal amount that a liter of water, salt solution, or plasma could hold under similar circumstances. To put it more vividly, to meet the needs of a resting man for oxygen, his heart would have to pump only 1¼ liters of blood each minute if *all* oxygen in the blood leaving the lungs were unloaded in the tissues and venous blood were oxygen free. But if the circulating fluid was plain water, salt solution, or even plasma, the heart would have to pump 84 liters each minute to transport the same amount of O_2!

Perhaps a brilliant chemist will someday concoct a synthetic, nontoxic chemical that would carry and release O_2 just as well as hemoglobin does, but would he also be able to incorporate the third amazing property of hemoglobin, the capacity to transport a waste product, carbon dioxide (CO_2), away from the tissues and to the lungs for elimination? The release of O_2 from oxyhemoglobin in the tissues actually speeds the transfer of CO_2 from tissues into blood; and when this venous blood, now poor in oxygen and rich in CO_2, reaches the lungs, the release of CO_2 from blood to air promotes the combination of fresh O_2 with hemoglobin!

It's pretty hard to improve on nature in general, and no one has yet done so for the fantastic actions and interactions involved in the loading and unloading of O_2 and CO_2 in lungs and tissues. For example, it is not an accident that hemoglobin is locked up inside red blood cells rather than riding free in the plasma in which the red cells float. It has been known since the 1930s, through the work of British physiologist Francis Roughton, that hemoglobin accomplishes its unbelievably speedy action only in concert with a special enzyme, or catalyst, that exists largely within the red cells and speeds the rate of conversion of CO_2 into carbonic acid, the first necessary step in carrying CO_2 in both red cells and plasma to the lungs for release there. It is well that nature not only devised hemoglobin but also deliberately packaged it and its special chemical helpers within bags or membranes, the red blood cells; if large numbers of red cells are damaged and spill their insides (hemoglobin, enzymes, potassium, etc.) and fragments of their outsides into circulating plasma, serious reactions occur.

Sir Joseph Barcroft, a twentieth-century physiologist, summarized the supreme importance of hemoglobin to man by writing, "But for hemoglobin's existence, man might never have attained any activity which the lobster does not possess, or had he done so, it would have been with a body as minute as the fly's."

So it must have appeared unwise to Gibbon to spend time looking for a better carrier for O_2 than hemoglobin. Hemoglobin had capacity to spare. The trick was to get O_2 into close contact with hemoglobin in blood. August Krogh, a Danish physiologist, studied the movement of gases, such as O_2, across living membranes and learned that gases travel by a process called diffusion. Molecules of gases are constantly in random motion. If molecules of a particular gas are more concentrated in one region than in another, there are more molecular collisions and more motion. Although the molecules of this gas are in motion in all regions, the net effect is that gas diffuses from regions of higher concentration and greater motion to regions of lower concentration and less motion. So in the real lung, where O_2 is in high concentrations in air sacs, O_2 will move from the air side of each sac to the blood side, and there rapidly combine with hemoglobin. In the real lung, where CO_2 is in high concentrations in venous blood, CO_2 will move to the air side and be excreted on the next expiration.

The amount of O_2 transferred each minute is so great that the great British physiologist John S. Haldane was sure about seventy years ago that the lung had to *secrete* at least some O_2 into the blood by an active process (just as stomach cells secrete hydrochloric acid). But he turned out to be wrong, for diffusion of gases is an extremely rapid process over *very* short distances, and the tissues in the lung that separate air from blood are exceedingly thin. Electron microscopy has now shown that in places these tissues are less than 4 millionths of an inch thick. In addition, the surface area of this tissue must also be enormous, which it is; in the human lung, nature has constructed a surface of 70 square meters, or 40 times the total area of a man's skin. On one side is continually renewed fresh air, and on the other continuously flowing venous blood with its red cells moving in single file, their hemoglobin ready to soak up O_2.

If one wants to imitate nature, one must first inquire how nature managed to put this huge air–blood surface into lungs that occupy only about 8% of the body's volume. First, let us look at the air side. Here nature has used the method of folding, over and over again (Fig. 2.22). If one constructs a lung with a smooth inner surface, its area is small; however, if one creates a plicated or folded surface, the surface area is now very much larger; and if one creates folds on each of the initial folds, over and over, and over again, there is scarcely a limit to the inside area that can be created in a lung whose outer dimensions remain the same.

Nature's second trick on the air side is to distribute evenly the fresh air drawn into the lungs on each inspiration so that each air sac gets its fair share. This requires an elaborate system of branching tubes. After fresh air is drawn through the nose or mouth into and through the pharynx and larynx (the "voice box"), it enters the main air pipe, the trachea. The ancients called this the windpipe, probably because they believed that air drawn into the lungs acted like a wind and cooled the hot blood in the heart or lungs. The trachea subdivides into two main bronchi, one to each lung; each of these subdivides into two bronchioles, and each of these into two more, and so on until at the eighteenth subdivision there are 262,144 respiratory bronchioles (Fig. 2.23). These subdivide further and further into millions of smaller ducts that lead, at the twenty-fourth subdivision, into 300 million alveoli or air sacs, each about $\frac{8}{1000}$ of an inch in diameter (Fig. 2.24). The collective walls of these air sacs is the air side of the 70-square meter membrane separating air and blood.

We have already looked at the blood side (Fig. 2.2). It attains its huge surface by dividing and subdividing large tubes into smaller and smaller ones until the vessels are barely wide enough (3/10,000 of an inch) to permit red blood cells to slip through in single file; there are about 600 million of these capillaries and they completely enmesh the air sacs (Fig. 2.25).

Gibbon's job obviously became one of creating as vast a surface as he could for air (or O_2) to come into contact with blood and to make the film of blood as thin as possible. Then if the circulating fluid contained red cells, its hemoglobin quickly soaked up the O_2 as soon as it diffused within range.

Some oxygenators had been devised as early as the nineteenth century for use in physiology laboratories. The first type was the *bubble oxygenator*. In this type, many fine bubbles of air or O_2 come into direct contact with blood. In its earliest and most elementary form, this method required nothing but shaking blood and air together in a closed flask. A simple method, still in use, allows fine bubbles of O_2 to enter the bottom of a tall glass cylinder full of blood; the bubbles rise through the blood and combine with hemoglobin on the way up and out. The second type was the *film oxygenator* (Fig. 2.26). In this type air or O_2 again comes into direct contact with blood, but a special device spreads the blood into a very thin film on the wall of a chamber in which the film is exposed to air or O_2; the devices used have been many and quite ingenious. The third type was the *membrane oxygenator*. This is the only apparatus that mimics the lungs in that blood and air are separated by a membrane that favors diffusion of O_2 and CO_2 but prevents direct contact of gas and blood.

The first bubble oxygenator was used in 1882, but was unsafe because the bubbles turned the blood into foam, and foam blocks small blood vessels. Bubbles of gas from an artificial lung are especially dangerous, because the blood, with its bubbles, does not go through the

A

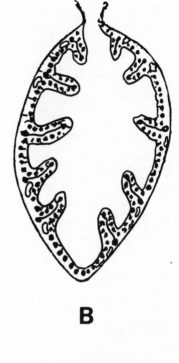

B

Figure 2.22.   Schematic representation of increasing the surface area
for gas exchange without a change in
the lung volume. Lung (A) is the
simplest; it has only one air sac.
Black dots represent pulmonary
capillaries in the wall of the air sac.
Both the number of capillaries and
the area of the air sac in close contact with capillaries are small. Lung
(B) has a greatly increased air–blood
surface created by adding ten partitions (invaginations), each of which
contains additional capillaries. Lung
(C) has a still greater air–blood surface created by adding thirty-one
partitions to (A); ten of these have
sixty-seven additional projections,
each with additional capillaries. It is
impossible to illustrate the hundreds
of millions of air sacs and pulmonary
capillaries of the human lung that
provide a surface area of 70 square
meters for gas exchange, almost
40% of the area of a tennis court.

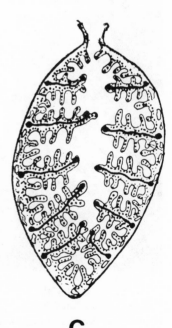

C

Figure 2.23. Cast of the bronchial tree of a lung of a 26-pound beagle at autopsy. One can see the intricate and multiple branchings of the windpipe (trachea) into bronchi and then into bronchioles that lead into more than 262,000 respiratory bronchioles that in turn conduct fresh air into about 300 million air sacs.

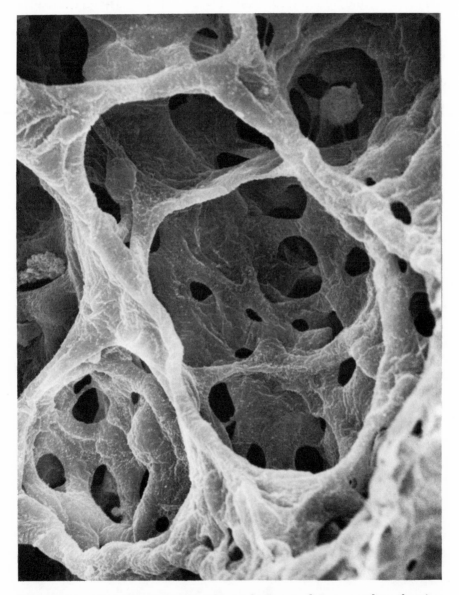

Figure 2.24. Mouse lung (×4,000). This is what inspired air passes through as it enters a vast number of branches of the bronchi until it reaches a gas exchange surface, the most distant and smallest openings, where fresh air is in close contact with venous blood flowing through the pulmonary capillaries.

patient's lung, whose pulmonary capillaries were designed to trap foreign particles and bubbles, but goes directly into the arterial circulation
(see p. 25), including the coronary arteries and the vessels of the
brain, where gas bubbles block fine blood vessels and cause damage to
cells of the heart and brain.

Lee Clark and his associates solved the foam problem in 1950, when
they found that silicone products both stuck to the oxygenator chamber
and broke up the foam in the blood. Once the blood was oxygenated,
the bubbles vanished and the danger of bubbles reaching and blocking
the vital circulations of the heart and brain also vanished. But someone
first had to invent silicones; this was done by Frederic Kipping in 1905,
with no thought in mind of an artificial heart–lung machine.

The first film oxygenator was used in the laboratory of Max von

**Figure 2.25.   Greatly enlarged picture of pulmonary capillaries (C) in intimate rela-
tion to air-filled sacs, or alveoli (A). In living animals the tiny capillaries are filled
with red blood cells in single file. Blood and air are separated by a very thin barrier
of tissue (T).**

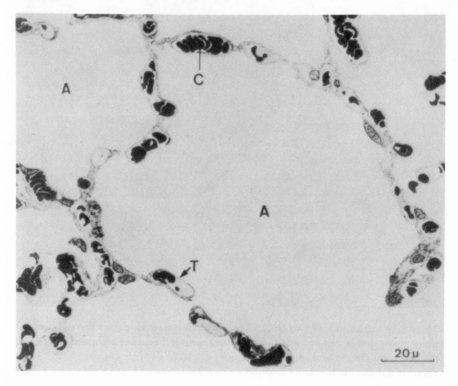

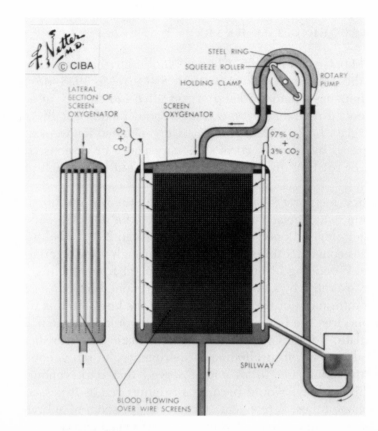

A

B

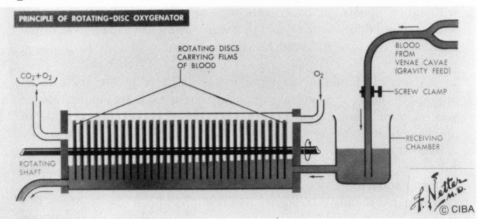

Figure 2.26.   Two types of film oxygenator. The one in (A) uses the principle of Gibbon's screen oxygenator, in which blood flows downward over fine wire screens surrounded by 97% oxygen and 3% carbon dioxide. The one in (B) is a rotating disc oxygenator. The rotating discs dip into a trough of blood and carry a thin film of blood on their surfaces into the O_2 above the trough. There hemoglobin combines with O_2. Blood is well oxygenated when it reaches the outflow tube of the oxygenator.

Frey and Max Gruber in 1885. Charles Lindbergh (the same Lindbergh who flew the Atlantic), working with Alexis Carrel in 1935, designed a special pump–oxygenator to keep organs alive indefinitely in a sterile environment; it operated by spreading venous blood over the smooth surface of glass bulbs and kept isolated organs alive for weeks. Other devices spread blood on vertical stationary plates or screens, rotating cylinders, or rotating discs that dipped in and out of a trough of blood (Fig. 2.26).

The first membrane "vividiffusion" apparatus was used in 1914 by Abel's group, who devised an "artificial kidney" for dogs 42 years before Willem Kolff devised one for man (Figs. 2.27 and 2.28). Abel used collodion tubes connected in parallel and ran through them arterial blood, kept liquid by adding hirudin, the anticoagulant from leeches, so that substances excreted by a normal kidney but retained by a diseased kidney could diffuse out of the blood and out of the body. In this way, the device could free the body of substances that would be toxic if allowed to accumulate. Very much later (1944), Kolff made Abel's artificial kidney clinically useful; in preliminary experiments, he ran venous blood through his cellophane tubes and observed that dark venous blood entering his "kidney" would become a brighter red as it passed along the cellophane tubes. A few years later Kolff devised a membrane oxygenator. By that time, the plastics industry was a giant and could respond with tubes, sheets, or bags made of a wide variety of materials that allowed rapid diffusion of O_2 and that were inexpensive enough to throw away after one use to avoid transmitting viral infections to the next patient.

A special membrane oxygenator was designed in the 1970s in an attempt to mimic the natural pulmonary circulation. Its unique feature was an 8-inch-long bundle of 16,000 parallel hollow fibers made of "polycarbonate siloxane copolymer"; the wall thickness of each was only 8/100,000 of an inch and the inside diameter of each of these microtubes was only 8/10,000 of an inch. Such a unit, only a few inches in diameter and 8 inches long, had a surface area of almost $1\frac{1}{2}$ square meters (as compared to only 0.05 square meter if it had been one empty tube 8 inches long and 3 inches in diameter). Blood flowed through the 16,000 fibers, and 5 liters per minute of O_2 flowed in, through, and out of the chamber that enclosed the bundle.

So in 1935 Gibbon had his choice of three types of man-made oxygenators: a bubble oxygenator, a film oxygenator, and a membrane oxy-

A

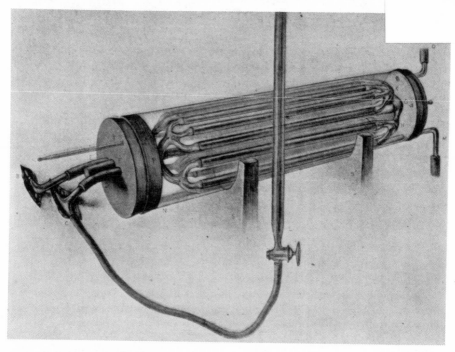

Figure 2.27.   Abel and his colleagues at Johns Hopkins built an
artificial outside-the-body kidney (A)
for animals in 1914, using collodion
(now replaced by cellophane) for the
tubing. Blood passed through the
thin-walled plastic tubes and eliminated excess waste materials into
the surrounding fluid. They used
hirudin obtained from leeches to
keep the blood liquid while passing
through the apparatus. A diagram-
matic representation of the tube
branching is shown in (B). This process of "vividiffusion," used here to
exchange small molecules across
membranes, is the same as that used
later in oxygenators.

B

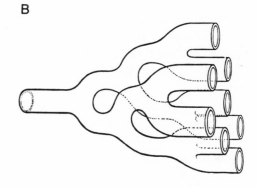

Figure 2.28. A membrane-type oxygenator. Kolff and his co-workers rediscovered the artificial kidney in 1944. They noted, by chance, that blue venous blood entering the thin-walled tubes became bright red toward the end of the coil. This observation led them to build an artificial oxygenator based on diffusion of oxygen across a thin membrane into blood flowing through the membranous tube. A cylinder made of varnished laths (left) rotates so that its lower part passes through a tub (filled with a rinsing liquid if used as an artificial kidney, or with flowing oxygen if used as an artificial lung). A segment of the rotating cylinder (right) shows the cellophane tubes wrapped around it.

genator. Gibbon chose a film oxygenator. But he had problems oxygenating enough blood fast enough with his early model. Two of his associates licked the problem in 1950. Gibbon had been using a hollow smooth metal cylinder that revolved in a vertical position. He maintained a thin film of blood on its inner surface, holding it there by centrifugal force, and blew O_2 on this film as it continuously moved from the top to the bottom of the cylinder. His associates, by covering the smooth inner surface with a wire screen to create turbulence in the blood film and a much greater surface area, were able to oxygenate eight to ten times as much blood each minute.

Gibbon now had safe blood, a suitable pump, and a gas exchanger that could oxygenate blood fast enough to support life in an adult man, and he had the full cooperation of Thomas Watson (president of IBM) and his engineers to put the apparatus into a compact, portable form. The time was now the early 1950s and time for Gibbon to create defects in the hearts of animals so that he could practice correcting these and perfect his own surgical techniques before performing open heart surgery in man, using his new heart–lung machine. Once he was satisfied in the surgical research laboratory, he moved to the hospital operating room.

He operated upon his first patient in 1952; it was a 15-month-old baby who died shortly after completion of the operation. Death was not due to technical failure of the apparatus, but to an incorrect preoperative diagnosis. Gibbon waited until May 6, 1953, before he operated upon a second patient. She was 18-year-old Cecelia Bavolek and both she and her mother knew of the earlier failure, but they also knew of Gibbon's phenomenal success in the following twelve months in the laboratory in repairing heart defects in animals. With great courage, she agreed to the operation. She was connected to the heart–lung machine for 45 minutes; for 27 of these minutes, it was the sole source of her circulation and respiration. Her recovery was smooth and she remains in good health to this day.

For a time Cecelia Bavolek had a difficult emotional adjustment. During the first year, she was flooded with phone calls asking for interviews and public appearances. She changed her telephone number to an unlisted one to diminish the annoyance, and avoided all publicity about the operation. Some years later, however, she overcame her reticence, and on the tenth anniversary of her operation she became the Heart Queen of the American Heart Association for the year 1963 and received an award presented by Lyndon Johnson (Fig. 2.29).

Figure 2.29.   Cecilia Bavolek, American Heart Association's Heart Queen for 1963 (tenth anniversary of Gibbon's first successful operation), accepting an award from Vice-President Lyndon Johnson.

The story of open heart surgery began on October 4, 1930, at Massachusetts General Hospital in Boston when Edith S. died because of a massive pulmonary embolism. Although Edith S. could never know it, her death led Gibbon to devise the outside-the-body heart–lung machine and it, in turn, started the explosion of open heart surgery and truly corrective operations that have saved thousands of lives each year since 1953. Maly Gibbon (Fig. 2.30) wrote some years later that she had always wished that the family and friends of Dr. Churchill's patient might know how many thousands of lives had been saved because Edith S. lived and died *when* and *where* she did. After a long search through old records had failed to uncover the hospital records of Edith S., Dr. Churchill's widow finally found them in 1974 in the one remaining carton in the Churchill attic. In it, Maly Gibbon found the name, address, and phone number of Edith S.'s husband. It took some months before Maly could gather her courage to call the number and decide what to say. She did call, a woman answered (Edith S.'s daughter), and Maly identified herself as the wife of Dr. Gibbon, one of the surgeons who had taken care of her mother 44 years previously. That was as far as she got. The daughter, to Maly's dismay, angrily remembered him well "as the man who killed my mother" and refused to see or talk with Maly.

Still determined that the daughter should know the story, Maly

Figure 2.30.   Maly and Jack Gibbon relax in their rose garden (1972).

wrote her a long letter telling her that her mother's life could not possibly have been saved by the surgical techniques that existed in 1930, but that her death led directly to developing the heart–lung machine which saved the lives of many thousands of patients who required open heart operations and prolonged the quality of life of thousands of others.

Six months elapsed without any reply. Maly than received a card and a note: The card said, "Though words really can't begin to express my thanks for all your thoughtfulness, I hope this note will help convey the gratitude I send your way. Thanks so much," and the note added, "I only wish my father and brother had lived to read it."

Here is a classic case of the unawareness of the public of *how* advances in medicine and surgery have come about—and of the failure of physicians, scientists, and science writers to acknowledge the contributions of patients who *died* as well as those who *survived*. In retrospect, Edith S. also deserved a special medal from the American Heart Association.

As for Gibbon, he never did remove a blood clot from a pulmonary artery—the goal that led him to build a heart–lung machine. (The first successful use of his heart–lung machine to remove a clot from a pulmonary artery of a patient came in 1958 in Boston.) Note that as early as 1939, Gibbon wrote that if the entire circulation could be carried temporarily by an extracorporeal circuit, it was conceivable that a diseased mitral valve might be exposed to surgical approach under direct vision and that the fields of cardiac and thoracic surgery might be broadened. Somewhere along the line, he realized that the cardiac defects of a tremendous number of patients could be completely corrected once his heart–lung machine was perfected and gave the surgeon unlimited time to do reconstructive operations on congenital defects and diseased valves instead of quick, temporizing procedures. He also realized that the number of such patients was huge compared to those with massive pulmonary embolus. To his credit, he changed his direction toward total repair of heart disorders. It was fitting that he was the first to use his apparatus for successful open heart surgery.

3

Preoperative Diagnosis

I've told why and how John Gibbon came to build the artificial heart–lung machine and how it came to be used in open heart surgery. But successful operations on the heart required far more than a dependable pump–oxygenator; I'll give you a list in Chapter 4. But at the top of the list belongs something absolutely essential that deserves a chapter to itself. It is something that I've barely mentioned, something that tends to be taken for granted and therefore omitted even at the end of a very long list of credits. That something is *pre*operative diagnosis, knowing *before* opening the chest *exactly what is wrong with the heart or artery that needs repairing.*

May 6, 1953, is carved in granite as the date of the first *successful* open heart operation, quite appropriately performed by John Gibbon while the patient's own heart was completely bypassed by Gibbon's outside-the-body machine. But a day in March 1952, the date of Gibbon's first open heart operation, is *not* carved in granite (or even noted in a medical journal) because the preoperative diagnosis was incorrect. The patient, a 15-month-old baby, had severe heart failure that was due, in the opinion of everyone who examined the patient, to an abnormal opening between the right and left atria. At the operation, Gibbon's team carefully examined every square millimeter of the right atrium and could not find a hole. Autopsy showed that, instead of a hole, there was a huge, wide-open ductus arteriosus (Fig. 3.1), an artery that is normally open in the fetus (to conduct blood directly from the right ventricle to the aorta) but which should close soon after birth; in this baby it had not. The team had tried before the operation to catheterize the baby's heart (see p. 121) to be sure that their clinical diagnosis was correct, but the attempt had failed.

This is not the only case on record of incorrect diagnosis of a cardiac defect; indeed, the very first operation planned to open a partially closed pulmonary valve (by Doyen in 1913) failed because at operation the valve was found to be perfectly normal. There *was* a serious congenital defect, but it was a narrowing of the muscular tube between the right ventricle and the pulmonary valve, and Doyen could do nothing about such a defect in the few minutes allowed for the operation.

If you have ever been to a diagnostician, you know that he begins by listening to your own story: your present symptoms, their beginnings and their progression, and past illnesses and those of your immediate family. He then begins his examination by observing your body for clues that are visible (by inspection), he taps (by percussion) your chest and abdomen, and he listens (by auscultation) through a stethoscope applied to areas overlying your heart and lungs. He also feels (by palpation) your abdomen and your surface arteries and tests your eye and limb reflexes and the acuity of various senses. If you are someone suspected of having heart disease, he records the electrical activity of your heart using the electrocardiograph and looks at your moving heart and lungs through a fluoroscope by which X-ray shadows are projected on a screen instead of on photographic film. All these things a physician could do by 1910–

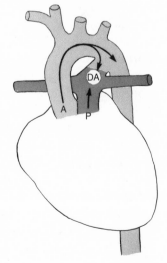

Figure 3.1. **In the fetus, the ductus arteriosus (DA) is wide open and the right and left pulmonary arteries are narrow. If, after birth, the pulmonary arteries dilate but the ductus does not close, blood from both the pulmonary trunk (P) and the aorta (A) flow into the low-pressure right and left pulmonary arteries and through the pulmonary capillaries. Gibbon's first patient had this defect, which defied diagnosis before the operation.**

1915, but it took a few centuries and a lot of interesting and important discoveries to get that far.

Clinical Diagnosis

Listening and looking and probably feeling were part of the physician's diagnostic equipment from ancient times, but percussion only came along in 1761, when a Viennese physician, Leopold Auenbrugger, wrote a small monograph, *Inventum Novum*. A number of factors combined to make Auenbrugger the first physician to introduce percussion into medical practice: First, his father was an innkeeper who regularly tapped the sides of his barrels to find out how much liquid and how much air was inside them; second, Auenbrugger was an accomplished musician with an excellent ear for pitch [he has among his publications the libretto for an opera, "Der Rauchfangkehrer" (The Chimney Sweep)]; and third, he chose medicine as a career instead of music or innkeeping.

As a physician, Auenbrugger realized that he could tell very little about the insides of the chest by feeling or looking at the outside. Then he remembered that the same was true about *looking* at a barrel, but when one tapped it over the fluid-filled part, one heard a dull, flat note, and when one tapped it over the air-filled part, one produced a resonant, "hollow" sound. Because the inside of the thorax contains a fluid-filled organ (the heart) with two air-filled organs around it (the lungs), Auenbrugger realized that one could, by percussion, outline the size of the heart and tell whether it was large or small, and whether any parts of the lungs were solid or fluid where normally they should be air filled.

This is easy to confirm for yourself. First, place the middle finger of one hand flat against your thigh and tap the middle of that finger with the tip of the other finger. You will hear a dull thud: The thigh is all skin, muscle, fat, bone, nerve, and blood—no air. Then repeat the procedure over your right chest, with your middle finger applied to the chest between two ribs: You will obtain a higher pitched, resonant sound. Repeat this over and over, but each time move the finger closer to the center of the chest. When you sense a dull thud, you are tapping over a fluid (a heart full of blood). If you mark on the skin all the transition spots from air to fluid, you will have the outline of your heart and will know its approximate size. A carpenter uses this same technique on a wall to find the solid wood studs that are equally spaced between air-filled interspaces. Doctor or carpenter, this method is Auenbrugger's percussion technique.

Auscultation (listening) through a stethoscope didn't come about until 1819, when a French physician, René Théophile Hyacinthe Laennec, wrote his landmark book, *Traité de l'auscultation médiate*. Physicians before Laennec had put their ear directly on the chest of a male patient to listen to sounds made by the beating heart and moving lungs (this was termed "immediate" listening instead of "mediate"), but the morals of the time forbade this practice on female patients; furthermore, the "immediate" sounds were muffled and indistinct, particularly in obese patients. Since necessity is the mother of invention, Laennec invented (Fig. 3.2). He wrote in 1819,

In 1816, I was consulted by a young woman labouring under general symptoms of a diseased heart, and in whose case percussion and the application of the hand were of little avail on account of the great degree of fatness. I happened to recollect a simple and well-known fact in acoustics, and fancied at the same time that it might be turned to some use on the present occasion. The fact I allude to is the augmented impression of sound when conveyed through certain solid bodies, as when we hear the scratch of a pin at one end of a piece of wood, on applying our ear to the other. Immediately, on this suggestion, I rolled a quire of paper into a [tight] sort of cylinder and applied one end of it to the region of the heart and the other to my ear, and was not a little surprised and

Figure 3.2.   Laennec's stethoscope. It was essentially a wooden cylinder with a center hole, almost 1 centimeter in diameter, drilled through the entire length. As shown in longitudinal section, it was constructed in three parts and could be easily taken apart (nineteenth century physicians carried the dismantled stethoscopes in specially constructed top hats). (a) the "stopper" that was applied to the patient's chest, (b) the middle section, (c) the section applied to the physician's ear, and (c′) the threads on (c) that allow for easy connection and disconnection with (b). Laennec's figure 4 shows the "hidden" part of (a) with its brass tube that fits into (b).

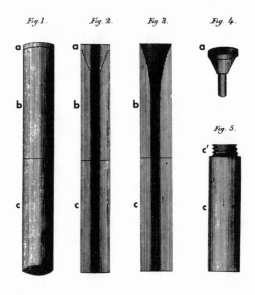

pleased, to find that I could thereby perceive the action of the heart in a manner much more clear and distinct than I had ever been able to do by the immediate application of the ear.

Laennec had invented the stethoscope and had solved two problems with one simple instrument: the moral one, because his stethoscope acted as a "mediator" between his ear and the patient's chest (the technique was called "mediate auscultation") and so eliminated direct ("immediate") contact of ear and skin; and the technical one, because it amplified faint sounds coming from the heart and lungs. Actually, it soon had more medical uses (e.g., listening to gurgling in the abdomen, a sign of intestinal activity; listening to a fetal heart beating within a uterus within an abdomen; identifying abnormalities in arteries near the surface of the body by hearing abnormal sounds; and measuring blood pressure by the arm cuff–stethoscope method), and, of course, it soon became a status symbol that certified to the patient that the bearer was indeed a physician! Again a discovery intended for physicians found nonmedical uses: Plumbers use a stethoscope to locate leaks in underground water pipes, safecrackers use it to hear the tumblers fall in place, and bomb squads use it to detect the ticking of the timing device of concealed explosives.

Although Laennec is best known for his invention of the stethoscope, he did far more than that. The stethoscope did, of course, permit physicians to hear murmurs, scratching, or rubbing sounds, clicks, clacks, snaps, thrills, and swishes, but Laennec realized that one learns very little from these noises unless one knows exactly what physical abnormality within the heart or lungs is causing these fascinating sounds heard outside the chest.

Because one cannot know what is an *abnormal* sound until one knows what is normal, Laennec began by becoming familiar with the sounds he heard during each cycle of a *normal* heartbeat (systole, or contraction; and diastole, or relaxation). If blood flowed through all of the cardiac chambers continuously and steadily (which it never does in a normal heart), one would hear only an unvarying swish as when water runs at a constant rate through a pipe. But different sounds occur when heart chambers are contracting and valves are opening, are open, or closing. During diastole, blood is running from the atria into the ventricles because the tricuspid and mitral valves are open; no blood flows from the pulmonary artery or aorta into the ventricles because the pulmonic and aortic valves are shut. When systole begins and blood pressure in the right and left ventricles rises, first the tricuspid and mitral valves to the aorta close tightly and then the pulmonic and aortic valves open. These changes can be linked to special sounds.

Laennec then had to recognize unusual sounds and identify their origin. These could come from unnatural openings in the wall between the two atria or between the two ventricles, or from diseases of any one or more of the four valves. Normally the valves close with amazing precision (they are absolutely leakproof) and open widely to permit free flow of blood. But they can become leaky (regurgitant) and permit backflow, or scarred and narrowed (stenotic) and offer only a small opening for forward blood flow; under these circumstances, unusual sounds occur.

What Laennec did was make careful notes of his detailed examinations of living patients with disease of the heart or lungs or both, using all of his senses, plus Auenbrugger's percussion and his own stethoscope. Then (and this is the important part) he correlated these observations with the acute anatomic defects he found at autopsy in the patient. He thus connected the new science of pathology with the new science of physical diagnosis. From this came a more precise system of making accurate diagnoses *during* the patient's life. Soon many physicians became interested in linking unusual sounds or pulsations with actual structural abnormalities in the heart. They learned that a murmur with specific characteristics (one that was continuous, crescendo, or diminuendo, that is, increasing or decreasing in loudness) at specific points on the chest wall (Fig. 3.3) meant a specific disorder of the aortic, mitral, pulmonic, or tricuspid valve and that the character of pulsations at the wrist indicated the presence of cardiac abnormalities. So medical textbooks now list more than sixty murmurs, thirteen of which bear the names of the physicians who first described them. It takes an educated ear to differentiate between these, but each has a special diagnostic value.

What Laennec did for the precise diagnosis of abnormalities of the cardiac valves and diseases of the lung, Maude Abbott and Helen Taussig did for the congenital disorders of the heart. True, there were isolated autopsy reports as early as 1672 by Nicolaus Steno in Denmark that described anatomic defects in the hearts of "blue babies," and in 1888 Etienne Louis Fallot showed that almost three-quarters of "blue babies" (babies that were still blue even after they began to breathe

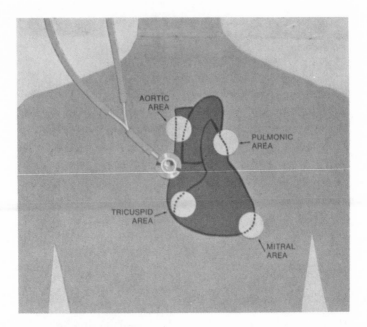

Figure 3.3. Modern physicians usually first place their stethoscope over certain areas of the chest most likely to yield normal or abnormal sounds associated with the four cardiac valves, then search for unusual sounds elsewhere.

normally) had a combination of four congenital defects that came to be known as the tetralogy of Fallot: a hole in the wall between the right and left ventricles; narrowing of the pulmonary artery; an unusually thick-walled right ventricle; and an aorta that was connected to both right and left ventricles instead of only to the left, as a normal aorta should be. But most physicians then believed that the congenital heart diseases comprised so many different malformations that the most a physician could hope for was help in sorting out *congenital* from *acquired* heart disease, and that actual diagnosis of any specific malformation during life was beyond human powers.

The first big step was taken by Maude Abbott, who classified a multitude of congenital disorders—all of which had previously appeared to be different—into twenty-four types recognizable at the autopsy table. Abbott was born in Quebec in 1869. In those days, Canada thought that women were not worth educating, but by the time she was ready for college, McGill University had opened a women's branch, Donalda College. Abbott was in the third class of women admitted to the new college and was graduated with high honors. Now, however, she was up against the McGill School of Medicine, whose faculty adamantly refused to admit women. The medical faculty of Bishop's College (a rival of McGill) who had just decided to admit women, came to her rescue and invited her to enroll in their first class. She was graduated in 1894, studied in Europe for four years, and in 1898 returned to work at the Royal Victoria Hospital in Montreal.

In 1900 she met Sir William Osler and this meeting determined her career. Osler was a firm believer in the power of pathology to advance the science and practice of medicine, and he urged her to study to the fullest the specimens in the McGill Medical Museum. The result was her lifetime's devotion to analyzing and classifying hearts with puzzling congenital defects. Her study was published first as a 100-page chapter on congenital heart disease in Osler's 1908 *Practice of Medicine* (after that, McGill University relented and gave her an honorary M.D. degree in 1910), and then in final form as a 1936 American Heart Association monograph based on more than 1,000 cases. Her critical analysis replaced disorder with order and permitted a clinical study of individual congenital defects. For example, her description of ninety-two patients who had died with a wide-open ductus arteriosus (see Fig. 3.1) permitted cardiologists to make correct diagnoses on most living patients, a necessity before surgical attempts to modify or correct the lesion could be uniformly successful. She lived to see the beginning of modern cardiovascular surgery in 1939, and died the next year at the age of 71.

What Maude Abbott did for classification of congenital heart disease as seen at postmortem examination, Helen Taussig, a pediatric cardiologist at Johns Hopkins Hospital, did for *bedside* diagnosis. She too, though a quarter of a century later, encountered somewhat the same problems that Maude Abbott had in getting her medical education. She went to Radcliffe College for two years and then transferred to the University of California at Berkeley, where she received her A.B. degree in 1921. She then considered a career in medicine, but at that time President Lowell of Harvard was utterly opposed to admitting women to Harvard Medical School. Her father suggested that public health was a more suitable occupation for a woman, so she applied to the dean of the new School of Public Health. The dean told her that she would be permitted to study there, but not to work for a degree. "Who is going to be such a fool as to spend two years studying medicine and two years more in public health and not get a degree?" Taussig asked. "No one, I hope," said the dean, to which she replied, "Dr. Rosen, I will not be the first to disappoint you." So she took courses in anatomy at Boston University, where she studied under Alexander Begg, dean and professor of anatomy. He was so impressed by her ability that two years later he urged her to transfer to Johns Hopkins Medical School to complete her medical training. Hopkins did accept women students and did give them an M.D. degree. This was due, in large part, to Elizabeth Garrett, a wealthy donor who provided most of the money needed to build the medical school in 1893, with the understanding that women would be admitted as students *on an equal basis with men.* So Taussig did get her M.D. degree at Hopkins, but then the department of medicine wouldn't (or didn't) accept her as a medical intern. This proved to be fortunate for the world of medicine, because she switched her goals to pediatrics and then to pediatric cardiology. While working in this field, she sorted out the various types of congenital heart disease in living patients and established an art of clinical diagnosis. Equally important, from her knowledge of pathophysiology she conceived of a surgical procedure that, without opening the heart, would provide more oxygen to the blood of "blue babies" and prolong their lives and permit them greater activity.

When Helen Taussig was put in charge of pediatric cardiology at Hopkins in 1930, her professor told her that if she wanted to amount to something in her specialty, she had to become an expert on malformations of the heart. He gave her a fluoroscope and an electrocardiograph (ECG) and ordered her to use these two instruments fully to study the heart of every patient with an abnormal heart, which she did. She learned how to diagnose congenital defects and to suggest surgical procedures to save or prolong lives. So now we must ask, When, where, and how did the fluoroscope and the ECG enter the medical picture?

X Rays

X rays and the fluoroscope were discovered in December 1895 not by a physician, but by a physicist—and not by a physicist studying practical, applied problems that might be useful in medicine, but by a scientist concerned with the esoteric problem of the emission of cathode rays in a vacuum tube.

On November 8, 1895, Wilhelm Conrad Roentgen, professor of physics at the University of Würzburg, passed the discharge from a large induction coil through an evacuated Crookes tube. The apparatus was in a completely darkened room and the tube was covered with black cardboard; nevertheless, at each discharge he observed that a paper screen covered with a fluorescent material became brightly illuminated. He soon found that not only black cardboard but all substances permitted the passage of "X rays" (as he named them), but—and this is all important—to differing degrees: A bound book of about 1,000 pages offered no hindrance, glass containing lead offered some, and lead itself, if at least 1.5 millimeters thick, almost completely blocked X rays. Most remarkable was Roentgen's observation that "if the hand be held before the fluorescent screen, the shadow shows the bones darkly with only faint outlines of the surrounding tissues" (Fig. 3.4).

He reported this in a December 28, 1895, paper and then orally, along with an actual demonstration, on January 23, 1896, before the

A   B

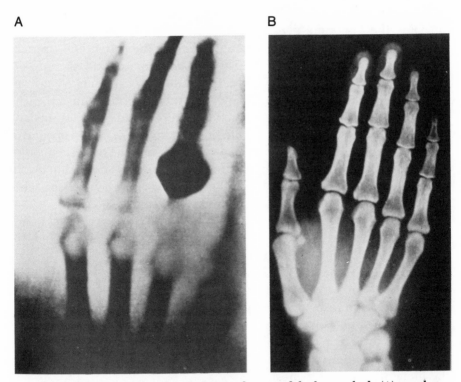

Figure 3.4.   Roentgen's first X-ray picture of a part of the human body (A) was that of his wife's hand, with a large ring clearly visible on one finger (1895). The X ray of a hand (B) taken a few months later (in 1896) in Vienna shows the rapid improvement in the technique of photographing tissues, such as bone, that stop X rays (such tissues are called "radio-opaque").

Würzburg Physical Medical Society in Germany. The response of the public was electric. X rays became front-page news in newspapers throughout the world. No medical discovery has ever been so universally acclaimed and so quickly put to medical and scientific use. The supply of commercially available Crookes tubes quickly ran out, but almost anyone who knew a little about physics could easily assemble the equipment at little expense and go to work. Within the first year (1896) more than 1,000 scientific papers and 50 books were published dealing entirely with Roentgen's rays! A new journal, *Archives of Clinical Skiagraphy* (shadow writing), appeared in the spring of 1896, edited by Sydney Rowland, still a medical student. The Roentgen Society was formed in June 1897, and Roentgen was a shoo-in for the first Nobel Prize in physics, awarded in 1901.

The diagnostic uses of X rays in medicine were immediately apparent. For the first time ever, physicians could "look inside" patients, without a surgical operation or even undressing the patient! Of course, X rays were used at once to diagnose broken bones. And as early as April 1896, Dr. F. H. Williams reported to the Association of American Physicians his study of the size, shape, and motion of the human heart. Harmless liquids were soon discovered that were called "contrast media" because, like bone, they stopped the new X rays (were "radio-opaque") and stood out in contrast to soft tissues of the body. Physicians could visualize arteries, veins, and the entire gastrointestinal tract using these media; with the advent of cardiac catheterization, they could also "see" the chambers of the heart and the coronary arteries.

The use of X rays spread quickly from medical to nonmedical uses. Even by 1897, they had been used, or their use had been suggested, to distinguish real gems from artificial ones, to discover the fraudulent introduction of mineral substances into textile fabrics to increase their weight, to discover the contents of packages in the parcel post without opening them, to recognize explosives and contraband in baggage (some sixty years before their routine use in airports), to age and oxidize alcohol, to test insulation used in the construction of cables, and to ascertain cohesion in welding (eighty years before their use to discover defects in the metal wings of jet planes).

It was hard to conceive of "radiation toxicity" when, unlike bullets, X rays zipped through tissues and came out again, leaving no holes, not even microscopic ones. Thomas Edison was intrigued and first tried "photographing" the brain. When that yielded nothing of interest, he became fascinated with the idea of making fluorescent light bulbs and began to use modified Crookes tubes as light bulbs, but the results were disastrous. Edison noted, "I started in to make a number of these lamps, but I soon found that the X ray had affected poisonously my assistant, Mr. Dally, so that his hair came out and his flesh commenced to ulcerate. I then concluded that it would not do, and that it would not be a very popular kind of light, so I dropped it."

Dally died in 1904 at the age of 39, the first fatality from X-ray "poisoning" in the United States. In April 1898 the Council of the Roentgen Society in England had appointed the first committee to collect information on the alleged injurious effects of X rays. One of the five-man group reported in 1899,

We may, I think, safely assert that the length of exposure necessary to produce any injury is at least three or four times that required to obtain a radiograph with the improved apparatus now at our disposal, even where the most opaque parts of the body are concerned, and then only when the patient is specially susceptible to the electrical forces which cause the injury.

To the best of my knowledge there were no "ban the X ray" marches at the turn of the century, nor any citizen uprisings against technological advances applied to medicine. Perhaps this was because the first report of *curing* cancer by X-ray therapy came in 1899, and the first report of *causing* cancer by X rays in 1902.

Over the course of the last eighty years, there has been increased awareness of the potential harmful effects of X rays and of the need for shielded equipment, rooms, patients, physicians, and assistants, and of limiting the time and area of exposure. Properly used, X rays remain one of the main weapons for curing cancer or limiting its spread. If the public had voted in 1896 to keep or ban X rays, knowing then as much about them as we know in 1980, I believe the vote would have been to use them. I am not sure how today's public would vote; the tremendous publicity concerning the dangers of radiation has made today's public wary of X rays.

If ever any discovery belonged to one man and one man alone, surely it was the discovery of X rays. But read what Sylvanus Thompson said in the first presidential address in 1897 before the new Roentgen Society:

In the history of Science, nothing is more true than that the discoverer—even the greatest of discoverers—is but the descendant of his scientific forefathers, is always and essentially the product of the age in which he is born. Roentgen himself has frankly avowed the ancestry of his discoveries. He himself has stated that, being aware of the existence of unsolved problems respecting the emission of cathode rays in and by an electrically stimulated vacuum tube, he had for a long time followed with the greatest interest the researches of Hertz and of Lenard, and had determined, as soon as he should find the necessary leisure, to make some researches of his own. Behind Roentgen then, stand Lenard and Hertz; behind Hertz stand Crookes, and Varley, and Hittorf, and Sprengel and Geissler; and so back to Hauksbee, and Boyle, and Otto Guericke, into the beginnings of modern science as it emerged from the vain imaginings and occult mysteries of Mediaeval night. . . .

Was Roentgen's discovery an accident? . . . . It cannot in any sense be called accidental; it was the result of deliberate and directed thought. He was looking for something—he knew not precisely what. And he found it. *Fortunate* the discovery may well be deemed, but not *fortuitous.*

As I mentioned earlier, discovery is not only preceded by discoveries, but leads to additional discoveries. The science of using X rays has undergone continual change since 1895: from an apparatus that a physicist could put together in a few hours, to cineradiography (X-ray movies), to X-ray therapy, and in 1973 to a method (computerized tomography, or CT) that can produce images of cross sections of any part of the body. The first Nobel Prize in physics went to Roentgen (1901) and the 1979 Nobel Prize in *medicine* went to Godfrey Hounsfield and Allan Cormack for construction of the amazing diagnostic instrument, the CT scanner, which combines the power of X rays with modern computer science (Fig. 3.5). Will the CT device, with its price tag of $800,000 in 1980, take the place of conventional radiography and many other tests? Will the CT, still in its youth, be replaced by even more sophisticated (and more expensive) devices? Will these marvels lower the costs of medical diagnosis, or will they be add-on tests that raise the costs? It will take five to ten years to find out.

Conventional X rays and CT scans are very important diagnostic techniques but each has the same drawback: the potential for damaging tissue cells. A new technique that makes use of nuclear magnetic resonance (already abbreviated to NMR) and which has no known harmful effects is now in use in about a half a dozen medical centers in the United States; it probably will be at work in all major medical centers in the United States within a few years (despite the price tag of 1.5 million dollars). Like the CT scan, NMR can be used to generate images of slices of any part of the body.

In this technique, the patient is inserted in a body-size chamber equipped with a large magnet. The patient is immersed in a magnetic field, up to 4,000 times the magnetic force of the earth, that causes

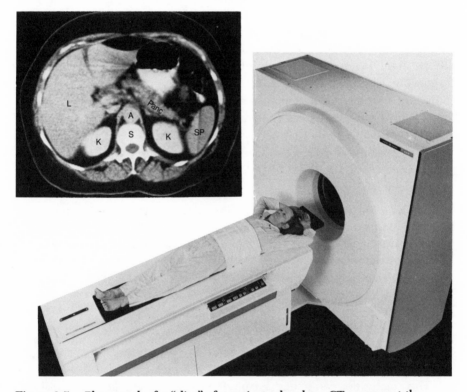

Figure 3.5.   Photograph of a "slice" of a patient taken by a CT scanner at the level of the patient's kidneys: K, kidneys; L, liver; Sp, spleen; Panc, pancreas; A, aorta; and S, spine. Below, a 1980 model of a CT scanner. An X-ray tube rotating about the long axis of the body projects X rays through a patient at a very large number of angles as the patient on a litter is moved into the tunnel. A detector rotating opposite the X-ray tube records the differential absorption of the rays at each angle; this information is processed by a computer to reconstruct a detailed two-dimensional image of a "slice" of the patient's body. The word *tomography* is derived from two Greek words, *tomos*, a cut or section, and *graphein*, to write.

alignment of the hydrogen nuclei in his body, as well as of other nuclei with odd numbers of protons and neutrons and hence a net spin. When the patient is subjected to energy of just the right phase and radiofrequency, the spins of these nuclei can change direction, absorbing energy in the process. This energy is subsequently reemitted at a characteristic radiofrequency and the signal is picked up by a receiver. The characteristics of the signal depend on the number of hydrogen or other nuclei present. The data go into a computer, which then plots the distribution of the nuclei responsible for the emission.

The technique clearly has enormous potential. Dramatic images of the brain and nerve tissues, better than comparable CT images, have already been obtained. Moreover, it may be invaluable in assessing conditions involving muscles, particularly damaged heart muscle, and in diagnosing multiple sclerosis and other diseases that affect the fatty compounds surrounding the nerves. Nuclear magnetic resonance has the advantage of using no X radiation, but a psychological disadvantage of a name that includes the word *nuclear*.

It is worth adding here a "Letter to the Editor" of *The New York Times* (December 19, 1982) from Leon Lederman, Director of the Fermilab, Batavia, Illinois:

A Nov. 28 news article by Jane Brody, 'Magnetic Device Lifts Hopes for Diagnosis Without X-ray,' treated front-page readers to a cogent account of a revolutionary medical diagnostic technique: nuclear magnetic resonance, or N.M.R. Your business section and many Wall Street publications have long been much taken with the predicted near-billion-dollar market for this remarkable scanning device.

What is not made clear to either set of readers is that N.M.R. is a classic example of the payoff of basic, abstract, pure research.

The N.M.R. technique was invented by E. Purcell (Harvard) and F. Bloch (Stanford) in 1946, based upon the atomic resonance work of I. I. Rabi (Columbia). All three were awarded Nobel Prizes for their work.

Their motivation was to understand the structure of atomic nuclei, making use of the magnetism associated with nuclei in a highly magnetic environment of spinning and orbiting electrons. The evolution of the medical application involves large superconducting magnets which were developed in high-energy accelerator laboratories in the 1960s in the course of research on the fundamental properties of matter.

This example of benefits to society of basic research—in better medicine and in taxes returned to the Treasury—needs to be told and retold; it is not easy to hold the attention of policy makers.

X-Ray Movies

The combination of X rays with motion pictures is almost essential today in diagnosing disorders of the heart and blood vessels; several hundred thousand X-ray motion pictures of coronary arteries are now taken yearly in the United States. The technique required not only the invention of X rays, but also that of motion pictures. If I asked who invented motion pictures, most of you would reply without hesitation, "Thomas Edison." Actually, the inventor was Eadweard Muybridge, an English-born, San Francisco-bred photographer who was director of photographic surveys on the Pacific Coast for the U.S. Government. Muybridge tells how he became involved in motion pictures:

In the spring of the year 1872 . . . there was revived in the city of San Francisco a controversy in regard to animal locomotion, which we may infer, on the authority of Plato, was warmly argued by the ancient Egyptians, and which probably had its origin in the studio of the primitive artist when he submitted to a group of critical friends his first etching of a mammoth crushing through the forest, or of a reindeer grazing on the plains.

In this modern instance, the principal subject of dispute was the possibility of a horse, while trotting—even at the height of his speed—having all four of his feet, at any portion of his stride, simultaneously free from contact with the ground.

The controversy started in 1872 when Governor Leland Stanford, who owned one of the finest stables in the country, presumably made a $25,000 bet with a friend that all four feet of a trotting horse are at some time during a stride simultaneously off the ground. Now it was agreed that this was not so when a horse ambled or walked, and that it was so when a horse cantered, galloped, or leaped (jumped); the sole subject of dispute was the position of all four feet in a *trotting* horse because human eyes could not settle the dispute. So Stanford asked Muybridge to find the truth by photography. Muybridge noted,

The problem before [me] was, to obtain a sufficiently well-developed and contrasted image on a wet collodion plate, after an exposure of so brief a duration that a horse's foot, moving with a velocity of more than thirty yards in a second of time, should be photographed with its outlines practically sharp.

In those days the rapid dry process—by the use of which such an operation is now easily accomplished—had not been discovered. Every photographer was, in a great measure, his own chemist; he prepared his own dipping baths, made his own collodion, coated and developed his own plates, and frequently manufactured the chemicals necessary for his work. All this involved a vast amount of tedious and careful manipulation from which the present generation is, happily, relieved.

There were no motion pictures in 1872 and most still photographs were made on glass plates. It occurred to Muybridge that a series of photographic images made in rapid succession at predetermined intervals of time would answer the question. Leland Stanford provided an outdoor laboratory at his Palo Alto farm (now occupied by Stanford University). Muybridge set up several banks of twelve to twenty-four stereoscopic cameras in a line parallel to the track on which the horse would trot at a predicted speed. When the horse reached position 1, which was opposite camera 1, Muybridge pressed a button that clicked the shutter of camera 1 and, by a "programmed" electric motor with eleven or twenty-three additional contacts, he exposed successively, at the proper time, the photographic plates of cameras 2 to 12 or 2 to 24. Muybridge then mounted his glass plates on discs; when he rotated these, he had a very satisfactory visual image of a miniature horse trotting along. By mounting plates made by his stereoscopic cameras on two discs and rotating them at equal speeds, he could also produce three-dimensional effects. The last four frames of Fig. 3.6 show clearly that all four hoofs of a trotting horse are at some point simultaneously off the ground, and presumably Leland Stanford became $25,000 richer.

Figure 3.6.   Six frames from an 1872 "moving picture" of a trotting horse.

Later, Provost William Pepper, along with trustees and friends of the University of Pennsylvania, raised funds for Muybridge to continue his work on man, land animals, and birds in motion. In 1887 Muybridge published an eleven-volume work, *Animal Locomotion*, that contained more than 100,000 individual photographic frames. In 1882 a French physiologist, Marey, improved Muybridge's multiple-camera system by using a single camera, a strip of photographic film, and a succession of moving figures; in 1893 Edison used a moving strip and a lantern for projection, patented these, and became known as the "inventor" of motion pictures.

Muybridge later noted,

It may here be parenthetically remarked that on the 27th of February, 1888, the author, having contemplated some improvements of the zoöpraxiscope [his name for the apparatus] consulted with Mr. Thomas A. Edison as to the practicability of using that instrument in association with the phonograph [invented by Edison] so as to combine, and reproduce simultaneously, in the presence of an audience, visible actions and audible words. At that time the phonograph had not been adapted to reach the ears of a large audience, so the scheme was temporarily abandoned.

The combination of such an instrument with the phonograph has not, at the time of writing, been satisfactorily accomplished; there can, however, be but little doubt that in the—perhaps not far distant—future, instruments will be constructed that will not only reproduce visible actions simultaneously with audible words, but an entire opera, with the gestures, facial expressions, and songs of the performers, with all the accompanying music, will be recorded and reproduced by an apparatus, combining the principles of the zoöpraxiscope and the phonograph, for the instruction or entertainment of an audience long after the original participants shall have passed away.

Muybridge also recognized the value of his work to photographers, artists, sculptors, animators, anatomists, and exercise and muscle physiologists, but probably never dreamed of its future importance in pinpointing specific defects in the heart and arteries of man.

The Electrocardiograph

About a decade after the discovery of X rays came the electrocardiograph (ECG). Essentially the ECG amplifies and records the electrical activity for various parts of the heart muscle. For all of this century, every schoolchild has learned about electricity and I suppose many of them thought that, like apple pie and ice cream, it's been around forever. Indeed, it *has* been around forever, but its important roles in industry, in running our homes, and in running our bodies has been known for only a hundred years.

The ancients certainly knew of the phenomena associated with electricity. They knew of it as lightning and of its incredibly destructive power capable of toppling giant trees and killing living creatures. They knew also that rubbing amber vigorously gave it the property of attracting and holding (by static electricity) lightweight objects. They also experienced shocks generated by electric fish, such as the torpedo fish and the electric catfish, and it is believed that the Greeks used such shocks to treat disorders such as headache, epilepsy, and the pains of childbirth.

The story of electricity illustrates how interactions both among scientists in several disciplines and between basic and applied scientists led not only to tremendous advances in basic and applied biology and medicine but also to the practical harnessing of electricity as an indispensible source of energy. Originally static electricity was a curiosity and a fun game; not until 1600 did any scientist study systematically the phenomena of electricity. The first to do so was the English scientist William Gilbert, who, around 1600, coined the terms *electricity*, (from *elektron*, the Greek word for amber) and *charged body*; he also differentiated between conductors ("electrics") and insulators ("nonelectrics"). The first electric machine was devised by Otto von Guericke in 1672, when he was 70 years old; it generated electricity by a rotating globe that rubbed against the hand. Electricity was first stored in 1745 when von Kleist, Bishop of Pomerania, transferred the charge generated by an electric machine to a glass bottle; this, greatly improved in design, became the famous Leyden jar that served for years as the storage place for generated electricity.

Then came Benjamin Franklin's famous discovery. Franklin, the foremost scientist in the American colonies, first established that the charge in atmospheric lightning was identical to that produced by electric machines. This he did in his famous kite and key experiments between 1746 and 1752, described in Fig. 3.7. In a somewhat lighter vein, Franklin wrote,

"It is proposed to put an end to them [electrical experiments] for this season, somewhat humorously, in a party of pleasure on the banks of Skuylkil. Spirits,

Oct. 19, 1752.

A S frequent mention is made in the news papers from *Europe*, of the fuccefs of the *Philadelphia* experiment for drawing the electric fire from clouds by means of pointed rods of iron erected on high buildings, &c. it may be agreeable to inform the curious that the fame experiment has fucceeded in *Philadelphia*, though made in a different and more eafy manner, which is as follows :

Make a fmall crofs of two light ftrips of cedar, the arms fo long as to reach to the four corners of a large thin filk handkerchief when extended ; tie the corners of the handkerchief to the extremities of the crofs, fo you have the body of a kite ; which being properly accommodated with a tail, loop, and ftring, will rife in the air, like thofe made of paper ; but this being of filk is fitter to bear the wind and wet of a thunder guft without tearing. To the top of the upright ftick of the crofs is to be fixed a very fharp pointed wire, rifing a foot or more above the wood. To the end of the twine, next the hand, is to be ty'd a filk ribbon, and where the filk and twine join, a key may be faftened. This kite is to be raifed when a thunder guft appears to be coming on, and the perfon who holds the ftring muft ftand within a door, or window, or under fome cover, fo that the filk ribbon may not be wet ; and care muft be taken that the twine does not touch the frame of the door or window. As foon as any of the thunder clouds come over the kite, the pointed wire will draw the electric fire from them, and the kite, with all the twine, will be electrified, and the loofe filaments of the twine will ftand out every way, and be attracted by an approaching finger. And when the rain has wet the kite and twine, fo that it can conduct the electric fire freely, you will find it ftream out plentifully from the key on the approach of your knuckle. At this key the phial may be charged ; and from electric fire thus obtained, fpirits may be kindled, and all the other electric experiments be performed, which are ufually done by the help of a rubbed glafs globe or tube ; and thereby the famenefs of the electric matter with that of lightening completely demonftrated.

B. F.

Figure 3.7. Letter from Benjamin Franklin to Peter Collinson in England describing his famous 1752 kite and key experiment. The results of many scientific experiments in the eighteenth century were still transmitted by way of letters instead of by publication in journals.

at the same time, are to be fired by a spark sent from side to side through the river, without any other conductor than the water; an experiment which we some time since performed, to the amazement of many. A turkey is to be killed for our dinner by the electrical shock, and roasted by the electrical jack, before a fire kindled by the electrified bottle: when the healths of all the famous electricians in England, Holland, France, and Germany are to be drank in electrified bumpers, under the discharge of guns from the electrical battery.

Amazingly, all of Franklin's speculations eventually came true.

Franklin has been regarded by many Americans as the printer–publisher–newspaper editor–author of *Poor Richard's Almanacks*. Others have put him in the category of a practical inventor—of the lightning rod, the Franklin stove, and bifocal glasses. Some regard him as a great colonial statesman—a special envoy to Great Britain, Ambassador to France, and an author of the Constitution. Others remember him as a founder of the Philadelphia Academy (forerunner of the University of Pennsylvania) and of the American Philosophical Society. But his international reputation was that of one of the century's great scientists (equal in the minds of some to Isaac Newton), author of *Experiments and Observations on Electricity Made at Philadelphia in America* (one of the most widely reprinted scientific books of the mid-eighteenth century), a member of the elite Royal Society of London (and winner of its Copley Medal), and one of the eight foreign associates of the Royal Academy of Science in Paris. He was for France a symbol of enlightenment and freedom that won French financial and military aid for the Colonies during the American Revolution and for Franklin the epigram "He snatched the lightning from the skies and the sceptre from tyrants."

His scientific philosophy might be summarized by his answer to a question he was asked as he witnessed the first ascent of a hydrogen balloon in France. The question was, "What good is it?"; his answer was, "What good is a newborn baby?" (This quotation is often attributed to Michael Faraday, who used it about fifty years later.)

But electricity was still used largely for its entertainment value, for example, to discharge the contents of a Leyden jar through 180 gendarmes linked hand to hand in one continuous circuit and to observe the almost instantaneous reactions to each of the electric shock. The first real shift to the *science* of electricity and the first hint of the *usefulness* of electricity (both in learning and in doing) came from basic experiments on the mechanism of contraction of frog muscle. Here, indeed, is an example of the power of fundamental experiments in biology. Out of "just for the sake of learning" came the Industrial Revolution and the Age of Electricity.

In 1756 Leopoldo Caldani discharged the contents of a Leyden jar in the direction of a frog muscle that, with its nerve, had been dissected completely free from the frog; the muscle twitched. Electricity quickly became the popular topic of the day, especially in scientific circles. John Walsh and John Hunter established that the effect of the discharge of an "electric fish," the torpedo, was the same as that from a Leyden jar. Hunter did a beautiful dissection of the electric organ of the torpedo (Fig. 3.8) and showed that it consisted of about 470 hexagonal or pentagonal columns, about $\frac{1}{4}$ to $1\frac{1}{2}$ inches high, $\frac{2}{10}$ of an inch in diameter, with each column containing about 150 thin partitions—obviously a biological storage battery. Hunter also observed a fantastically rich network of nerves in the electric organ and proposed that these nerves were

subservient to the formation, collection or management of the electric fluid . . . and that the will of the animal does absolutely control the electric power of its body; which must depend on the energy of its nerves. How far this may be connected with the power of the nerves in general, or lead to any explanation of their operations, time and future discoveries alone can fully determine.

Future experiments were not long in coming. Luigi Galvani, a student of Caldani, continued the experiments with electricity and frogs. In one of Galvani's early experiments, around 1780, he dissected a frog and placed it on the same table as an electric machine, though at a considerable distance from it (Fig. 3.9). It happened that one of his assistants, by chance, lightly applied the point of a scalpel to the nerves running to the muscles of the frog's legs. Suddenly all the muscles of the limbs contracted violently or, as we would now say, were "galvanized" into action. Another assistant thought he observed, at the time this phenomenon occurred, that a spark had been discharged from the conductor of the electric machine. The experiment was repeated over and over again and Galvani noted that violent contractions of the limbs occurred in the individual limb muscles only at the very moment that the sparks were discharged. Galvani then tried to repeat Franklin's experiments of tapping an electrical charge from lightning to determine whether atmospheric electricity also caused contraction of the frog muscles. He skinned some frog legs and suspended them from an iron balustrade using a copper wire that passed under the nerves of the frog muscles. Galvani found that frog muscles so suspended often contracted

A

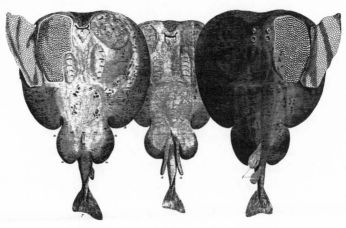

B

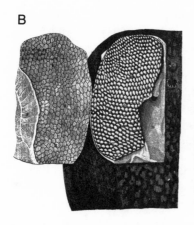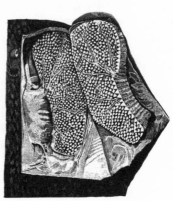

C

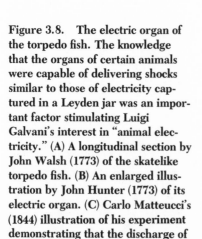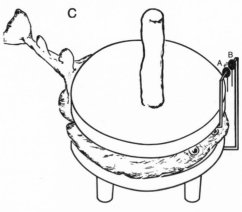

Figure 3.8. The electric organ of the torpedo fish. The knowledge that the organs of certain animals were capable of delivering shocks similar to those of electricity captured in a Leyden jar was an important factor stimulating Luigi Galvani's interest in "animal electricity." (A) A longitudinal section by John Walsh (1773) of the skatelike torpedo fish. (B) An enlarged illustration by John Hunter (1773) of its electric organ. (C) Carlo Matteucci's (1844) illustration of his experiment demonstrating that the discharge of a marine torpedo can make a spark cross a gap. The electric fish is sandwiched between two metal plates; each plate has an upright rod with a ball at its tip. When the fish discharges its electric organ, an electric spark jumps the gap between the two metal balls.

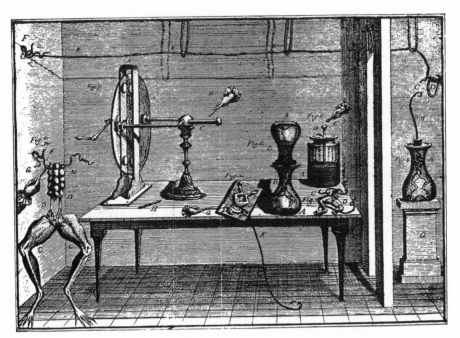

Figure 3.9. Galvani's drawing of his friction machine for producing electric currents. In the lower left is an oversized sketch of the lower limbs of a frog; a hand (far left) holds a scalpel that touches the nerve trunks leading to the limb muscles.

at times when there was neither a discharge of electricity from his man-made electrical machine nor one from atmospheric electricity. This led Galvani to conclude that the muscle contraction was due to "animal electricity," an accumulation of electricity within a muscle that could be discharged under appropriate conditions and which caused the muscle to contract.

Galvani's conclusion was wrong, and it started a controversy between Galvani and Alessandro Volta. Controversy in science often accelerates discovery, and the Galvani–Volta battle was one of the most wonderfully productive disputes the world has ever known, because it led to the development of two entirely new sciences: One was the science of electrophysiology and the beginning of many studies of the role of electricity in body function, including the electrical activity of the heart and nervous system; the other was the science of electrochemistry, whose first product was the development of a practical method for generating and storing electricity in the "voltaic" pile or battery, composed of alternating plates of dissimilar metals (Fig. 3.10).

What did Volta see that Galvani failed to see? Galvani *did* see that

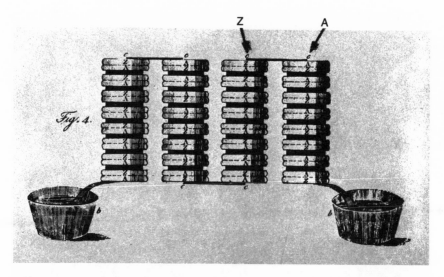

Figure 3.10. The "voltaic pile," Alessandro Volta's arrangement for producing a continuous flow of electricity. Discs of two dissimilar metallic conductors (A, silver; Z, zinc) stacked in contact with one another and a moist conductor (here discs of brine-soaked paper) generate enough electricity to give a mild shock to anyone who might touch the apparatus.

every time his frog's feet swung toward and touched the balustrade, the muscle contracted, but he *failed* to see or recognize the importance of the copper wire, attached at one end with the frog's leg, coming in contact with the iron railing at that very moment. Volta saw the *contact* and it meant to him that generation of electric current had resulted from the contact of two dissimilar metals.

Galvani, determined to prove his theory of "animal electricity" and show that he wasn't all wrong, conducted further experiments in which he was sure that there was no contact of any type with metal. This he did in 1797 with two frog muscles and no metal wires or instruments (Fig. 3.11). Each muscle was still connected to its nerve, but the nerve of each was cut in two several inches away from its muscle. When the cut end of one nerve touched the second nerve, both of the limbs would contract. In a second type of experiment, he demonstrated that a frog muscle placed on the electric organ of an eel contracted only when the eel moved and discharged its electric organ.

Sixty years later, Rudolph von Kolliker and Heinrich Müller established the basis for present-day electrocardiography. They placed the cut end of a nerve–muscle preparation not on another leg muscle, but on the surface of a beating heart, and observed that the leg muscle con-

Figure 3.11.   In 1797 Galvani showed that when the cut end of one sciatic nerve touches the surface of another sciatic nerve, both limbs contract. Because no metals or electric machines or lightning were even remotely present, he proved the existence of animal electricity. Wherever there were frogs and wherever two dissimilar metals could be fastened together, people saw with their own eyes the marvelous revival of dead limbs. Physiologists thought they grasped in their hands their dream of a vital force; physicians thought no cure impossible; and even corpses were galvanized to prevent premature burial.

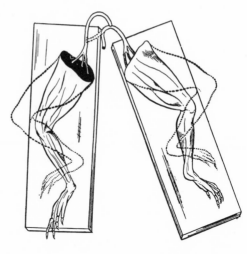

tracted with every heartbeat (Fig. 3.12). Obviously, the contraction of heart muscle was associated with a flow of electricity that stimulated the nerve leading to the muscle. It must have been a small flow, but luckily the current was detected and stepped up by a biological amplifier—a

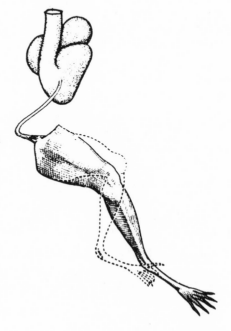

Figure 3.12.   With each contraction of the frog heart, von Kolliker and Müller found that the muscle of a frog's leg twitched once and, in sensitive preparations, three times when the motor nerve to the leg muscles was laid on the frog heart. This was the first electrocardiogram. The electric current accompanying each beat of the heart stimulated the motor nerve, which in turn stimulated the leg muscle to contract.

responsive nerve and muscle of a frog. In very sensitive frog leg preparations, the frog leg twitched three times during every cardiac cycle,
corresponding to what we now know as the three waves of the electrocardiogram, P, QRS, and T. But what clinical electrocardiography needed
to detect these very small currents was a very sensitive galvanometer
and one more readily available and durable than part of a living frog.

The great advance in *practical* electrocardiography came about in
1897, and from events completely unrelated to physiology or medicine.
There was at that time great interest in communication by transatlantic
and other underwater cables, but there was no device sensitive enough
to receive and amplify dispatches sent over them. Lord Kelvin had
devised galvanometers, but the problem with these was that Kelvin had
fixed a mirror to the string (to amplify a light beam) and the mirror,
having weight and inertia, couldn't record the response to a rapidly
changing current. Clement Ader (1897) invented a new type of galvanometer, a string galvanometer that needed no mirror; he recorded the
movement of the string directly on moving photographic film. It worked
successfully on one cable running from Brest to St. Pierre and on another
from Marseilles to Algiers. Having little mass, the string had a high
frequency of response and could follow 600–1600 signals per minute.

So it was the need for more rapid and better communication over
long distances that led to Ader's invention, and it was Ader's galvanometer that gave Willem Einthoven something that he could modify for
recording the ECG of man. In 1903 Einthoven made Ader's galvanometer far more sensitive by using an extremely thin quartz string,
1/10,000 of a millimeter in diameter, unburdened by the added mass of
either Kelvin's mirror or Ader's heavier string. He magnified 660 times
the moving shadow of the string, using a microscope, and projected the
shadow onto the slit of a special recording camera 6 feet away. Einthoven also made the ECG a quantitative instrument. He built it so that
the photographic plate moved at a speed of 25 millimeters per second
(1 millimeter of the record represents 0.04 second), and set the ampli-
fication of recorded voltage so that a 1-millimeter deflection of the string
was equivalent to 0.1 millivolt of electromagnetic force. I mention these
details because his construction and calibration not only made this
instrument the first practical tool for faithful recording of the electrocardiogram, but it made tracings from it comparable in any country or laboratory (Fig. 3.13). Einthoven also demonstrated the usefulness to
medicine of telemetry (measuring at a distance, transmitting signals from

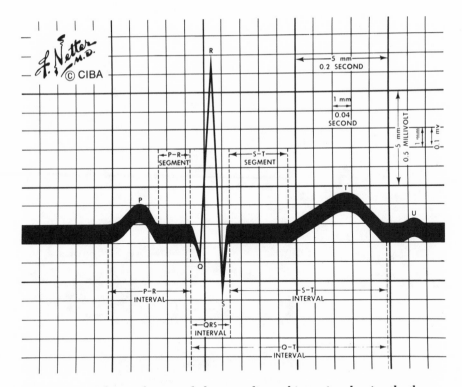

Figure 3.13.   Schema of a normal electrocardiographic tracing showing the three
main waves, P, QRS, and T. Wave P occurs at the beginning of the contraction of the
atria; QRS represents the excitation of the ventricles; and T is the recovery phrase.
The electrocardiogram is recorded on a grid of horizontal and vertical lines that seem
to clutter up the electrical tracing, but they are necessary for making quantitative
measurements. The recording paper moves at a rate so that the distance between
two vertical lines equals 0.04 second, and the apparatus is calibrated so that the distance between two horizontal lines equals 1 millivolt. This system was devised by
Einthoven 80 years ago and is still in use in laboratories and hospitals today.

the body to a distant recorder). The bulk of his original instrument was
such that it could not be moved to the hospital, and his first ECG's were
recorded by telemetry over 1500 meters of wire run between the university hospital and Einthoven's physiology laboratory. Einthoven's first
ECG's were really "telecardiograms," now used widely in long-distance
cardiological consultations and those required by paramedics in emergency ambulances. The brilliant success of Einthoven's instrument
started a whole new science for the specialty of cardiology and won for
Einthoven the Nobel Prize in 1924 (Fig. 3.14).

    Willem Einthoven began his scientific life in the renowned Eye
Hospital in Utrecht, Holland. His first research problems had nothing

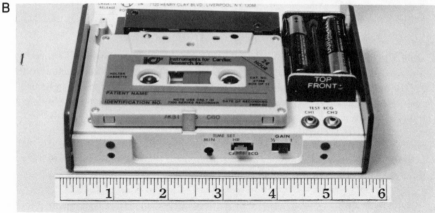

Figure 3.14. Einthoven's original electrocardiograph (A), built by him in his physiological research laboratory, weighed 800 pounds, occupied parts of two rooms, and required five people to operate. Modern engineering and development has miniaturized the electrocardiograph (B) so that it is easily portable. The Holter recorder shown here is worn around the waist, is less than 6 inches long, weighs less than 2 pounds, continuously records the electrical output of the heart for as long as 48 hours, and automatically pinpoints dangerous abnormal rhythms, heart block, and temporary cardiac arrests. It is especially useful for detecting irregular heartbeats in a patient whose heart insists on beating rhythmically during a physical examination in the physician's office.

to do with electrocardiography. One was a study of the elbow joint, and the other of stereoscopic vision. In 1885 he became professor of physiology at the University of Leyden. His first important work there again had nothing to do with the ECG; instead, it was the first major study done on the bronchial tree! He then turned his attention to optics; possibly it was an interest in the electric responses of the eye to stimulation by light that led him to explore methods for measuring extremely small electric currents there and then later in the heart. It's pretty hard to plan advances in medicine. No one would have put his money on Roentgen to find X rays, or on Einthoven to have made possible clinical electrocardiography.

Einthoven, like Roentgen before him, pointed out how new scientific discoveries came about. In accepting the Nobel Prize, Einthoven said,

Innumerable other workers in the field of electrocardiography have gained great merit. We cannot now name them all but we conclude with a reference to the happy circumstance that investigators of the whole world have worked together. A new chapter has been opened in the study of heart diseases, not by the work of a single investigator, but by that of many talented men, who have not been influenced in their work by political boundaries and, distributed over the whole surface of the earth, have devoted their powers to an ideal purpose, the advance of knowledge by which, finally, suffering mankind is helped. Among them the English investigator Thomas Lewis, who has played a great part in the development of electrocardiography, deserves special mention. It is my conviction that the general interest in ECG would certainly not have risen so high, nowadays, if we had had to do without his work, and I doubt whether without his valuable contributions I should have the privilege of standing before you today.

Einthoven was generous in giving credit not only to scientists who preceded and followed him, but also to his laboratory assistant, Van der Woerd, who designed many of the intricate parts of Einthoven's original string galvanometer. When Einthoven returned from Stockholm in 1924 with the Nobel Prize, he began a search for Van der Woerd, who had retired years before. He learned that Van der Woerd had died but had two surviving destitute sisters living in genteel poverty in a kind of alms house. He finally found them and gave them half of the award money ($20,000), which he felt Van der Woerd's services were worth in helping develop the string galvanometer.

Electrocardiography did not *end* with the invention of an instrument; it *began* with it. Once again, as with Auenbrugger and Laennec, someone had to establish what a *normal* electrical tracing looked like and what it meant, and then someone, or many, had to determine the meaning of *abnormal* tracings in relation to specific defects or changes in the heart—correlating changes recorded from skin electrodes with structural changes in the heart. Between 1883 and 1907, scientists discovered that the heart had a natural pacemaker that created rhythmic impulses whether the heart was in or out of the body (though *in* the body the pacemaker could be influenced by nerve impulses from the brain). Figure 3.15 shows how precise measurement of the time (in hundredths of a second) required for the impulse starting at the natural pacemaker to reach different portions of the heart permitted mapping of the normal pathway for activating atria and ventricles to contract. The impulse first spreads throughout the atria. When it reaches a node between the atria and ventricles (the A-V node), it is delayed for a little more than $\frac{1}{10}$ of a second; it then spreads in a special conducting system throughout both ventricles and activates the ventricular muscle to contract. Delay in the A-V node has a purpose; it ensures that normally the ventricles contract only after the atria have finished their contraction.

Figure 3.15. The heart's own pacemaker is located in the sinoatrial (S-A) node. It transmits rhythmic impulses that spread linearly throughout the muscles of the two atria, causing them to contract; impulses also impinge on the atrioventricular (A-V) node, stimulating it to activity. This, after a delay of about 0.1 second, stimulates a nervelike network of ventricular muscle fibers, the bundle of His; the right and left branches of this bundle (indicated by large arrows just below the A-V node) send fibers, as shown, to all parts of the two ventricles, causing their muscles to contract in sequence, beginning at the bottom and moving upward. The numbers indicate the time (in fractions of a second) it takes an impulse to travel from the S-A node to a particular point. The modern artificial pacemaker can take over the func-

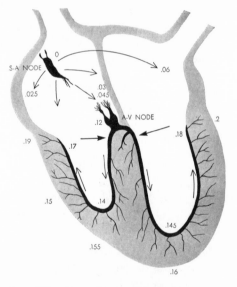

tion of the natural pacemaker when the latter is damaged, inhibited, or blocked. (From "The Heart" by Carl J. Wiggers. © 1957 by Scientific American, Inc. All rights reserved.)

The course of the pathways in ventricular muscle ensures that the ventricle doesn't contract all at once, but sequentially as the impulse reaches different muscle fibers, so that the heart empties from the bottom of the cavity upward. Once the ventricles have contracted (systole), they rest (diastole) while blood flows into them from the atria and the great veins. The ECG tracing records all of these events and many more, such as specific changes that point to occlusion of a coronary artery and damage to or death of part of the heart muscle.

Einthoven by himself does not "equal" ECG. It took a dramatic celestial event, lightning, an electric fish, a kite and a key, a Leyden jar, frogs legs swinging in a gentle Italian breeze, the transatlantic cable, and scientists of many countries to produce the electrocardiograph, and then, scores of brilliant cardiologists, starting with Sir Thomas Lewis, had to determine normal patterns and relate deviations from these to specific structural and functional changes in the heart—all this to make the ECG a valuable and precise diagnostic test.

No one working in 1895–1903 with Crookes tubes or animal electricity had any thought of cardiac or vascular surgery. Roentgen certainly never thought of using X rays as a way of producing pictures of blood vessels (as he had of bones) or of the interior of the heart. Einthoven never used his ECG to investigate and classify congenital heart disease, and Sir Thomas Lewis' main interest was in diagnosis and in learning the genesis of abnormal rhythms of the heart. But the many who preceded Helen Taussig gave her, usually unknowingly, the tools to study congenital heart disease and contributed to the surgical repair of congenital defects.

The Cardiac Catheter

It turned out that precise diagnosis of defects in the architecture of the heart, its valves, and main arteries and veins often required more information than could be provided by using the fluoroscope and studying the electrical pattern of the heart muscle. For example, it required knowing the blood pressures in the four cardiac chambers, and the amount of oxygen in the blood on the two sides of the heart; these data could point to abnormal openings between the right and left heart that allowed mixing of blood directly between the two where there should be none, or to constrictions (obstructions) where there should be none.

To obtain such information, one had to get an instrument inside the heart: It had to be a hollow tube that one could use first to withdraw samples of blood from atria or ventricles to measure the amount of O_2 in these and then, through the same tube, to measure blood pressure in these chambers; it had to be flexible so that it could be guided and coaxed around bends and curves in the veins leading to the atria and within the heart itself; and it had to be a barrier to X rays (its wall must contain substances that blocked X rays; such as lead or barium) so that the cardiologist using a fluoroscope could see the tube, in contrast to soft tissues, and know where the tip was at any moment. The answer was the cardiac catheter (originally used to explore the ureter, the tube that connects the kidney with the urinary bladder).

If one were to ask a hundred knowledgeable medical students, Who first catheterized a living heart? When? And why?, I believe that at least ninety would answer the "who" part with "André Cournand" or "André Cournand and Dickinson Richards," who popularized its use in the United States, the "why" part with "to diagnose cardiac disorders," and the "when" part with "1941." All three answers would be wrong. Cournand himself has pointed out that it was his famous countryman Claude Bernard, the great nineteenth-century physiologist, who first passed long glass thermometers down the carotid artery into the left ventricle and down the jugular vein into the right ventricle of animals, and that he did this to settle an argument over whether body heat originated in the lungs (it did not). The year was not 1941, but 1844, almost a hundred years before Cournand's first experiments. A few years after 1844, Bernard pushed hollow glass tubes into the ventricles and measured blood pressure there. Then, in 1861, two French physiologists, Jean Chauveau and Etienne Marey, systematically guided catheters into the two atria and two ventricles of animals to make continuous and fairly accurate measurements of blood pressure in the cardiac chambers.

But no one performed such studies on man for almost seventy years. Initially, physicians were fearful that touching the human heart with any foreign body, such as a probe, would cause cardiac standstill and death. Later, when that fear was shown to be unfounded, it was pretty difficult to guide a catheter without X-ray vision, and there were no X rays until 1896, and no really good X rays and fluoroscopes (for fine work) until 1916–1918, when William Coolidge, working in General Electric Company's Research Laboratories, devised a far more powerful X-ray tube. Then, in the early 1900s, so many "safe" uses for X rays were being explored by physicians that using X rays to guide a catheter into the heart (even if someone had already devised a radio-opaque catheter) must have been at the bottom of a very long list.

As most always happens, historians disagree on who first catheterized the heart of man. In 1912 a team of German physicians passed a catheter into the arm and leg veins of one of them and into those of patients, and advanced the arm catheter as far as the thorax and the leg catheter into the lower vena cava; but they either didn't have (or didn't use) radio-opaque catheters or X-ray equipment, and so there are no permanent pictures to show the actual location of the tip. The Nobel Prize committee and cardiologists in general gave credit to Werner Forssmann as the first to guide a catheter into a human heart (his own), prove it was there by taking an X-ray picture of it in place (Fig. 3.16), and demonstrate that it wasn't a high-risk procedure by doing it not only once, but at least six times on himself without stopping his heart or even producing irregular beats.

Who was Forssmann? You might guess that he was a research cardiologist or a physiologist, but he was neither. Actually, he had just finished medical school and passed his state examination in 1929. In that year he went to the August Victoria Home at Eberswalde near Berlin for clinical instruction in surgery. In July of 1929 he inserted a well-lubricated ureteral catheter into his own arm vein, slid it in 65 centimeters by feel alone, and then walked "a fairly long way" down the hall and then down one flight of steps to the X-ray department, where he had a photograph taken of the catheter lying in his right atrium. He then slipped it out and his famous experiment was finished. There was no resistance to sliding it back and forth; he experienced no pain.

Why in the world did he do it? In his 1929 report, Forssmann gave his reasons:

In sudden emergencies threatening the patient with cessation of heart activity, that is, in conditions of acute collapse, heart ailments, or even anesthetic accidents, or cases of poisoning, quick local medical treatment must be undertaken. Often the only way to save the patient is to attempt an intracardiac injection (aiming a long needle through the chest wall at and into a right or left ventricle) which is occasionally successful. Nonetheless, intracardiac injection remains a dangerous procedure; in numerous cases it has led, upon puncture of the heart wall, to injury of the coronary blood vessels and their branches, bleeding into the pericardium, and death by compressing the heart within its pericardial sac. Likewise, injury of the pleura can cause a fatal pneumothorax

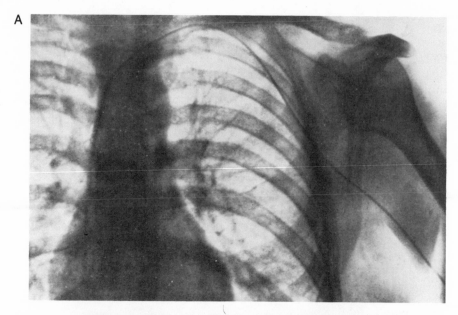

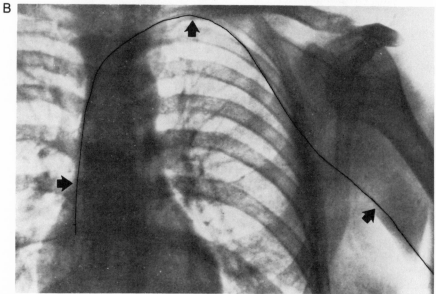

Figure 3.16. An X ray (A) showing the tube (catheter), then in use for entering the urinary bladder and ureter, that Forssmann pushed into the right atrium of his own heart—the first human heart catheterization. The X ray in (B) has been deliberately reproduced as a faint image of that in (A), to show the course of the catheter (see arrows).

(air between the chest wall and the lung). Incidents of this sort make it necessary to delay intracardiac injections until the last moment, resulting in loss of valuable time for application of medicine at the heart itself. These experiences compelled me to look for a new way, a less dangerous way, to penetrate into the heart, and I tried the *catheterization of the right side of the heart from the venous system.*

Later he wanted to use the catheter to record electrocardiograms from within the heart, but Professor Wilhelm His, famous for his discovery of part of the system that conducts nerve impulses from the A-V node to the ventricles (see Fig. 3.15) discouraged him from attempting this. Today it is an acceptable and valuable test.

Forssmann had still another idea for his catheter: to use it to outline the cavity of the heart (cardiogram) or the channel in arteries and veins through which blood flows (angiogram, from the Greek words *angeio*, meaning blood vessel, and *gramma*, meaning drawing). He reasoned that if he could inject through his catheter, close to the heart or blood vessel, a radio-opaque liquid and then quickly take an X-ray picture, there would be enough contrast between his liquid and the surrounding tissue to get a good picture of the heart and vessels. This time, Forssmann gave no one a chance to discourage him and made his trail-blazing angiograms in 1931.

However, he had the great misfortune to have continued his postgraduate education under Germany's great (and authoritarian) surgeon Ferdinand Sauerbruch. Many years later in *Experiments on Myself: Memoirs of a Physician in Germany,* Forssmann wrote,

Every time I attempted to talk to the Old Man [about the work on right heart catheterization] I got the feeling that independent thinking was regarded as a dangerous threat. This applied not only to scientific questions but also to problems with patients. An extraordinary inflexibility of thought reigned over the department, a rigid dogma based upon the teachings of Sauerbruch. Any divergent opinions were considered heresy. . . . I often wondered why Sauerbruch's surgical department, in itself so excellent, produced so many dull and uninspired doctors. Later I found the answer in a biography of Peter the Great by the eighteenth-century Russian historian M. M. Sherbatov. "How could men remain virile and steadfast when in their youth they had trembled before the rod of their superiors and been praised only for servility?"

Later, when Forssmann ventured to express to Sauerbruch the hope that he might qualify for a lectureship, Sauerbruch responded, "You might lecture in a circus about your little tricks, but never in a respectable German university." And when Forssmann protested quietly, Sauerbruch screamed, "Get out! Leave my department immediately!" He did, and returned to Eberswalde, where he had done his 1929 cardiac catheterization. In presenting the Nobel Prize to Forssmann in 1956, Swedish Professor Liljestrand commented,

His later disappointment must have been all the more bitter. It is true that the method was adopted in a few places—in Prague and in Lisbon—but on the whole Forssmann was not given the necessary support; he was, on the contrary, subjected to criticism of such exaggerated severity that it robbed him of any inclination to continue. This criticism was based on an unsubstantiated belief in the danger of the intervention, thus affording proof that—even in our enlightened times—a valuable suggestion may remain unexploited on the grounds of a preconceived opinion.

Roentgen's discovery was instantly known throughout the world; Forssmann's experiment on himself was not, even though his report was published in a widely read German medical journal. Most everyone believes that cardiac catheterization was forgotten between 1929 and 1941, when Cournand published his first report. Actually, this belief does an injustice to radiologists, for whom those twelve years were very busy ones. As mentioned earlier, on several occasions Forssmann injected a radio-opaque liquid through a catheter into dogs' hearts, as well as his own, but was unable to obtain enough contrast between the chambers of the heart and its wall to serve a useful purpose. But in 1931, Egas Moniz and his group in Portugal injected a contrast material into the right atria of patients and immediately took X-ray pictures of the blood vessels in the lungs; the next year they put a tube in a carotid artery and took X-ray pictures of the cerebral vessels. Heuser in Argentina and Ameuille in France took more pictures of the pulmonary circulation in 1936; because Ameuille studied a hundred patients without a fatality, he pretty well demolished once and for all the old concept that touching a human heart with anything at all would cause cardiac standstill. Then in 1937 in Cuba, Castellanos and his group showed for the first time that cardiac catheterization was not just a "circus trick"; they made a precise diagnosis of a congenital heart defect during the life of a patient. So taking X-ray pictures of the heart and arteries using special contrast fluids (angiocardiography) was well developed as a diagnostic method by the radiology profession at least a decade before the cardiac surgeons were ready for it.

Cardiac catheterization became a generally acceptable procedure in America after the studies of Cournand and Richards in New York in the 1940s; in England, McMichael and Sharpey-Schafer gradually gained reluctant acceptance for its use. Brannon, Weens, and Warren in Atlanta showed its further clinical value in 1945 in diagnosing abnormal openings between the two atria in four adults. Then in the same year Richard Bing joined Helen Taussig and the famous "blue baby" team at Hopkins to set up a catheterization laboratory devoted solely to pinpointing with precision a wide variety of defects in the hearts of children. The catheter then found clinical and scientific uses in most every part of the body— the coronary and cerebral arteries, the aorta, the arteries of the arms and legs, the kidneys, and the liver—to provide angiograms, highly selective X-ray pictures of the arterial system to a variety of organs by injecting contrast media directly and selectively, in high concentration, into the artery in question.

I have answered the question of *who* first used this new technique in man and *when;* I have said *why* Forssmann used it, initially and later, but not *why* Cournand and Richards did. Most physicians believe that they used it first to study circulatory shock in World War II or to diagnose heart failure. Not true; they were not cardiologists looking for a new test of the state of the patient's heart and circulation, but clinical physiologists interested in a basic research problem of whether the distribution of air to the millions of air sacs of the lungs matched the distribution of blood delivered to them through millions of pulmonary capillaries. To answer their scientific question, they had to know the oxygen and carbon dioxide content of venous blood that had come back to the heart through the two venae cavae and which had mixed in the chambers of the right side of the heart. This they could learn only by passing a catheter into the right heart, drawing out samples of mixed venous blood, and analyzing these chemically. So it was to answer a basic physiological question that Cournand and Richards began their studies that generated thousands of additional studies which made a diagnostic catheterization laboratory a requirement in almost every hospital in this country.

What is a cardiac catheterization laboratory? Physicians and patients think of it in terms of a patient lying on a hard table with a long plastic tube entering his arm vein and ending in his heart. But it involves a lot more. Figure 3.17 shows what else is in that laboratory; in condensed form, it shows almost four decades of progress in devising and improving new techniques and apparatus (to get more information and ensure safety), each of which is an interesting story in itself. Some were generated by discoveries of a basic nature (completely unrelated to medical diagnosis or cardiac surgery), and some were generated by industry.

Once cardiovascular catheterization was found to be safe, many uses were found for the technique. Selective visualization of coronary, cerebral, renal, and limb vessels became essential to establish the precise location of obstructions when surgeons learned how to replace blocked arteries with open ones. Cardiologists also built an electrical pacemaker into a cardiac catheter so that in an emergency a stopped or very slow heart could be paced through electrical wires hooked into the heart muscle, without ever opening the thorax. Others added a recording electrode to a cardiac catheter so that cardiologists could record ECGs directly from the bundle of His that carries the natural pacemaker's stimulus from the A-V node to the ventricular muscle (see Fig. 3.14). The catheter has also been used to deliver radioactive isotopes to any desired area of the circulation for precise diagnostic study, and it will soon be used to deliver specific antibodies to the region of a malignant tumor in man.

Echoes and Echocardiography

In recent years, a new way of examining the structure and performance of the heart has evolved from the use of echoes. Though we may not realize it, we are all familiar with three types of echoes: those coming from audible sound waves, those from radio waves, and those from ultrasound waves, which have such high frequencies—above 20,000 cycles a minute—that maybe most dogs can hear them but most humans cannot.

The first type of echo, resulting from audible sound waves, has been around forever, wherever there have been hills and valleys. We all know that at certain favorable locations a shout of "hello" is followed in a very short time by an echoed "hello." The original "hello" sent out sound waves that bounced off a mountain or hill and returned as an echo. The phenomenon has always been great fun for yodelers in the

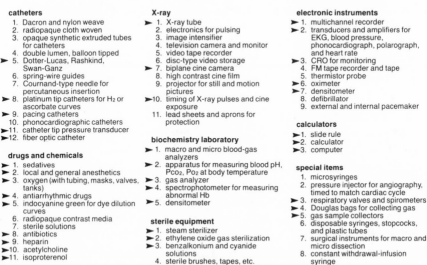

catheters

1. Dacron and nylon weave
2. radiopaque cloth woven
3. opaque synthetic extruded tubes for catheters
4. double lumen, balloon tipped
► 5. Dotter-Lucas, Rashkind, Swan-Ganz
6. spring-wire guides
7. Cournand-type needle for percutaneous insertion
► 8. platinum tip catheters for H_2 or ascorbate curves
► 9. pacing catheters
10. phonocardiographic catheters
►11. catheter tip pressure transducer
►12. fiber optic catheter

drugs and chemicals

► 1. sedatives
► 2. local and general anesthetics
► 3. oxygen (with tubing, masks, valves, tanks)
► 4. antiarrhythmic drugs
► 5. indocyanine green for dye dilution curves
6. radiopaque contrast media
7. sterile solutions
► 8. antibiotics
► 9. heparin
►10. acetylcholine
►11. isoproterenol

X-ray

► 1. X-ray tube
2. electronics for pulsing
3. image intensifier
4. television camera and monitor
5. video tape recorder
6. disc-type video storage
► 7. biplane cine camera
8. high contrast cine film
9. projector for still and motion pictures
►10. timing of X-ray pulses and cine exposure
11. lead sheets and aprons for protection

biochemistry laboratory

► 1. macro and micro blood-gas analyzers
► 2. apparatus for measuring blood pH, Pco_2, Po_2 at body temperature
► 3. gas analyzer
► 4. spectrophotometer for measuring abnormal Hb
►5. densitometer

sterile equipment

► 1. steam sterilizer
► 2. ethylene oxide gas sterilization
► 3. benzalkonium and cyanide solutions
4. sterile brushes, tapes, etc.
5. scrub and preparation solutions

electronic instruments

► 1. multichannel recorder
► 2. transducers and amplifiers for EKG, blood pressure, phonocardiograph, polarograph, and heart rate
► 3. CRO for monitoring
4. FM tape recorder and tape
5. thermistor probe
►6. oximeter
►7. densitometer
8. defibrillator
9. external and internal pacemaker

calculators

►1. slide rule
►2. calculator
►3. computer

special items

1. microsyringes
2. pressure injector for angiography, timed to match cardiac cycle
► 3. respiratory valves and spirometers
► 4. Douglas bags for collecting gas
►5. gas sample collectors
6. disposable syringes, stopcocks, and plastic tubes
7. surgical instruments for macro and micro dissection
8. constant withdrawal-infusion syringe

Figure 3.17. One usually thinks of cardiac catheterization as a simple procedure: a patient lying on a table with a long, flexible tube slid up an arm vein, coaxed around curves, and into the right atrium, right ventricle, or pulmonary artery. Alternatively, the catheter can be passed into an *artery*, against the stream, for selective injections into branches of the aorta such as limb arteries or the arteries supplying the heart, brain, or kidneys.

Actually, a tremendous number of devices and techniques are also needed besides a catheter to obtain maximal information about the patient, to analyze or record the information, and to provide for the safety of the patient. Many of the items required applied research and development by universities or industry; many more represent application to the catheterization laboratory of fundamental knowledge in biology, chemistry, and physics uncovered by those whose interests were simply to learn more—like those who climbed Mount Everest because it was there to be climbed. An arrowhead before an item indicates that it was a product of basic research; items not marked are the result of development and engineering.

Swiss Alps, but of little practical use until the speed of sound in air was measured. The accurate measurement of the speed of sound depended first upon knowing the speed of light. The latter was estimated as early as 1676 by Roemer, a Danish astronomer who was studying the motion of the satellites of the planet Jupiter. Each of these satellites is a moon that revolves about Jupiter, much as our moon revolves about the Earth. Once during each of its revolutions each satellite passes behind Jupiter and thus disappears from our view for a few hours. This phenomenon gave Roemer a marker. By measuring the time between two successive disappearances of the same satellite, Roemer found that it took $42\frac{1}{2}$ hours to traverse one complete orbit. If the Earth is in position A during successive eclipses of this satellite (Fig. 3.18), we should expect the next eclipse $42\frac{1}{2}$ hours later, and the next one $42\frac{1}{2}$ hours after that. Since, however, the earth is revolving in its own orbit about the sun as it leaves position A and moves steadily farther and farther away from Jupiter, the light coming from Jupiter will take longer to reach Earth, so that the eclipses of this satellite of Jupiter will recur at intervals slightly greater than $42\frac{1}{2}$ hours. Roemer noticed in 1676 that when the earth was farthest away from Jupiter (at position B), the eclipse of Jupiter's satellite began nearly 1,000 seconds late. He reasoned correctly that this 1,000-second delay was the time taken by light to travel the additional distance from A to B. This distance is the diameter not of the earth, but of the earth's orbit around the sun, then believed to be about 140 million miles. Using these figures, Roemer calculated that the speed of light must be 140,000,000/1,000 or 140,000 miles per second. Roemer's values were lower than today's values (because the 140 million mile figure was wrong), but he did make the first scientific measurement of the speed of light and proved that it was a finite figure.

In 1878–1880, Albert Michelson, an American physicist, measured the velocity of light with great precision; it was 186,324 miles per sec-

Figure 3.18.   Roemer's method for measuring the velocity of light.

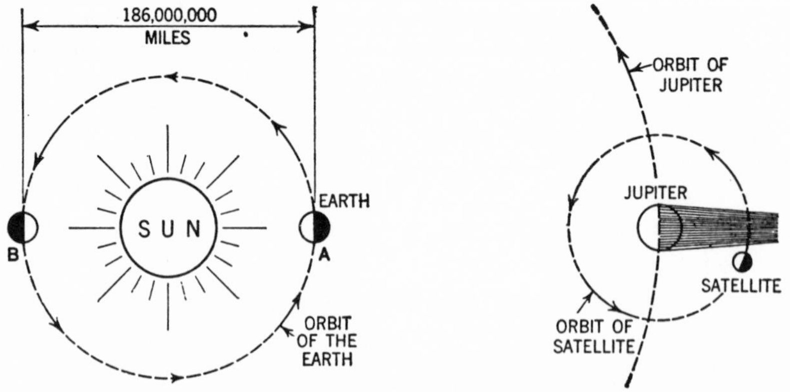

ond. For his research on light, lasting over several decades, he became the first American to win a Nobel Prize (1907). Once one knew the fantastic speed of light (even approximately), one could roughly estimate the speed of sound by measuring the time between a lightning flash and the thunder it created. Once gunpowder became available, the speed of sound could be measured more accurately by noting the time between the flash and the roar of distant cannon fire, and by actually measuring the distance between the cannon and the recording eye and ear.

When man knew the number of feet that sound waves travel in a second in air at a given temperature, then the number of seconds between the first hello and its echo provided the information needed to calculate the distance between the hello-er and the obstruction that bounced the hello back.

The second type of echo, coming from radio waves, is relatively recent in terms of world history and world science. Radio waves had to await the great discoveries of Faraday, Henry, Maxwell, Hertz, Crookes, J. J. Thomson, and others in the late 1800s and early 1900s—the discovery of how to generate electricity and the existence of electromagnetic fields and radio waves. The practical use of echoes from radio waves bouncing off an object in air dates only from the 1930s. The technique was called *ra*dio *de*tecting *a*nd *r*anging ("radar" for short—as Ritchie Calder noted, an appropriate name for an echo, for "it spells the same both ways"). Robert Watson Watt, a descendent of Sir James Watt, inventor of the steam engine, began thinking about radio waves in World War I when the British wanted him to detect storm cloud formations so that British aviators could avoid them. When World War I ended, Watt went off to the Sudan to study the radio characteristics of tropical thunderstorms. In 1934, when the construction of a huge, modern German Luftwaffe threatened the security of England, till then an island easily protected by its navy, Watt, then director of England's Radio Research Station, really went to work on "radiolocation" and within a year showed that it was practical. England then embarked on a vast, highly secret project.

Radar must rank with gunpowder and the longbow among military discoveries that changed the course of history. During World War II, Germany had overrun France, and what remained of the British Army had retreated into England, waiting for the Luftwaffe to bomb the British Isles into surrender. When the Luftwaffe finally came, their formations had been spotted even before they left their bases in France. They had been followed as they left their bases and assembled at their rendezvous point in the air, and finally as they flung themselves across the English Channel in their "surprise" assault on Britain. But there was no surprise; radar had already told the British pilots the number and location of the planes and even the height at which they were flying. The rest is history. A relatively small number of British fought back the massive Nazi air attack; a secret weapon (which the Germans were not using effectively even by the end of the war) had kept Europe and Britain from becoming Germany, and Watson Watt became Sir Robert or, as his friends called him, "Sir Echo."

Somewhere along the line a historical footnote should be made on two astute observations by men whose names few have ever heard. One was by some British Post Office engineers who had no difficulty in their regular transmissions of radio messages except for a curious interference that occurred whenever aircraft came in for nearby landings; the radio waves were obviously hitting the planes and bouncing back. The other was by an American, Albert Hoyt Taylor, Chief Physicist of the U.S. Naval Research Laboratory. In the early 1920s Taylor noted distortions in his radio transmissions when a ship steaming up the nearby Potomac river got in the line of transmission. He reported these findings to his superiors, but they were not interested in them until 1930, when they instructed him to "investigate the use of radio to detect the presence of enemy vessels and aircraft." My guess is that if Taylor had been a university research professor of physics, he would have worked out the principles of the radar in a few years—but he was in the navy. There has been some question of who discovered radar. I don't know who had the *idea* first, Taylor or Watson Watt, but certainly the British team developed a practical unit first; the Americans helped by producing huge numbers of the original unit for the British, and later more and more advanced devices for all of the Allies.

The third type of echoes, coming from high-frequency "ultrasound" waves, must have been around as long as there have been bats and caves. One of the marvels of nature is that bats, believed to be blind, can fly at top speed in utter darkness and yet find and catch tiny insects, flying at their top speed. The bats accomplish these feats in caves that have irregular, rough walls, ceilings, and floors, and even projecting stalactites and stalagmites. The mystery of the "blind" bat was cleared up in 1938. Donald Griffin, then a graduate student in biology at Harvard, brought together in one laboratory several bats and an apparatus that could generate and detect ultrasound. He soon showed that his bats emitted sounds with frequencies between 30,000 and 70,000 cycles per second that are inaudible to the human ear, and that they possessed their amazing navigational skill only when they could both emit these high-frequency sounds and detect the waves reflected back from objects in their path. It would have made a fascinating story if Griffin's studies of echolocation in bats (even though he was studying ultrasound and not radio waves) had led directly to the invention of radar and to winning the "Battle for Britain" in the 1940s, but such was not the case. Physicists and engineers began to study radar at about the same time as Griffin studied bats (between 1935 and 1940), and the studies of man-made and bat-made echolocation proceeded independently. It would also have made a fascinating story to say that the study of blind bats led to the development of sonar for detecting underwater objects, but again the practical military use of sonar (*so*und *n*avigating *a*nd *r*anging) came first—to detect enemy submarines. (Radar is ineffective in deep water, though of inestimable value in spotting surface warships and surfaced submarines).

Interest in detecting underwater objects was originally generated by the ship-versus-iceberg problem. This was dramatized when the *Titanic,* highly publicized as the first "unsinkable" ship, sank after colliding with an iceberg in 1912. Underwater detection then became a matter of national survival during World War I, with the beginning of unrestricted submarine warfare. In 1914 the only way of detecting a submerged submarine was to lower a hydrophone, an underwater microphone, and amplify the noise emitted by idling submarine engines; the hydrophone became useless when U-boat commanders learned to shut off their engines. But, thanks largely to the work of French physicist Paul Langevin, sound waves could, by the end of World War I, be bounced off the ocean floor (to determine the depth of the ocean) and then be "pinged" off any object, such as a submarine, above the floor to determine its depth (Fig. 3.19). Today, when there are few submarines cluttering the oceans, modern fishing fleets use sonar to find large schools of fish. In medicine, the use of echo techniques has made possible a new diagnostic technique called echocardiography that makes use of ultrasonic echoes.

Echocardiography has achieved great popularity in a few years because it is simple, relatively inexpensive, painless, presumably harmless, and "noninvasive." "Noninvasive" is medical jargon for "no needles,

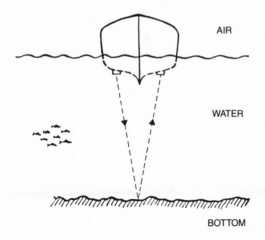

Figure 3.19. This is the simplest use of echo sounding: measuring the distance from a boat to the bottom of the sea by directing sound waves downward and noting the time for their return (sonar). The echo method is useful in medical diagnosis because many biological tissues reflect sound waves. However, because the distances between the skin and deeper tissues or organs in the human body are small, medical diagnosis requires the use of very short pulses (ultrasound) to distinguish the locations and shapes of the reflecting tissues.

no injections, no scalpels, no tubes slid into veins, no enemas, etc." Actually, the test is *not* noninvasive, because ultrasound waves, even though the human ear cannot hear them, do indeed pass through the skin and muscles of the thorax and the heart with a frequency of more than 20,000 cycles per minute. Industry, which uses ultrasound to detect flaws in metal, is more accurate in its terminology and calls ultrasonic echolocation "nondestructive" testing. One should point out here that X rays once fit the definition of a "noninvasive" test because their passage through tissues produced no gross or even microscopic changes in surface or internal cells (see p. 100). So far, ultrasound, in the frequency range used for the test, has produced no known harmful effects on living cells or tissues. Let us hope that it will prove to be as harmless as the stethoscope, even fifty years from now.

Of what use is echolocation to the cardiac surgeon? How does ultrasound tell a physician what's wrong with a patient's heart? Sound waves are applied to a small area of the patient's chest. Sound travels more slowly in gases than in liquids and more slowly in liquids than in solids. The waves travel forward at the same rate in a uniform medium; when all of them enter tissue of a different density (e.g., liquid instead of gas or heart muscle instead of blood), they still travel together, but at a different rate. Whenever the waves hit substances of different density, for example, at a liquid–solid interface, some of the sound energy bounces back, as an echo at different rates and can be detected at the surface of the body. By systematically aiming the beam at each part of the heart, a picture (Fig. 3.20) can be constructed of the outer muscle wall of the

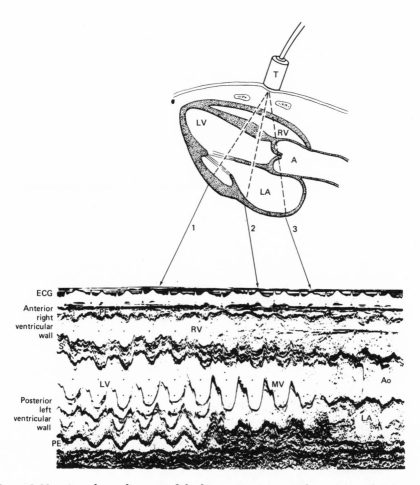

Figure 3.20. An echocardiogram of the heart. From a transducer (T) on the chest wall, ultrasound beams are sent through the heart at different angles to obtain reflections from different parts of the heart such as the left ventricle (LV), leaflets of the mitral (MV), aortic, tricuspid, or pulmonary valves, and right ventricle (RV). By studying what appears to be a completely chaotic record of reflected echoes, the cardiologist can reconstruct the anatomical outlines of these structures and make a specific diagnosis of abnormal structures.

heart, of its blood-filled cavities (every change in density providing another echo), and of the contours of the valves. So the cardiologist can use echoes to detect heart size, wall thickness, the shape of the cavities, defects in valves, and abnormal openings between the right and left heart.

Echocardiography was probably a spin-off of Griffin's study of the blind bat. To complete the circle, some scientists are now providing portable ultrasound sending and receiving sets for blind people, to replace the white cane and Seeing Eye dog.

It is fascinating that the practical use of echoes began with esoteric, "useless" research (astronomers studying eclipses, basic scientists who wanted to know the speed of light), the sinking of an "unsinkable" ship by an iceberg, and physicists' calculations of the speed of sound (in air and in water) and the velocity of radio waves. Echo science was then put to practical use in the two world wars by engineers to locate military targets, and it now has "spun off" a new test for detecting heart disease, a device for guiding the blind, and a way for commercial fishermen to make a better living.

The diagnostic methods discussed have, for the most part, solved an important problem facing every cardiac or vascular surgeon—knowing exactly what he is going to find when he and the patient come together in the surgical operating room. But the cardiac surgeon needed to know even more before he cut and stitched!

4

Open Heart Surgery

Once the correct diagnosis has been made and the cardiologist and the cardiac surgeon have agreed that an operation has far more chances of benefiting the patient than harming him, we move into the operating room (the "O.R." or "operating theatre," as some call it). As we look around the operating room, we see what the surgeon must have at hand before he can do a predictably successful operation, and it's a great deal more than what is needed for cardiac catheterization (see Fig. 3.17). Some special apparatus that we've already discussed are there: Gibbon's heart–lung machine (or a more recent version of it) is needed if the operation requires that the surgeon stop the heart and open it for more than a few minutes, and the electrocardiograph is there for continuous recording of the electrical activity of the heart (but, in the O.R. it is now displayed on a television screen for all to see). But there are many more things in the operating room. What immediately strikes the observer is that everyone—surgeon, anesthetist, nurses, residents, orderlies—is wearing a sterilized cap, mask, gown, and rubber gloves. Instruments and sponges are in packs that have been sterilized; all covers and drapes have been sterilized. The operating room is as spotless and clean as modern man knows how to make it; it would even satisfy an advertising manager promoting Product X on television to produce a germfree bathroom.

Antisepsis

The scene described above was not always so. There were not always sterile caps, gowns, masks, and gloves (Fig. 4.1); there were not always sterilized instruments and sponges or even disinfectant sprays. In fact, a very bitter and sometimes tragic battle was waged in the nineteenth century to make the operating room germfree, and it was finally won only in the late 1880s.

The cast of characters in the great drama of the late 1800s included men now in the Hall of Fame but then doubted, scoffed at, or even reviled. First came Oliver Wendell Holmes, the elder, who, as early as 1843, years before the germ theory of disease was established, stated his belief that childbed fever was contagious. Then came Ignaz Semmelweiss of Vienna, who in 1847 confirmed Holmes's belief, again before the germ theory of disease was proposed and accepted. A little later Louis Pasteur insisted that germs (bacteria) do not pop up out of all sorts of nonliving material and do not generate spontaneously, but, like all other creatures, arise only by reproduction from similar existing creatures; later he demonstrated that specific germs cause specific diseases. Then John Tyndall, a physicist, went to Pasteur's rescue in the great battle over germs; his weapon was completely unpredictable, but powerful: It was a light-scattering device (Fig. 4.2) that could guarantee the presence or complete absence of otherwise invisible particles in air (including floating bacteria). Finally, Lord Lister, an early and strong believer in Pasteur's germ theory, went to work with a passion in the surgical operating room to make it germfree and thereby prevent wound and surgical infections. Robert Koch also used his very rigid, unassailable criteria to prove to all disbelievers that tubercle bacilli did indeed *cause* tuberculosis and that the germ and the disease could be transmitted from one individual to another.

These men, today acclaimed as great scientists, did not have an easy time in the 1800s. Oliver Wendell Holmes, professor of anatomy and physiology at Harvard Medical School, pronounced in 1843 that childbed (childbirth) fever was contagious and whatever caused the disease was usually carried from patient to patient by physicians. He advised all physicians to wash their hands in calcium chloride after they had taken care of a patient with childbed fever. He was attacked by Charles Meigs, professor of midwifery at Jefferson Medical College in Philadel-

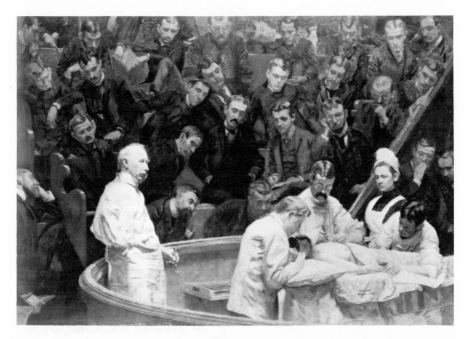

Figure 4.1. The famous painting of the Agnew Surgical Operating Room (University of Pennsylvania) by Thomas Eakins (1889) shows no sign of cap, mask, or gloves on the operating team. An eager, unscrubbed audience is leaning over the railing, almost touching the surgeon and perhaps breathing on the patient's open wound. (Note the painter has included his own portrait at far right.)

Not appreciated in his own time (1844–1916), Eakins is usually referred to today as the greatest painter this country has ever produced. It is said that certainly he was *the* great American realist painter and that no one else has ever got American scenes and faces down on canvas with such authority. One art critic wrote, " 'Best' is a big word, but if there are better American paintings than these, I, for one, cannot for the moment think which they are."

However, Eakins' insistence on realism and faithfulness led to his financial and even artistic undoing as a portrait painter in the 1800s. It is said that his lifelong earnings were only $15,000 (less than the worth of any one of his canvases today). Honors finally came to him late in life, but he never forgave the public's attitude toward him. When awarded a gold medal by the Pennsylvania Academy (which earlier had dismissed him from its faculty), he appeared for the ceremony dressed as a cyclist, took the medal, and then cycled to the Philadelphia mint and turned in the medal for $75 in currency. His life story reads like that of some now-famous scientists.

phia and by Hugh Hodge, professor of obstetrics at the University of Pennsylvania. Hodge begged his students to divest their minds of the fear that they could ever carry the dreadful virus. Meigs scorned Holmes's deductions as characteristic of the "jejune and fizzenless vaporings of

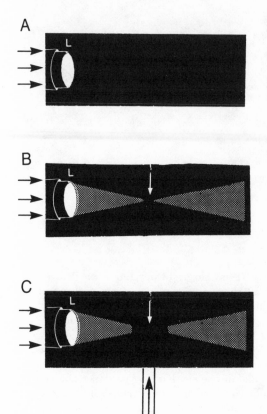

Figure 4.2. (A) When Tyndall, using a lens in the wall of a box, focused a beam of light on the center of the box, the box remained completely dark if he had first removed from the box all particles, including the finest, by the use of filters with infinitesimally small pores. This proved that light waves were invisible until they impinged on particles in their path and these reflected and scattered the light. Tyndall's experiment demolished the theory of spontaneous generation, because no organisms ever appeared or grew in a box in which his beam did not scatter light. (B) When fine, floating dust particles were added to the box and light waves again focused through a lens on the center of the box, each particle reflected and scattered the light waves to produce cones converging on and diverging from the center (white arrow). The expanding cone of light to the right is what one sees in a completely darkened (and dusty) movie house when the projector is turned on. (C) When a man blew his expired air through the center of the light path (through tube below), a dark area appeared; this was evidence that the human airways had filtered all particles from the inspired air and the air then expired from the air sacs of the lung was particle free and probably also bacteria free.

sophomore writers" (Holmes's medical critics were not above attacking his literary talents as well) and added that he preferred to attribute the deaths to "accident, or Providence, of which I can form a conception, rather than to a contagion of which I cannot form any clear idea, at least as to this particular malady."

Undoubtedly, Holmes had antagonized members of the medical profession by suggesting that they were carriers of death, and his scientific observations further drew scorn because he was "a sophomore writer."

Holmes's allegations were not based upon anatomic and clinical observations; he had little or no obstetric experience to back his assertions. Acting the role of a barrister pleading the cause of martyred mothers, he declared,

The balance must be struck boldly and the results declared plainly. If I have been hasty, presumptuous, ill-informed, illogical; if my array of facts means nothing; if there is no reason for any caution in the view of these facts, let me be told so on such authority that I must believe it, and I will be silent henceforth, recognizing that my mind is in a state of disorganization. There is no quarrel here between men, but there is deadly incompatibility and exterminating warfare between doctrines. Let the men who hold opinions look to it: if there is any voluntary blindness, any interested oversight, any culpable negligence, even in such a matter, and the facts shall reach the public ear, the pestilence carrier of the lying-in chamber must look to God for pardon, for man will never forgive him.

Sir William Sinclair commented,

Holmes conferred immense benefits on humanity by devoting his literary genius to attracting attention to puerperal [childbirth or childbed] fever and trying to suppress the practices which brought childbed fever in their train.

But, actually, Holmes *said* that childbed fever could be prevented; Semmelweiss *proved* that it could be.

In 1847 Ignaz Semmelweiss of Vienna independently proposed that childbed fever was contagious (though his book was not published until 1861). It was well known that many more pregnant women died in one particular hospital ward in Vienna that was attended by students and physicians than in a similar ward supervised exclusively by female nurses (who never attended autopsies). Even patients, on entering the hospital, pleaded to be admitted to the latter ward. Semmelweiss reasoned that the students and physicians examined their living patients immediately after coming from the morgue where they had done autopsies on women who died of childbirth fever. He instituted a strict routine that all hands about to touch patients must first be thoroughly washed in a solution of chlorinated lime. Mortality from puerperal sepsis fell at once from 12 to 3% and later to 1%. But his revolutionary doctrine, like that of Holmes, incriminated obstetricians as the carriers of disease and death, and aroused fierce opposition from medical authorities, including the great German pathologist Rudolf Virchow. Semmelweiss, ostracized, denounced, and ridiculed, died eighteen years later in an insane asylum, ironically, of a bloodstream infection, perhaps one of those same killers whose existence he had, without success, tried to identify and prevent. In an appendix to his 1861 book, Semmelweiss had written,

When I, with my present convictions, look back upon the past, I can only dispel the sadness which falls upon me by gazing into the happy future when within the lying-in hospitals, and also outside of them throughout the whole world, only cases of selfinfection will occur. . . . The conviction that such a time must inevitably sooner or later arrive will cheer my dying hour.

How in 1847 could one have ensured that Semmelweiss' theory be given an objective evaluation? If the Emperor of Austria had assembled a Viennese Imperial task force on puerperal sepsis, would it have given Semmelweiss a chance to prove his theory? I doubt it, because even men with the greatest minds in any century have experienced difficulty in believing in the existence of creatures or their parts that they cannot see, feel, hear, or smell. Virchow would probably have been chairman of the emperor's task force and, though an eminent scientist, he had a closed mind on the matter of germs and contagion.

Joseph Lister, later Lord Lister, an English surgeon going along happily in the mid-1800s working on scientific problems concerned with muscles, nerves, blood clotting, and anesthetics, read Pasteur's famous papers of the 1850s and 1860s on fermentation and the germ theory of disease. He at once became an ardent admirer of Pasteur's, a staunch advocate of his beliefs, and dropped his other interests to apply Pasteur's belief to surgical practice. In 1875, Lister wrote,

The Germ Theory supposes that germs are omnipresent in the world around us and are sure to gain access to any exposed organic substance, and develop there if it proves to be a favorable bed. These organisms, minute though they appear to us, form no exception to the general law of living things, i.e., that they originate from similar beings by parentage. The philosophical investigations of Pasteur long since made me a convert to the germ theory and it was on the basis of this discovery that I founded the antiseptic treatment of wounds in surgery.

Lord Lister was the right man at the right time for four reasons: First, he was already a respected scientist; second, he read widely (his reading included "natural philosophy," as physiology was then called, and highly controversial articles in basic biology); third, he came out strongly on the right side of the controversy; and fourth, he was a surgeon accustomed to taking immediate action and he set out at once to eliminate germs from the operating room.

Lord Lister's attempts to achieve antisepsis in surgical operating rooms met with determined attacks from hospital administrators who saw the reputations of their hospitals being destroyed, and from physicians who still disbelieved the germ theory of infection. It is interesting that the one physician who was most influential and persistent in disparaging Lister was James Simpson, discoverer of chloroform, who, when he had introduced chloroform into obstetrics and surgery only a few years earlier, was denounced by the clergy, both from the pulpit and in pamphlets, on the grounds that anesthetics were decoys of Satan. Apparently, having been attacked without reason does not deter one from attacking another without reason.

Lister established the technique of "antisepsis" (attacking germs) using chemical agents. He first used carbolic acid (phenol) to destroy any germs present in or on instruments, bandages, the surgeon's hands, the patient's skin, incisions, and deeper wounds. In his operating room the technique led to greatly reduced mortality and many fewer infections after operations. In 1864 and 1866, of 35 patients who required amputation of a limb, 16 died (46%); in 1868 and 1869, after Lister introduced his antiseptic system, of 33 patients who required amputation, only 6 died (18%).

Actually, Lister was not committed to the use of one particular chemical substance such as phenol to achieve *anti*sepsis, but he was committed to a *principle*—no matter how it was achieved—that germs don't belong in an operating room. Later, when he realized that phenol damaged tissues and interfered with wound healing, he switched to milder antiseptics and finally to the *a*sepsis concept (*preventing* germs from entering the operating room) as opposed to *anti*sepsis (*killing* those already there). In 1887, when Lister finally gave up as ineffective his antiseptic spray (similar to ones now advertised daily on our television screens for "purifying" our kitchens and bathrooms), he stated that he regretted that he had ever used and advocated it. Lister wrote in 1890,

As regards the spray, I feel ashamed that I should have ever recommended it for the purpose of destroying the microbes of the air. If we watch the formation of the spray and observe how its narrow initial cone expands as it advances, with fresh portions of air continually drawn into its vortex, we see that many of the microbes in it, having only just come under its influence, cannot possibly have been deprived of their vitality. Yet there was a time when I assumed that such was the case, and, trusting the spray implicitly as an atmosphere free from living organisms, omitted various precautions which I had before supposed to be essential.

Asepsis brought with it the use of sterile caps, masks, and gowns, as well as the use of sterile rubber gloves.

The first suggestion for the routine use of sterilized rubber gloves in the operating room came some thirteen years before Semmelweiss's "clean hands" campaign. It came from a young Hoboken physician, Richard Cooke, who wanted to protect the surgeon's hands from "the most malignant virus of his patient." A second suggestion came in 1840–1842 from Dr. Thomas Watson of London, but his goal was to protect the patient from the surgeon's hands, which could not be completely germfree, even with vigorous scrubbing, and which obviously could not be boiled to be sterilized. Watson hoped for a glove "which should be impervious to fluids and yet so thin and pliant as not to interfere materially with the delicate sense of touch required" by the surgeon.

The rubber surgical glove actually came into use in 1889, but not to protect the surgeon from the patient's germs, nor the patient from the surgeon's germs. William Halsted, first professor of surgery at the new Johns Hopkins Medical School, tells how they came into use:

In the winter of 1889 and 1890—I cannot recall the month—the nurse in charge of my operating room complained that the solutions of mercuric chloride produced a dermatitis of her arms and hands. As she was an unusually efficient woman, I gave the matter my consideration and one day in New York requested the Goodyear Rubber Company to make as an experiment two pair of thin rubber gloves with gauntlets. On trial these proved to be so satisfactory that additional gloves were ordered. In the autumn, on my return to town, the assistant who passed the instruments and threaded the needles was also provided with rubber gloves to wear at the operations. . . . This assistant was given the gloves to protect his hands from the solution of phenol (carbolic acid) in which the instruments were submerged rather than to eliminate him as a source of infection.

According to Halsted, the assistants in time became "so accustomed to working with gloves that they also wore them as operators." Soon observations of an impressive reduction in infected incisions made the use of sterile gloves mandatory.

It took a little while for antisepsis and asepsis to become fully accepted in surgical operating rooms (see Fig. 4.1, painted in 1889). But eventually they were universally accepted. By 1927, on the occasion of the Lister Centennial, Lord Moynihan, President of the Royal College of Surgeons, was able to say of Lister, "Nothing of which this world has knowledge has rescued so many lives, spared so much suffering, lifted so heavy a load of apprehension and sorrow from human hearts as has the work of this Quaker hero. For him I have justly proclaimed that he has saved more lives than all the wars of the ages have thrown away." Certainly, without Lister the specialty of surgery could not have flourished during the long period between the discovery of anesthesia and the advent of chemotherapy and antibiotics.

Anesthesia

Successful operations on the heart require more than precise diagnosis, the heart–lung apparatus, and asepsis; they also require general anesthesia and all of the expert professional skill of a relatively new specialist—the medically and scientifically trained anesthesiologist. Thanks to him, you can go to sleep the night before your scheduled cardiac operation and wake up the next day in a special recovery room, with no recollection of ever having been in or out of an operating room.

It was not always so. Figure 4.3 shows the "Operation Bell" from the London Hospital in 1791. The inscription on the base reads, "Prior to the discovery of anaesthetics, this bell was rung before a Surgical Operation to summon attendants to hold the patient still."

Why have we heard so little about the patient's suffering during operations before 1846, the first year in which ether was deliberately given to produce "surgical" anesthesia? Someone has written a little story to explain this. The story starts by quoting a fable about how many paintings depict battles between a lion and an unarmed man, with man always emerging as the victor. A lion asked an artist why artists always show man as the victor, though in fact this was rarely the case. The artist replied simply, "Lions do not paint." And so it is in the operating room: The surgeon, and never the patient, writes the notes describing the event. The story ends:

We read of the skill and intrepidity of the operator, of difficulties met and overcome, and of victories snatched, as it were, from the very jaws of impend-

Figure 4.3. The Operation Bell, London Hospital, 1791—a poignant recollection of surgical procedures before the days of anesthesia.

ing defeat; but we hear little of the tortures of the victim under the life-saving process, or, in an unsuccessful case, of the gradual subsidence of agonizing cries hushed in the silence of death.

How and when was anesthesia discovered? Probably the state of anesthesia was achieved many times after 1774, the year in which Joseph Priestley first prepared nitrous oxide; but for many years no one, including Priestley, ever knew that nitrous oxide was an anesthetic gas. Nitrous oxide was known as laughing gas because it produced a sense of exhilaration in those who inhaled it, and laughing gas parties (Fig. 4.4) were fashionable in the early 1800s. At any one of these parties many an inebriated fellow may have fallen and hit his head on the floor with a thud; he felt no pain, but he did not connect the absence of pain with the inhalation of nitrous oxide. As Winston Churchill said, "Men occasionally stumble over the truth but most of them pick themselves up and hurry off as if nothing had happened."

The first person to realize that something had happened was Humphrey Davy at the Pneumatic Institute in Bristol, England. Near the end of July 1799, Davy, then a 19-year-old student, prepared and inhaled large quantities of nitrous oxide. He wrote of his experience:

In cutting one of the unlucky teeth called *dentes sapientiae* [wisdom teeth], I experienced an extensive inflammation of the gum, accompanied with great pain, which equally destroyed the power of repose, and of consistent action. On the day when the inflammation was most troublesome, I breathed three large doses of nitrous oxide. The pain always diminished after the first four or five inspirations. As nitrous oxide in its extensive operation appears capable of

Figure 4.4.   Caricature published in 1808 satirizing the effects of inhaling nitrous oxide. These guests at a nitrous oxide "party" are saying, "What a concatenation of Ideas," "This World's a little dirty Planet / And I'll no longer help to Man it," "I feel disposed to Merryment," and "Nothing exists but thought." The caption at the bottom states, "Effects of breathing Nitrous Oxyd—the only genteel way of getting Drunk."

destroying physical pain, it may probably be used with advantage during surgical operations.

This was a note on p. 556 of Davy's book *Concerning Nitrous Oxide* (published in 1800) and it seems that no one read past p. 555 or, if anyone did, he didn't realize the importance of those few words. Davy himself was a chemist and not a physician or surgeon. It was not until 1844 that an American dentist named Horace Wells used nitrous oxide for painless dentistry.

Davy became director of the Pneumatic Institute and his young apprentice was Michael Faraday. Some years later, when Davy was asked what he considered to be his greatest discovery, he unhesitatingly answered, "Michael Faraday." Michael Faraday became one of Britain's greatest scientists. Among his minor accomplishments were some observations he made in 1818 on ether. He observed,

In trying the effects of the ethereal vapour on persons who are peculiarly affected by nitrous oxide, the similarity of sensation produced was very unexpectedly found to have taken place. One person who always feels a depression of spirits on inhaling the gas, had sensation of a similar kind produced by inhaling the (ether) vapour.

No one immediately used ether to produce anesthesia, but when some youngsters in 1842 asked Dr. Crawford Long, who practiced medicine in the small town of Jefferson, Georgia, for some nitrous oxide for a "laughing gas" party, Long said he hadn't any but would give them some ether, which he said was just as good. Long never wrote about the 1842 event until 1849, when he said,

I gave it to the gentleman who had previously inhaled it, then inhaled it myself and afterwards gave it to all persons present . . . its inhalation soon became quite fashionable in this country. I noticed my friends, while etherized, received falls or blows, which I believe were sufficient to produce pain on a person not in a state of anesthesia and on questioning them, they uniformly assured me that they did not feel the least pain from these accidents.

On March 30, 1842, Long administered ether anesthesia while he removed a tumor from the back of the neck of a patient who had repeatedly postponed the operation for fear of pain. When informed that the operation was over, the patient was incredulous until Long showed him the excised tumor.

Many people before must have noted the analgesic effects of ether but "picked themselves up and hurried off as though nothing had happened." Some call Long's observation "serendipity," a word coined by Horace Walpole in 1754. It *was* serendipity, but as Walpole *really* defined his new word, and not as now used by those who have never actually read Walpole's letters. Walpole defined it as "making discoveries, by accidents *and* sagacity, of things which they were not in quest of." The important word in Walpole's definition is *and*. Louis Pasteur put it in different words when he wrote in 1854 that "chance favors the prepared mind." Purely accidental happenings are one thing; an accidental observation falling on a prepared *and sage* mind is quite a different thing.

Long, who used ether first in 1842, did not publish his observations until 1849 because he wanted to make sure that lack of pain was not due to hypnosis or "mesmerism," still a popular "ism" at that time. As a result, William Morton, who anesthetized a patient in the now famous "Ether Dome" at Massachusetts General Hospital in 1846, gained priority because Henry Bigelow of Boston promptly published an account of this use of ether in the same year. James Simpson of Edinburgh added a third general anesthetic agent, chloroform, in 1848. But there were three very important happenings in the world of anesthesia in addition to these discoveries.

Sigmund Freud is remembered best as the father of psychoanalysis, but he also did the first scientific study of cocaine as a drug. As a result, he was quite familiar with its properties, except its most important one—its action as a local anesthetic. Carl Koller, a young ophthalmologist, was an associate of Freud's and had learned much about cocaine from Freud. Koller's daughter tells her father's account of his famous 1884 discovery:

"Upon one occasion," my father said, "another colleague of mine, Dr. Engel, partook of some [cocaine] with me from the point of his penknife and remarked, 'How that numbs the tongue.' I said, 'Yes, that has been noticed by everyone that has eaten it.' And in the moment it flashed upon me that I was carrying in my pocket the local anesthetic for which I had searched some years earlier. I went straight to the laboratory, asked the assistant for a guinea pig for the experiment, made a solution of cocaine from the powder which I carried in my pocketbook, and instilled this into the eye of the animal."

Koller's young assistant concluded the story:

"Now it was necessary to go one step further and to repeat the experiment upon a human being. We trickled the solution under the upraised lids of each other's eyes. Then we put a mirror before us, took a pin in hand, and tried to touch the cornea with its head. Almost simultaneously we could joyously assure ourselves, 'I can't feel a thing.' We could make a dent in the cornea without the slightest awareness of the touch, let alone any unpleasant sensation or reaction. With that the discovery of local anesthesia was completed. I rejoice that I was the first to congratulate Dr. Koller as a benefactor of mankind."

Koller was not the first to note that local application of cocaine had a numbing effect. It had already been mentioned at least four or five times in reports or at meetings, but no one made any use of these observations. In fact, in the textbook of pharmacology that Koller used as a medical student, an underlined sentence stated that "on account of an anesthetizing effect on mucous membranes, it might deserve experimental trial in quite a number of diseases." The difference between Koller the student and Koller the young ophthalmologist was that as the latter he knew that finding a local anesthetic was essential for progress in his surgical specialty: "Chance favors the prepared mind."

Cocaine was immediately put to worldwide use to anesthetize the cornea, then to block accessible nerves to produce local anesthesia elsewhere. Cocaine in the 1880s was indeed a gift to medicine of Koller's "prepared mind." However, cocaine, taken by mouth, was a stimulant. (Its adrenalin-like actions will be discussed later.) There were wondrous tales from Peru of its effect on Peruvian Indians, who, by chewing the native coca leaves, could do heavy work for long hours without fatigue. Cocaine (or coca, as it was then called) became an ingredient of many medicinal remedies (Fig 4.5) and, for six years, a component of a new, extremely popular drink (Coca-Cola). Within a decade physicians learned of the addictive properties of cocaine (about the same span of time required to discover the destructive effects of X rays) and cocaine was soon replaced by safer local anesthetic agents for regional and spinal anesthesia. Coca-Cola kept its famous tradename, even though the company thought it wise to omit the cocaine.

The second happening was the use of curare in the operating room as an adjunct to general anesthesia. Native medicines and poisons have always intrigued scientists. One of these poisons was curare. South American tribal witch doctors, with elaborate secret ceremonial ritual, collected the stems of curare plants, made these into a brew, strained it, and then boiled it down to a gumlike thickness; they then dipped arrowheads into the gum and allowed them to dry. The native hunters thus had poisoned arrows, which they fired into tasty animals, such as deer, and killed them not by the lethal action of the arrow, but by that of its poison. The animal, once hit by an arrow, continued to run for a while, and then weakened and dropped in its tracks because of muscle paralysis; it soon died because its respiratory muscles were paralyzed. Now you should ask, What good is poisoned meat to an Indian tribe? I do not know how, but the Indians found that the meat was safe to eat even though it contained curare. Because it paralyzed all of the deer's

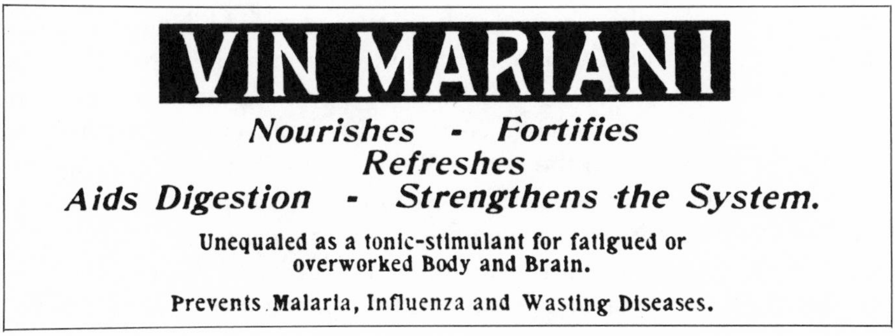

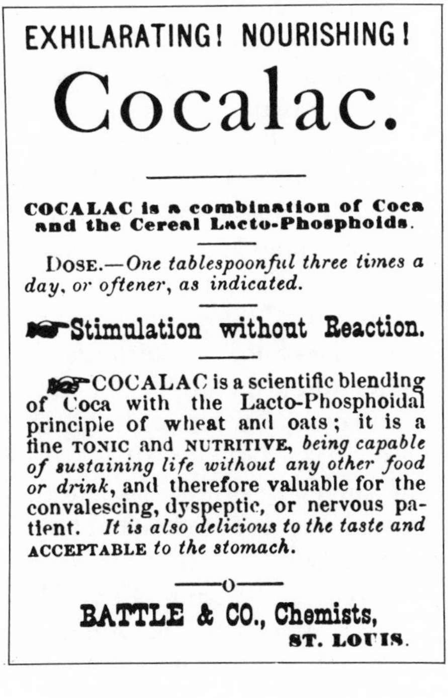

Figure 4.5.   Advertisements for Vin Mariani (cocaine in wine) and Coca-lac in newspapers around 1885. Coca was the common name for cocaine at that time. Note the italicized statement, "capable of sustaining life without any other food or drink." Coca-Cola contained cocaine until 1903.

muscles, the curare at the tip of the arrow must have entered the animal's circulating blood, but, fortunately for the Indians, curare is one of a small group of drugs not absorbed into the blood through the gastrointestinal tract of man. These same primitive tribes also realized that their favorite plant food, the cassave, contained a deadly poison (cyanide) that could be completely inactivated by heating, leaving a nutritious meal behind. Primitive tribesmen were either very astute observers or fearless clinical investigators, or had food tasters, or all three.

Claude Bernard, the brilliant French physiologist, became interested in poisons, and in 1854, in a beautifully analytic study, showed that curare in small doses had only one important biological action—it blocked the transmission of motor impulses from brain to muscle so that the muscle was paralyzed (though the muscle would still contract if stimulated directly by an electric current). In short, curare had only one highly specific action in the body: Without actually paralyzing any muscle itself or any of the nerve fibers leading to it, it prevented impulses coming down motor nerves from the brain from *activating* muscles; that is, it blocked the neuromuscular junction. Bernard's analytic study was in fact the beginning of a new medical science called pharmacology. Such a highly selective chemical substance as curare usually serves an important function for its host. Snake venoms and the electric organ of the eel inactivate or kill the enemy; but the usefulness of curare to its plant is unknown, unless it is absorbed through the intestinal tract or skin of pests that attack the curare plant.

When did curare become a useful drug instead of a useful poison? In 1932 Ranyard West deliberately injected curare into patients to treat muscle spasm, and in 1940 Abram Bennett used this poison to prevent excessive muscle contractions during electroconvulsive shock therapy in patients with mental disorders. Two years later Harold Griffith and Enid Johnson used it to supplement general anesthesia. Why would a muscle poison be of use in anesthesia? Because surgeons can do their job much better when the body's muscles are relaxed. The surgeon can ask the anesthetist to accomplish this by giving deeper and deeper anesthesia; this is risky, because it takes the patient closer and closer to death. Or the surgeon can ask the anesthetist to keep the anesthesia just light enough to prevent pain and to produce the additional relaxation of skeletal muscles by adding curare.

Why did Claude Bernard do his long-remembered research on curare? Was it to relieve muscle spasm so that a surgeon could set a fractured leg more expertly? Was it to control the violent spasms of an epileptic during a severe fit? Was it to relieve the agonizing muscle contractions caused by the poison strychnine? No, he was not a physician or a surgeon, but a professor of physiology. He was not looking for any medical use; he just "wanted to know."

During the long lag between 1856, when Bernard discovered the highly specific action of curare in the body, and 1942, when it became a useful drug in the operating room, the results of Bernard's 1856 experiments were not simply "useless knowledge." First, they had tremendous educational value: Tens of thousands of young scholars and medical students were forced to think. I still remember my introduction to pharmacology when I was a second-year medical student in 1931–1932. The first laboratory experiment in that course (before we heard a single lecture on drugs) was that we repeat Bernard's curare experiment. Our instructions, and challenge, were, "Given a live frog, a rubber band and an electric stimulator to activate nerves and muscles, determine precisely where curare produces its highly specific action of paralyzing muscle." A tough assignment? Maybe, but that's all Bernard had and all that he needed in 1854, plus a keen analytic mind. And, indeed, a student can answer the question, as Bernard did, by putting a wide rubber band about one thigh tightly enough to shut off circulation to the frog's limb (Fig. 4.6), but not tightly enough to damage the nerve, and then injecting curare into the frog's abdomen, from which it quickly enters

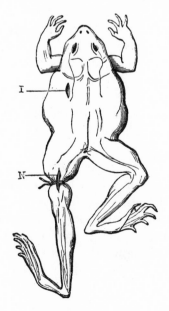

Figure 4.6.   Claude Bernard's sketch (1854) of a frog he had prepared to study the site of action of curare. He first tied a ligature around the frog's thigh at *N* (tightly enough to stop blood flow but not enough to damage the nerve to the leg). After he injected curare at *I*, each muscle in the frog twitched when stimulated directly by an electric shock, but only the muscles below *N* twitched when stimulated indirectly by electric current applied to their nerve.

the bloodstream and has access to all body tissues with a blood supply. Almost at once, all of the frog's muscles relax and fail to respond even to electrical stimulation of *nerves* leading directly to them—except for the muscles in the leg that has no blood supply and therefore received no curare. (The frog does not die when its muscles of breathing are paralyzed, because oxygen can diffuse directly into the frog's body through its moist skin.) So far, so good—no circulation to the leg, no muscle paralysis in that leg. The problem now becomes one of eliminating every possible site of action of curare except one: It cannot act on motor nerve fibers, because those to the bloodless limb are exposed to curare above the rubber band; it cannot act on muscle itself, since all of the frog's muscles still contract when stimulated *directly* by an electric current. The site of action therefore must be the junction between motor nerve and muscle. It is good to make a medical student learn how to think and to solve problems instead of simply telling him the answer in a lecture or textbook. A good physician is going to have to solve problems for the rest of his life, and a good time to start is during his basic science courses in medical school.

Another lesson from the curare experiment was that it showed dramatically that a drug or poison with access to *all* tissues and cells of the body can, in controlled concentrations, act highly selectively on only a *single* part of a cell—in this case, a specialized part of muscle that normally reacts by contracting when a nerve impulse reaches it. This concept has been tremendously important in shaping our present concepts of the functioning of the entire neuromuscular system and in designing drugs to increase or diminish certain functions. Today the study of cell receptors for hormones and drugs is one of the most active fields in biomedical research.

Curare has been replaced by better muscle relaxants, and ether by better anesthetics, but using these called for men and women with expert judgment and training to be in charge of all of the patient's body not directly in the surgeon's operative field. This brings us to the third happening in the control of pain—the shaping of a new specialist called the anesthesiologist. For a long time anesthetics were administered by a nurse or by a surgeon's assistant. As long as the anesthetist had only to pour ether on a cone and to keep the patient's airway open, not much specialized training was required. Only few physicians became anesthetists, and most of them did it part time to earn money, possibly because they were unsuccessful in the general practice of medicine. In 1938 there were six medical schools and hundreds of hospitals in Pennsylvania, but there were only three diplomates of the American Board of Anesthesiology in the entire state; in that year a full-time physician–anesthetist at a university hospital received a salary of about $3,500 a year for full-time work, and no extras.

Because of the tremendous advances in surgery, anesthesia, and intensive care, a change had to come about; it did, in the 1940s. The modern anesthesiologist now has to do a lot more than pour ether: He chooses, for each patient, between inhalation anesthesia, spinal anesthesia, and intravenous anesthesia and decides whether to use curare-like compounds as well. Furthermore, surgeons, at long last, were opening the thorax for surgical operations on the heart or lungs and someone had to manage proper ventilation of the patient's lungs if the artificial heart–lung was not being used, or to inflate them properly when it was used (Fig. 4.7). Both during and after operations, patients need transfusions of blood or infusions of plasma or substitutes, along with

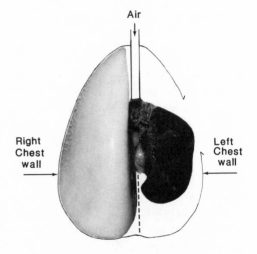

Figure 4.7. The vertical dashed line represents the mediastinum, a thin partition separating the contents of the right and left sides of the chest. The pressure is always *sub*atmospheric in a normal closed chest, because the elastic lung tries to retract and pull away from the chest wall. In this diagram the right half of the chest wall is intact and maximally expanded; the lung contained in it adheres closely to the inner wall of the chest and is fully inflated. The other half of the chest wall has been opened widely and atmospheric pressure has collapsed this lung and it soon becomes airless—the dreaded pneumothorax (air in the thorax) that baffled and discouraged thoracic surgeons until the 1930s. An anesthesiologist can maintain any degree of inflation desired (from moderate to full inflation) by applying continuous or intermittent positive air pressure through a tube inserted in the airway; the tube permits him to control the right and left sides separately or both at once, and prevent atmospheric pressure from displacing the contents of the thorax toward the closed half of the chest.

continuous monitoring of respiration, circulation, and reflex activity. In short, there was need for a clinical cardiovascular, respiratory, and neurophysiologist–pharmacologist as part of the surgical team. The greatest wish come true for a cardiac surgeon is to have a highly trained professional colleague take care of all the patient's organs except the one he is operating on, so that he can devote himself entirely to his surgical procedures, assured that everything else is being managed as well as possible.

Even so, physician–anesthesiologists had a rough time for a decade or more, because some surgeons had a tendency to be arrogant and demanding and created almost a master–servant relationship. But anesthesiologists eventually developed into a strong academic group, with their departments independent of the departments of surgery and of equal academic status.* Indeed, quite a few anesthesiologists became deans and vice-presidents of medical schools and occupied a rung on the academic ladder higher than their professors of surgery. Respect at last!

Elective Cardiac Arrest

Surgeons perform a wide variety of operations upon the arteries and heart. Obviously, if the operation is on an artery in a limb or the abdomen, the surgeon does not stop the heart and use an artificial heart–lung machine, and some operations on or near the heart itself do not require opening the heart. However, an operation to repair defects in the heart muscle or its valves does require opening the heart.

No surgeon could possibly perform a delicate operation to repair a cardiac defect while the heart is in motion, especially in an infant, whose heart is twisting, turning, and contracting up to 115 times per minute. So the heart must be motionless during the operation on the heart itself. This raises two questions: How can one stop a human heart with complete (100%, not 95%) assurance that one can start it again, and how long can organs and tissues live without blood flowing through them?

Let's start with the first question. Over the past century, physiologists have found many ways to stop the heart, ways that still allow it to start again. In 1846 the Weber brothers in Germany found that stimu-

---

*In 1983, in 112 medical schools throughout the United States, there are 99 departments called "anesthesiology" and 13 called "anesthesia," but the training and responsibilities of "anesthesiologists" and "anesthetists" are identical.

lation in the neck of the tenth cranial nerve that runs from the brain to the heart and to many other organs (appropriately named the vagus or vagabond or *wandering* nerve) temporarily causes the heart to slow down or even stop beating completely. Later on, an apparently useless bit of research uncovered the fact that electrical stimulation of the vagus nerve to the heart causes release of a special chemical substance, acetylcholine, at the finest terminals of the vagus nerves, and it is the released acetylcholine, rather than an electric spark, that bridges the gap between the anatomical end of the vagus nerve and the anatomical beginning of the heart muscle.

Acetylcholine is a transmitter, a chemical released at a nerve ending in an arm or leg muscle, in salivary glands, or in bronchi, gut, or heart, that transmits a message from the brain to specific cells. Activating the natural pacemaker (the sinoatrial node) of the heart by acetylcholine means only one thing to the node: Slow down or stop the heart. Activating an arm muscle means "contract." This might once have been classified as a bit of "useless knowledge," but not to the cardiac surgeons, because in the 1950s one of them found that synthetic acetylcholine injected into the coronary arteries that supply blood to the heart muscle stopped the heart physiologically, and the arrest was under the surgeon's control because cardiac arrest continued only as long as they allowed acetylcholine to remain in the coronary artery system.

To go back again to the nineteenth century, in 1883, Sidney Ringer, the British physiologist, found another way to stop a heart electively. He was trying to keep hearts alive, after removing them from the body, by perfusing their coronary arteries with blood substitutes such as various salt solutions. He had a difficult time, but eventually found that with too much calcium, the heart contracted too tightly; with too much potassium, the heart relaxed and stopped. Ringer discovered the effect of calcium and potassium salts largely to satisfy his curiosity, but he also had a little luck that turned into Walpole's "serendipity." He had been perfusing plain salt solution (sodium chloride and water) through the coronary arteries of isolated hearts of animals; the hearts all weakened and died. But one day they didn't. Detective work by Ringer showed that his laboratory technician that day had run out of pure distilled water and, rather than bother to prepare a fresh batch, had used water directly from the New River. Ringer immediately obtained a sample of the river water and analyzed it; it contained many mineral salts, including calcium and potassium. This started him on an investigation of what salts, and in what concentrations, made the isolated heart beat longest. Ringer finally hit upon a proper balance of potassium, calcium, and other salts (later he added glucose for nutrition). This, the famous "Ringer solution," known to every biology student in high school, keeps isolated hearts beating outside the body for long periods, and army surgeons in World War I, before the era of citrated blood, also kept bleeding soldiers alive by infusing Ringer's salt solution intravenously. But in his work Ringer found another way of stopping a heart electively: by decreasing the calcium concentration in the nutrient fluid, increasing its potassium concentration, or both. Cardiac surgeons made good use of this knowledge in the 1950s.

As far back as 1812, a French physiologist, Le Gallois, made two more discoveries: One was that the heart and brain of newborn animals survived far longer than those of adults of the same species when all their blood flow was cut off; the other was that cold-blooded animals survived longer than warm-blooded ones of the same age when the circulation of blood was stopped. These were not useless observations, because cardiac surgeons in the 1950s found that lowering the body temperature (hypothermia) of the entire patient allowed the patient to survive longer periods of cardiac arrest and permitted the surgeon more time for working with a nonbeating heart. Surgeons also found that selective hypothermia of only the heart, achieved by perfusing the coronary arteries with colder and colder solutions, provided a way of greatly decreasing the needs of the heart for energy, and that such selective hypothermia could safely slow down or stop the heart. Cells and tissues do not necessarily die when the heart stops; they die when there is an insufficient supply of blood, with its nutrients, to meet their energy needs. When active cells receive no blood flow, they have no choice but to use up their own reserves, then those in nearby capillary blood, and then to consume their own structural tissues—and this is when cells die and cannot be revived. So, stopping the heart by cooling both it *and* the whole body is a reversible stoppage, because the needs of cells for energy decrease to a minimum when they are cold enough (as in a hibernating animal). Such cells do not deteriorate.

Another way of stopping the heart is to apply an electrical current directly to the ventricle. It has long been known that electrocution kills by causing cardiac arrest. Actually, the heartbeat does not stop completely: The muscle fibers quiver continuously instead of beating rhythmically, but the movements are weak and uncoordinated and serve no useful purpose, because the fibers exert no force and the heart ejects no blood. This state of muscle is called fibrillation; individual muscle fibrils still contract, but they do not beat vigorously, in unison, or in proper sequence. Fibrillation of *atrial* muscle is not dangerous because coordinated contraction of the atria is not essential for life. However, fibrillation of the ventricles is dangerous, and death follows in a few minutes because the ventricles can no longer pump blood around the circulation. Therefore it seems a bit scary to stop the human heart deliberately by causing ventricular fibrillation, thought to be irreversible; but in the 1940s and 1950s, physiologists and surgeons learned how to reverse it, by using, of all things, a second jolt of electricity.

How and when did we learn that ventricular fibrillation could be reversed? Surely some of the credit belongs to the Consolidated Edison Company of New York City, whose management was distressed over accidental electrocution of its linemen. Having no research staff of its own, the company turned in 1926 to the Rockefeller Foundation in New York, who in turn approached several research groups to ask them if they would work on the problem. One team was at Johns Hopkins University: Orthello Langworthy, a neurologist, and William Kouwenhoven, an electrical engineer. In 1928 they began studies on the effects of electric shocks delivered to rats. Two years later, William Howell, professor of physiology at the same school but not one of the team, called them to his office and showed them a translation of work done in France in 1899 by Prévost and Battelli, who had not only produced but also reversed ventricular fibrillation in dogs. The French workers reported that they could readily produce fibrillation by a weak alternating current (AC), and could then reverse it just as readily by giving the dog a strong countershock with direct current (DC). Professor Howell did not ask Langworthy and Kouwenhoven whether they had read the paper; he simply asked them if the claim was true! Because they did not answer his question until 1933 (their answer then was, "Yes, it is true"), one can safely assume that neither they nor anyone else interested in electrocution and ventricular fibrillation had ever heard of the work of Prévost and Battelli. In several instances I have mentioned long lags (thirty-four years here) between an initial discovery of some importance and its rediscovery by others. Sometimes there are specific reasons for a lag. Between 1600 and 1948, there were few researchers and little financial support for their work. As a consequence, many fascinating discoveries were never followed up because there were so many new things to learn and so few people engaged in scientific research. This probably explains this thirty-four–year lag. It is worth noting that the Prévost–Battelli work came to light because Howell, a physiologist interested in blood coagulation, translated the French papers into English for the defibrillation team to read; this is a lesson in how to accelerate medical research.

At any rate, work then started in earnest on defibrillation. Carl Wiggers, professor of physiology at Western Reserve University in Cleveland got into the problem sideways. A world-famous cardiovascular physiologist, Wiggers had not been concerned with ventricular fibrillation because he was fully engaged in studying the coronary circulation in animals. But events compelled him to study fibrillation. His research involved setting up over many hours an elaborate preparation, only to have the day's work end unexpectedly by the occurrence of ventricular fibrillation. So Wiggers decided he had to learn the genesis of ventricular fibrillation and how to reverse it if he was to succeed with his work on the coronary circulation.

He knew of Kouwenhoven's work and made several visits to him. In 1940 Wiggers and his associate, René Wegria, demonstrated clearly that an electric shock caused the ventricle to fibrillate only when the current was applied during one very small part of the cardiac cycle that they labeled the "vulnerable phase." However (and this is very important), an electric current reaching any part of the right or left ventricle at any other time caused a vigorous coordinated contraction. So, though an electric shock *can* cause fibrillation, it can also—if properly timed during the cardiac cycle—stop fibrillation and initiate rhythmic beats.

Wiggers presented his work and ideas on what started and stopped ventricular fibrillation to physiologists and surgeons in the 1940s, but they had been brought up on the notion that ventricular fibrillation equalled death, and only one, Claude Beck, a cardiac surgeon in Cleveland, became genuinely interested. Beck put defibrillating devices in his operating room and established an elaborate procedure to be followed whenever ventricular fibrillation occurred in a patient in the operating room. The first five attempts at defibrillation failed, but Beck persisted. On his sixth try he successfully defibrillated the heart of a patient and from that time on this equipment became essential in all operating rooms and cardiac catheterization laboratories, because it was in these locations that ventricular fibrillation was most apt to occur and be treated successfully.

The effects of electric shocks on the heart are confusing, so let us summarize them: If a heart is beating rhythmically, an electric shock can cause fibrillation if it strikes in the "vulnerable period"; alternating current is more apt to strike in a vulnerable period because it strikes 60 times each second. However, if a heart has already stopped completely or is already fibrillating, one no longer worries about *causing* arrest or fibrillation. The job is now to produce regular cardiac beats. A jolt of either AC or DC can cause the heart to contract all at once; when the heart relaxes and the fibers are all in a state of rest, they can then respond to impulses from the heart's own pacemaker.

A technique for putting electrodes directly on the ventricles of a patient whose thorax was already open or that could be immediately opened was invaluable to the cardiac surgeon in his well-equipped operating room. However, it scarcely helped Consolidated Edison and its lineman who was electrocuted at the top of a pole miles away from the nearest hospital. The fibrillation problem went from France (Prévost and Battelli) to Baltimore (Howell and Kouwenhoven) to Cleveland (Wiggers and Beck) and then back to Baltimore when the Edison Electric Institute of New York asked Kouwenhoven in 1951 to design a *portable* defibrillator that could work in the field on a patient with a *closed chest*, a machine that the electric companies could put in every line truck. Kouwenhoven began work on this in 1952–1953. Howell had died and Langworthy had gone into the practice of psychiatry, but Alfred Blalock, Hopkins' cardiac surgeon, now offered facilities to Kouwenhoven in his department of surgery. He developed a useful closed chest defibrillator for dogs and then for human use (an AC type) and reported on it in 1957. These were the forerunners of the paddles paramedics apply to the patient's chest to restart a stopped heart.

In the meantime, Paul Zoll in Boston had developed his own AC defibrillator for use with a closed chest, and he reported on this in 1956. Fate is often unkind. Kouwenhoven was almost first with a defibrillator for use in a patient with an open chest (but was beaten by Beck), and he was almost first with a portable defibrillator for use in a patient far away from an operating room (but was beaten by Zoll). A few years later, however, Kouwenhoven, with his associates James Jude and Guy Knickerbocker, was indeed first with a technique for resuscitating a completely stopped heart in a closed chest by rhythmic mechanical compression (inaccurately called "massage") of the thorax to transmit a mechanical stimulus to the ventricle and also to create pressure on all sides of it to force the ventricle to empty and restart a circulation. It is interesting that their main incentive to develop this new method was to prolong the period during which circulation could be maintained and the patient kept alive until an external electric defibrillator could be brought to the patient. Their technique, combined with mouth-to-mouth resuscitation, is now standard for cardiopulmonary resuscitation (CPR)—something that can be done at once, anywhere, for a patient dying of cardiac arrest, but with a heart muscle too good to die.

Again, we must ask, why did closed chest mechanical resuscitation of the heart take so long to discover? For decades physiologists whose experimental work or laboratory teaching required the use of cats, dogs, or rabbits had been faced with sudden cardiac arrest or ventricular fibrillation in these animals. They learned that it was not necessary to open the thorax, grab the heart, and rhythmically squeeze it manually to generate aortic blood pressures sufficient to produce adequate flow of blood through the coronary and cerebral circulations; this could be done just as well through the intact chest wall. Boehm had shown in 1878 that by rhythmic, forceful compression of the intact chest wall, he could raise arterial blood pressure from zero (atmospheric pressure) to 50–120 mmHg (millimeters of mercury) in cats whose hearts had stopped. Tournade described the technique again in 1934. Why was it not applied to man then? One reason was that physiologists rarely write scientific papers describing tricks of their trade that everyone is already using in his own laboratory. But a further problem was that the shape of the animal thorax is quite different from that of the human thorax. Manual squeezing of the narrow, flexible chest of a dog or a cat is an obvious and easy thing to do, but the human chest is wide, flat, and more rigid, and one certainly could not squeeze it with one or two hands, as one could the thorax of a cat.

However, no one told Kouwenhoven, Jude, and Knickerbocker all the reasons why it could not be done in man, so they went ahead and did it. They began by working on cadavers in the morgue, within 45 minutes of death of the patients, before rigor mortis set in and the chest became immobile. For months they practically lived in the morgue to be sure to be there when there was any chance of measuring the effects of compression of the closed chest. They found that the human chest *could* be compressed and that blood could be impelled into the aorta, but they also found that excessive pressure led to serious damage to the ribs, breast bone, and internal organs. Over months they learned how to compress the heart between the lower sternum and the vertebrae without damaging the thorax and abdominal structures. They then tried their technique on living man and again it worked. And now, as I have already noted, it is a standard component of the American Red Cross' technique for cardiopulmonary resuscitation.

When the cardiac surgeon has deliberately produced cardiac arrest by using acetylcholine or potassium, all he need do to restart the heart is to wash the chemical out of the coronary circulation or compress the heart itself by hand. Or, if he had produced fibrillation electrically, all he must do is deliver an electric countershock, or warm the heart if he had cooled it. When a heart suddenly quits outside of an operating room, closed chest manual compression is invaluable until an electrical defibrillator becomes available.

Earlier I had asked two questions critical to open heart surgery: How can one stop the human heart? And for how long can organs and tissues live without blood flowing through them? I've given answers to the first question. There are many answers to the second question, because newborn survive longer than adults and cold bodies survive longer than warm ones (for example, completely submerged individuals survive longer in ice cold water than in heated pools). But each organ and tissue also has a different survival time, depending upon the source of its energy and on how much it needs in relation to how much is initially stored within its cells and in nearby capillaries. Immobility on an operating table decreases energy needs; so do general anesthesia and cooling of the body. The cerebral cortex, which gets its energy largely from glucose, dies irreversibly after 4–6 minutes of zero blood flow at normal body temperature, but the lower brain centers controlling respiration and circulation can be revived after 25–35 minutes, the spinal centers after 40–60 minutes, and the heart after 10–15 minutes—and all can survive longer if deliberately cooled before the heart is stopped. If adequate supplies of blood are available and an artificial heart–lung machine is used, the heart can be stopped for hours; if only hypothermia is available, the safe time period is much shorter; if none of these is available, the surgeon must "get in and get out."

So this greatly increased store of knowledge in many fields—antisepsis and asepsis, anesthesia and pain relief, mechanisms that permit reversible cardiac arrest, and knowledge of the survival times of bloodless organs at different temperatures—has enabled cardiac and vascular surgeons to go into a previously forbidden field—open heart surgery.

Congenital Defects

So far we have been involved with hundreds and even thousands of people in many professions, people who lived in many different countries, and in different centuries who made cardiac surgery possible. Now we come to those who made it happen, the cardiac surgeons themselves.

The diagnosis has been made, an operation is indicated, anesthesia (with or without neuromuscular block) has been given, the thorax opened, and the heart stopped. Now the patient belongs to the surgeon, who has available to him a wide variety of old and new knowledge, techniques, instruments, and materials.

Modern cardiac surgeons have a right to feel proud of their accomplishments. In 1896 Stephen Paget wrote in his book *Surgery of the Chest,*

Surgery of the heart has probably reached the limits set by nature to all surgery: no new method and no new discovery can overcome the natural difficulties that attend a wound of the heart. It is true that heart surgery has been vaguely proposed as a possible procedure and that it has been done in animals, but I cannot find that it has ever been attempted in practice.

Paget, of course, was wrong, but Niels Bohr, the great Danish physicist, is credited with saying, "It is very difficult to predict—especially, the future!"

Who were responsible for changing Paget's rather bleak prediction? Cardiac surgery started with an assault on the birth (congenital) defects. Some of these are genetic in origin, inherited or inborn malformations of the heart and great vessels. Some are not inherited but are due to something having gone wrong with the developing fetus during its life in the uterus. The normal fetal heart is not simply a miniature adult heart; it has a different design because the fetus gets its oxygen and nutrition from its mother, and not from its own lungs and alimentary tract. For 9 months the fetus grows inside its mother's uterus, immersed in a sac filled with amniotic fluid. So immersed, it has no access to outside air and no possible way to bring oxygen into its own lungs and from them into its blood. The fetus depends entirely upon the mother's placenta, which is attached to the inside wall of her uterus and connected to the fetus through the umbilical vessels. The mother's heart pumps her blood through a vast pool of blood in her placenta, and the fetus' heart pumps fetal blood through a vast capillary network (Fig. 4.8) immersed in this maternal pool, separated from the mother's blood by only the thinnest membranes. Oxygen diffuses from maternal blood into fetal blood, carbon dioxide diffuses from fetal blood into maternal blood, and everything else that the fetus needs, or needs to get rid of, passes from or to the mother's circulation, or into the surrounding amniotic fluid.

If the lung of the fetus doesn't oxygenate its blood or eliminate its own carbon dioxide, it doesn't make sense that the right ventricle of the fetus should, as in the adult, have to do the work of pumping all of the venous blood through the pulmonary circulation before the left ventricle distributes it throughout the body. The lung does need *some* blood during fetal life, largely for nutrition and growth, but this is only about one-tenth of the total blood flowing through the veins to the heart. In fact, that's about all the lung gets. How is this accomplished? For one thing, the fetal heart has a large oval opening (the "foramen ovale") between the right and left atria and much of the fetal blood goes directly through this hole to the left heart, without entering the right ventricle at all (see Fig. 4.9). For another, the right and left branches of the main pulmonary artery are small, but the main artery has a third (and very

Figure 4.8. Projections from the developing fetus grow into the placenta and push into pools of maternal blood supplied by the mother's uterine arteries. The fetal capillary projections are equivalent to the adult's pulmonary circulation; the maternal blood pool is equivalent to the adult's alveolar gas. (From "The Placenta" by P. Beaconsfield, G. Birdwood, R. Beaconsfield. © 1980 by Scientific American, Inc. All rights reserved.)

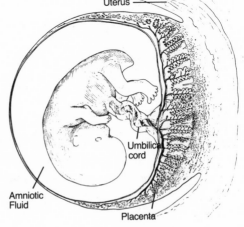

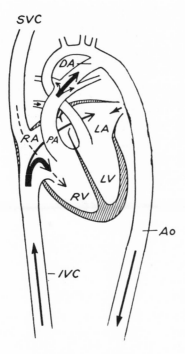

Figure 4.9. The fetal circulation differs from the adult circulation in several important ways. Oxygenated blood coming from the placenta flows into the inferior vena cava (IVC) and then into the right atrium (RA). Here it splits into two streams: The larger stream enters the right ventricle (RV) and much of this then flows through a unique fetal artery, the ductus arteriosus (DA), into the aorta, instead of going through the lungs (the pulmonary arteries to the fetal lung are very small). The lesser stream in the right atrium goes through an oval opening between the right and left atria (also unique to the fetus) and bypasses the pulmonary circulation. (To simplify this diagram, the four cardiac valves and the lungs have been omitted.)

large) branch, the ductus arteriosus (see p. 91), that connects directly with the aorta and conducts blood into it, bypassing the lungs.

But then suddenly the fetus is no longer connected to its mother by an umbilical cord and becomes a baby. The cardiovascular–pulmonary events that occur at the birth of a baby are by far the most dramatic of its lifetime. These are wondrous in their magnitude, diversity, and timing; one might well call them miraculous. At the birth of a baby a physician or midwife is present to clamp the umbilical cord, tie it, and cut it in two. But it's rather wonderful that every newborn mammal becomes separated from its umbilical cord and mother at birth—without undue hemorrhage—even when an obstetrician is not present!

Once the cord is clamped, the newborn infant can no longer depend on its mother for oxygen; it must very soon breathe on its own or die. What events make it breathe? Some of these are the multiple, strange, and varied sensory stimuli that for the first time bombard the respiratory and associated centers of the previously insulated newborn: Sounds beat against its ears; bright lights shine into its eyes; its tissues experience the effects of gravity; the limbs move and nerves sensitive to stretch are excited; the skin experiences cold, touch, and pain; and odors assail the nose. When the fetus is floating in warm fluid in the uterus, the immersion reflex prevents normal breathing; but once the baby is in a dry environment, this reflex is no longer active. At the same time, the tissues of the newborn baby are using blood O_2 without replenishing it and are adding CO_2 without eliminating it; blood O_2 falls, blood CO_2 rises, and these changes stimulate breathing.

Some or all of these events at birth almost always make the newborn baby take its first breath, and then its second, and so on. The oval opening in the wall between the right and left atria closes shortly after birth so all venous blood returning to the right reservoir must go to the right pump and then through the pulmonary circulation (now wide open) to be oxygenated by the now functioning lungs. The ductus arteriosus constricts gradually after birth, and usually closes completely within 10–12 hours.

If you are excited by miracles, then contemplate these two. The first is the miracle of a single fertilized ovum changing into heart, lungs, circulation, blood cells, brain, nerves, liver, kidneys, spleen, eyes, nose, mouth, limbs, skin, and endocrine and sex organs—all maturing at the right time for the survival of a whole, intact, and healthy newborn baby! The second is the miracle of birth, with everything happening in precise and correct order with split-second timing.

But if the two miracles don't occur exactly as they should, the newborn baby has congenital defects. Some of these are due to improper scheduling of events at or near the time of birth: For example, the foramen ovale doesn't close when it should, the pulmonary circulation doesn't open widely when it should, and the ductus arteriosus doesn't close when it should. But some defects occur long before birth. Another common defect is the tetralogy of Fallot (the famous "blue baby"; see p. 169), which consists of four main malformations: a thick-walled right ventricle, failure of the pulmonary artery to widen, failure of the ventricular septum to close, and a misplaced aorta that connects with both the right and left ventricles. Another common congenital defect is a narrowing or severe constriction of the aorta at the point where the ductus arteriosus formerly emptied into it (this constriction is medically known as "coarctation" of the aorta). In addition, there are rare but serious malformations of the ventricular walls and valves and improperly placed large veins and arteries closely related to the heart. In all, about 25,000 babies are born in the United States each year with congenital heart disease. Correction of an open ductus arteriosus requires simply tying off an open vessel coming from the heart; there is no need to open the heart. Correction of other defects may require extensive repair of the wall between the right and left sides of the heart (closing openings that don't belong there) or actually switching arteries and veins from where they shouldn't be to where they should be. For careful reconstruction of such hearts, long periods of open heart surgery may be needed, and for this the heart–lung machine is essential.

The first surgical operation on the heart was the famous "blue baby" operation in 1945. (Two important operations on large arteries preceded this—the closure of an open ductus arteriosus in 1939 and the repair of a constricted thoracic aorta in 1945—but these were vascular and not cardiac surgery; see Chapter 5.)

You will remember Helen Taussig who, turned down for admission to Harvard Medical school and denied the privilege of working for a degree at the Harvard School of Public Health, went to the Johns Hopkins School of Medicine and there became an expert in diagnosing congenital heart disease. She was quite rightfully concerned about the fate of "blue babies," babies who after birth were continuously blue because most of their venous blood went directly from the right ventricle to the left ventricle (through an abnormal hole in what should have been a solid partition) and this blood never got into and through the pulmonary arteries and capillaries of the lungs to be oxygenated.

Normally the ductus arteriosus constricts within an hour after birth, but it can remain open much longer when the blood of newborn babies is not well oxygenated. Taussig noted that blue babies, apt to have delayed closing of their ductus, got worse when it began to close. She reasoned that although in the normal fetus blood flows from the right ventricle to the pulmonary trunk to the ductus and into the aorta (see p. 166), in blue babies flow goes in the reverse direction: from the aorta into the ductus (because one of the congenital defects in blue babies is a marked narrowing of the pulmonary artery, which stays constricted after birth when it should open widely). So blue babies are better off with a fifth defect, an open ductus, because the aorta sends blood backward to the lungs through the right and left pulmonary artery branches.

If Gibbon's heart–lung machine had been perfected by 1941, it would have allowed time for complete correction of the four main defects in blue babies. But it was wartime and Gibbon's machine would not be ready for some time. Taussig had to think of a way to keep the babies alive. She reasoned that there must be some way to create an open ductus to get some aortic blood to flow through the pulmonary circulation and become better oxygenated. So she went to Boston to urge Dr. Robert Gross, the world expert on ligating the ductus arteriosus, to see if he could *construct* an artificial duct, a vessel that would conduct poorly oxygenated blood in the baby's aorta back into the pulmonary artery and through the lungs—to pick up more oxygen. Gross answered that he was interested in tying off ducts, but that he was not in the least interested in creating new ones and advised her to return to Baltimore to "stay where you are wanted." In later years Taussig reminisced that this was the second time she would be eternally grateful to Boston for its rebuffs, because in 1941 Alfred Blalock came to Hopkins to be its chief surgeon.

Taussig watched Blalock in his experimental laboratory joining the end of a subclavian artery (a branch of the aorta) to a nearby artery and asked him why he could not connect it to a pulmonary artery in a blue baby (Fig. 4.10). On November 29, 1944, he did so; the child improved, and soon most of the blue babies in the United States were en route to Baltimore for the new life-prolonging operation. They were not cured, because the hole still remained between the two ventricles, but they became pinker and grew bigger and stronger. Someone might have raised the ethical question in 1945 whether this surgical procedure was worthwhile. Lord Brock, a great British cardiac surgeon, answered this question when he described the lectures of Taussig and Blalock in 1947 in the Great Hall of the British Medical Association. The hall was still completely dark after the last lantern slide had been shown when, as Brock wrote:

Suddenly a long searchlight beam traversed the whole length of the hall and unerringly picked out on the platform a Guy's Hospital nursing sister, dressed in her attractive blue uniform, sitting on a chair and holding a small cherub-like girl of 2½ years with a halo of blonde curly hair and looking pink and well; she had been operated on at Guy's by Blalock a week earlier. The effect was dramatic and theatrical and the applause from the audience was tumultuous. It was a Madonna-like tableau, a perfect climax to an impressive lecture on an epoch-making contribution and left nothing more to be said by the lecturer. No audience could have failed to have been convinced or satisfied by this summation and no one there could possibly forget it.

The blue baby operation kept the babies alive and alert. In 1953 John Gibbon's artificial heart–lung was at last functioning, and in that year he performed his first successful operation, using a complete cardiac bypass.

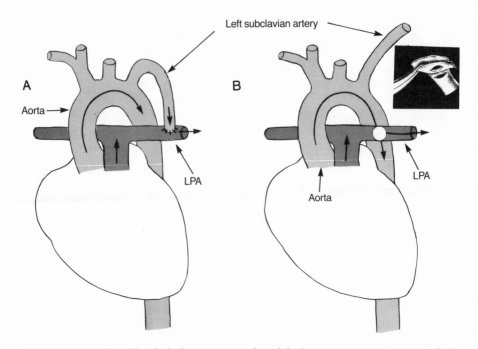

Figure 4.10. The "blue baby" operation. The Blalock–Taussig operation provided relief (palliation); it did not repair and cure. (A) shows the construction of an artificial "ductus" by connecting the left subclavian artery (main artery to left arm) to the left pulmonary artery (LPA). Arterial blood reaches the left arm through other arteries. The right subclavian could have been joined to the right pulmonary artery instead. (B) shows the creation of a direct connection between the descending aorta and the left pulmonary artery. The surgeon makes a slit in bottom side of the left pulmonary artery (in the region indicated by the white dot) and a similar one in the topside of the aorta just under the left pulmonary artery. The two openings are then sewn together, creating an open connection between the two arteries (see inset for the apposition of the two openings). This also routes additional blood into the pulmonary arteries for supplementary oxygenation in the lungs.

In 1953 and thereafter, a lot of babies that had undergone the "blue baby" operation were now ready for complete and final repair, which never could have been attempted without an artificial heart–lung machine and a completely quiescent heart. From about 1955 on, even the most complicated cardiac abnormalities could be reconstructed so that the heart was as good as new. Temporary solutions gave way to complete reconstruction, even of all four defects of the blue babies.

There is a small footnote to this story. The historic Blalock operation—sewing a branch of the aorta into a pulmonary artery—had been pictured forty years earlier in Ernst Jeger's 1913 *Surgery of the Blood*

Vessels and Heart" in Chapter 4, entitled "The Importance of Vascular Surgery for Experimental Medicine." Jeger had not proposed the operative procedure for any specific purpose; he just wanted to see if, in a laboratory experiment, he could run aortic blood through a pulmonary artery for additional oxygenation in the lung. Taussig's dedication to her blue babies and Blalock's love of experimental surgery fully justified Jeger's "fooling around."

New Valves for Old

Since the early years of this century, surgeons have wanted to operate on narrowed (stenotic) heart valves. Obviously, total replacement of a badly diseased valve—cutting out the old and stitching in the new— was the ideal operation, but this, like intracardiac repair, had to wait for Gibbon's heart–lung machine (1953). From time to time, a surgeon made a stab (literally) at widening a stenotic valve. Théodore Tuffier, a French surgeon, tried in 1912 to open a stenotic aortic valve by pushing his finger into it through the intact wall of the much tougher aorta. In 1925 Henry Souttar made an incision in the left atrial appendage of a 19-year-old girl with mitral stenosis and enlarged the mitral orifice with his finger. The patient recovered, but Souttar never performed the operation again. Many years later, as Sir Henry, he stated his reasons in two letters he wrote to two American surgeons:

At the time, it was an article of faith with Physicians that the valves were of no importance and that the only thing that mattered was the condition of the cardiac muscle. [That was the teaching of Britain's leading cardiologist, Sir James Mackenzie.] In that atmosphere I was naturally unable to obtain another case, in spite of this one complete success. It was a pity but easy to understand. . . . Although my patient made an uninterrupted recovery, the Physicians declared that it was all nonsense and in fact, that the operation was unjustifiable. In fact it is of no use to be ahead of one's time! . . .

It was a pity, but progress in science requires repeated challenges to "authority." (Sometimes "authority" seems merely to be synonymous with "author," *any* author, right or wrong.)

By 1928, ten patients with mitral stenosis, one with pulmonary stenosis, and one with aortic stenosis had been subjected to operations to enlarge the opening of these valves. The operations included dilatation by the surgeon's finger, slitting open the leaflets of a stenotic valve, or removing a segment of it. Nine of the patients died without ever leaving the hospital, and a tenth died 4½ months later.

But valvular disease was too important a problem to set aside; almost 2 million Americans have rheumatic valvular disease, mild to severe.

The first bright, new idea came from Dr. Charles Hufnagel, at Georgetown University, who was interested in seeing what a surgeon could do about a leaky aortic valve, one that permits much of the blood pumped into the aorta by each beat of the left ventricle to leak back into the empty ventricle during diastole, thereby greatly increasing the size and work of the left ventricle. Because he had been working with plastic tubes to replace diseased segments of the aorta, he thought of building a plastic valve to put into the aorta, a valve that would stop backflow, even though the leaky valve remained in place. He designed and built a wide variety of valves (many in his basement at home) and gained experience inserting them in the aortas of numerous experimental animals. Finally, he decided to try it in a patient. Such a plastic valve would not work if the aortic valve was stenotic (but had to remain in place), but should work optimally if the valve was leaky and if he could place the plastic valve as close as possible to the natural but diseased valve. Technical difficulties prevented him from placing it where he wanted to, that is, at the very beginning of the aorta near the left ventricle. At this point he might have given up. But he settled for reducing backflow instead of eliminating it; he put his valve in the thoracic aorta, where it could do no more than prevent regurgitation of blood from the lower half of the body. His first operation was in 1952, about a year before Gibbon's first operation using the heart–lung machine, and it was as successful as he had hoped.

Now we see the convergence of two novel ideas that came to fruition within a year of each other. One was Hufnagel's idea of *replacing* bad valves with good ones (instead of blindly poking or slashing at them); the other was Gibbon's heart–lung machine. Gibbon's machine gave the cardiac surgeon time and a bloodless field in which to do delicate surgical repair; Hufnagel gave the cardiac surgeon the concept of going beyond attempts at repair and instead removing diseased valves and replacing them with artificial valves.

Gibbon's heart–lung machine scored its dramatic "first" in 1953. After this achievement, backed by John Kirklin's solid success with Gibbon's apparatus at the Mayo Clinic, cardiac surgeons literally swarmed into the business of valve replacement. The heart–lung machine allowed a surgeon to replace any or all of the four cardiac valves, if he had the right replacements. New valves could be natural, normal valves (removed from patients who died of noncardiac causes) preserved until ready for use; they could come from animals, such as pigs; or they could be synthetic. Since human heart valves must open and close about 40 million times a year, it was not a simple matter to devise a man-made valve whose leaflets could move back and forth more than a billion times over a man's life span without fracturing, thinning, or warping, especially since synthetic valves lack the unique feature of living cells—the ability to replace their own damaged or dead cells and to effect repair that is inevitably needed with time. But durability for the normal life expectancy of the patient is only one requirement for a synthetic valve. There are many others:

The valve must not allow blood to clot on it, or if this has already happened, must not permit the clot to break off as an embolus.

It should open with little resistance so that its presence does not force the heart to do more work to pump blood through it.

It should close quickly, gently, and effectively so that blood cannot flow backward.

It should open and close noiselessly.

Its contour, size, and shape must not interfere with the function of surrounding organs and tissues.

It should be easy to store and readily available in a wide variety of sizes to fit the opening created by removing the diseased valve.

It should be easy to attach permanently to the patient's heart, even though the tissues of the heart are diseased.

It must be easy to sterilize.

It must not cause a foreign body reaction or damage any of the components of blood, such as red or white cells, or plasma proteins.

Obviously, collaboration between surgeons and industry's engineers was needed and led to many varieties of valves. The first attempts were made to replace aortic valves, because these were easier to construct and implant. Construction of an artificial mitral valve (that between the left atrium and left ventricle) proved to be more difficult. Unlike the aortic valve, which is swept clean beat by beat with the strong surges of blood from the left ventricle, the mitral valve is more apt to collect blood clots on it because of the lower pressures and decreased velocity of flow leaving the left atrium. Such clots may completely obstruct the orifice or may break away and lodge elsewhere to obstruct flow through arteries supplying the heart, brain, or kidney.

The first sustained clinical successes were achieved by Albert Starr and Lowell Edwards at the University of Oregon. In 1958 Edwards, an engineer, told Starr that he wanted to build an artificial implantable heart. Starr, the surgeon, thought that this was too ambitious a project for a start and suggested that he begin by building a mitral valve, and then go on from there. Edwards designed a ball-in-a-cage valve (Fig. 4.11), like that in a diving snorkle. During forward flow, the ball moved toward the apex of the cage, uncovering an orifice for blood to flow forward; when forward flow stopped, the ball seated itself on the rim of the orifice and prevented backflow. The ball was made of Silastic (silicone rubber) and the cage was cast as one piece of a stainless steel alloy by Precision Metalsmiths of Cleveland. (I am mentioning the industries involved to show the interest and cooperation of a variety of companies in solving a medical problem). The cage was then machined, ground, buffed, and electropolished until a mirror-smooth finish was obtained. The seat was a ring of Teflon cloth, provided by U.S. Catheter and Instrument Company, padded with silicone foam rubber obtained from Dow Corning and designed for sewing into the opening between the left atrium and the left ventricle after the diseased mitral valve had been removed. After extensive tests in dogs, Starr used the synthetic valve to replace the diseased mitral valve in eight patients; six survived and returned to a useful existence. Starr was not the first to replace a diseased valve with a man-made valve, but his work had a great impact on cardiac surgery, because his valve was elegantly machined and worked consistently well.

Starr had never conducted laboratory research as an undergraduate or medical student, and spent no time in an animal laboratory during his internship at Hopkins or surgical residency at Presbyterian Hospital in New York. But of great importance to his later research was that in undergraduate school he was taught to think for himself, to doubt the printed word, and to place great reliance on his own thought processes. His early training with Blalock, followed by several years in a research atmosphere at New York's Presbyterian Hospital, where the staff was continually questioning, reinforced his spirit of independent thinking.

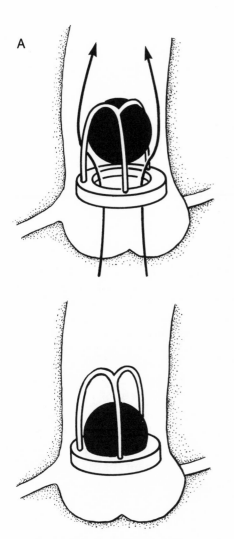

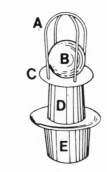

Figure 4.11. One of the earliest, and most successful, artificial heart valves was the Starr–Edwards caged-ball valve (A) that permitted blood to flow forward with little resistance during systole and prevented backflow during disastole. The cage is made of silicone-coated stainless steel, and the ball of a silicone–plastic compound (Silastic). The valve at the top is in the open position; at the bottom, it is in the closed position. (B) Diagram of a nineteenth century bottle stopper using the ball-and-cage valve principle: (A) cage for (B) ball that fits into (C) seat leading to (D) tube surrounded by (E) cork. (Redrawn from Williams, U.S. Patent no. 19323, February 9, 1858.)

He also had the good fortune and wisdom to work in close collaboration with an engineer and a splendid team of imaginative and vigorous cardiologists at the University of Oregon.

Since the introduction of Starr's successful mitral valve there has been a steady succession of different valves; at times it seemed as though there was "a valve of the month." There have been flat valves, ball valves, disk valves, pivoting valves, sleeve valves, and two-and three-leaflet valves—made of Teflon, Dacron, Silastic, polyurethane, polyvinyl, Stellite, stainless steel, titanium, and other materials—and, of course, natural valves from pig hearts (Fig. 4.12).

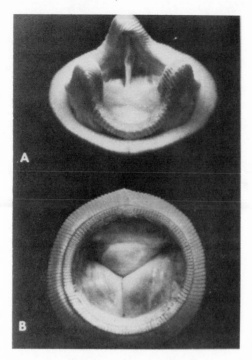

Figure 4.12. View of aortic outflow (A) and aortic inflow (B) in a pig's three-cusp heart valve. The valve can be preserved and be ready when needed to sew into the opening created by removing a diseased human heart valve.

Obviously, the ultimate goal of cardiologists is to *prevent* disease of valves, not to replace valves once deformed. Two great advances in chemotherapy (penicillin for the treatment of syphilis and prophylactic treatment of acute rheumatic fever) may soon eliminate much valvular disease. In the meantime, the incredible achievements of cardiologists, surgeons, engineers, and physiologists are keeping large numbers of patients alive and in vigorous health.

5

The Master Seamsters

In June 1894 Sadi Carnot, President of the French Republic, was assassinated by an Italian anarchist—not by a bullet, but by a knife that severed a large vein in Carnot's abdomen. The attending surgeons decided that, because a large blood vessel had been slashed, nothing could be done to save the president. A young intern in a French hospital insisted that Carnot could have been saved if surgeons only had known how to sew up blood vessels as they did skin, intestines, muscle, and tendons. The young intern was Alexis Carrel; the Carnot assassination led to his career decision to learn how to perform vascular surgery—not surgical procedures to remove or tie off hemorrhoids or varicose veins in legs or thighs, but those that could correct life-threatening disorders of arteries.

Fortunately, during his internship he worked under the great French surgeon Mathieu Jaboulay, a pioneer in developing techniques to repair injured arteries. In 1896 Jaboulay had successfully united the two ends of a severed carotid artery of a donkey. But by 1900, practicing surgeons had sutured only nine human arteries "successfully" and success in 1900 meant only that the vessel was still open at the end of the operation; all nine of these "successes" became obstructed later. It was not a popular field that Carrel entered when he began his experimental work on vascular suture in 1901, but Carrel believed that he knew the technical deficiencies in 1900 and how to correct them.

Who was Alexis Carrel? He was born in Lyons, France, in 1873. Beginning in 1890, he first went to medical school at the University of

Lyons for three years, then spent two years in hospital service, one year in military service, and five years in internship in hospitals in Lyons. From 1901 on, he devoted himself to experimental vascular surgery.

Why did he succeed when others had failed or had serious problems? One reason was his manual dexterity; Carrel attributed this to instruction he received from Mme. Leroudier, a superb embroidress in Lyons who gave him lessons at her home during his internship. Another was his insistence on avoiding damage to vascular tissues by using extremely fine, smooth needles (here he got help from a "lace woman" in Lyons) and by using special thread lubricated with Vaseline. A third was the exceedingly strict aseptic techniques he used in his operations—more rigid than those used by Lister and far more demanding than those then in use by surgeons in any other specialty.

But Carrel's research was done in the United States and not in his homeland. Why did Carrel leave Lyons and clinical medicine and surgery? In May 1903 he accepted an invitation to travel with the trainload of the sick in the annual pilgrimage to the shrine at Lourdes, in part to attend to the sick and in part as a medical scientist and a skeptic to observe firsthand the allegedly miraculous cures. En route, Carrel examined a gravely ill girl, Marie Bailly, who, to Carrel, appeared to be dying of tuberculous peritonitis, a disease that had killed both of her parents. The next day, because this patient was unconscious and too sick for the usual immersion, she was sprinkled with a bit of holy water from the pool. That afternoon she began a remarkable recovery and lived in religious service until 1937 (she came within seven years of outliving Carrel!). Carrel, although mystified and dumbfounded, dutifully reported his observations to the medical community in Lyons. He was attacked by the clergy for being unduly skeptical and by his medical colleagues for being unduly gullible. One of his surgical colleagues told him that he would now never pass his surgical examination. In May of 1904, he left France for the New World, initially Canada.

In November of that year, Carrel went to Chicago, where he first worked with surgeon Carl Beck and then accepted a position in physiology at the University of Chicago. G. N. Stewart, chairman of that department, was a cardiovascular physiologist, still famous today for his 1897 method for measuring blood flow. But Stewart was also somewhat of an experimental cardiovascular surgeon; indeed, in 1910 he devised a famous clamp (which in 1946 became the "Potts clamp") that permitted flow to continue through a lateral channel in a large artery while the other channel remained bloodless so that a surgeon could cut and stitch it (Fig. 5.1).

Stewart assigned Carrel to work with Charles Guthrie, a young physiologist seven years Carrel's junior. They worked together for a 21-month period between November 1904 and August 1906, although their direct association lasted for only 12 months, because Guthrie was on sabbatical leave at the University of Missouri for 9 of the 21 months. During the Chicago period, they jointly wrote twenty-eight scientific papers, Carrel an additional five, and Guthrie two more (on cardiac resuscitation). It was obviously a highly productive collaboration. They reimplanted and transplanted arteries, veins, kidneys, thyroid glands, ovaries, and even a thigh.

In 1906 Carrel went to work in the new experimental surgery unit

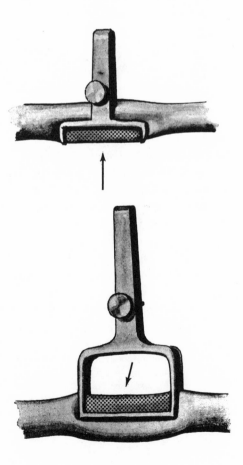

Figure 5.1.   Stewart's clamps (1910) that allow blood flow to continue through the open part of an artery while the closed-off portion (dotted area) is operated upon without loss of blood. In 1907 Carrel had achieved the same result by placing fine sutures along the artery where Stewart placed his clamps. In the 1940s, surgeons used these clamps in one of the "blue baby" operations (see p. 170).

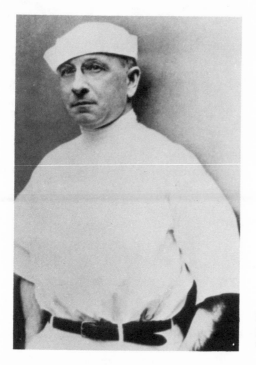

Figure 5.2. Alexis Carrel at the Rockefeller Institute after World War I.

at the Rockefeller Institute for Medical Research in New York (Fig. 5.2). Between 1901 and 1910, Alexis Carrel, using experimental animals, performed every feat and developed every technique known to vascular surgeons today (except for using a dissection microscope and inserting tubes and valves made of synthetic materials). He reunited vessels, inner lining to inner lining; he sutured artery to artery, vein to vein, artery to vein, and did this end to end, side to side, and side to end (Fig. 5.3). He used patch grafts, autografts and homografts,* rubber tubes, glass tubes, metal tubes, and absorbable magnesium tubes. He devised his own nontraumatic needles, clamps, and lubricated sutures. He even performed a coronary bypass operation on a dog using a carotid artery that he had preserved by refrigeration in saline solution. He replaced arteries with veins in dogs, transplanted organs, limbs, and even a heart,

---

*An autograft or autotransplant is a transfer of tissue or an organ into a new position in the same person or animal; when a cardiac surgeon removes a segment of a superficial vein in the patient's own leg and uses it to replace a diseased coronary artery, he is performing an autograft. A homograft or homotransplant is a transfer of tissue from one member to another of the same species (e.g., man to man, dog to dog); a heterograft or heterotransplant is a transfer from one species of animal to another (e.g., heart valves of a pig transplanted to the heart of a man).

and so proved that surgically it was possible, and even easy, to transplant organs. On top of it, he did all this in an era that long antedated anticoagulants such as heparin and antibiotics such as penicillin. Carrel won the Nobel Prize in 1912, and he won it not for some obscure, esoteric research, but "in recognition of his work on vascular suture and the transplantation of blood vessels and organs."

Gibbon started his research on a heart–lung machine because he believed it could save the life of patients with a massive pulmonary embolus, but he ultimately used his device for much broader purposes, the repair of cardiac defects. Similarly, Carrel, although he began research on vascular surgery because an assassin's knife severed a deep abdominal vein in the French president, soon found that once he had conquered the technical aspects, his research led to far broader problems and applications.

Carrel's early research dealt with devising techniques for successfully joining arteries and veins. In retrospect, this early phase almost seemed to have been the first part of a grand plan that he could have

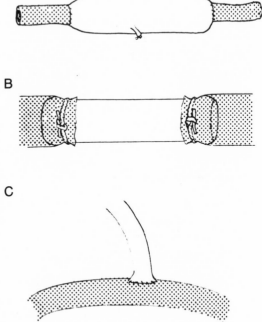

Figure 5.3.   (A) Carrel's transplantation of a vein to fill a gap between the ends of a severed artery (1906). (B) A tube made of gold-plated aluminum used as an arterial "graft" (1912) (plastic materials were unknown in Carrel's day). (C) A vein grafted on to the side of an artery (1906); the same technique is used today for coronary bypass operations. In each sketch the stippled tube is an artery or portions of one. (By permission of *Surgery, Gynecology & Obstetrics*.)

conceived in the mid-1890s and carried forward logically step by step to its climax in the late 1930s. Once he knew how to suture vessel to vessel, he was ready for the second part: how to excise and *re*implant organs and then how to *trans*plant organs.

For this he had to know how long he could deprive different organs of their blood flow and still be sure that they would survive and function normally when he restored flow. This obviously led him to wonder whether organs could survive longer if he perfused them with special fluids instead of letting them remain bloodless. Because each organ had a different function, he reasoned that each required a unique perfusion fluid to retain its optimal function. If he could find it, it would lead logically to the third part of the grand plan: keeping organs alive indefinitely. In other words, were tissues, ideally fed and watered in a perfect environment, essentially immortal? This led him to cell, tissue, and organ culture and, in the 1930s, in collaboration with Charles Lindbergh, to the first germfree pump–oxygenator (Fig. 5.4).

So much for the grand plan of Carrel's scientific career. Now let me tell you a bit more about his achievements that led to the 1912 Nobel Prize. Carrel could successfully suture any vessel to any other, even though they were less than "a matchstick in diameter." Part of his success was a new surgical trick—"triangulation." His technique was to sew along straight lines, which was far more precise than sewing around a circle. He did this by placing three sutures, each 120° apart, on the circumference of the cut circular ends of a vessel and then pulling them in opposite directions (Fig. 5.5), he could convert an arc into straight lines and then sew together one-third of the circumference. He then repeated the trick for each of the other two thirds.

Part of his success was also due to his conviction that even *slightly* infected vessels healed poorly or not at all. Sterling Edwards wrote of Carrel's technique:

His laboratory rooms, necessarily guarded against bacterial contamination, acquired the aura of a sanctuary where masked acolytes clad in black gowns and caps performed the aseptic mysteries of experimental surgery and tissue culture. Early in his career Carrel adopted black surgical gowns and drapes for his operating table to cut down glare and give better visibility to the tissues upon which he performed his extremely delicate operations. People from other laboratories, fearing to carry infectious germs into the laboratory, did not drop in for casual visits and never learned what was going on, except when specially invited.

Figure 5.4.   Carrel continued into the 1930s his attempts to keep whole organs alive by perfusing their arteries with special fluids. Charles Lindbergh, the aviator, became interested in this project and, in Carrel's laboratory, designed and constructed this germfree pump–oxygenator (1938). It is still in use in some laboratories as the best available system.

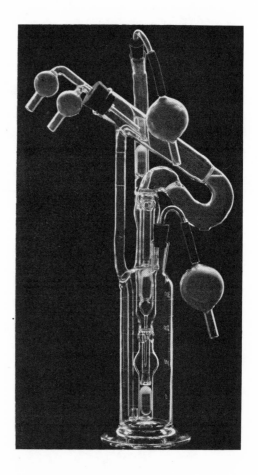

Lindbergh wrote in 1973 why he began his work in Carrel's lab in the early 1930s:

"My wife's older sister had developed a seriously defective heart valve as a complication of rheumatic fever. I had asked her doctor why surgery would not be beneficial. He replied that the heart could not be stopped long enough to permit a surgical operation. I asked why an artificial heart could not be used during the operation. He said he didn't know, and showed little interest in the problem. I asked other doctors. To my amazement, none of them could tell me, and none seemed to have much interest until I came to . . . the French surgeon Alexis Carrel.

"He said he had been trying for years to develop an apparatus similar to an artificial heart, one that would perfuse living organs isolated from the body. He showed me two mechanical devices that had been successful. I told him I thought I could construct a better perfusion apparatus. He replied that I would be welcome to the facilities of his department in the attempt to do so.

"My original objective in working with Carrel was to develop a successful perfusion apparatus as a step toward an artificial heart. My interest in such an apparatus soon became secondary to my interest in Carrel himself and the elements of life he worked with. Since childhood, I had been fascinated by questions of life and death. How mechanical, how mystical was life?

Did all existence end with death, or in some way extend beyond? Suppose an old head were grafted onto a young body, could wisdom and knowledge thus be combined with eternal youth? Carrel had explored all of these questions in his mind and laboratories, and both had become available to me.

"I spent midnight hours with my microscope in the Department's incubator room studying living cells that had once composed a body. They could be kept alive forever in Carrel's culture flasks. Why, then, did the body they came from have to die? Since every body consisted of trillions of such individually-living cells, why should one think of oneself as an individual? But if man was not an individual, what was he?"

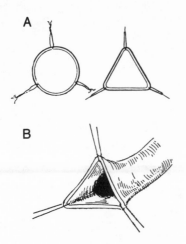

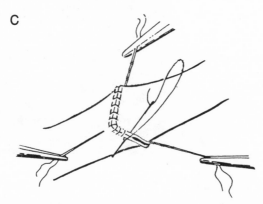

Figure 5.5. Because of the difficulty in sewing around circles, Carrel devised a triangulation technique. (A) Schema showing how the cut edge of a circular vessel is transformed into a triangular one by placing three equidistant threads in it and pulling in three directions. (B) After the threads are in place on both ends of the severed vessel, one edge of the triangle can be sewed shut. (C) Continuing tension on the threads enabled Carrel to sew easily along the other two straight edges of the triangle.

It was obvious that in the early 1900s Carrel was approaching the modern germfree atmosphere required for the survival of patients who have few or no defense mechanisms against bacteria.

Carrel did far more than sew together arteries or arteries and veins. A full decade before the first attempt to preserve whole blood (see p. 68), Carrel recognized the importance of preserving tissues (e.g., blood vessels) outside of the body so that they would be available whenever needed.

In 1910, Carrel wrote,

The graft must be taken from an amputated limb, or from the fresh cadaver of an executed criminal or of a man killed by accident. But such an opportunity will certainly not occur precisely when a graft is needed for an operation. The grafts, therefore, must be kept in storage and be ready for use when necessary.

Such a preservation of vessels outside of the body can be obtained by placing them in a condition of latent life. . . . The metabolism being completely stopped, the duration of the period of preservation could be indefinite. I began in 1906 some experiments on the preservation of arteries in cold storage. It was found immediately that a dog's carotid artery could be preserved outside of the body at a low temperature for several days and transplanted without suffering degeneration of its muscle fibers.

This long antedated the famous Houston artery bank of the 1940s.

And in 1912, he wrote,

The results obtained by Tuffier [on bone, cartilage; and peritoneum], Magitot [on the cornea], and myself demonstrated that human tissues preserved in cold storage could be used in human surgery. A supply of tissues in latent life would be constantly ready for use and the tubes containing the tissues could even be sent, in small refrigerators of the type of vacuum bottles, to surgeons who would need them. It would simplify very much the transplantations of skin, bone, and other tissues which are more and more used in human surgery.

Then Carrel went on to show that reimplantation or transplantation of organs was *technically* simple. Christiaan Barnard was the first to transplant the heart of one man to another, in 1968, but Carrel and Guthrie did it in the dog as early as 1905. Carrel described it and transplantation of both the heart and lung in 1907:

The heart was transplanted in several different ways. This is an example: The heart of a small dog was extirpated and transplanted into the neck of a larger one. The circulation was re-established through the heart, about an hour and 15 minutes after the cessation of the beat; 20 minutes after the re-establishment of the circulation, the blood was actively circulating through the coronary system. An opening made through the wall of a small branch of the coronary vein led to an abundant hemorrhage of dark blood. Strong fibrillar contraction soon occurred. Afterward contractions of the auricles appeared, and about an hour after the operation, effective contractions of the ventricles began.

However, unlike Barnard in 1968, Carrel appreciated the problem of tissue rejection. As early as 1912, he stated,

But it is not yet known whether surgeons will ever be able to perform a homoplastic transplantation with permanent success . . . it will only be through a more fundamental study of the biological relationships existing between living tissues (. . . to recognize individuals, if such exist, between whom organs can be interchanged with impunity) that the problems involved will come to be solved.

He also anticipated kidney transplantation long before the first successful operation in man. In 1907 he wrote,

In a case of a dog with kidney disease, it would be a rational procedure to substitute for one of its kidneys a sound kidney extirpated from some normal dog. . . . But the question of the transplantation of organs on man is difficult and very far from settled. In some exceptional cases it would be possible perhaps to use the kidneys of a man killed by accident. Also the organs of the anthropoid apes are perhaps able to tolerate human plasma.

In 1912 he was able to write,

A female dog, in which both kidneys had been removed [and one replaced] continued to live in perfect health for two years and a half, at the end of which time she died of a disease unconnected with the operation. The re-implanted kidney was normal. These experiments thus served to show that the extirpation of a kidney, its perfusion in Locke's [salt] solution, the complete interruption of the circulation for a period of 50 minutes and the subsequent suturing of its vessels and of its ureter did not occasion any interference with its function, even after a considerable interval of time. It was thus shown grafting of an organ is possible.

This remarkable man also pioneered in using a length of an animal's own vein to replace a similar length of an artery. He wrote that the ideal way to treat damaged or obstructed segments of arteries would be to remove the diseased portion and then, because end-to-end suturing (artery to artery) would be impossible because the gap would be too long, to interpose between the cut ends of the artery a segment of the neighboring vein, or of some other vein, for example, the superficial leg vein or a neck vein (see Fig. 5.3). He even fashioned leakproof tubes from the animal's own peritoneum, the membrane that lines the abdominal cavity and some of its contained organs, much as surgeons today have used body membranes to create delicate cardiac valves. But he also noted in 1912 that "on human beings, it is always possible to find on the patient himself a segment of a vein suitable for transplantation." This technique, of course, is now routine in performing the relatively new coronary artery bypass operation in man—removing a segment of the patient's own accessory (but not essential) leg vein to use as a substitute for a clogged coronary artery (Fig. 5.6).

Carrel even thought of and performed the now-famous coronary bypass operation. He wrote in 1910,

In certain cases of angina pectoris, when the mouth of the coronary arteries is calcified, it would be useful to establish a complementary circulation for the lower part of the arteries. I attempted to perform an indirect anastomosis [connection] between the descending aorta and the left coronary artery. It was, for many reasons, a difficult operation. On account of the continuous motion of the heart, it was not easy to dissect and to suture the artery. In one case I implanted one end of a long carotid artery, preserved in cold storage, on the descending aorta. The other end was passed through the pericardium and anastomosed to the peripheral end of the coronary, near the pulmonary artery. Unfortunately, the operation was too slow. Three minutes after the interruption of the circulation, fibrillary contractions appeared, but the anastomosis took five minutes. By massage of the heart, the dog was kept alive. But he died less than two hours afterwards. It shows that the anastomosis [connection] must be done in less than three minutes.

Figure 5.6.   Repair or reconstruction of obstructed coronary arteries. (A) Using selective coronary arteriography (see Figs. 5.7 and 5.8), the surgeon identifies the site of the main obstruction and makes sure that there is no additional obstruction further on. (The obstructed artery is blackened). Then he removes part of a long superficial, accessory vein (stippled tube) from the patient's own leg or thigh to avoid incompatibility with tissue from a donor, makes sure that the venous valves face in the right direction, and uses it to bypass the obstructed segment. (B) One end of the vein is sewed to the side of the aorta, and the other end to the cut end of the open coronary artery beyond the obstruction. (C) An implant from the aorta onto the side of the unobstructed far end of the coronary artery. The modern-day coronary bypass operation using the superficial (nonessential) saphenous vein is almost identical to that published by Carrel in 1906 (see p. 181).

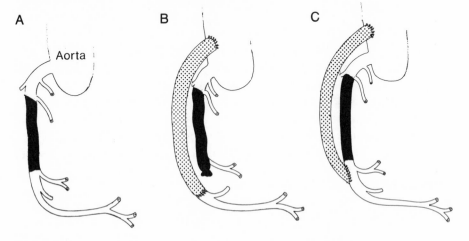

Carrel, of course, did not have a Gibbon heart–lung machine to give him additional time; indeed, the basic knowledge needed to build Gibbon's machine was largely unknown in the early 1900s.

Carrel also speculated on surgical procedures to improve impaired circulation to the brain:

We tried to increase the circulation of the brain by directing a strong current of red blood through the internal jugular vein, the peripheral end of this vein being anastomosed [joined] to the central end of the common carotid artery. After this operation no clinical troubles occur in the dog; a dog operated on five months ago is living in good health, but it might not be the same in man.

(The jugular vein has no valves and can conduct blood in either direction.)

Carrel and Guthrie also recognized in the early 1900s that vessels transplanted from another animal or species no longer lived and grew but simply served as fibrous tubes—as a framework or scaffolding that eventually became covered by a membrane of the recipient's own cells. But, even before new cells from the patient lined the donated tube, the vessels remained watertight, or at least bloodtight, and were admirable conduits for blood. These experiments laid the groundwork for the use in the 1950s of cloth tubes to replace obstructed arteries.

From Carrel to Clinical Vascular Surgery

Four of every ten deaths each year in the United States are due to serious arterial diseases; these include narrowing or complete obstruction of arteries by clots, atherosclerosis, or both. The obstructions may be in the arteries supplying the heart muscle (causing coronary occlusion, also called a heart attack or myocardial infarction), in arteries to the kidney (causing a special form of high blood pressure; see p. 308), in arteries leading to the brain (causing stroke), or in arteries of the extremities (resulting in pain, ulceration, or gangrene). The defects also include aneurysm (a thin ballooned-out pouch that develops at a weak point in an artery which can burst and lead to fatal hemorrhage) and mechanical injuries that pierce or sever arteries, leading to serious bleeding.

Considering the huge "consumer market" for surgical repair of arteries, one might have expected instantaneous worldwide embrace of

Carrel's techniques and suggestions, such as that accorded to Roentgen's discovery of X rays. But this was not to be. George Crile, a Cleveland surgeon, did use Carrel's technique in the early 1900s to give direct, artery-to-vein blood transfusions, but the discovery of citrate as an anticoagulant and of the technique of storing liquid blood in "banks" led to widespread use of indirect transfusions, and therefore to the demise of the transfusionist.

Why didn't Carrel himself, a highly qualified surgeon, make the leap from his experimental laboratory to the hospital operating room? Basically because he was primarily a research scientist interested in life processes, and he used his techniques largely to have control over the arterial inflow and venous outflow of individual organs, to study what maintained life in isolated organs. I believe he used his surgical skill on a patient only once in the United States—in 1908—when he was asked to transfuse a 5-day-old infant bleeding from hemorrhagic disease of the newborn. She was the daughter of a prominent surgeon, whose brothers were also well-known physicians. Carrel was persuaded to try to rescue the dying infant. He was able to give her a blood transfusion by surgically connecting her father's radial (wrist) artery to her leg vein. This delicate surgery was performed on a kitchen table. The bleeding ceased promptly, the infant recovered, and the story of this lifesaving happening was reported in the daily papers as the "first successful blood transfusion in New York City," which it was not. However, the publicity, emphasizing that the surgeon had acquired his skill by experiments on animals, helped turn the tide against a strongly supported bill of the antivivisectionists about to be passed by the New York State legislature.

Despite Carrel's unique achievements, the vast majority of American physicians and surgeons today believe that vascular surgery and organ transplantation sprang, like Athena from the skull of Zeus, full-grown from the skulls of imaginative, daring, and skillful surgeons of the 1940s and 1950s. This odd situation requires analyzing why the work of America's first Nobel laureate in medicine had to wait thirty years to become one of the great modern advances in surgery. When questioned nowadays, vascular surgeons (and there are hordes of them) give a variety of reasons for not recognizing or quoting Carrel's work. It is true that he was French-born, and that some of his early papers were in French, but the great majority were written in English. His work on experimental vascular surgery was written in English and published in highly respected and widely read journals: *Journal of the American Medical Association*

(18 articles), *Journal of Experimental Medicine* (25 articles), *Science* (7 articles), *Surgery, Gynecology and Obstetrics* (5 articles), *Annals of Surgery* (3 articles), *Transactions of the American Surgical Society* (3 articles), and the *Bulletin of the Johns Hopkins Hospital* and *British Medical Journal*. In its October 19, 1912, issue the British weekly *The Lancet* commented editorially as follows:

And there is a further advance in the surgery of the blood vessels which is, perhaps, even more surprising. Carrel has shown that a portion of artery may be preserved in cold storage for several days or even weeks before transplantation, and yet it will live. Nay more, although as a rule the tissue of one animal will not grow in the body of an animal of a different species, yet Carrel has found that these portions of blood vessels of dogs can be transplanted from cold storage with success into the bodies of cats. None who have followed with interest these new advances in surgery can doubt that they contain immense possibilities, *and the application to man of the methods learned in animals cannot be long delayed* [italics added].

Carrel worked in one of the best known and most highly respected scientific laboratories in the world—the Rockefeller Institute for Medical Research in New York City. It *is* true that he discouraged casual visitors to his laboratory, but he did invite the top men in the American surgical profession—George Crile, Rudolph Matas, John Murphy, and Harvey Cushing—to his laboratory at the University of Chicago in 1905 to watch demonstrations of his surgical techniques. In addition, Carrel lectured at Johns Hopkins Medical School in 1905 and met all the great surgeons at Hopkins and the University of Pennsylvania before he visited New York City.

Although he did not actively seek public recognition, he was the first scientist working in an American laboratory to win the Nobel Prize in medicine; the award was duly headlined in American newspapers, specifically his successful vascular surgery and transplantation of organs.

There are some legitimate reasons for the long lag between discovery and clinical use. Carrel was an exquisitely gifted surgeon. He worked in a special, nearly germfree operating room on clean arteries; he practiced matchless aseptic techniques because he knew that even a minor wound infection prevented healing of arterial wounds. The years 1914–1918, immediately following his experimental work, were World War I years, fought on the muddy and infected farmlands of France, and wounds were treated in less than ideal, frontline hospitals by less than ideally trained surgeons. Possibly some young surgeons tried to repair mangled arteries and failed completely, as even Carrel might have.

But that should not have prevented postwar surgeons in the 1920s and 1930s from tackling "clean," elective procedures, such as replacing clogged arteries with wide-open vein transplants, or removing aneurysms and filling the gap with a transplant, or even performing a kidney transplant in a twin dying of terminal disease of both kidneys.

I believe three factors prevented clean vascular surgery in these decades: First, there was no heparin to prevent clotting after the operation; second, there were no antibiotics to prevent or battle postoperative infections; and third, there was no dependable technique for preoperative X-ray diagnosis of the precise structural defect to be repaired. Clinicians were convinced that arteriosclerosis was a patchy process, unpredictable in its locations, and hence it was impossible to pinpoint the precise site of vascular obstruction. Heparin became commercially available in 1934, chemotherapy of infections in 1936–1937, and X-ray diagnosis (arteriograms) also in the 1930s (Figs. 5.7 and 5.8).

I suspect that there was a fourth factor responsible for the lag, but I dare only whisper this: I believe that many surgeons had not *read* Carrel's articles and did not even know of his Nobel Prize-winning work. I suspect this because of fifteen top-rated vascular surgeons in the period

Figure 5.7. For sharp X-ray visualization of a specific artery and its branches, a contrast medium must be injected into the artery close to the suspected partial obstruction. A special catheter is inserted into an artery of an arm or leg and pushed upstream against the flow of blood, aimed at a renal, coronary, or cerebral artery. The sketch shows a catheter designed to be pushed up the abdominal aorta and then actually into the orifice of the left coronary artery. A catheter with a different configuration can be guided to the beginning of the right coronary artery.

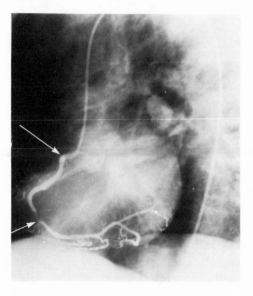

Figure 5.8. A coronary angiogram. Before performing a coronary artery "bypass" operation, the vascular surgeon requests that a test be done to determine if there is significant obstruction in any of the coronary arteries and, if so, exactly *where* it is. Here a long catheter has been pushed up the abdominal aorta (the long white tube on the right side with a long loop at the top) into the aortic arch and then into the right coronary artery. The catheter itself stops at the upper of the two arrows; from there on the white lines are the image of radio-opaque liquid injected through the catheter tip. The lower arrow represents a significant block in a segment of the right coronary artery. The left coronary artery was open in this patient. I doubt that Forssmann in 1929 ever dreamed that his catheter (or a modification of it) would find its way into hundreds of thousands of patients each year for this purpose.

1939–1955, only three (Potts, Harkin, and Hufnagel) referred to Carrel's published articles; the other twelve did not, even though some of them repeated Carrel's experiments almost step by step.

Despite the long lag, Carrel's techniques were rediscovered in the 1940s and, as one surgeon later put it, "almost every surgeon who had a dog and a surgical resident at his disposal began an investigation" on designing or replacing diseased heart valves or arteries. The result was that cardiac surgery and vascular surgery—macro or micro—became the most exciting branch of modern surgery, involving adult cardiac surgery, newborn cardiac surgery, bypassing obstructed coronary arteries, cerebral vascular repair, and replacing obstructed arteries with healthy vessels to kidneys or obstructed or diseased aortas or arteries to the four limbs.

If we divide vascular surgery into two periods—Carrel and post-Carrel—the second period began in 1938. It began on August 17, 1938, when Robert Gross in Boston performed a "first" on a 7-year-old girl by tying off her ductus arteriosus, which had remained open since birth (Fig. 5.9). This was hailed as a landmark in vascular surgery, but I confess that I do not know why. Maude Abbott (see p. 96) had already reported on a series of ninety-two patients who had come to autopsy with an open duct as the sole congenital defect; Helen Taussig had already learned how to diagnose such patients clinically. Actually, Dr. John Hubbard, a cardiologist, had made the diagnosis of an open duct in this particular child and urged Dr. Gross to tie it off.

It was not really the first such operation. Dr. John Strieder had performed a similar operation on March 16, 1937, at the Massachusetts Memorial Hospital, only two miles from Gross' operating room at Children's Hospital. It's true that both operations took place in Boston, "where Lowells speak only to Cabots and Cabots speak only to God," but Strieder's article did appear in the May 1938 issue of the *American Heart Journal* 3 months before Gross' operation and 11 months before Gross' report appeared in print. It is also true that, although Strieder's

Figure 5.9.   Surgical closure of a patent (open) ductus arteriosus. This duct, normally open in the fetus, should close shortly after birth. Figure 3.1 (p. 91) shows the problem that occurs when a ductus remains open after birth. Surgeons may correct this defect by either (A) simply tying off the open vessel or (B) tying off the ductus at its two ends (near the pulmonary artery (P) and near the aorta (A) and then cutting the ductus in two between the two ties.

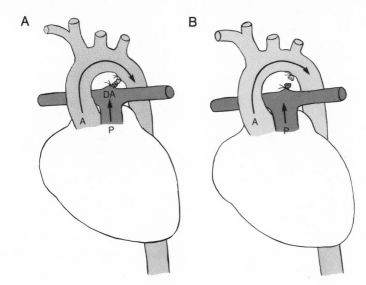

operation was successful, his patient died 4 days later, not because of an unsuccessful operation, but because of the spread of bacterial infection from a previously localized site in the ductus.

Most important of all, Dr. Ian Munro, also of Boston, had outlined in great detail the anatomical details and surgical approach to close an open duct, and he urged surgeons to undertake the simple task of slipping a ligature under the open vessel and tying it off; this report was published in 1907 in a well-known American surgical journal that must certainly have found its way to Boston, because Strieder quoted it in 1938, even though Gross did not in 1939.

Furthermore, no new concepts were involved in his operation. Gross simply tied off an artery and did not even touch the heart, let alone open it (it was *vascular* and not *cardiac* surgery). There was no new contribution to the knowledge of the heart and vessels. His operation did not interfere with the heartbeat or with aortic blood flow. It appeared to involve a simple technical procedure of opening the thorax (done many times previously for various types of thoracic surgery) and ligating a vessel near the heart, and detailed steps for the operation itself had been proposed and published thirty years previously.

However, at about the same time (1938) surgeons began to develop an operation to correct another congenital defect, coarctation* (narrowing or constriction) of the aorta just beyond the arch. This was really quite a challenge, since the operation required opening the thorax, clamping the aorta, cutting out the constricted part of the aorta, and reconnecting the cut ends of the aorta by sutures (Fig. 5.10). But fortunately for the future of vascular surgery, clamping the aorta in such a patient did not really mean completely depriving the lower parts of the body of its blood supply, because the wisdom of the body somehow or other sees to it that over a period of years the patient sprouts a new set of arteries from the aorta both above and below the narrowing (Fig. 5.11). Clarence Crafoord in Sweden recognized that this additional circulation existed and successfully clamped the aorta above the constriction, removed the narrowed segment, and joined the upper and lower ends of the aorta together again, and so a second congenital vascular defect was conquered.

Coarctation is a perfect example of medical jargon; two commonly used words—*narrowing* and *constriction*—obviate the need for this "scientific" term.

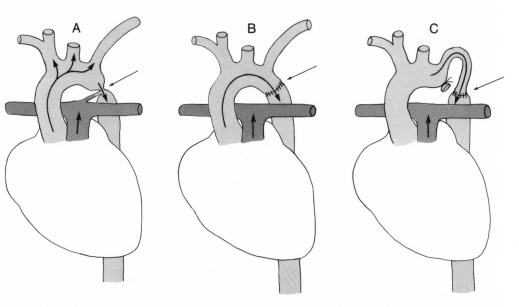

Figure 5.10.   Repair of coarctation (constriction) of the aorta. (A) The narrowed portion of the aorta, which is usually at the point where the ductus arteriosus (now just a fibrous cord) connects with the aorta. Numerous new arteries that have sprouted above the constriction and joined with newly formed arteries below it are not shown here (see Fig. 5.11). (B) The technique used for removing the narrowed segment and stitching together the upper and lower cut ends of the aorta. (C) An alternative procedure in which the left subclavian artery is cut, swung around and down, and joined to the lower cut end of the aorta (the upper cut end is tied off). This ability to mobilize an artery intended for one purpose and use it to correct a nearby defect in another artery proved to be valuable in many types of vascular operations. Parts formerly supplied by the subclavian artery now get their blood from accessory arteries.

Spare Parts

When the vascular surgery boom arrived and a new breed of experimental vascular surgeons sprang up, some remarkable new techniques appeared, unknown even to Carrel. One of these was the production of "spare parts." A surgeon who had to remove only a small segment of an artery would simply sew the cut ends of the artery together again, but when the diseased segment that was removed was long or contained a branch, pulling the cut ends together was no longer possible or sufficient, and the surgeon needed another solution. The first solution was to make use of earlier techniques—to establish a *blood vessel* bank to store healthy arteries removed from accidentally killed people. DeBakey

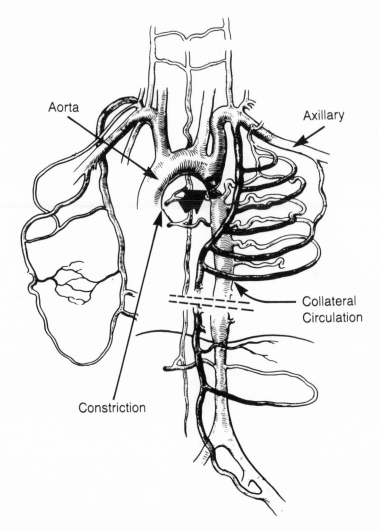

Figure 5.11. Constriction (coarctation) of the aorta decreases blood flow to the tissues normally supplied by it; deprivation of blood flow, especially in the young, acts as a stimulus for many new, smaller arteries to grow into the deprived tissues. Here many new vessels have grown downward from arteries above the constriction to supply arterial blood to the lower part of the body. The aorta and its main branches within the chest are shown here in light gray; the additional collateral vessels are dark gray or black.

and his enterprising group in Texas in the 1940s took a commanding lead in vascular surgery for a while, because they set up a unique Carrel-type vessel bank. It seems that a Houston coroner was perfectly willing to surrender his prerogatives at nights and weekends and allow

DeBakey's residents to perform autopsies on fatal accident cases that came to the morgue at these inconvenient times. As a result, the Houston team soon built up an extensive bank of preserved arteries and many patients requiring elective operations on vessels flew to Houston to become beneficiaries of its warehouse. But two problems arose: One, patients needing arteries soon outnumbered even Houston's supply of healthy, nonsclerotic arteries (one should not put a 75-year-old artery in a 40-year-old patient); and two, patients came in all sizes and arterial defects occurred in many locations, so a diseased artery might require a straight tube, a Y-tube, or a tube with right-angle side branches, again, all of different sizes.

This time the solution was a brand new one—the use of artificial arteries—though it was based on earlier research by Carrel and Guthrie. Arthur Blakemore and Arthur Voorhees in New York discovered that a synthetic material, Vinyon N cloth, could be fashioned into tubes that could be sutured onto arteries as a satisfactory conduit for blood as soon as the pores of the cloth became sealed with platelets and fibrin. To make certain that the tube was the right size and had the correct number, size, spacing, and angles of branches, the surgeon, after exposing an arterial aneurysm, measured the size and shape of graft required, and a seamstress just outside the operating room quickly constructed a cloth tube on a sewing machine. Once again, as in Carrel's early training, medicine benefited from the talents of a seamstress. Then the graft was sterilized and inserted.

Another unexpected benefit came from a patient, Arthur Hanisch, who was on the receiving end of one of DeBakey's transplants. In 1954 Hanisch, president of a pharmaceutical company who also had associations with the knitting industry, immediately saw an important role for industry in the design of cloth tubes. He suggested that DeBakey get in touch with Tom Edman, professor of knitting technology at the Philadelphia College of Textiles and Science, and he financed a project for developing cloth arteries. Edman tested many fabrics and weaves and suggested Dacron as a good bet, because it could be knitted by machine into seamless tubing, either straight or forked (Fig. 5.12).

The problem of creating a no-kink tube that could span an elbow, hip, or knee joint was solved by surgeon Sterling Edwards and textile engineer James Tapp of the Chemstrand Corporation, a synthetic textile company in Alabama. For several months they worked with different concentrations of formic acid and so varied the stiffness of nylon tubes,

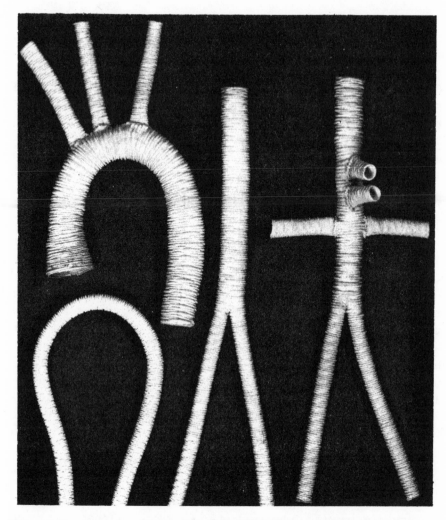

Figure 5.12. Knitted grafts to replace the arch of the aorta and the abdominal aorta, and a flexible tube capable of bypassing an artery across a freely moving joint.

trying to eliminate the kinking on bending. Nothing worked. Purely by accident one day, Tapp was removing a braided tube from the glass rod he used for dipping the graft in the solvent when he noticed that it assumed a crimped configuration if the two ends were compressed toward each other, something only a braided tube will naturally do. He allowed one of the tubes to set with this crimping and realized that this could eliminate the kinking, just as it does in flexible drinking straws. With great excitement, he sent one to Edwards for testing. Edwards was skeptical that a crimped tube would work in the bloodstream, because all research work going on at that time in the synthetic graft field suggested that an extremely smooth inner lining was necessary to prevent thrombosis. But he gave it a try and was delighted when crimped, small-caliber (6-millimeter inside diameter) grafts uniformly stayed open in dogs. Examination of these grafts only a few days after implantation showed that the thin layer of fresh clot that lined all grafts had leveled out the irregularities of the crimps and a smooth lining was present. In the fall of 1954, the first opportunity came to test this graft clinically. A patient with the main artery to his thigh destroyed by a gunshot wound required a 5-centimeter graft. A braided, crimped nylon tube was inserted and functioned well, even though the patient flexed his hip with every step.

Artificial heart valves went through a valve-of-the-month phase for several years. Similarly, artificial arteries went through an artificial artery-of-the-month period, with arteries made of a wide variety of smooth and rough synthetic materials with different degrees of porosity and durability.

In addition to the fabrication of artificial arteries, the design of new instruments also played an important role in permitting vascular surgeons to do finer and finer work in more and more inaccessible locations; Mueller's surgical instrument catalog devoted *157 pages* of illustrations and descriptions of special instruments devised by or for vascular surgeons.

The Advent of Microsurgery

Another major advance came with the advent of vascular microsurgery. Vascular surgeons had worked on larger arteries, but shied away from the smaller ones. Stitching together very small vessels (1–2 millimeters in diameter) required a whole new way of operating: microvascular surgery, the surgeon operating while looking through a microscope and using extremely delicate and fine instruments and needles. It all began in 1960 with a young experimental surgeon named Julius Jacobson.

Jacobson told me in 1972 how he came to use the microscope as an aid to vascular surgery:

In 1959 I completed a seven-year residency at New York's Presbyterian Hospital and stayed on there for a short while as an attending surgeon. In 1960 I was appointed the Director of Surgical Research at the University of Vermont, intending to study the factors that determine why new blood vessels grew where needed.

Just before leaving Presbyterian Hospital, I wandered into one of the Ear, Nose and Throat operating rooms and was allowed to look through the Zeiss microscope they were using. [Otologists were the first to use a microscope in the operating room.] I'm sorry to say that there was no sudden recognition of its potential value in vascular surgery.

Some months later, on my arrival in Vermont, one of the pharmacologists asked for help in making the carotid artery of a dog completely nerve-free. The only way to really accomplish this with certainty was to divide a segment of the vessel and sew together the divided ends. In attempting to do this, it was immediately evident that the problem was not in the ability of the hand to do but rather the eye to see. I borrowed a Zeiss microscope from the operating room and began to look at severed small arteries. The experience was very much like looking at the moon for the first time through a powerful telescope; I saw a wealth of previously unappreciated detail for the first time and minor surgical errors became glaringly apparent. I should add at this point that before going to medical school I had worked in cell physiology under Dr. L. V. Heilbrunn, and had also spent several summers at the Woods Hole Marine Laboratory in Massachusetts. I interject this because, in thinking back, it becomes obvious to me that I probably would not have attempted to interpose a microscope between my eyes and the surgical field had the use of dissecting microscopes not been second nature to me by that time.

Now we know why microvascular surgery began in 1960. A surgeon, fascinated by research because of stimulating experiences at Woods Hole Biological Laboratories and working with an inspiring general physiologist, Lewis Heilbrunn, was asked by a pharmacologist to lend his technical skill to help solve a basic problem on the sensitivity of denervated arteries to various drugs. Conventional surgical techniques then available to him were obviously inadequate, but instead of his saying, "Sorry, it's impossible," he came up with microvascular surgery. To be certain that all the nerve fibers that run in its wall were cut, he had to cut the entire artery in two. Then he had to sew the artery together again, and that required the use of a microscope (Fig. 5.13).

We still don't know why a Jacobson didn't come along in 1930, 1940, or 1950. Maybe there wasn't anyone with the same combination of surgical and research training, inquisitiveness, patience, and willingness to help a couple of basic scientists get along with an esoteric problem.

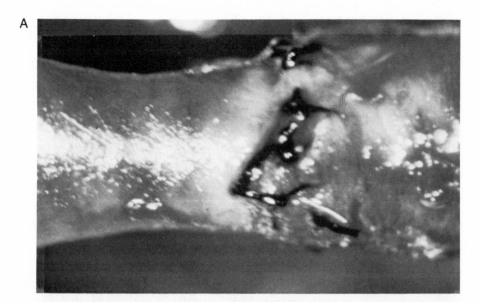

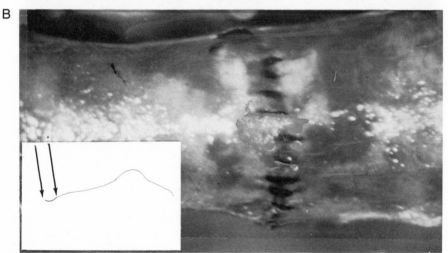

Figure 5.13.　Microsurgical technique. For microsurgery, extremely small needles are used and very fine thread (finer than human hair) is actually built into the end of the needle to eliminate the eye and the need to thread it. The stitching is done by a surgeon looking through a microscope. (A) A limb artery of a small animal was severed cleanly and the cut ends joined together *without* the aid of a microscope. The view here is the result of the surgery as seen through a microscope (×18). (B) A similar artery in the opposite limb was severed and joined together by a microvascular surgeon using his accustomed microscope. Each artery before enlargement measured about ⅛ of an inch in diameter. In the inset (lower left) is a fine needle with attached thread. The microneedle (curved line between two arrows) is about ⅛ of an inch; the wavy line to the right of the arrows is the ultrafine thread. The use of microsurgical techniques prevents small errors (see the suture line in the upper artery) that lead to failure of the operation in small vessels.

Microsurgery has now led to a considerable number of spin-offs to many fields: reconstruction of a ligated vas deferens (first performed by Jacobson) or of a Fallopian tube, restoration of minute arteries in the brain, union of severed nerves or of a ureter, and suturing back in place a severed hand or finger.

As is often the case, scientific progress in a special field, here vascular surgery, resulted from contributions from unexpected sources: an embroidress, a "lace lady," a cardiovascular physiologist, a patient, a coroner, a knitting technologist, the plastics industry, a microscope manufacturer, an otologist, a summer research experience with a general physiologist, a pharmacologist, and, most unexpected of all, a surgical genius.

Prevention of Arterial Disease

The ultimate goal of medicine is to prevent disease for a lifetime by having every potential patient swallow a single harmless, inexpensive tablet that requires neither hospitalization nor loss of time from one's job; a shining example is the prevention of polio by an oral vaccine. With cardiovascular diseases, we're far from this goal. The American Heart Association has estimated that in 1983 the total cost of cardiovascular disease to the nation will be $56.9 billion, including costs of precise diagnosis, hospitalization, medical and surgical bills, intensive care units, nursing care, and lost income from the job. There is nothing immoral about this huge bill; we have it because very expensive diagnostic tests and surgical operations—brilliant lifesaving achievements— have for the most part preceded discovery of preventive measures. Physicians and surgeons must take care of urgent, immediate problems while scientists are struggling to learn the cause and prevention of these disorders.

What preventive measures *do* we have in 1983? The main causes of disease of cardiac valves are acute rheumatic fever (which is associated with one type of streptococcus), other infectious diseases that affect valve leaflets, and congenital defects. Acute rheumatic fever can now be prevented or checked early in the disease by long-term administration of a penicillin derivative; the number of patients with diseased valves caused by rheumatic fever has declined decade by decade. In 1950, 22,000 Americans died of rheumatic heart disease; in 1980, the number of deaths was only 8,000 and will almost certainly continue to decline. If treated promptly, other infectious diseases (syphilis and bacterial endocarditis) that affect heart valves will have little or no opportunity to distort cardiac valves to the extent that surgical operations are necessary. Some congenital heart disease can be prevented by measures such as immunizing (before conception) would-be mothers against German measles and prohibiting their use of drugs known or believed to cause fetal abnormalities.

What progress has been made in the prevention of arterial disease? Very little. If you scan the causes of all 1,986,000 deaths in the United States in 1980, you'll find that arterial disease is way at the top of the list. Of deaths from all causes, 1,012,150 (51% of the total) were attributed to diseases of the heart and blood vessels; 737,300 (37% of the total) were assigned to two diseases: heart attack (coronary artery obstruction) and stroke (block of arteries to the brain). But heart attack and stroke are simply names that physicians, pathologists, or coroners give to the final cause of these deaths. If we are to prevent these diseases, we must know the *primary* "cause of death"; in some cases, the cause is a blood clot or a hemorrhage, but in most it is atherosclerosis, making this disease the number one killer of Americans. If we want to know how to prevent or reverse heart attacks or strokes, we must concentrate our efforts not on the heart or brain, but on learning the genesis of atherosclerosis and on finding answers to the question, what transforms the smooth inner lining of a healthy artery into a lumpy surface (Fig. 5.14) that eventually obstructs one or more essential channels for blood flow (Fig. 5.15) to the heart muscle or brain?*

I'm willing to wager a large sum that if you ask a hundred well-

---

*The terminology used today (arteriosclerosis and atherosclerosis) is confusing, so let me try to clarify it. In the early 1800s physicians named the disease "hardening of the arteries," because at autopsy they saw only end stages of the disease, in which calcium had entered these lumps (see Fig. 5.14) and hardened them. Then, unhappy with "lay language," physicians invented a proper medical name of Greek derivation, "arteriosclerosis" (using the Greek *skleros*, meaning hard).

In the late 1800s, pathologists found cholesterol, a fatty substance, in these lumps, were convinced that arteriosclerosis began with fat deposits, and created a new name, "atherosclerosis" (*athere* is Greek for gruel or a soft porridge). In so doing they created confusion, first because the word *atherosclerosis* completely omits any reference to arteries, where the disease occurs, and second, because the two parts of the new name are self-contradictory—*athero* means mushy and *sclerosis* means hard! Arterial atheroma might be a better name, because it identifies the site of the disease (in arteries) and indicates that initially the lumps consist of mushy material (cholesterol) or a benign tumor (*oma*) of muscle cells, or both. However, as shown in Fig. 5.15, other tissues and cells invade these lumps, including platelets, blood clots, fibrous tissue, calcium, fibrin, and macrophages (scavenger cells) that may eventually completely block the channel for blood flow.

At the moment very few realize that the first half of the word *atherosclerosis* contradicts the second half. Under mild protest, I'm using the popular name, atherosclerosis, in this section.

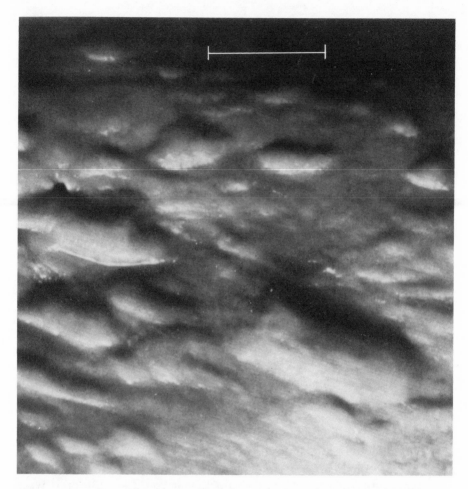

Figure 5.14. Photograph of the inner surface of an atherosclerotic human aorta. The numerous lumps ("plaques") of various sizes are accumulations of material under the inner lining of the aorta. When these become large enough in smaller vessels, they can significantly decrease the inside diameter of the vessel and favor clot formation. Most coronary and cerebral artery obstructions are due to an increase in size of these lumps. The scale (upper right) represents 1 centimeter.

The term *atherosclerosis* has largely replaced *arteriosclerosis* and *hardening of the arteries* to describe the encroachment of nodules or plaques upon the channel of an artery (see p. 203).

educated adults what causes atherosclerosis, most all will answer cholesterol (or fat or saturated fat) in the diet. Yet recently a congressional committee asked Dr. Robert Levy, then director of the National Heart Institute, "Is there any scientific evidence that ingestion, by otherwise

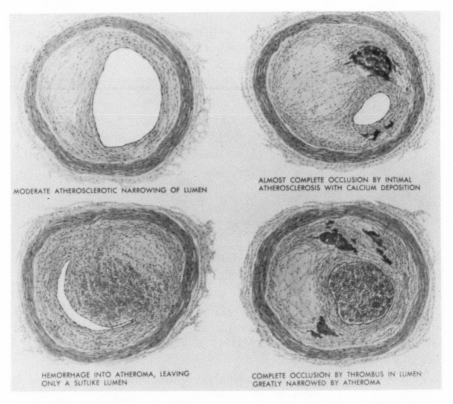

MODERATE ATHEROSCLEROTIC NARROWING OF LUMEN

ALMOST COMPLETE OCCLUSION BY INTIMAL
ATHEROSCLEROSIS WITH CALCIUM DEPOSITION

HEMORRHAGE INTO ATHEROMA, LEAVING
ONLY A SLITLIKE LUMEN

COMPLETE OCCLUSION BY THROMBUS IN LUMEN
GREATLY NARROWED BY ATHEROMA

Figure 5.15. Progression from a normal arterial wall and open channel to one whose channel (lumen) is completely closed: (A) an artery with a partly obstructed tube lined with normal cells, surrounded by a ring of normal involuntary muscle cells; (B) further occlusion by atheroma or by a tumor of muscle cells; (C) almost complete closure; and (D) complete obstruction, probably by a blood clot.

normal individuals, of a diet restricted in cholesterol will prolong life or reduce the incidence of mortality due to coronary artery disease?" Levy replied simply, "No, sir." This "no, sir" does not mean that cholesterol has nothing to do with atherosclerosis; it means that the disease is not a simple one, but involves numerous factors.

Further realization of the complexity of atherosclerosis comes from the American Heart Association's list of factors that increase the risk of acquiring it: a diet high in saturated fats, high blood pressure, diabetes and chronic increase in blood sugar, smoking cigarettes, obesity, infrequent and insufficient muscular exercise, coffee, stress and tension, oral contraceptives in women, and just being a male for men. Remember, however, that "risk factors" are just that; they are not necessarily *causes* of disease, but circumstances that statisticians have found to be associated with an increased frequency of a disease. Risk factors may be "fellow travelers" that aggravate a disease or accelerate it, or they may be present independently of the true cause or causes and simply act as "markers." If atherosclerosis had a single cause (such as polio virus for poliomyelitis), the Heart Association would simply have pronounced, "Eliminate cholesterol from your diet," and stopped at that.

Let's start with cholesterol, because physicians have associated it with atherosclerosis for more than a century. Cholesterol is a fat (chemically termed a "lipid"). By definition, lipids are insoluble in water and practically insoluble in blood plasma. In order to travel through the bloodstream to all cells in the body, lipids are invariably joined to a protein and thereby become lipoproteins. There are many different lipids and hence many different lipoproteins. These can be separated into different groups because each has a different density. This makes it easy, using special centrifugation techniques, to classify lipoproteins. The pertinent classes, with their abbreviations, are very low density (VLDL, the second L standing for lipoprotein), low density (LDL), high density (HDL), and very high density (VHDL). Cholesterol with its protein is a low-density lipoprotein (LDL).

Cholesterol is essential to normal body function in several ways. It is an essential component of cell membranes and, being a *sterol*, is necessary for the formation of steroid hormones such as testo*sterone*, adrenal cortical steroid hormones, andro*sterone;* it is also needed for the formation of bile. Presumably it has no unique function in arterial walls beyond the fact that these, being living tissues with living cells, require cholesterol for the formation and maintenance of cell membranes.

So why has cholesterol become the villain in the atherosclerosis story? First, because LDL is always present in blood; second, because it's always present in the arterial wall; third, because it's always found "at the scene of the crime," in atherosclerotic streaks or lumps (see Fig. 5.16); and fourth, because atherosclerosis is more common in patients with a high level of LDL than in those in whom LDL is at normal or low levels. A special instance of the fourth case is a very rare disease characterized by a level of blood cholesterol that is four to six times normal (the disease has the impressive name of familial hypercholester-olemia) and severe atherosclerosis that occurs at an early age (children with this disease may have coronary artery occlusion as early as 10 years of age). As Daniel Steinberg put it, it seems that, at least in this genetic disease, cholesterol must be a cause in itself that does not require the existence of other contributing risk factors; these children do not have high blood pressure, are not diabetic, are not obese and have not yet begun to smoke cigarettes. Of course, one may still argue that a second, as yet unidentified, genetic factor causes the atherosclerosis and that the high level of cholesterol in blood is only a "marker" or a red herring.

Let's discuss now how cholesterol gets inside the arterial wall. The wall is composed of living cells that require nutrients and oxygen for growth and repair. Like most cells in the body, they receive their blood supply through the usual system of artery, arterioles, and capillaries (capillaries to blood vessels are called vasa vasorum—"vessels of ves-sels"). But capillaries on the outer wall of an artery have difficulty sup-plying cells deep in the wall, because the inner wall of an artery is exposed to a pressure (arterial blood pressure) that is much higher, both in systole and diastole, than capillary blood pressure. The inner lining of the arterial wall is exposed to very rapid blood flow at high pressure, but the inner wall has an intact, nonporous, layer of cells (endothelial cells) that prevents blood or plasma from leaking into the arterial wall itself.

However, there are ways by which substances in blood can get into the wall of an artery. One way is by sacs, whose openings are first on the blood side, where they collect material for transfer and then turn 180° to dump their collection inside the arterial wall. (This is a micro

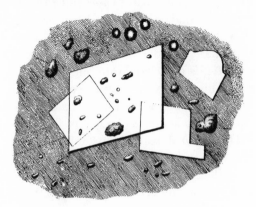

Figure 5.16. Vogel in 1847 found deposits of cholesterol, geometri-cally shaped crystals, in the aortic wall of an 84-year-old man. The small round deposits are fat or fat droplets (×200).

version of the old-time turning-box that was set in the wall of convents; when the opening of the box faced the outside, it accepted letters—or even an unwanted baby—and brought them inside, all by a 180° turn of the box. No one ever opened a door.) Biologists today call the process they see "endocytosis."

Another way is by specific receptors on endothelial cells or on smooth muscle cells that bind only one specific component of blood and transfer it to the inside of the cell. We now know that there are LDL receptors throughout the body, including the endothelium of arteries; these can grab LDL in the bloodstream and transfer it to the smooth muscle cells in the arterial walls. (We believe now that these LDL receptors are specific for the protein joined to cholesterol to produce a lipoprotein rather than for cholesterol itself.) Recently Michael Brown and Joseph Goldstein at Dallas have shown that familial increase in plasma cholesterol is a genetic disease that causes a defect in regulating cholesterol metabolism and a deficiency in LDL receptors that allows cholesterol to rise to high levels in circulating blood.

Most persons exposed to popular science articles believe that all cholesterol in the body comes from their food. *Some* does, but human cells can also make their own cholesterol by metabolic processes. If the cholesterol absorbed from the gastrointestinal tract is sufficient to supply the cells, the cholesterol factories inside the body shut down; if the supply is insufficient, they go to work again. The mechanism for regulating internal production of LDL is pretty good, but even if it shuts down completely, it has no control over what comes into the blood from the gastrointestinal tract and then to the LDL receptors. So the cholesterol content of cells in arterial walls is a matter of balance between how much is formed within the cell plus what enters the wall through the arterial blood, on the one hand, and the amount used by the cell plus that which leaves the cell, on the other hand. Entering the cell is not the final stop for LDL; there is also an outflow of LDL to the liver, where it is converted into bile and excreted into the small intestine.

This brings us now to consider the "good guys" versus the "bad guys." The bad guys are LDLs that enter the arterial wall in excess of the metabolic needs of its cells. The good guys, we now believe, are the HDLs (*high*-density lipoproteins) that remove cholesterol from the arterial wall and send it to the liver for elimination. So not all lipoproteins are villains; HDLs are antiatherosclerosis and hospital laboratories are now measuring HDL as well as LDL levels in patients' blood.

We now know, as a result of modern techniques used by cell biochemists, that LDL receptors can be good guys. When LDL receptors in all tissues in the body are actively at work, they soak up plasma LDL and keep it at a low level; when these are deficient (as they are in the inherited disease of increased blood cholesterol), plasma LDL rises and the arterial wall receives more cholesterol.

None of the preceding explains why lumps rich in cholesterol form mainly in the walls of arteries and not uniformly throughout the body. The answer is probably that the cells of the arterial wall are more vulnerable than other tissues, both to poor blood supply and to mechanical trauma. High blood pressure within the artery may reduce blood and oxygen flow to cells in the arterial wall and so damage its muscle cells. But the arterial wall is also vulnerable because of the incessant rises and falls of blood pressure, undergoing low diastolic (with little stress and stretch) to high systolic pressure (with considerable stress and stretch) 70 times a minute, or 36,792,000 times each year.

Micro damage could occur more frequently in coronary arteries, because, being on and in the heart, they are subjected to all the changes in size and shape of the heart with each beat and the wide alterations in pressure inside and outside the coronary arteries during each contraction–relaxation cycle of the heart muscle.

Minute damage to the lining of arteries (resulting from trauma or infection with bacteria or viruses) may be an important factor in the genesis of atherosclerosis. Whenever there is a break in the lining of an artery, several events can occur. One is a greater likelihood that substances in blood, such as LDL, will enter the arterial wall and increase its lipid content; another is that platelets are apt to adhere to breaks in the lining (see p. 69) and to each other, resulting in formation of clumps. Platelets, however, are more than mechanical plugs; they contain a variety of chemical substances (Fig. 5.17). One of these is known to favor the entry of LDL into the arterial wall and permit them to accumulate there; another is a growth factor now known to accelerate the growth of the muscle cells within the arterial wall. Once thought to be only an accumulation of fatty substances, the lumps of atherosclerosis are now known to include masses of tumors consisting of overgrown smooth muscle cells. Furthermore, when tissue cells are damaged, calcium often enters dying cells and hardens the lumpy masses.

Do we know enough about the rise and decline of lumpy lesions to recommend treatment or preventive measures? It's difficult to get rig-

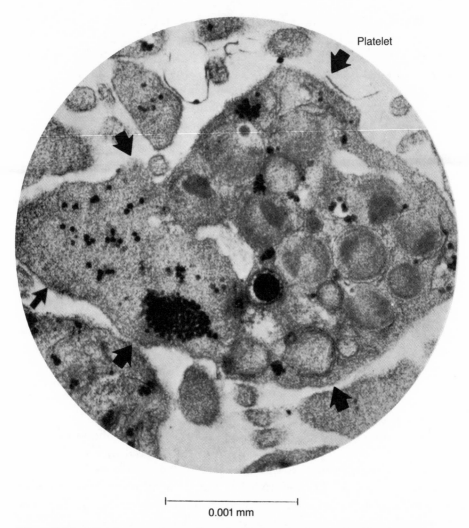

Platelet

0.001 mm

Figure 5.17. Platelets are the smallest of cells that circulate in the blood. Long
known to be important in stopping bleeding from capillaries by physically plugging
holes in these small vessels, and in blood clotting by releasing a chemical substance
that favors blood coagulation, cell biologists and chemists are now finding additional
roles for these inconspicuous cells. A look at the internal structure of human platelets
(magnified 50,000 times by an electron microscope) shows it to be a complex chemical
factory and storehouse containing many substances still to be identified. Arrows show
the boundaries of the platelet.

orous proof that regimen X, Y, or Z will prolong a patient's life or reduce or eliminate his chances of getting severe atherosclerosis, because this requires carrying out well-controlled, long-term studies, with strict adherence of the participants to a prescribed course. For example, even the dramatic bypass operation that replaces clogged coronary arteries with healthy veins has been validated only for its short-term effects and no one knows yet how long these substitute tubes or vessels will function. The first coronary artery bypass operations were performed in 1968, and then they were only a few. It takes ten years to find out how many bypasses are still open after ten years. It takes years to learn whether, in those patients whose transplanted vein remains open, atherosclerosis develops in smaller branches beyond the site of repair. It takes careful planning of cooperative studies to learn objectively whether patients who have had a bypass operation feel better and live longer than similar patients who declined the operation. And with new materials and techniques being introduced each year, objective evaluation of the need and usefulness of the basic procedure becomes more and more difficult. All of this means that we still don't have all the answers on the uniform effectiveness and long-term cost of these very expensive procedures.

Life would be very much simpler for the clinical investigator if there were a simple, safe, inexpensive, repeatable test (such as the measurement of blood pressure) to determine the size of one or more atherosclerotic lumps in living patients subjected to different types of diets, drugs, or other procedures. Such tests are on the way; one includes obtaining images of the artery in question without the use of X rays, another uses X rays to determine the size and shape of small fatty lesions in skin or tendons that closely resemble the atherosclerotic lumps in arterial walls.

Drug therapy to reduce high cholesterol levels to normal is now a possibility. Recently John Kane and Richard Havel in San Francisco have shown for the first time that in patients with inherited high levels of blood cholesterol, a combination of two drugs can decrease very high levels not by 20 or 30%, but all the way down to normal: One drug is colestipol, a substance that binds bile acids and increases their excretion; the other is niacin (nicotinic acid), long known to be the antipellagra vitamin, but now known to have the unrelated action of decreasing high blood cholesterol levels. This combination also decreases cholesterol deposits in the Achilles tendon, another objective sign of the effectiveness of this new drug therapy. This is a beginning; it's far too early to recommend daily treatment of large groups of patients, all of whom would require the drugs for years.

Much more basic research is needed to clarify new theories and obtain agreement on the factor, or factors, that cause atherosclerosis or pave the way for it. More research is also needed to find out why 63% of our population does *not* die of clogged arteries, and why patients who have never smoked, are not obese, and exercise regularly still may have coronary artery disease. Scientists tend to study patients who *have* a disease, and not those whose defense or regulatory mechanisms have allowed them to avoid disease. Edward Jenner discovered vaccination against smallpox in 1796 because of a dairymaid who *did not* and *could not* contract the disease. When discovery reveals the cause for sure, work on how to prevent or shrink atherosclerotic plaques may eliminate the need for much of present-day vascular surgery.

6

120 / 80 or Bust?

On April 12, 1945, Franklin D. Roosevelt, three months into his fourth term as President of the United States, suddenly complained of an agonizing headache and within a minute or two became unconscious. Two hours later he was dead. The cause of his death was massive brain hemorrhage due to rupture of an artery that had been weakened by high blood pressure.

As President of the United States, he had available to him the very best physicians in civilian life as well as in the armed forces. Had they been treating him for some years? If so, why did antihypertension drugs fail to lower his blood pressure? The course of history, especially Soviet–American relations, might have been drastically altered had treatment been successful and had Roosevelt completed his fourth term as president.

Before answering these questions, let me define arterial blood pressure. The pressure in the main arteries is defined by two numbers. The higher number is the pressure measured at the peak of left ventricular contraction, when the heart has just ejected several ounces of blood through the open aortic valve into the aorta (see p. 44); it is called *systolic* pressure from the Greek verb for contract. The lower number is the pressure measured at the end of the resting period of the ventricle; during this period the aortic valve leaflets are closed, and arterial blood cannot flow back into the left ventricle and must flow forward through arteries, arterioles, and capillaries into veins; it is called *diastolic* pressure from the Greek word for dilate, because during its resting phase, the relaxed left ventricle dilates as blood flows passively into it from the left atrium to load the left ventricle for its next contraction.

The normal systolic arterial blood pressure is about 120 millimeters of mercury, which means that contraction of the left ventricle has generated a pressure that can raise a column of mercury 120 millimeters (mm) in a vertical tube; the normal diastolic arterial pressure is about 80 mmHg (the chemical symbol for mercury is Hg). Medical shorthand has abbreviated all this to "normal BP = 120 / 80." Although it is confusing to their patients, physicians do not use the correct word *pressure* (which is what they measure) when it is high or low, but instead use the terms *hypertension* or *hypotension,* using *tension* in the physical meaning of a stress on the arterial wall and not in the everyday meaning of mental or nervous tension or strain.

Now back to my first question: Had Roosevelt's physicians been treating him for long? Charts containing all medical information about Roosevelt between 1932 and 1944 were stored in the U.S. Naval Hospital in Bethesda, Maryland; after his death these could not be found. However, we do know for certain the following dates and numbers for his blood pressure:

July 30, 1935	136 / 78
April 22, 1937	162 / 98
November 30, 1940	178 / 88
February 27, 1941	188 / 105
March 27, 1944	186 / 108
April 1, 1944	200 / 108
April 4, 1944	226 / 118
April 9–June 14, 1944	196 / 112*
November 18, 1944	210 / 112
November 27, 1944	260 / 150
April 1–10, 1945	170 / 88 to 240 / 130**
April 12, 1945	300 / 190

*Average.   ** Low to high.

These numbers suggest that his blood pressure was normal in 1932, when he began his first term, because by today's standards it was still within normal limits in 1935. It then rose moderately between 1935 and 1940 but was still "high normal" from 1937 to 1940 (Fig. 6.1). From that

Figure 6.1. Franklin D. Roosevelt in 1939, looking the picture of radiant good health with a blood pressure of about 162/98 to 178/88.

time on he had a fluctuating but always abnormally high blood pressure; in short, he had severe hypertension. As is usually the case in patients with mild to moderate hypertension, and often the case in patients with severe hypertension, Roosevelt had no symptoms related to his heart or circulation between 1935 and 1944. This is why hypertension is often called "the silent disease."

Now for my second question: "Why did antihypertension drugs fail to lower Roosevelt's blood pressure?" The answer is short and simple: As late as 1945 there were no effective antihypertension drugs; and it is likely that had there been one, physicians would have hesitated to use it for fear of doing serious harm. Cardiologist Edward Fries wrote, "At the time I came into the picture in 1946, drug treatment of hypertension was considered to be a foolish procedure verging on charlatanism." So in 1945, physicians did not treat hypertension itself, but only its serious complications, when these broke the silence.

What are the manifestations that demand treatment? The left ventricular muscle, when forced to develop higher pressures as the disease progresses, becomes thicker and thicker, just as the arm muscles of a weight lifter become bulkier with ever-increasing exertion. Physicians in the late 1940s looked upon such an enlarged heart with thick walls as a favorable response to a bad disease. But they also knew that long continued effort by some hearts could lead to failure of their muscle fibers and that this manifestation did require treatment.

Roosevelt had one such episode of heart muscle failure in 1944, when he was 62 years old. His physicians treated him with bed rest for one to two weeks, "avoidance of irritations and tensions of his office," digitalis (to strengthen the heart muscle), a light diet with restricted use of salt, curtailment of cigarette smoking and use of codeine to relieve cough, sedatives to ensure a good night's sleep, gradual weight reduction, and mild laxatives to avoid straining. The treatment was effective; the episode subsided in two to three weeks and Roosevelt went back to work.

High blood pressure can also manifest itself by direct damage to the patient's arteries caused by excessive stretching and a shearing force. Such injury favors the development of arterio- or atherosclerosis that narrows the channels in vital vessels (see p. 204) such as those to the heart muscle, kidneys, and brain, and can lead to such serious complications as heart attack, kidney failure, or stroke. Or it can lead to actual rupture, usually of cerebral arteries, and hemorrhage. Roosevelt had no signs of arterial damage until the final, fatal episode, the sudden bursting of a cerebral artery.

Even with his continuing hypertension, Roosevelt was not an invalid between his 1944 illness and his abrupt death in 1945. The record shows that quite the opposite was true. He made one trip to Hawaii to confer with Admirals Nimitz and Leahy and General MacArthur on strategy for winning the war against Japan. He did not go there directly, but went first to Chicago, where the 1944 Democratic National Convention was in progress. He then went on to San Diego, where he accepted the nomination for a fourth term. Instead of returning directly from Hawaii to the White House, he went first to Alaska, and then to Bremerton, Washington. In September he met with Churchill in Canada to plan a knockout blow against Japan. In October he campaigned for the presidency. In January 1945 he gave his fourth Inaugural Address and two days later set out for Malta (for conferences with his chiefs of staff and Churchill) and then went on to Yalta for the historic conference with Stalin. He returned from Yalta via Egypt, where, near Ismalia, he conferred with King Farouk of Egypt, Emperor Haile Selassie of Ethiopia, and Ibn Saud, King of Saudi Arabia, and then went to Alexandria to meet again with Churchill. So his physicians in the 1940s appear to have followed the right course, up to and including April 11, 1945, but, in hindsight, *not* on the next day, with its swift, catastrophic ending.

Today there is a vigorous, nationwide campaign to record blood pressure in every American, whether he has symptoms of severe hypertension or not, to treat vigorously everyone (a group estimated at 37 million adults) whose blood pressure is above 160 systolic or 95 diastolic, and to obtain the patient's commitment to continue treatment. Ironically, the concept of early detection and drug treatment of even slight hypertension began in the late 1940s (after Roosevelt's death) and gathered momentum in the late 1950s, when a new drug, hydrochlorothiazide (Hydrodiuril) became number one on the list of physician-prescribed drugs in the United States. The campaign to detect and attack high blood pressure is now at its peak.

Why was the answer to "Should physicians treat high blood pressure?" *no* for centuries up to the 1950s and then an emphatic *yes* thereafter? A very large number of discoveries came between the yes and the no, most of which promoted better understanding of the heart and circulation, of the forces that pumped blood, of the resistance to blood flow through small arteries, and of the mechanisms that regulated these. It's worthwhile to recount some of the events that, over several centuries, replaced ignorance with knowledge, as well as events that effectively held back progress, and of the long battle between discovery and authority. It's worthwhile if only to emphasize that knowledge and authority are not synonymous.

Measurement of Blood Pressure

It's obvious that a physician couldn't decide if treatment was worthwhile until he knew whether his patient really had high blood pressure. That meant that he had to be able to measure pressure in arteries, and not just once, but repeatedly. True, for ages physicians had felt the patient's pulse at his wrist and labeled it hard or soft, but *knowing* that a patient's blood pressure is high and that it is getting higher or lower means knowing numbers—the systolic and diastolic blood pressures. Until the early 1700s, no one had ever *measured* arterial blood pressure, in man or in any other animal. Then an English clergyman, Stephen Hales, was the first to make precise measurements of blood pressure. He probably made the first of these in 1707, on a variety of animals, with the help of a good friend, William Stukeley, while both were at Cambridge; Hales was a divinity student and Stukeley a medical student. But in 1709 Hales became perpetual curate in the parish of Teddington and lived there for the remainder of his eighty-three years; in this quiet, out-of-the-way parish on the Thames (now a residential section southwest of London), he continued, by himself, to make his remarkable measurements.

Why did a clergyman measure blood pressure? He wasn't a physician; he wasn't especially interested in medicine or in the heart or circulation. He was interested in knowledge for the sake of knowledge; his was undirected research, not goal directed, not mission oriented, and not applied. What he really wanted to learn was what governs the flow of fluids—in particular, what makes sap rise from the bottom to the top of a tree. But initially he couldn't figure out a way to get an answer. While pondering on sap and trees, he decided to measure the rise of sap in animals, the vertical height to which the heart could pump arterial blood (Fig. 6.2). In a typical experiment, he tied a brass tube into a main artery of an animal, usually a horse, then connected the other end of the brass tube to a long glass tube; he used nature's accordion tubing, the flexible windpipe of a goose, as the connector. He then held the glass tube vertically and allowed arterial blood to rise in it. How long a tube would he need? For a pressure of 200 mmHg of blood, he would need a tube 200×13.6 (the specific gravity of mercury) or 2,720 millimeters, which is about 9 feet long.

With this tube he learned many things. He learned, of course, how

Figure 6.2.   Reverend Stephen Hales and an assistant measuring blood pressure in a horse in the early 1700s. (Hales' book, *Vegetable Staticks* contains numerous original illustrations, but his *Haemastaticks* has none. This illustration was drawn by Elizabeth Cuzzort for *Medical Times* in 1941 after she found pictures of Hales' house and church, did considerable research on eighteenth century apparel, and read carefully Hales' written description of his experiments.)

high the blood went up the tube, but he also saw it bounce up and down with systole and diastole, and he saw the effects of deep breathing, struggling, and discomfort. He also removed ounce by ounce 17 quarts of blood and saw the horse's blood pressure fall from 8 feet 3 inches to 2 feet 4 inches high. He measured the pressure in the great veins and in the pulmonary artery, the volume of the cavity of the left and of the right ventricle, and the volume and velocity of blood ejected from the heart during each beat. Not bad for a clergyman interested in botany! He also made measurements and calculations on the total area of all the tiny air sacs in the lungs of a calf and figured it as 150 square feet, or ten times the body surface. (Today we believe this area, calculated for an adult man, to be five to seven times greater, but Hales' was a remarkably good 1720 estimate.)

But Hales really wanted to measure the rise of sap in plants. In 1720, quite by accident, he cut off a stem of a vine too near its "bleeding" time. He bandaged it by tying a piece of bladder tightly over the cut stem, but he found that instead of stopping the oozing, the bladder became more and more tightly distended. Now he knew that he could get actual numbers by attaching his long glass tubes, designed to measure blood pressure, to the cut stems and measuring how high the sap rose in them (Fig. 6.3). He then went on to determine the factors controlling the flow of sap, including transpiration ("perspiration" through leaves) and root pressure. Serendipity? Yes, but as Horace Walpole originally defined the word. Incidentally, because sap rose very much higher in tall plants and vines than blood did in a tube in an animal's artery, Hales had to devise mercury-filled U-tubes to measure sap pressure. So an eighteenth century clergyman made two great scientific discoveries: one of fundamental importance to botany and the other of fundamental importance to medicine and physiology. Hales also taught us that great discoveries come in unexpected ways, and from unexpected professions and disciplines, and that they come even without a request from a royal Task Force or commission appointed by the King. Some have called him the most important English scientist of the eighteenth century.

About a hundred years elapsed between Harvey's discovery of the circulation of the blood and Hales' measurement of arterial blood pressure, and another hundred years passed before the latter was widely adopted in physiological laboratories throughout Europe and England. Harvey's discovery met with bitter opposition for forty or fifty years;

Hales' did not—it simply was not put to use. Why not? Maybe it was because his "laboratory" was the great outdoors, which could accomodate tubes 9 feet high, whereas others worked indoors, in rooms with ceilings. Maybe physiologists didn't read Hales' *Vegetable Staticks,* in which he described his *mercury* manometer. In 1828 a French medical student, Jean Léonard Marie Poiseuille, popularized the use of the mercury manometer and U-tube. Was he interested in hypertension? No, he simply wanted to know where the resistance to blood flow was in the circulation of animals and, especially, whether there was really a considerable resistance to flow through a normal aorta from its beginning at the left ventricle to its end in the lower abdomen. All good physiologists in 1825 claimed that there was; Poiseuille thought otherwise. To prove his view, he needed good instruments to measure blood pressure—good manometers. If the aorta offered resistance to blood flow, blood pressure should decrease along the aorta. It was obvious to Poiseuille that a 9-foot glass tube was a pretty inconvenient and fragile instrument for measuring blood pressure in an indoor laboratory that had a ceiling only 7 feet high. Whether he "invented" or rediscovered it, he used mercury in a U-tube and calculated that he could reduce the tube length to 1/13.6 of 9 feet and have a manageable, 8-inch, portable instrument. His

Figure 6.3. Hales' drawing of a measurement of the rise of sap in limbs of a tree. Here one long limb, bent to a horizontal position, has a manometer (a U-tube containing mercury) tied into each of three branches.

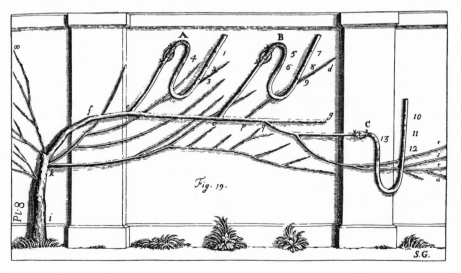

U-tube mercury manometer was used to measure blood pressure for the next 100 years in every student laboratory in Europe and America; this is why we record arterial blood pressure in millimeters of mercury instead of feet and inches of blood. Poiseuille found blood pressure to be almost identical at the beginning and at the end of the aorta in a supine animal, and so proved that there was no measurable resistance in the aorta. This meant that normally the main resistance to arterial blood flow had to be in the small arterioles; as we shall see later, this was a key finding in devising treatment of high blood pressure. He then went on to formulate a law governing the resistance to flow of liquids through such small vessels. Esoteric? Not clinically useful? Perhaps, but his research introduced an instrument absolutely essential for studying the circulation, and the equally important concept of variable resistance in blood vessels.

In 1847 a German physiologist, Carl Ludwig, then professor of comparative anatomy at the University of Marburg, put a float atop Poiseuille's mercury column and added a horizontal scribe that recorded blood pressure continuously (see Fig. 6.4). In this way he obtained continuous curves: The variations in height measured ups and downs in blood pressure, and the horizontal distance measured time. This was the beginning of moving pictures of blood pressure; it enabled Ludwig to record on paper and then analyze carefully and at length continuous tracings of systolic and diastolic blood pressure and heart rate, instead of depending upon visual memory of rapidly changing pressures and heart rate. Of course, it also provided permanent records of changes in blood pressure that occurred when he stimulated nerves or injected drugs into the circulation, records that are essential in a study of factors that regulate heart rate and blood pressure.

Like Hales', Ludwig's contributions to medical science were many. In 1865 he became professor of physiology at the University of Leipzig and director of its new Physiological Institute. There he collected a group of brilliant students who, with Ludwig, formulated the first concept of how the kidney separates urine from blood flowing through that organ, learned the location of nerve centers in the brainstem that regulate heart rate and blood pressure, devised an instrument to measure blood flow to organs, perfused isolated organs with defibrinated blood (see p. 59), and discovered sensory nerve endings in the beginning of the aorta that regulated the level of arterial blood pressure.

Actually, as cardiovascular physiologists became more sophisti-

Figure 6.4. Ludwig's blood pressure recorder (1847). An artery is connected at (A) to a manometer that is identical to Poiseuille's original instrument. Arterial blood pressure pushes mercury downward in column B and upward in column C. A light float with an attached vertical wire rests on top of the mercury in column C; it rises and falls with each rise and fall of arterial blood pressure. At the top of the wire is a cross-wire or scribe (D) that rests lightly on a rotating cylinder or drum (E) covered with paper blackened with a coat of soot. The blood pressure (in mmHg) at any moment is the distance in millimeters of the scribe above 0, times 2, because the total column of mercury supported by the blood pressure is the distance between the top of the mercury in both sides of the U-tube. Simple gears (F) put in motion by gravity rotate the drum at a constant speed. The scribe makes a continuous white line by scratching away the soot; the paper is then removed and varnished to be made into a permanent record (see the portion of a record mounted above the drum).

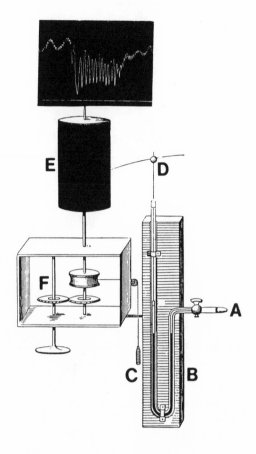

cated, Poiseuille's mercury manometer became an unsatisfactory instrument for research, though it has always remained the standard against which all new manometers must be tested for accuracy. The problem with using mercury for *research* on blood pressure was that a column of mercury has mass and inertia and therefore can't move quickly enough to record the true systolic peak and true diastolic trough of blood pressure, data needed to measure the dynamics of cardiac contraction. Scores of new manometers were devised in the nineteenth century for use in animals and even a few for use in humans. Some of those for humans were simply impractical, some gave inconsistent numbers, some yielded very consistent numbers that were incorrect, and some were pretty good instruments.

But the direct methods of measuring pressure used in the laboratory require inserting a needle or tube into an artery ("invading" the body), and even though we now have a wide variety of elegant and accurate devices for measuring blood pressure in man, through a needle, tube, or catheter in an artery or in the heart, these are also "invasive." None could be used routinely or repeatedly on every patient in a physician's office to follow the course of the disease and the effects of treatment on blood pressure. Something else had to be devised.

Finally, in 1896, Scipioni Riva-Rocci, a physician in Turin, Italy, learned how to make accurate and reproducible measurements of human *systolic* blood pressure with a wide, inflatable arm cuff. His goal was practical: to learn more about diagnosis, prognosis, and progression of cardiovascular disease. What Riva-Rocci did was inflate a rubber cuff around the upper arm (measuring the cuff pressure all the while) to find the pressure on the outside of the brachial artery that would just obstruct it completely and stop arterial blood flow to the lower arm so that he could no longer feel a pulse in the artery at the wrist. This pressure he considered to be systolic blood pressure.

Riva-Rocci's was a long report that gave full credit to everyone who preceded him (a rare happening in those days). He even apologized for not having seen earlier Rabinowitz's modification of Basch's instrument:

Not until my apparatus already had been completed did I become aware of the modification, my ignorance of it being the consequence of my unfortunate habit of not keeping up with the literature on a subject before I undertake new ventures. I hope the reader will forgive me on the score of the vastness and diffusion of the current literature on any given subject.

Note his dismay at being unable to keep abreast of the vast literature—in 1896! The immensity of the scientific "literature" (a euphemism for anything published in a scientific journal or book) and the impossibility of a scientist reading enough of it to keep up-to-date has been commented on frequently. Riva-Rocci's comment was written in Italy in 1896. Here is a sample from America:

In modern times, the constituent branches of medical science are so expanded that they are not acquired by any physician in a lifetime, and still less by a student in medical school. The same is true even of many individual branches. We do not believe that 'a scheme of scientific instruction should embrace the whole science and no part shall be omitted', nor that 'a well-digested plan of lectures should embrace all that is known'. Medical science has at this day become so unwieldy and contains so much that is unnecessary—at least to beginners—that the attempt to explain to students the whole, is likely to result in their learning but little.

This was dated July 10, 1850, and is an excerpt from the *Report on Medical Education* by the medical faculty of Harvard University; signers include the name of Oliver W. Holmes, professor of anatomy and physiology.

Here is another sample, this one from England:

The multitudinous facts presented by each corner of Nature form in large part the scientific man's burden today, and restrict him more and more, willy-nilly, to a narrower and narrower specialism. But that is not the whole of his burden. Much that he is forced to read consists of records of defective experiments, confused statement of results, wearisome description of detail, and unnecessarily protracted discussion of unnecessary hypotheses. The publication of such matter is a serious injury to the man of science; it absorbs the scanty funds of his libraries, and steals away his poor hours of leisure.

Dated 1899, it is an excerpt from the presidential address to the British Association by Professor John Langley, owner and editor of the *Journal of Physiology*.

But back to the measurement of blood pressure in man. In 1905, Nikolai Korotkoff of Leningrad (Fig. 6.5), using only a single paragraph (written in Russian), told his readers how to measure both systolic and diastolic pressures in humans. Korotkoff proposed listening to sounds instead of feeling a pulse or lack of it:

The sleeve [cuff] of Riva-Rocci is placed on the middle ⅓ of the arm toward the shoulder [Fig. 6.6]. The pressure in the sleeve is raised quickly until it stops the circulation of the blood beyond the sleeve. Thereupon, permitting the mercury in the manometer to drop, a child's stethoscope [to match the diameter of the artery] is used to listen to the artery directly beyond the sleeve. At first no audible sound is heard at all. As the mercury in the manometer falls to a certain height the first short tones appear, the appearance of which indicates the passage of part of the pulse wave under the sleeve. Consequently, the manometer reading at which the first tones appear corresponds to the maximum pressure. With a further fall of the mercury in the manometer, systolic pressure murmurs are heard which change again to a sound (secondary). Finally, all sounds disappear. The time at which the sounds disappear indicates a free passage of the pulse wave; in other words, at the moment the sounds disappear, the minimum blood pressure in the artery exceeds the pressure of the sleeve. Consequently, the reading of the manometer at this time corresponds to the minimum blood pressure.

Figure 6.5. Korotkoff, pioneer
vascular surgeon, was the first to
devise a method to measure systolic
and diastolic blood pressure in man
simply, accurately, and repeatedly.

Korotkoff devised this method because he needed it for a specific use in his surgical practice. He was one of a new crop of vascular surgeons who were accustomed to using a stethoscope to determine whether a mass was solid tissue or a locally distended artery full of swirling blood (an aneurysm). He decided that he could also be more accurate by listening with a stethoscope than by feeling a pulse in another situation: when a tourniquet around a limb had completely shut off blood flow through the artery under it. As he put it,

The absence of pulsations in the peripheral vessels is not indicative of the fact that the artery is completely occluded, its channel obliterated. In this respect, our hearing is a better guide. . . . Immediately below a completely compressed artery (with obliteration of the channel) no sounds are heard. As soon as the first drops of blood escape from under the site of pressure, we hear a clapping sound very distinctly. This sound is heard when the compressed artery is released, and even before the appearance of pulsation in the peripheral branches. Hence, whenever I had to shut off a vessel, I proceeded with auscultation of the artery immediately below the site of pressure in order to check the compression and found [it] extremely useful for this purpose.

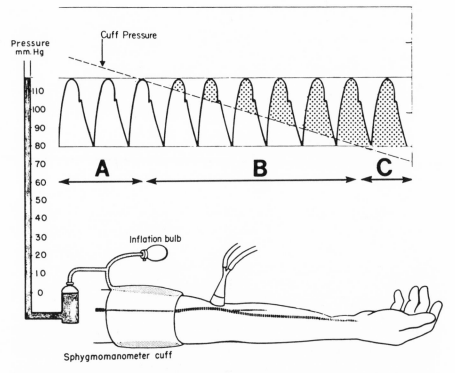

Figure 6.6. The principle of Korotkoff's method. A cuff around the patient's upper arm is inflated to a pressure well above the patient's systolic blood pressure. At this time (A), the physician listening with a stethoscope over the artery just below the cuff hears no sounds because no blood flows past the cuff. He then gradually decreases the pressure in the cuff. When it falls below systolic pressure in the artery (B), blood at peak pressure pushes past the cuff (see shaded areas) and sets the arterial wall into vibration at each beat, which can be heard using the stethoscope. When cuff pressure falls below diastolic pressure (C), blood flow is now continuous in the artery and sounds disappear.

At any rate, it took an Englishman, a Frenchman, a German, an Italian, and a Russian 172 years to go from the measurement of blood pressure in a horse to accurate measurement of systolic and diastolic blood pressure in man. But at last physicians no longer "measured" blood pressure by deciding whether the pulse at the wrist was hard or soft, and how hard and how soft. In 1905 physicians could obtain actual numbers for blood pressure, numbers that allowed the study of hypertension to become a science. Even though the *British Medical Journal* in that same year argued that by using these new devices "we pauperize our senses and weaken clinical acuity," the new method began to be used widely.

Hypertension: A New Disease

Why, with physiologists in every university in Europe, Great Britain, and America measuring blood pressure daily in their laboratories, had there not been an insistent demand for a device that clinicians could use day in and day out on their patients? Probably because leading physicians and pathologists in the nineteenth century were convinced that it was unwise and indeed dangerous to lower abnormally high blood pressure. This dogma was due in large part to the first description, in 1836, of a severe kidney disease, by Dr. Richard Bright of Guy's Hospital in London. The disease, soon to be called "Bright's disease," was fatal; autopsies in 100 patients showed hard, contracted kidneys and in more than half the wall of the left ventricle of the heart was thick. Because about two-thirds of those with large hearts had no disease of their heart valves that might have caused the heart to work harder and its walls to become thicker, Bright attributed the enlarged heart to disease of blood vessels in the kidneys. As Bright put it, the kidney disease "so affects the minute and capillary circulation, as to render greater [cardiac] action necessary to force blood through the distant subdivisions of the vascular system."

In 1856 Ludwig Traube, a leading German pathologist, confirmed Bright's findings and advanced the concept that the increased cardiac work was nature's way of compensating for diseased and narrowed blood vessels in the kidneys: The heart produced a higher aortic blood pressure and this pushed more blood through the kidney, permitting the kidney to form enough urine to excrete the body's waste products and so keep the patient alive, in other words, the high blood pressure was "essential" for life. In 1877 Julius Cohnheim, another prestigious German pathologist, promoted Traube's "compensatory hypertension" theory in his text on pathology. This is a classic instance of great authorities, "Geheimrats," in this case pathologists, holding back medical progress by their authoritative pronouncements (that happened to be wrong!). It's a particularly informative instance, because Traube is recognized as the founder of experimental pathology in Germany and it was he who published the first journal that reported only results obtained by the new experimental method.

And so physicians accepted a hard pulse as indicative of hypertension and the notion that this was nature's way to compensate for Bright's disease. This meant accepting the dogma that only harm could result from meddling with blood pressure. If some nonbeliever had the courage to lower blood pressure in a patient with a "hard pulse" to see whether he got better or worse, he had no effective, harmless procedure available to test his conviction. So hypertension was considered to be the hero whose task was to defeat the villain, Bright's disease, and it didn't make sense to physicians to eliminate the hero when there was no other to take over.

But patients with Bright's disease did die and physicians could not have regarded compensatory hypertension as a *cure*. Yet when the patient's heart was strong and didn't fail when forced to work harder, high blood pressure could prolong his life. When a nineteenth century patient had a hard pulse and a large heart, his physician regarded him as being pretty fortunate.

When physicians were convinced that a hard pulse equalled high blood pressure, that it occurred only in patients with Bright's disease, and that nothing could be done about that disease, there was no urgency to measure blood pressure in their patients. Thomas Huxley said that the great tragedy of science was the slaying of a beautiful hypothesis by an ugly fact. Sir William Gull and Henry Sutton in London in 1872 and Frederick Mohamed, a resident medical officer at Guy's Hospital in 1874, supplied the ugly fact. They described patients who in life had "hard" pulses and at autopsy had marked enlargement of the left ventricle but neither obstruction of their aortic heart valve (which might have made the heart work harder) nor kidney disease. So hypertension could occur either along with kidney disease (to be discussed later) or in patients with perfectly healthy kidneys. At last, hypertension could be studied as a disease all by itself. And when Riva-Rocci and Korotkoff devised a simple, repeatable, painless, and harmless method for measuring blood pressure in man, they made it possible to study the prevalence of this new disease—high blood pressure—in the population and to chart its natural history.

Theodore Janeway, a New York physician, began this gigantic task in 1903. He became involved because he believed "that neither clinical studies of nearly a century nor experimental investigation of nearly half a century had succeeded in elucidating the real cause of hypertension." Why did Janeway succeed? In part, let me answer as my professor of obstetrics did when I, as a student, asked him why pregnancy lasted 9 months instead of 8 or 10. He gave a succinct answer: "When an apple is ripe, it falls." The cuff made the time ripe for Janeway. Furthermore, he and his father had a large private practice and didn't need to depend upon other physicians. They had 7,872 patients between 1903 and 1912, and the younger Janeway measured systolic blood pressure in each one. Because Korotkoff's method was not published until 1905 and because physicians modified criteria for determining diastolic blood pressure every few years for a while, Janeway reported only his measurements of systolic pressure. He found that at one time or another, more than one in nine had a systolic blood pressure of 165 mmHg or more (he decided that a pressure greater than 160 mmHg was abnormally high). He preferred not to tackle the question whether high blood pressure causes cardiovascular changes or results from them. However, he did give the disorder the dignity of a unifying name. He wrote, "The most prominent symptoms associated with high blood pressure are circulatory rather than renal. The disease underlying high arterial pressure is predominantly a disease of the circulatory system, and is best designated hypertensive cardiovascular disease." He also noted that the average duration of life, after patients developed *symptoms* associated with high blood pressure, was 4–5 years. Major causes of death were heart failure, kidney failure, stroke, and angina pectoris.

What effect did Janeway's mammoth study have on the treatment of hypertension? Immediately, not much. Some of the great physicians were still more impressed by how long a few patients could live with very high blood pressure than by how much it shortened the life-span of most. Janeway himself wrote that he had one patient with a systolic blood pressure of 280 for more than ten years. Dr. James Paullin, later to become one of Roosevelt's physicians, wrote in 1926 that he had a patient who lived for seventeen years with a blood pressure that never fell below 200 mmHg. Philadelphia's Dr. David Reisman pointed out in 1931 that, though high blood pressure is not conducive to longevity and on the whole is no blessing, he cared for a patient from age 72 to 97 years whose blood pressure ranged between 220 and 274. Alex Burgess of Providence wrote as late as 1948,

It is quite evident that an elevated systolic pressure is not, of itself, an unfavorable prognostic sign. Five patients in whom a reading of over 300 was recorded on one or more occasions actually showed an average duration of life slightly in excess of the normal.

And physicians were not impressed by the efficacy of available treatment. Boston's Soma Weiss believed that hypertension should be moderated only slightly if at all lest blood flow to vital organs become inadequate. Reisman was not enthusiastic about drugs; in life-threatening episodes he recommended (1931) that three leeches be applied to the bone behind the ear as "an almost sovereign remedy."

A look into two of the highly respected American texts of medicine of that era, Sir William Osler's and Russell Cecil's, shows that each did have a section on arterio- (or athero-) sclerosis and that each did state that hypertension favors the development of arteriosclerosis and heart failure; however, neither had much to say about *treating* hypertension. Osler's 1919 edition (the last that he wrote himself) still had no separate section on hypertension; he mentioned it under arteriosclerosis, as a cause of it. Cecil's first edition (1927) had no separate section on hypertension and didn't mention its treatment. The second edition (1930) did; it recommended as treatment "physical and mental rest," "physiotherapy," "phenobarbital—[but] drugs are disappointing."

It seems that two major studies were still needed to convince the medical profession that hypertensive patients should be treated and treated vigorously. One was needed to settle, once and for all, whether hypertensive patients met with disaster if they *were* treated vigorously enough to decrease their blood pressure; the other was needed to determine the added risk to patients if they were *not* treated.

Treating Hypertension with Neurosurgery

For real progress in treatment, someone had to prove that one could lower blood pressure in a severely hypertensive patient without making him worse and hastening his death. There was one form of hypertension—*malignant* hypertension—that progressed rapidly toward death, and clinicians could do nothing for patients with it. Because the patient with malignant hypertension and his neurosurgeon could lose nothing but might find a cure or at least a beginning toward effective treatment, neurosurgeons decided to try to lower blood pressure in patients with "incurable" malignant hypertension. But why a neurosurgeon?

The rationale for a neurosurgical approach was established in 1851 and 1852 by two French physiologists, working quite independently of each other and neither looking for a treatment for human hypertension. They were interested in the role of the sympathetic nervous system in narrowing and widening small arteries (more later on about the sympathetic nervous system). Claude Bernard observed in 1851 that cutting the sympathetic nerves to the ear of a rabbit led immediately to increased warmth of that ear, visible dilation of blood vessels of the ear, and the appearance of new vessels not previously visible. A rabbit's ear is ideal for this study because it is thin—almost translucent—and blood vessels can be seen and measured while shining a light through the ear.

In 1817, an American sailing ship called at Mauritius, lately ceded by France to Britain. It carried a sailor named Brown, who fell in love with and married a local girl named Séquard. Mr. Brown sailed away and he and his ship were lost in the Pacific. His son, whom he had never seen, was destined to become one of the most remarkable medical scientists of the last century. His name was Charles Edouard Brown-Séquard. Like Benjamin Franklin, the New World's foremost scientist, he was equally at home in America, England, and France. Indeed, for a while Brown-Séquard was a professor of physiology at the Medical College of Virginia, then a professor of physiology and pathology at Harvard, and later professor of experimental medicine at the University of Paris. In London he was physician to the National Hospital in Queen's Square and a Fellow of the Royal Society. Brown-Séquard confirmed Bernard's observations and added some of his own. In 1852, Brown-Séquard reported in an American journal, *The Medical Examiner and Record of Medical Science,* that

if galvanism [direct electric current] is applied to the upper portion of the sympathetic nerve trunk after it has been cut in the neck [which in itself dilates blood vessels], the vessels of the face and of the ear after a certain time begin to contract; their contraction increases slowly, but at last it is evident that they resume their normal condition, if they are not even smaller. Then the temperature and the sensibility diminish in the face and the ear, and they become in the palsied side the same as in the sound side.

When the galvanic current ceases to act, the vessels begin to dilate again, and all the phenomena discovered by Dr. Bernard reappear.

I conclude, that the only direct effect of the section [cutting across] of the cervical part of the sympathetic, is the paralysis and consequently the dilatation of the blood vessels. Another evident conclusion is, that the cervical sympathetic sends motor nerve fibres to many of the blood vessels of the head.

Poiseuille had already studied the effect of narrowing arterioles on resistance to blood flow through them and the effect of increased resistance to blood flow upon blood pressure. Now Bernard and Brown-Séquard showed that stimulation of sympathetic nerves increased resistance to blood flow.

If two renowned French physiologists provided a rational basis for severing vasoconstrictor nerves, it was two equally renowned British physiologists who supplied the exquisite anatomical detail required for precise and correct surgical procedures on sympathetic nerves; again, neither was involved in research on human hypertension.

The first was Walter Gaskell at Cambridge, who in 1887 tackled the anatomy and function of the autonomic nervous system on a grand scale. The autonomic nervous system (from the Greek *autonomos*, "self-governing") has two separate parts, the sympathetic and the parasympathetic systems. Fibers in these systems originate in the brain and either enter nerves within the cranium or go down the spinal cord to be distributed to involuntary muscles and glands throughout the body. Voluntary muscles are those that are completely under your control. You can at will move your lips, hands, and legs (all by contraction of voluntary muscles). Involuntary muscles are different. As a rule you cannot voluntarily speed up or slow down your heart, narrow or widen blood vessels, or contract or relax bronchi or stomach or intestines (all involuntary muscles); the body is liberally supplied with sensory receptors that respond to touch, pain, stretch, chemicals such as O_2 and CO_2, and temperature, and in response to their signals can initiate appropriate reactions without your being aware of it. You also have muscles that act automatically most of the time but that you can at times control voluntarily; an example is the respiratory muscles, which usually work at a subconscious level but which you can control in such activities as holding your breath, overbreathing, singing, and talking.

The two divisions of the autonomic nervous system together govern most of our involuntary, automatic responses. Sometimes they control different territories; sometimes they affect the same organs and tissues. Here are two examples of joint control: Sympathetic nerve impulses speed the heart, whereas parasympathetic impulses slow it down; sympathetic impulses dilate bronchi, whereas parasympathetic impulses narrow them. Ideally, together these impulses create a nice balance.*

The second of the British pair, John Langley, also at Cambridge, found that he could selectively activate any part of the sympathetic nervous system by applying a weak solution of nicotine to the outside of each ganglion, and could selectively paralyze each ganglion by using a somewhat stronger solution. This enabled him to determine in living animals exactly what structures in the body received nerve fibers from each ganglion in the sympathetic nervous system, and what fibers must be cut to interrupt the flow of sympathetic nerve impulses to each. Langley didn't set out to study nicotine. He had, out of curiosity, become interested in the active ingredients of plants from distant countries. One of these was the South American Indian arrow poison curare (see p. 152); another was an Australian plant chewed by the natives; its active principle was piturine, which Langley later found to be almost identical in action to nicotine.

Gaskell, without anticipating the coming of neurosurgeons, had shown that the sympathetic nerve cells were conveniently collected in ganglia *outside* the bony vertebral column (which protected the spinal cord) like a string of beads on either side of the vertebrae (Fig. 6.7), and Langley had shown which ganglia sent nerve fibers to which blood vessels. So in 1913 it occurred to the French surgeon René Leriche to cut sympathetic nerves to limbs in patients who had poor blood flow to their arms or legs, and in the same year George Crile suggested, in the *Cleveland Medical Journal*, that it was time to cut sympathetic nerves in patients with hypertension. There was now enough knowledge to make possible and to justify surgical removal of specific sympathetic nerves in patients suffering from excessive constriction of arteries or arterioles in their limbs or in their circulation in general. So it was natural that surgical treatment of hypertension preceded drug treatment.

In 1925 a team at the Mayo Clinic, physician Leonard Rowntree and surgeon Alfred Adson, decided to do something about hypertension and selected a suitable patient for removal of lumbar sympathetic gan-

---

*This chapter deals in large part with the control of blood pressure by sympathetic nerves. Parasympathetic ganglia (not discussed here) are scattered throughout our viscera, buried in the tissue or organs they control. This main parasympathetic nerve, the vagus (vagabond or wanderer), is preganglionic and sends its fibers to clusters of ganglia in almost every tissue in the thorax, abdomen, and pelvic region. The vagus nerve does not enter the spinal cord, but takes its own path from the brain.

glia. Fully recognizing that the proposed operation was entirely experimental in man, the patient displayed great enthusiasm, stating that he was willing to undergo any procedure that offered hope of permanent or even temporary relief. The patient felt better and his blood pressure was lower for some months after the operation. Rowntree noted, "There was no change in volume or composition of urine; certainly the efficiency of the kidney was in no way impaired." Adson's next paper (1934) gave a follow-up on the 1925 experience and mentioned that the ultimate "results on blood pressure and ultimate outcome were not significant." The important result was, of course, that a period of lowered blood pressure did the patient *no harm*.

In the same year, Irvine Page, then at the Rockefeller Institute in New York City, entered the hypertension field and shattered the century-old dogma. It was fortunate for hypertensive patients that Page, after three years as head of the chemistry division of the Kaiser Wilhelm

Figure 6.7. A segment of the sympathetic nervous system. This illustration shows that sympathetic nerves coming from the brain run down the spinal cord (protected by bony vertebrae) but emerge to form their own "chains of ganglia" (a ganglion is a collection of nerve cells). There are two such chains running just outside the bony vertebrae—one on each side of the vertebrae and parallel to them—from the top of the thorax to the bottom of the abdomen. This figure shows only two of the vertebrae and three sympathetic ganglia related to them (of a total of fifteen ganglia on each side). It shows how Gaskell and then Langley could study sympathetic ganglia because of their accessibility, how neurosurgeons could remove several or all of the ganglia on both sides of the bony vertebrae without damaging other nerves, and how physiologists and pharmacologists could study them and learn how they transmit impulses.

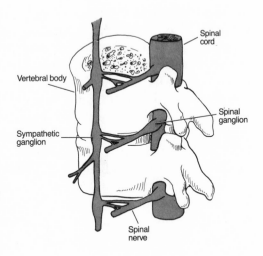

Institute, left Munich (with Hitler looming ominously on the horizon) and, in 1930, joined the associate staff of the Rockefeller Institute in New York. This was fortunate first because that institute was then the most prestigious in the United States. It was also a fortunate choice, because the institute's policy was to let its staff work on problems that each staff member thought were important. If all of the staff but one were working on infectious diseases and immunology, and that one (Page) wanted to work on blood pressure, lipids, or atherosclerosis, that was fine; the philosophy of the institute was that a good scientist shouldn't do what a committee directs, but what he himself thinks important. And the choice was also fortunate because all of the staff (clinicians and basic scientists) got together at lunch and shared their experiences, ideas, and critical judgment; this was a true learning program among scientists in many disciplines.

But most fortunate of all was that Donald Van Slyke was on the staff of the Rockefeller Institute and had just devised a urea clearance test to measure one of the functions of the kidneys. This was the golden age of renal physiology and the urea test produced the first respectable measure of renal function in man in actual numbers. Urea is a waste product of body metabolism that is carried in the blood to the kidneys to be excreted. Van Slyke's test calculated how much urea the kidney "cleared" from the blood each minute; this clearance depended in large part on how much blood flowed through the kidneys. Van Slyke's test was not a precise measurement of renal blood flow, but was the best guide available in the early 1930s.

Page rounded up six patients with hypertension. He stated the goal of the study clearly: "The object of the present investigation was to compare the efficiency of renal excretion when blood pressure was at a high level with that when it was reduced." He studied six patients whose blood pressure was initially high and then fell sharply. In two blood pressure came down spontaneously, in three he used drugs, and in one a surgeon denervated one kidney. What was responsible for the decrease in blood pressure was unimportant;* what was important was that systolic blood pressure decreased by 60, 102, 70, 100, 78, and 72 mmHg

---

*Page later remarked that "the problem was how to lower it. I was so short of means [to do so] that I used intramuscular injections of colloidal sulfur which, if I may say so, was a bit better than the extracts of mistletoe, cucumber seeds, garlic or even 'whiffless' garlic." It's hard today to believe how few useful drugs there were in the 1930s. We had not advanced very far beyond Oliver

Table 6-1. *Renal Function at High and Low Blood Pressure in Six Patients*

Patient	Diagnosis	Blood pressure[a]		Corresponding urea clearances (%)	
		High	Low		
1	Essential hypertension	210/120	150/100	63.9	69.2
2	Essential hypertension	230/124	128/88	39.8	38.3
3	Essential hypertension	290/137	220/108	42.4	60.6
4	Malignant hypertension	300/163	200/120	55.7	68.9
5	Chronic nephritis	210/106	132/80	52.5	62.1
6	Terminal Bright's disease	194/110	122/78	14.2	9.9

[a] Times between measurements of "high" and "low" values were 26, 7, 3, 8, 54, and 27 weeks, respectively.

in his six patients (see Table 6.1), but in none was there any significant change in urea clearance. He concluded, "Abnormal elevation of blood pressure in these cases does not appear to assist in maintenance of renal efficiency. This evidence does not support the compensatory theory of the cause of hypertension in patients suffering from nephritis or essential hypertension." Since it is unlike Page not to speculate on why lowering systemic arterial blood pressure did not decrease renal function, it is reasonable to assume that he must have thought at that moment of autoregulation of the circulation; he may well have mentioned this in

Wendell Holmes' memorable summary on May 30, 1860. Dr. Holmes listed the then existing weapons of life as follows:

Opium . . . a few specifics which our doctor's art did not discover . . . wine, which is a food, and the vapours which produce the miracle of anaesthesia.

As for the rest he thundered,

I firmly believe that if the whole materia medica, as now used, could be sunk to the bottom of the sea, it would be all the better for mankind—and all the worse for the fishes.

his manuscript only to have a journal editor delete it as speculation and therefore unfit for a respectable scientific journal to print! (*My* speculation).

Because lowering blood pressure in the main artery did *not* decrease renal function, obviously the small "resistance" vessels in the kidney had to dilate to maintain blood flow and preserve renal function. This phenomenon couldn't exist in cast iron pipes; it could and did exist in arterioles whose walls were not irrevocably hardened, and whose smooth muscle was alive and could relax and contract to changes in the environment (Fig. 6.8). Actually, autoregulation of the caliber of arterioles was proposed by Leonard Bayliss in 1902 as a mechanism by which small arteries could regulate blood flow through them to meet the needs of nearby tissues and cells, but his idea didn't attract much attention. Now physiologists agree that the phenomenon of "autoregulation" occurs to various degrees in all vascular beds in the body (Fig. 6.9). So the old, universally respected wisdom that lowering high blood pressure to normal would cause calamitous damage to body organs was at last discredited.

Every so often, we should stop and wonder how a young person decides to become a scientist and why he enters a particular field of science. The "oral history" (recorded on tape) has now become a popular technique for delving into the early motivations of now elder statesmen of science. I have done a bit of this myself, but I cannot erase from my memory a wondrous duet in *Gigi* in which aging Maurice Chevalier and Hermione Gingold reminisce about an early romance in "I Remember It Well." The words go as follows:

I can remember everything as if it were yesterday
We met at 9/*We met at 8*
I was on time/*No, you were late*
That dazzling April moon/*There was none that night, and the month was June*
Ah, yes . . . I remember it well.

So rather than rely completely on the memory of a senior scientist, I like to look at his first published independent effort. For Page, it was an article published in the *Journal of Biological Chemistry* in 1923, when he was a medical student. Obviously, he was interested in learning about living creatures and had this interest long before he knew about high blood pressure. The title of his article was

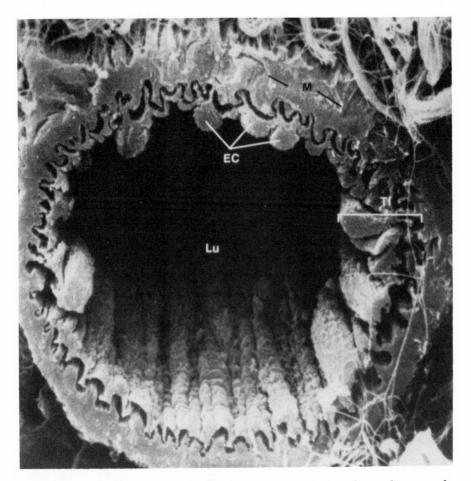

Figure 6.8. The "resistance" blood vessels. You are not looking down a long tunnel, but into an arteriole (magnified 3,915 times). The arteriole has a thin outer and inner layer, and most of the thickness of its wall consists of two or three layers of smooth (involuntary) muscle cells (M) that can contract, narrow the internal diameter of the tube, and increase resistance to blood flow. When the muscle cells relax, the internal diameter of the tube increases and resistance to blood flow decreases. The arterioles obviously are of great importance in regulating arterial blood pressure and blood flow to any organ or tissue. Their caliber can be regulated by sympathetic nerves, but also by local physical and chemical conditions (Lu, lumen or channel of arteriole; EC, inner lining of endothelial cells). (From *Tissues and Organs: A Text-Atlas of Scanning Electron Microscopy*, R. G. Kissel and R. H. Kardon. W. H. Freeman and Company. © 1979.)

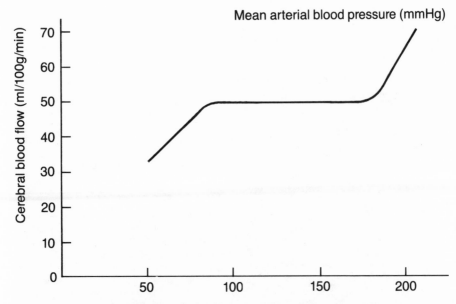

Figure 6.9. Autoregulation of blood flow to the brain. Note that blood flow to the brain changes only little as the blood pressure in arteries to the brain is varied over a range of 80–180 mmHg. This relative constancy of blood flow also occurs in the kidney and many other organs. It still occurs when all nerves to the kidney are cut, and even when the kidney is removed from the body. Therefore the control must be independent of nerves and blood-borne hormones and, accordingly, is termed "autoregulation." It is presumably due to local reaction of the small arteries (arterioles) to changes in their chemical environment or in the stretch of their walls as blood pressure rises and falls. Autoregulation stabilizes renal blood flow in the face of changes in renal arterial pressure.

ASTERIASTEROL—A NEW STEROL FROM THE STARFISH
AND THE STEROLS OF CERTAIN OTHER MARINE
ECHINODERMS.

By IRVINE H. PAGE.

(From the Lilly Research Laboratory, Woods Hole and Indianapolis.)
(Received for publication, June 11, 1923.)

And the opening sentence was

The present study was undertaken with the view to obtaining information of a chemical nature that might help to explain some of the curious differences that exist between the eggs of the starfish (*Asterias forbesi*) and other echinoderms; more especially those of the sea urchin (*Arbacia punctulata*) and sand dollar (*Echinarachnius parma*).

The title and opening sentence would have curled Senator William Proxmire's* hair, and if he had been on a peer review section of the National Institutes of Health judging an application for a research grant on sea urchins and sand dollars, surely he would have axed the proposed study on urchins as ridiculous and ludicrous and an outrageous waste of the public's money. Maybe Page would have fooled him on the sand dollars (after all, dollars *are* dollars), and research on sand dollars might have yielded clues to balance the federal budget; nothing else has. But the sea urchin man was indeed the one, ten to twelve years later, who put the treatment of hypertension on the right track for the first time and then kept in the forefront research on hypertension and its treatment for many decades; it was he who later discovered angiotensin, the most potent arteriolar constrictor known, forty times as potent as epinephrine in raising blood pressure. A lesson to be learned is to look at the man, and not the title of his project (most scientists change fields every ten or fifteen years anyway); look at the man and not for some immediate application of his work. Does he have new ideas? Does he have conviction? Is he willing to buck authority to test his ideas? Page had ideas, conviction, and persistence.

Page and the neurosurgeons had now opened wide the door to the treatment of hypertension. Who rushed through it? One would have been almost certain that it would have been research cardiologists and the big research-oriented drug companies. It wasn't; they had nothing to offer at the time. It was the neurosurgeons again: Adson once more, Heuer (with Page), Peet at Ann Arbor, Grimson in Chicago, Smithwick in Boston, Zintel in Philadelphia, and others. They started with partial removal of sympathetic nerves, then went on to almost total removal, then to total excision, and finally total excision of the sympathetic chain plus removal of the adrenal glands. The purpose of removing the adrenal glands was to eliminate the core of the gland, the part that produced adrenaline; to do this, one had also to remove the outer shell of the glands, the cortex, which produces hormones essential to life—a discovery made by Brown-Séquard in 1856. Removal of the whole gland became safe in 1934–1936, when scientists extracted, isolated, purified, and synthesized the cortical hormones so that physicians and surgeons

---

*Since 1975 U.S. Senator Proxmire has periodically given a "Golden Fleece Award" to scientists whose applications for government research grants were, in his opinion, completely irrelevant to the advance of biomedical science; that is, the scientist was fleecing the taxpayer.

could give them as substitute hormones to patients whose adrenal glands were absent or nonfunctioning.

For ten to twelve years, the neurosurgeons dominated the treatment of hypertension. They have now vanished from the hypertension scene without a trace, like the lost continent of Atlantis, but they served a useful purpose: They kept alive the knowledge that malignant hypertension was amenable to treatment and maybe even to treatment with drugs.

Treating Hypertension with Drugs

For treatment of hypertension to progress beyond surgical operations on patients with life-threatening hypertension, physicians needed less heroic measures. The answer, of course, was treatment by drugs.

In the 1980s, we have a choice not only of many drugs but of many categories of drugs: those acting to depress the sympathetic nervous system, in specific ways and to specific degrees; those acting directly on blood vessels to dilate them; those acting by increasing the excretion of salt (sodium, in particular) in the urine (diuretics, from the Greek word meaning "to increase the flow of urine"); and those acting through hormones (activating some and inactivating others).

The first group of drugs to be used clinically were those that suppressed the activity of the sympathetic nervous system. This was natural, because in the 1800s, although physicians were not greatly interested in knowledge of the circulation and the body's mechanisms for regulating blood pressure, physiologists were. Indeed, many of the very best had elected to study the heart and circulation and had uncovered a wide variety of nervous mechanisms capable of narrowing or widening arterioles, thereby increasing or decreasing resistance to blood flow through one or more parts of the body. But the real challenge came at the turn of the century with the discovery of epinephrine* (or adrenaline, as it is called in Great Britain). Epinephrine was discovered as a hormone, a substance secreted by the adrenal gland; it was named epinephrine because anatomically the adrenal gland sits on top of (*epi*) the kidney

---

*There are many names for this hormone because it was given "official" chemical names and also "trade" or "proprietary" names by the drug industry. The official British name is *adrenaline;* the official U.S. name is *epinephrine;* trade names include Adrenalin, Suprarenin, and Suprarenalin.

(*nephros*). Initially epinephrine aroused the interest of physiologists and physicians because endocrine glands were then becoming fashionable. Endocrine glands manufacture chemicals (hormones) that enter the bloodstream directly; they are not secreted through a duct into the alimentary canal as are saliva, gastric juices, and pancreatic juices. In 1885 Thomas Addison had described a disease characterized by profound weakness, and Brown-Séquard had proved it to be due to a deficiency of the adrenal gland. Then in 1882 and 1883 two surgeons in Geneva (J. and A. Reverdin, cousins) and one in Berne (Emil Kocher) studied the thyroid gland; they removed large goiters from forty-six patients and noted that they improved immediately, because the tumor masses no longer weighed down on tissues in the neck, but in a few weeks the patients began to suffer symptoms that we now know to be due to deficiency of the thyroid hormone. In 1884 Moritz Schiff removed the thyroid gland from the neck of dogs and transplanted it into the abdominal cavity; the dogs remained healthy.* In 1881 I. V. Sandström discovered the parathyroid glands, tucked away behind the much larger thyroid, and eleven years later, Eugene Gley, a French physiologist, discovered their function. Because glands were both cheap and fresh at the neighborhood butcher shop, even practicing physicians were intrigued by these organs and began to extract juices from them and do some experimental work at home or in their laboratories.

The discovery of epinephrine was first reported in the *Journal of Physiology* in a 1895 paper, forty-six pages long, by George Oliver and E. A. Schäfer. It is an erudite, highly scientific presentation; a much shorter account was given later on by Sir Henry Dale, which I like better:

In March 1894, I was still a boy, so that the story as I know it, came to me some seven years later from those who . . . were in the laboratory of the University College, London, at the time. And the story . . . was remarkable enough. . . . Dr. George Oliver, a physician of Harrogate (a summer resort) employed his winter leisure in experiments on his family, using apparatus of his own devising for clinical measurements. In one such experiment he was applying an instrument for measuring the thickness of the radial artery; and, having given his young son, who deserves a special memorial, an injection of an extract of the suprarenal adrenal gland, prepared from material supplied by the local butcher,

---

*The dogs remained healthy because capillaries grew into the thyroid gland in its new location and the gland was again able to secrete its hormones into circulating blood, just as it had in its original location.

Oliver thought that he detected a contraction or, according to some who have transmitted the story, an expansion of the radial artery. Whichever it was, he went up to London to tell Professor Schäfer what he thought he had observed, and found him engaged in an experiment in which the blood pressure of a dog was being recorded; found him, not unnaturally, incredulous about Oliver's story and very impatient at the interruption. But Oliver was in no hurry, and urged only that a dose of his suprarenal extract, which he produced from his pocket, should be injected into a vein when Schäfer's own experiment was finished. And so, just to convince Oliver that it was all nonsense, Schäfer gave the injection, expecting a triumphant demonstration of nothing, and found himself, like some watcher of the skies when a new planet swims into "his ken" watching the mercury rise in the manometer [see Fig. 6.10] with surprising rapidity and to an astounding height, until one wonders whether the float will

Figure 6.10.   Oliver and Schäfer (1895) injected an extract of adrenal glands and measured the effect on blood pressure in the femoral (hind leg) artery of an anesthetized dog. The tracing of the historic first injection described by Sir Henry Dale was not published in the 1895 report, but the authors state in their text, "The blood pressure may mount up to a height of from 2 to 5 times or more that which it had originally: indeed, even although we have employed an exceptionally long manometer, in more than one instance the mercury has been entirely driven out from the open end of the tube." In this figure, blood pressure rose from 52 (at A) to 208 mmHg (at B). This blood pressure tracing (obtained using Ludwig's mercury manometer; see Fig. 6.4) is a narrow band because the weight and inertia of mercury dampened the peak of the systolic pressure and raised the trough of diastolic pressure (except in a few sections, such as at C, when the heart rate was very slow). The white strip at the bottom left indicates the time of the injection.

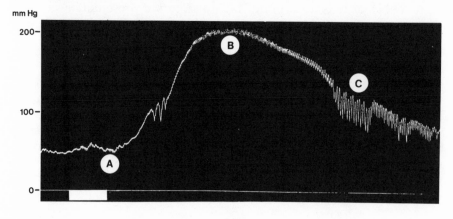

be thrust right out of the peripheral limb. So the discovery was made of the extraordinary active principle of the suprarenal gland, later found to come only from the medulla [the core] of the gland, and still later obtained as a pure, crystalline substance and variously named epinephrine or adrenalin.

Chemical Transmission of Nerve Impulses

The real importance of epinephrine was not that it could be used clinically to raise low blood pressure, but that it led to a completely new concept of the transmission of nerve impulses from the brain to all ramifications of the sympathetic nervous system. It overturned the age-old belief that nerve impulses from brain to tissue cells speed, without interruption, by an *electrical process*. Thanks to the discovery of epinephrine, and later of acetylcholine, we now know that there are two gaps in what was considered a continuous line: one where the nerve impulse arrives at an autonomic ganglion and another where the impulse arrives at its target cell. At these gaps, the nerve impulse is carried forward not by electric "sparks," but by the liberation of chemical transmitters. *Why* this is important in the treatment of hypertension will be discussed later; first, let us see *how* the discovery was made.

The synthesis of epinephrine as a pure chemical led to extensive study of the action of this hormone on all cells and tissues of the body and the remarkable finding that epinephrine had one and only one invariable characteristic: It acted solely on the heart, involuntary muscle, and glands "that are, or have been, in functional union with sympathetic nerve fibers." Thomas Elliott, then a graduate student in physiology at Cambridge, did a comprehensive study and published a 66-page report in 1904 that demonstrated tissue by tissue and organ by organ that whatever action epinephrine had on these, electrical stimulation of sympathetic nerves to each had the same effect, in the same direction, and, with few exceptions, to about the same degree.

In short, if epinephrine relaxed an involuntary muscle, so did stimulation of sympathetic nerves to that muscle; if epinephrine constricted it, so did sympathetic nerve stimulation; if epinephrine action was powerful, so was that of sympathetic nerve stimulation; if epinephrine action was weak, so was that of sympathetic nerve stimulation. To Elliott, such correspondence was not a coincidence but had a deeper meaning, that "adrenaline might then be the chemical stimulant liberated on each occasion when the [nerve] impulse arrives at the periphery." This was not the age-old concept of Galen, that nerves were hollow tubes and that a fluid or humor ran from the brain down to a terminal fiber and then acted on adjacent tissue; it was an entirely new concept, because the rapidity of nerve action demanded that epinephrine always be present and readily available at the finest nerve endings and be liberated almost instantaneously at the precise point where nerve is almost one with involuntary muscle cells, gland tissue, or heart muscle. If Elliott was right, then the universally accepted theory that conduction and transmission were electrical events from head to toe had to undergo radical revision to allow for a *chemical* (or chemicals) transferring or transmitting a nerve impulse whenever there was a gap to be jumped, even if it was only 0.000005 millimeter wide.

Elliott's observations applied only to the sympathetic nerve endings. What about endings in the other division of the autonomic nervous system, the parasympathetic nerves? Let Sir Henry Dale, later to become a Nobel laureate, tell the beginning of the story:

About 1913, an accidental observation of the unusual activity of a particular extract of ergot [a fungus which occasionally replaces the grain in rye] quickened anew my interest in phenomena suggesting a chemical, pharmacodynamic transmission of excitation at the junctional contacts between nerve-endings and cells. What was supposed to be an ordinary liquid extract of ergot had been sent to me [then working in the Wellcome Physiological Research Laboratory] for a routine control of its activity. When a conventional dose of this was injected into the vein of an anaesthetized cat, it caused a profound inhibition [slowing] of the heart-beat; I suspected, indeed, a fatal accident [injection of air into the vein] till recovery set in, and successive repetitions of the injection then caused the same sequence at every trial. Tests of this extract on other biological reagents, such as isolated loops of intestine, confirmed the presence in it of an unusual constituent, with actions suggestively resembling those of muscarine a poison from one species of mushrooms and muscarine, I thought, might perhaps turn up occasionally in a fungus like ergot. It was obviously impossible to pass an extract with such properties for therapeutic use, and I secured the whole batch of it for further investigation. My chemist colleague at that time, A. J. Ewins, succeeded thus in obtaining and purifying a few milligrammes of the abnormal active constituent, but it became clear that it could not be stable muscarine.

There seemed little hope then of further progress with the minute amount in hand, till I recalled into conscious memory an observation made some 8 years earlier by my late friend Dr. Reid Hunt, then in Washington.* Hunt and Taveau had found that when choline was acetylated [converted into acetylcholine], its depressor [blood pressure lowering] activity was enormously intensified, the unstable ester, acetylcholine, being some *ten-thousand times as active* as the parent choline. When Ewins, accordingly, made me some acetylcholine, its identity with our substance from the ergot extract was immediately put beyond doubt. And when the actions of this came to be examined in detail, they showed as suggestive a correspondence to the effects of other nerves [the parasympathetic nerves] as those of adrenaline had shown to the effects of the sympathetic nerves in particular. At that time there was no reason at all to believe that acetylcholine was a natural constituent of the animal and human body; but my late colleague, Dr. Dudley, and I found it there [in the spleen] some 15 years later, again by accident, when we were looking for something else.

Now there was good reason to believe with Elliott that the endings of sympathetic nerves liberated epinephrine, or something quite similar to it, directly onto sensitive cells, and it seemed likely, because of the strong correspondence noted by Dale between the actions of acetylcholine and stimulation of *para*sympathetic nerves, that terminal fibers in the latter system liberated acetylcholine. So these two chemicals might be responsible for exciting or inhibiting cells regulated by the autonomic nervous system.

But "good reason to believe" and "it seemed likely" do not constitute *proof* in science, although they are fully acceptable to faddists and cultists. Someone had to do a direct experiment to change a plausible concept into a fact. This meant nothing less than collecting whatever was liberated by nerve endings during stimulation of their nerve fibers, letting it flow through similar but nonstimulated tissues, and seeing whether it produced the same result as that produced by the electrical stimulus. But World War I came along and delayed the logical exploration of Elliott's and Dale's ideas.

It fell to Otto Loewi, a professor of pharmacology at the University of Graz in Austria, to do the crucial experiment in 1920. He described, forty years later, at the age of 80, how it came about:

* Reid Hunt was then chief of the Division of Pharmacology of the Hygienic Laboratory of the USPHS Health and Marine Hospital Service in Washington, D.C. It is not widely known that these two extraordinary substances—acetylcholine and epinephrine—were first synthesized or crystallized in pure form at the turn of the century in the United States (then "a scientifically backward country")—acetylcholine by Hunt and Taveau and epinephrine by Jokichi Takamine, a consultant for the Parke-Davis Company.

As far back as 1903, I discussed with Walter M. Fletcher from Cambridge England, then an associate in Marburg, the fact that certain drugs mimic the augmentary as well as the inhibitory effects of the stimulation of sympathetic and/or parasympathetic nerves on their effector organs. During this discussion, the idea occurred to me that the terminals of those nerves might contain chemicals, that stimulation might liberate them from the nerve terminals, and that these chemicals might in turn transmit the nervous impulse to the respective effector organs. At that time I did not see a way to prove the correctness of this hunch, and it entirely slipped my conscious memory until it emerged again in 1920.

The night before Easter Sunday of that year I awoke, turned on the light, and jotted down a few notes on a tiny slip of thin paper. Then I fell asleep again. It occurred to me at six o'clock in the morning that during the night I had written down something most important, but I was unable to decipher the scrawl. The next night, at three o'clock, the idea returned. It was the design of an experiment to determine whether or not the hypothesis of chemical transmission that I had uttered seventeen years ago was correct. I got up immediately, went to the laboratory, and performed a simple experiment on a frog heart according to the nocturnal design. I have to describe briefly this experiment since its results became the foundation of the theory of chemical transmission of the nervous impulse.

The hearts of two frogs were isolated, the first with its nerves, the second without. Both hearts were attached to cannulas filled with a little Ringer [saline] solution. The vagus [parasympathetic] nerve of the first heart was stimulated for a few minutes. Then the solution that had been in the first heart during the stimulation of the vagus was transferred to the second heart. It slowed and its beats diminished just as if its vagus had been stimulated. Similarly, when the [sympathetic] nerve was stimulated and the saline from this period transferred, the second heart speeded up and its beats increased. These results unequivocally proved that the nerves do not influence the heart directly but liberate from their terminals specific chemical substances which, in their turn, cause the well-known modifications of the function of the heart characteristic of the stimulation of its nerves [Fig. 6.11].

The story of this discovery shows that an idea may sleep for decades in the unconscious mind and then suddenly return. Further, it indicates that we should sometimes trust a sudden intuition without too much skepticism. If carefully considered in the daytime, I would undoubtedly have rejected the kind of experiment I performed. It would have seemed likely that any transmitting agent released by a nervous impulse would be in an amount sufficient to influence the effector organ. It would seem improbable that an excess that could be detected would escape into the fluid which filled the heart. It was good fortune that at the moment of the hunch I did not think but acted immediately.

For many years this nocturnal emergence of the design of the crucial experiment to check the validity of a hypothesis uttered seventeen years before was a complete mystery. My interest in the problem was revived about five years ago by a discussion with the late Ernest Kris, a leading psychoanalyst. A short time later I had to write my bibliography, and glanced over all the papers published from my laboratory. I came across two studies made about two years before the arrival of the nocturnal design in which, also in search of a substance given off from the heart, I had applied the technique used in 1920. This experience, in my opinion, was an essential preparation for the idea of the finished design. In fact, the nocturnal concept represented a sudden association of the

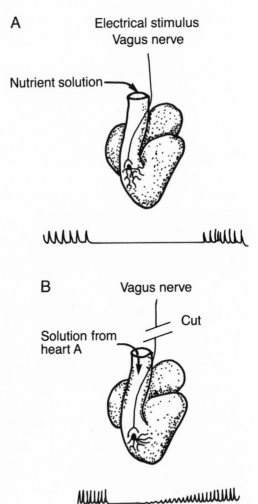

A   Electrical stimulus
Vagus nerve

Nutrient solution

B   Vagus nerve

Cut

Solution from heart A

Figure 6.11. Loewi's experiment on isolated frog hearts. He filled heart A with a nutrient solution and then stimulated the left vagus nerve to the heart; as expected, this slowed the rate of beating of heart A, producing a tracing similar to that beneath heart A. He then transferred the fluid within heart A to heart B (whose vagus nerve was cut and not electrically stimulated); heart B slowed as had heart A, producing a tracing similar to that beneath heart B. Loewi then repeated the experiment (tracing of the heartbeat not shown here), but this time stimulated the sympathetic nerve to the heart (the vagus nerve belongs to the *para*sympathetic division of the autonomic nervous system). This time, heart A speeded and fluid from it, transferred to heart B, caused it to speed similarly. Loewi had in one experiment discovered both chemical transmitters, later identified as acetylcholine and epinephrine.

hypothesis of 1903 with the method tested not long before in other experiments. Most so-called "intuitive" discoveries are such associations suddenly made in the unconscious mind.

Loewi's 1921 report didn't convince skeptics,* but he was stubborn and didn't give up. In 1926 he came back with a different type of proof. If a chemical substance liberated at the endings of the vagus nerve is responsible for slowing the heartbeat, something must turn off the chemical action or the muscle would beat more and more slowly until the heart stopped beating altogether. Loewi and Navratil found a special enzyme in nerve endings that almost instantly splits highly potent acetylcholine into inactive acetate and choline (he named the enzyme cholinesterase); this cuts off each response to a nerve impulse almost immediately and so permits a succession of contractions to follow a succession of nerve impulses (Fig. 6.12). In addition, they found that this enzyme can itself be inactivated by a drug, eserine, the active principle of the calabar or native African ordeal bean (Fig. 6.13); this preserved acetylcholine as active acetylcholine and let it accumulate to concentrations that permitted definite chemical analysis and proof of its existence, rigorous enough to satisfy the most demanding critic.

Actually, although Loewi was indeed right, he was unusually fortunate in several respects. "Looking back," said a Belgian colleague, Z. M. Bacq,

one must regard the choice of the amphibian heart by Loewi as being providential. For instance, the cholinesterase content in this organ is small compared to that in mammalian hearts, the low body temperature is favourable for the stability of acetylcholine, and working with [blood-free] saline avoids the cholinesterase in the red blood cells and plasma. Loewi had unwittingly combined the most favorable conditions to ensure the success of his experiments. The great merit of this exceptional man was his ability to follow a logical course and to accumulate convincing experimental evidence without paying too much attention to the criticism of his theory. The main thing is to have confidence in one's own view of the truth.

Feldberg, in Dale's laboratory in 1934, extended the theory of chemical transmission of impulses to all preganglionic autonomic fibers

---

*A good scientist is skeptical of others and expects others in return to be wary of his new ideas. Alfred North Whitehead said that every great idea sounds like nonsense when first pronounced, and Mark Twain remarked that the man with a new idea is a crank until the idea succeeds.

Figure 6.12. Electrical conduction versus chemical transmission. (A) Until 1921 physiologists thought that the nerve impulse went directly from brain to tissue as an unbroken electric current. (B) Loewi's 1921 experiment suggested that acetylcholine must be formed in nerve terminals; it is now known that acetylcholine is synthesized from acetate (1) and choline (2)—and stored there (3). The nerve impulse releases it into a gap (4) between the preganglionic fiber and the ganglion cell, and the acetylcholine then activates the ganglion cell (5) to send a new impulse down the postganglionic fiber. A few years later, Loewi realized that a special enzyme, cholinesterase (6), quickly splits active acetylcholine into inactive acetate and choline, to be recycled.

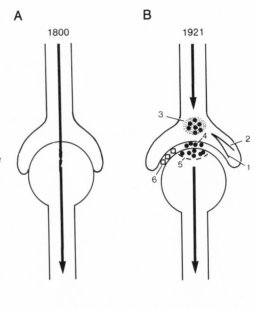

Figure 6.13. The calabar bean, a native ordeal bean of northern Africa, is now known to contain a chemical substance, eserine (or physostigmine) that blocks the enzyme that normally changes active acetylcholine into inactive choline and acetate. For this reason it prolongs and intensifies the effects of injected acetylcholine or that liberated from nerves. For many decades it has been used in treating glaucoma, myasthenia gravis, and sluggish activity of the intestinal tract.

and their appropriate ganglion cells, sympathetic or parasympathetic; here too the chemical substance responsible was acetylcholine. Then in 1936 Dale and Brown found that transmission of nerve impulses from motor nerve endings to voluntary muscle cells was also mediated chemically, again by acetylcholine (Fig. 6.14). Dale and Loewi won the Nobel Prize in physiology in 1936.

Several turning points in Loewi's career deserve comment. The first is that he originally intended to be a practicing physician. He received his M.D. degree in 1896 and in 1897–1898 served as an assistant at the City Hospital in Frankfurt. However, after seeing the high mortality rate in patients with advanced tuberculosis or pneumonia, he soon decided that he might do more good in a basic science department of pharmacology, where he had a chance to find a cure or prevention for then incurable diseases. He became a junior faculty member in pharmacology first at the University of Marburg and then at Vienna. In 1909 he became professor of pharmacology at the University of Graz. He never did work on chemotherapy or antibiotics, but had a long and distinguished career as a physiologist and pharmacologist.

The second turning point in Loewi's life came on March 12, 1938, a day after Hitler's Nazis marched into Austria. At three in the morning a dozen young storm troopers, armed with guns, broke into Loewi's bedroom, threw him into a prison wagon, and then into jail, where he was shortly joined by two sons, Victor and Guido. After being relieved by the Nazis of his Nobel Prize money (which he believed to be safe in a Stockholm bank), he was kept in prison for several months. He was then released, relieved of all remaining personal effects and property, and ordered to leave the country. He managed to get to England, then to Liège in Belgium, and finally in 1940 to New York, where he became a professor at New York University.

This second turning point for Loewi was also one for both German and American science: Germany expelled many of the top scientists in Germany, Austria, and Hungary, and German science sank to its lowest point in a century; the United States provided positions and facilities for many of the refugees and U.S. science reached a new peak. At this time, the inscription on the Statue of Liberty might well have been amended to "Give me your tired, your poor . . . and your persecuted scientists."

The discoveries of Dale, Loewi, Feldberg, and their associates created a revolution in physiology and pharmacology and especially in the drug treatment of hypertension. Why? What difference does it make to

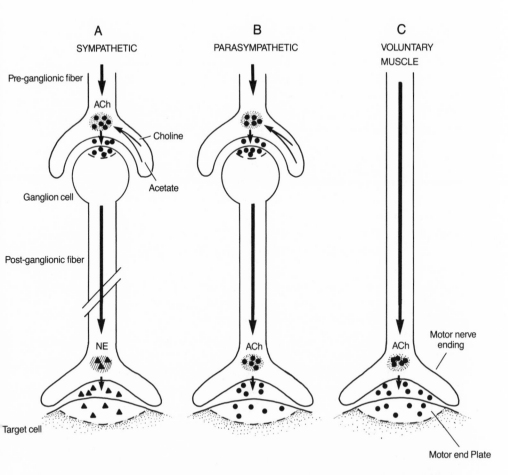

Figure 6.14.   Extension of chemical transmission to other parts of the nervous system. Acetylcholine was shown to transmit the nerve impulse from the preganglionic fiber to the ganglion cell in both the sympathetic (A) and parasympathetic (B) nervous systems. Quite unexpectedly, it was also shown to transmit impulses traveling down motor nerves to specialized receptors on voluntary skeletal muscle. (C) Acetylcholine is also the chemical transmitter at the postganglionic endings in the parasympathetic nervous system. However, acetylcholine is not involved in *postganglionic* transmission in the *sympathetic* nervous system; this is the responsibility of norepinephrine (to be discussed later). (The break in the sympathetic postganglionic fiber is to indicate that it may be very long—up to 30–40 inches—compared to the very short distances between the ganglion cell and the target cell in the parasympathetic nervous system.)

a patient if his nerve impulses travel from brain to blood vessel or heart wholly by an uninterrupted electrical process or in two steps and two processes—first, electrical conduction along intact nerve fibers, and then chemical transmission at gaps—just as long as the impulse gets to its

destination swiftly? It makes a tremendous difference. The very existence of chemical transmission raised fundamental questions that kept
many productive minds at work for years. How could chemicals appear
with fantastic speed at just the right place, at just the right time, and in
just the right amount, and then disappear just as quickly to allow transmission of the next impulse and the next in a long series? Chemical
transmission could and did provide a field day for physiologists, biochemists, and pharmacologists to devise ways of increasing, decreasing, or
modulating the activity of the autonomic nervous system by chemical
means. There were important questions for them to ask and answer,
such as the following:

    1.   What is the precise nature of the chemical transmitters at each
junction?

    2.   Where do the transmitters come from?

    3.   Where is the chemical transmitter stored?

    4.   Where and how is it released?

    5.   Where does it act on target cells in heart, involuntary muscle
fibers, or gland cells?

    6.   What happens to the chemical once it has acted?

    7.   Are there ways of preventing or intensifying one or more of
these chemical events by designing new drugs with specific actions?

    The answers to these questions changed the treatment of hyperten-
sion from surgical sympathectomy to treatment by drugs. Research proceeded so rapidly that by 1970 Professor Uvnas of Stockholm presented
three more Nobel prizes—to Julius Axelrod, Ulf Von Euler, and Bernard Katz, who had provided answers. Uvnas said in his 1970 introduction.

The work for which this year's Nobel Prize in Physiology or Medicine has been
awarded has its origin in earlier prize-winning discoveries. It was long assumed,
naturally enough, that the transmission of nerve impulses took place by physical means, in the same way as an electric current passes between two electric
cables. However, in the twenties, Henry Dale and Otto Loewi showed that
impulse transmission takes place by chemical means. At the nerve ending the
impulse releases a biologically-active substance which, in turn, induces electrical activity in the next nerve or the innervated structure. In this way the functional gap between the nerve terminal and the innervated structure is bridged.
As with all fundamental discoveries, the discovery of a chemical mediator in
nervous transmission led to revolutionary new thinking. Neurochemistry and
neuropharmacology developed into rapidly expanding branches of science.

What did the neurochemists and neuropharmacologists discover that made it possible to switch from *surgical removal* of the sympathetic nervous system to chemical modulation of the activity of sympathetic nerves? Let's start with the list of questions that I just posed and answer them for transmission from preganglionic nerve fibers to their autonomic ganglion cell (see Fig. 6.14).

The Autonomic Ganglia

1.   What is the precise nature of the chemical transmitter at autonomic ganglia? The electrical impulse speeding down a preganglionic sympathetic fiber to one of the ganglia in the sympathetic chain releases acetylcholine at the fiber's ending and it is the chemical transmitter. Unexpectedly, the chemical transmitter at parasympathetic ganglia is also acetylcholine, and this, as we shall see, leads to some difficulties in treating patients with hypertension.

2.   Where does the acetylcholine come from? From a chemical factory in the nerve terminals that continously manufacture potent acetylcholine from two inactive but readily available ingredients, acetate and choline, already present in the nerve terminals.

3.   Where is the acetylcholine stored? It is stored within microsacs (vesicles) in the nerve ending.

4.   How is acetylcholine released? The sac moves toward and into the outer membrane of the nerve ending; there it extrudes its contents, the acetylcholine molecules, into a gap or cleft between it and the ganglion cell, a gap so narrow (0.000005 millimeter) that it was a postulate and not a fact until the invention of the electron microscope.

5.   Where does acetylcholine act? Once in the gap, it attaches itself to one of many acetylcholine "receptors" on the surface of the ganglion cell (more will be said about receptors later). This union of acetylcholine and receptor initiates events within the ganglion cell that generate an electrically conducted impulse that travels the whole course of the postganglionic fiber to its target cell.

6.   What happens to the acetylcholine after it has done its job? Because a great excess of acetylcholine molecules is popped into the gap or cleft between the nerve ending and ganglion, the area must immediately be cleansed of its used and unused acetylcholine. Why? Because nerve impulses travel in trains; the second in a train releases a second

charge of acetylcholine, the third a third charge, and so on, and ganglion cell receptors must be ready to accept subsequent charges of the substance in order to trigger subsequent excitations. This cleansing or restoration process requires changing active acetylcholine back into two inactive components. This is accomplished by the naturally occurring enzyme cholinesterase strategically placed in the cleft itself, where it can accomplish its splitting act quickly and completely.

7.   Are there ways of preventing or intensifying one or more of these chemical events? Specifically, are there drugs that can modify chemical transmission at sympathetic ganglia to decrease sympathetic nerve activity and so lower blood pressure in a hypertensive patient? Your first thought might be of nicotine (see p. 234), because in 1889 Langley and Dickinson, using experimental animals, brushed a solution of nicotine directly onto each of the sympathetic ganglia and paralyzed each of the ganglia in turn.* Unfortunately, nicotine given orally or inhaled as a vapor cannot be used to paralyze the sympathetic nervous system of hypertensive patients because it paralyzes ganglia only in high concentrations.

Langley did note that stimulation of ganglia preceded paralysis, but he was much more impressed by the long-lasting and complete block that followed it. The tolerable dose of nicotine inhaled by man in tobacco smoke is quite low and far below that required to block ganglia; nicotine therefore is of no use in treating patients with hypertension.

However, chemists have synthesized drugs that will paralyze autonomic ganglion cells and do so without any preliminary stimulation at lower doses. One of the first of the wave of new antihypertensive drugs was such a chemical (Fig. 6.15): It was TEA (tetraethylammonium). TEA had been shown to block autonomic ganglia by Marshall in 1912, by Burn and Dale in 1915, and again in 1925 by Reid Hunt, then at Harvard. It prevented neither the formation of acetylcholine within the nerve terminal nor its release from storage sites, but it did block its effect on acetylcholine receptors on the surface of the ganglion cell. In 1946 George Acheson and Gordon Moe, also at Harvard, found in a dusty

---

*Most of us believe that it was Sir Walter Raleigh who introduced the American Indian tobacco plant into Europe. Actually, Nicholas Monardes, an Italian physician and entrepreneur living in Seville, was the first to transplant herbal products from the New World into European medicine. Although he never left Seville, he imported specimens of most every plant grown in Central America and established in Seville both a museum and a botanical garden for cultivating them. He was growing American tobacco in his Seville garden in 1558 while Raleigh was still a child in England; he was also the first physician to write about tobacco and curare.

closet a bottle of Hunt's 1925 TEA, and they demonstrated that it could indeed decrease blood pressure in hypertensive patients; they had performed the first medical sympathectomy! This was in 1946, one year after Franklin D. Roosevelt's death.

TEA wasn't a perfect drug for the treatment of hypertension because it had to be injected, its action was brief, and, although it blocked the response of sympathetic ganglion cells to incoming nerve impulses (as desired), it also blocked transmission of impulses to parasympathetic ganglia as well (not desired), acetylcholine being the chemical transmitter for both parasympathetic and sympathetic ganglia. This added effect on parasympathetic ganglia doomed TEA to be only a stop-gap drug, to be used only until more specific drugs came along. TEA did, however, serve three purposes: It was a useful drug to give to candidates for a surgical sympathectomy to indicate whether the operation was likely to lower blood pressure and, if so, by how much; it could be used in emergencies to lower blood pressure quickly; and it lent further encouragement to chemists and pharmacologists to maintain full speed ahead in the search for better drugs.

The next year came another "-onium" drug, hexamethonium, called C-6 because its chemical structure has a backbone of six carbon atoms. It was introduced by William Paton and Eleanor Zaimis in London. It

Figure 6.15. Action of drugs on autonomic ganglion cells. Drugs such as nicotine can stimulate autonomic ganglion cells in low concentration and block in high concentrations at (3). Tetraethylammonium (TEA) and hexamethonium (C-6) specifically block acetylcholine receptors (3) on both sympathetic and parasympathetic ganglion cells. Certain poisons block formation of acetylcholine at (1). Drugs such as eserine prevent splitting and inactivation of acetylcholine once released into the gap (2) and thereby prolong its action.

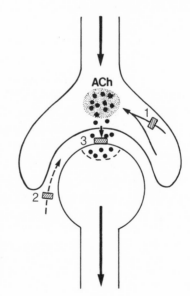

was more powerful and hence more valuable in emergencies, and lasted a little longer. Horace Smirk in Australia, among others, convincingly showed that its use slowed the progress of malignant hypertension, prolonged the patient's life-span, and lessened his symptoms. But both TEA and C-6 had to be injected and both caused a constellation of unpleasant side effects, predictable because a dose that blocked sympathetic ganglia also blocked parasympathetic ganglia. The "side effects" of C-6 were difficult for patients to live with, because they consisted of some or all of the following: too low a blood pressure on standing erect,* dryness of the mouth, cessation of gastrointestinal movement, difficulty in urination, loss of the eye's ability to adapt for near vision so that reading was difficult, impotence, rise in skin temperature, and cessation of sweating. It was as though suddenly the brain had no control over autonomic or automatic regulation of tissues and organs, and involuntary systems had to get along with purely local regulation. This was the era in which a powerful cure by drugs might be worse than surgical sympathectomy or no treatment at all in those patients with mild hypertension who, if untreated, had few or no symptoms.

The Postganglionic Fibers

Now let us use the same set of seven questions (p. 254), but this time provide answers that apply to the sympathetic *post*ganglionic fiber. First let us describe briefly the structure of the postganglionic nerve fiber. A single fiber leaving a sympathetic ganglion is about 0.001 millimeter in diameter and in most instances is the final nerve fiber that runs without interruption to its final destination; a fiber to blood vessels in the big toe might be as long as 36 inches.

Close to its end, it branches into many fine fibers (Fig. 6.16). If all the terminal branches of one nerve fiber were laid end to end, their combined length could be another 10 centimeters or even more. On each branch, like a string of microscopic beads, there are swellings, or varicosities, about 0.003 millimeter apart, that house the microchemical plants that produce and release the chemical transmitter. The combined

* Marjorie Bremner, in her murder novel *Murder Most Familiar*, made use of administration of hexamethonium and enforced standing erect to murder a captain of industry. W. D. M. Paton, who introduced hexamethonium into medical practice remarked, "Whether this is a beneficial or adverse effect, I leave to you."

Figure 6.16. At the top left is a schema of a sympathetic postganglionic fiber similar to that in Fig. 6.14, except that it shows a more accurate picture of the ending of the fiber; it branches into many fine terminals, each studded with varicosities. It is in these that norepinephrine (NE) is manufactured. The main drawing is a schematic representation of a single varicosity, greatly enlarged (a varicosity is actually less than 0.00001 millimeter long). A series of chemical reactions, each speeded up by a different enzyme, produces dopa, then dopamine, and the latter is transformed into NE within the storage sacs or vesicles. A nerve impulse causes these sacs to move toward the membrane of the varicosity and disgorge their NE into the gap between the varicosity and the tissue cell. Here special alpha or beta receptors grab onto and bind NE. The binding triggers chemical reactions that initiate the cell's characteristic activity. Unused NE either returns to the varicosity (uptake), enters nearby blood capillaries, or is destroyed by specific enzymes.

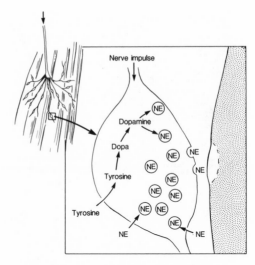

terminal fibers of a single nerve fiber may contain about 26,000 of these swellings. Inside each of these are about 1,500 sacs (vesicles) and these modulate the activity of about 1,000 cells. Each sac may store about 15,000 molecules of the chemical transmitter. The fine nerve terminals from one ganglion cell thus contain approximately 4 trillion molecules of the transmitter, or about 300 times the amount contained in the parent ganglion cell. Figure 6.17 shows the density of the transmitter in the terminal nerve fibers surrounding an arteriole with two branches.

Now, with this anatomic background, let us answer our seven questions.

1. What is the precise nature of the chemical transmitter released at the sympathetic postganglionic terminals? It is *not* acetylcholine, as at the preganglionic fibers in both sympathetic and parasympathetic nervous systems. In 1904 Elliott proposed that it was epinephrine because of the faithful reproduction by epinephrine of effects of stimulation of sympathetic nerves throughout the body. Actually, we now know that it is *nor*epinephrine. Norepinephrine was first prepared in 1904; it was a close relative of epinephrine, but it never recieved any

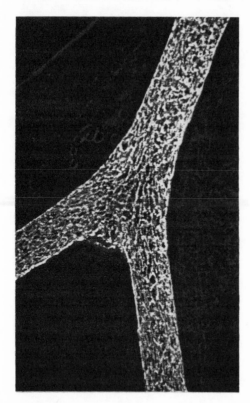

Figure 6.17. The sympathetic postganglionic network enmeshing a branching arteriole revealed by a microscopic technique for identifying specific chemicals within cells. Norepinephrine within cells treated with formaldehyde fluoresces a yellow-green color and can be distinguished from naturally fluorescent tissues.

serious attention because no one had ever found it to occur naturally in the body until 1946.

We now know that both epinephrine and norepinephrine are natural constituents of the body. The adrenal medulla (the core of the adrenal gland) produces and stores mostly epinephrine. In emergencies the gland releases it into the circulating blood as a hormone; as such, it acts on many cells in the body to produce a coordinated response. The sympathetic postganglionic endings, however, produce only norepinephrine.

Why does the body need both circulating epinephrine and locally released norepinephrine? Harvard physiologist Walter Cannon believed that the sympathetic nervous system is a defense mechanism that prepares a threatened animal for "fight or flight." Such an emergency function would best be served by pumping more blood to voluntary muscles (achieved by increasing the force and rate of cardiac pumping and *dilating* arterioles to the limbs), increasing the flow of fresh air to the lungs (by relaxing bronchioles), and shutting down activities not immediately essential to survival (gastrointestinal movements, formation of urine, skin blood flow). For such coordinated whole body action, a hormone, such as epinephrine, secreted by the adrenal gland directly into circulating blood and quickly distributed to all parts of the body is ideal. However, for precise regulation by the sympathetic nervous system of individual parts of the body when there is no whole body emergency, nerves serve the purpose better. Norepinephrine liberated from sympathetic nerve endings, activated by messages from the brain, is an ideal regulator of the heart alone, of blood vessels alone, or of bronchial diameter alone. An example of sympathetic regulation of one body function is conservation of body heat when man is exposed to cold; closing superficial blood vessels in the skin and stopping the flow of warm blood through them shuts off a radiator (a system designed to lose body heat) without altering the activity of the heart, kidneys, muscle, and other organs.

The discovery of norepinephrine as the terminal sympathetic transmitter was made in 1946 by Ulf Von Euler, a Swedish scientist distinguished enough to receive a Nobel award. (The Swedes, who select the Nobel Prize winners in physiology or medicine, practice "reverse chauvinism" in considering the award of Nobel Prizes to their own countrymen.) Von Euler was probably "genetically determined" to be a Nobel Prize winner: His father won the 1929 Nobel Prize in chemistry, his grandfather was professor of chemistry at Uppsala and discovered two new chemical elements, and his mother was a professor of botany and of geology. Ulf Von Euler could justifiably have been awarded two Nobel Prizes: one for his proof that norepinephrine is the chemical transmitter in the sympathetic nervous system and another for his discovery of an important new class of chemicals called prostaglandins.

2. Where does the norepinephrine come from? It is made in the varicosities of the sympathetic nerve terminals by a local synthetic process* that is somewhat more complicated than the production of acetylcholine by ganglion cells. Most of the chemical events were worked out at the National Institutes of Health by Julius Axelrod, another Nobel

---

*We don't obtain our epinephrine and norepinephrine directly from the food we eat; even if we went on a diet of braised adrenal glands, the epinephrine and norepinephrine in them would not be absorbed through our gastrointestinal tract. Our norepinephrine is synthesized from simpler materials by our body's cells, largely in the adrenal medulla and sympathetic nerve endings. It may dismay some of you that, for the most part, we really are not "what we eat" but, rather, what our body's cells manufacture from the food and drink that passes across our gastrointestinal tract, enters blood and lymph, is distributed bodywide to tissues and organs, and there processed into needed chemicals.

laureate. Key enzymes produced in the ganglion cell itself slowly find their way down the center of the long nerve fiber into the vesicles in the nerve terminals, where they transform the amino acid phenylalanine into storage granules of norepinephrine, each granule about 0.001 millimeter in diameter.

Figure 6.18 shows the chemical building blocks of norepinephrine in schematic form. Tyrosine, formed in the body from the amino acid phenylalanine, crosses the membrane of the varicosity into its interior. There begins a series of enxyme-prodded chemical reactions that produce successively dopa, dopamine,* norepinephrine, and epinephrine. In the adrenal medulla the same biochemical processes produce some norepinephrine, but for the most part the reaction proceeds further to form epinephrine; in the sympathetic nerve endings, however, the process stops when it produces norepinephrine.

3.   Where is norepinephrine stored? Norepinephrine (NE) granules are stored locally in sacs inside the varicosity until needed.

4.   How is the stored NE released? Upon receiving the appropriate nerve impulse, the sacs move into the membrane of the varicosity and spill their norepinephrine molecules into a gap, or microcleft, between the nerve ending and norepinephrine receptors on the surface of heart muscle or arteriolar muscle (Fig. 6.19).

5.   Where does NE act on target cells? It immediately adheres or is bound to special adrenoceptors† on the membranes of the tissue cell. The interaction of NE and its receptors sets into motion a series of events that triggers the cell to carry out its unique function (to be discussed later).

6.   What happens to NE once it has acted? More transmitter molecules are normally released than needed and the fate of this excess is important. The processes involve breakdown of NE by enzymes into inactive components, leakage of NE into capillaries and then into the circulating blood, and a new process called "reuptake." "Reuptake" is choice jargon because norepinephrine was never taken up by varicosi-

---

*Here are two brilliant examples of "spin-offs": dopa (in the form of L-dopa) is now used to control Parkinson's disease of the brain, and dopamine is itself a chemical transmitter in the brain and, in addition, a useful dilator of kidney arterioles in the treatment of circulatory shock.

† Sir Henry Dale, in an attempt to ensure precision in the use of words, introduced new words: *adrenergic*, to label nerves that act by production and release of norepinephrine; *adrenoceptors*, to label receptors that specifically bind epinephrine or norepinephrine; *cholinergic*, to label nerves that act by production and release of acetylcholine; and *cholinoceptors*, to label receptors that specifically bind acetylcholine.

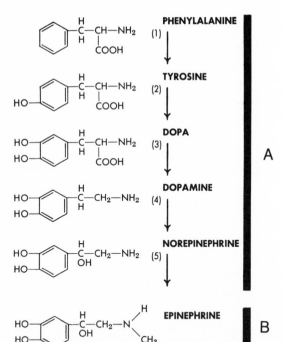

Figure 6.18. The conversion of phenylalanine to tyrosine to dopa to dopamine to noradrenaline and adrenaline. Process A occurs within postganglionic terminal varicosities; B is an additional reaction in the adrenal medulla. Those of you who have some knowledge of chemistry will see that epinephrine has an NH—CH₃ group at the right (the CH₃ group is often abbreviated as R), whereas norepinephrine has only an NH₂ group. Since norepinephrine has no CH₃ group (or *no R* group), it is called *nor*epinephrine; these two compounds are often abbreviated as E and NE.

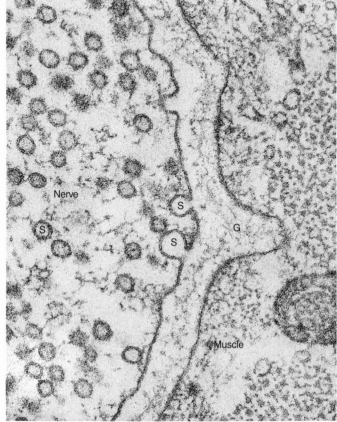

Figure 6.19. Acetylcholine-containing sacs (S) in the nerve ending move toward and merge with the nerve cell membrane and then release their contents into the gap (G) between nerve and muscle (the muscle shown here is skeletal muscle). This image, magnified 230,000 times, was captured by freezing the tissue within a thousandth of a second after stimulating it electrically.

ties of the nerve terminal in the first place; just plain *uptake* would be a better term for the excess NE that returns to varicosities.

However, the uptake, or return to the nerve ending, is an important process because, if blocked (as by some drugs such as cocaine), a single nerve impulse or train of impulses produces prolonged and exaggerated effects as the NE piles up at adrenoceptors. For example, it has been known through the 1910 work of Otto Loewi, though no one then knew why, that if one injects norepinephrine, then cocaine, and then the initial dose of norepinephrine, the second dose of norepinephrine produces a rise in blood pressure that is two to three times greater— both in magnitude and duration—than that produced by the first dose. This occurs because cocaine prevents the uptake and storage of norepinephrine by sympathetic nerve endings and norepinephrine continues to act on target cells. Failure of uptake also explains another phenomenon, namely, that when sympathetic nerves have been cut and time has been allowed for the death of their terminal branches, the response to intravenous epinephrine or norepinephrine is also greatly *increased* ("denervation hypersensitivity")—this time because there simply are no functioning microsponges in nerve endings to soak up and store NE and prevent its action on target cell receptors.

The answer to the seventh question, How can one make useful antihypertensive drugs based on chemical—as opposed to electrical— transmission of nerve impulses? has been answered for drugs acting on sympathetic ganglia, but we must postpone answering it for the sympathetic postganglionic endings on target cells until we amplify our brief answer to the fifth question (p. 262) and discuss in some detail the very important question of cell receptors.

In 1890, a 5-year-old English lad, Alfred Clark, impressed his elders by making calculations of the cubic capacity of Noah's ark (using dimensions provided in the Bible) and comparing it with his calculation of the volume of a pair of elephants housed in the ark. Though there is no record of this, I wager that the lad also pondered over the question of the relative sizes of a doctor's pill and a human body and wondered how the pill accomplished its mission when put inside a body 250,000 times as large.

In 1918, at age 33, Clark became professor of pharmacology at University College, London, and 15 years later, when professor at Edinburgh, wrote a small book (*The Mode of Action of Drugs on Cells*) with a tremendous impact: It was the first attempt to relate the molecular dimensions of drugs to the surface areas of target organs and theorize on the mechanism of action of drugs. For example, he determined the minimal dose of a digitalis-like drug needed to act on the frog heart and then he calculated two numbers. First, using known dimensions of molecules, he calculated the number of molecules in this dose and the maximal surface area they could cover if spread out in the thinnest possible layer, a layer one molecule thick. Second, he estimated the number of cells in a frog heart and calculated their combined surface area. He found that drug molecules sufficient to produce a response could not have covered more than $\frac{1}{6000}$ of the surface of the cardiac cells. For calculations on acetylcholine, he found that the surface of one heart muscle cell was 10 trillion times greater than that of an acetylcholine molecule. As Clark put it, the acetylcholine molecules would look like a small gnat sitting on a huge whale. Even if 10,000 molecules of acetylcholine were necessary to activate this single cardiac cell, they would cover only one-billionth of the cell's surface. Because body cells are so very much larger than drug molecules, Clark concluded that "drugs must exert their action by uniting with certain specific receptors in or on the heart cells and these receptors must form only an insignificant proportion of the total surface of the cells." In brief, cell functions must be initiated by molecules combining with small active patches of chemicals on the cell's surface.

Much earlier, in 1878, Paul Ehrlich became interested in the staining of animal tissues by dyes and was awarded his doctorate in medicine on the basis of this work, which incidentally was made possible by the discovery of aniline dyes by W. H. Perkin in 1853. Before Perkin, there were innumerable coloring materials or dyes, all of natural origin—from fruit, flowers, leaves, stems, roots, seeds, berries, the bark of trees, and from insects and mollusks. Perkin prepared the first synthetic dye of known chemical composition—a purple dye christened mauve; he obtained it from aniline in coal tar and so began a huge synthetic chemical industry. He made his discovery at the age of 18, in 1856, in a simple laboratory in an outdoor shed; 50 years later he became Sir William Henry Perkin. Perkin's discovery provided Ehrlich with a varied supply of dyes, of known chemical composition, that he could use to stain living tissues and organs of animals.

Ehrlich, then at the Berlin Clinic, recalled that his professors told him to dissect dead bodies and learn all of their parts; instead he took small bits, made very thin slices of each, and stained them with a variety of Perkin's new dyes. Then he thought that he would learn even more by injecting dyes into living animals and seeing if they sought out any special tissues. He was especially impressed by observing that methylene blue dye went primarily or only to nerve endings. His reasoning was sound: If one dye went to only one tissue, he should be able to find a dye that shunned all animal tissues and cells but, instead, preferred to settle on or in bacteria. He developed his concept of a "magic bullet," a guided missile that, once introduced into the body, would seek out and attach itself to a specific cell type (native to the body) or even to a specific foreign bacterium or parasite which had invaded the body. Most scientists of Ehrlich's time scoffed at this belief and contended that it was impossible to find a chemical that would selectively kill microbes within a living body without killing most if not all of the body's cells as well, but, unlike his contemporaries, Ehrlich believed in highly specific cell receptors.

He worked first with trepanosomes that caused sleeping sickness, and then with the spirochetes of syphilis. He was obsessed by his conviction and methodically tested chemical after chemical—100, 200, 300, 400, 500, 600 of them. Most anyone else would have stopped; Ehrlich didn't and compound 606 (ansphenamine, or Salvarsan) was worth the tremendous effort. It killed spirochetes and became the first effective antisyphilis drug. Compulsively, Ehrlich kept on and found an even better one, number 914 (neoarsphenamine). Not only did these arsenic compounds kill spirochetes and cure or arrest syphilis, but they opened the door for research in bacterial chemotherapy and the later discovery of the sulfa drugs and antibiotics. Remember, though, that the discovery of aniline dyes by an 18-year-old boy was also necessary for Ehrlich's success.

We now know that Ehrlich was wrong in one respect. The drug is not a guided missile programmed with instructions to find the right receptor; instead, the *receptor* is programmed to grab from its immediate environment the specific substance it must combine with to trigger its cell to appropriate activity. We also know that it is the receptor that determines the nature of the cell's activity, and not the particular substance that activates it. Ehrlich received the 1908 Nobel Prize for his studies on immunity, and not for his discovery of chemotherapy against two parasitic diseases, syphilis and sleeping sickness. He did manage, however, in his 1908 Nobel lecture, to include some remarks about *arseno*receptors, his all-consuming research interest at that time!

So the question the inquisitive child asks has its answers: It takes only a minute amount of a drug relative to the size of a cell, organ, or body to be effective, because the molecules need attach themselves to only a minute part of the cell surface. Drug molecules, properly designed, go to the right cells because of a unique binding that takes place between the drug molecules and molecules in the "active patch" or receptor on the cell surface. Once activated, it is the receptor that tells the cell what to do.

The receptor concept became medically important when pharmacologists observed certain puzzling effects of epinephrine and tried to explain them. In 1937 Walter Cannon believed that the effects of epinephrine could be best explained by postulating that there were actually two different kinds of epinephrine; he called them sympathin E (E for excitatory) and sympathin I (I for inhibitory). There was some justification for Cannon's classification, because epinephrine was "excitatory" (it constricted smooth muscle in small arteries and stimulated the heart) and it was also "inhibitory" (it dilated bronchioles and relaxed the involuntary muscle of the gut and of some blood vessels); so, epinephrine simply had to exist in two forms. But in 1948 Raymond Ahlquist, a pharmacologist at the Medical College of Georgia, thought that Cannon's hypothesis was muddling understanding in the field rather than clarifying it. Why, said Ahlquist, must there be two forms of epinephrine? Why not two slightly different types of receptors on tissue cells? After all, epinephrine was simply the trigger that activated the cell receptor; from then on it was the receptor and its specific mission that counted. Maybe one type of receptor fired off an excitatory response and a slightly different type fired off an inhibitory response. He noted that one very close chemical relative of epinephrine, phenylephrine (the bottle in your medicine cabinet that's labeled Neosynephrine), is purely excitatory—it constricts small blood vessels (and dilates none) and so it is used locally as a nasal decongestant. On the other hand, another close relative of epinephrine, isoproterenol (which you know as Isuprel), dilates bronchioles and arterioles and has no constrictor effects. So Ahlquist turned the explanation of epinephrine around: Epinephrine is one substance (not two), but it can act on two different receptors, which he, as he quipped later, "with great originality named *alpha* and *beta* adrenoreceptors." Not everyone believed Ahlquist and, indeed, the *Journal of Pharmacology* turned his manuscript down (it was published in a physiology journal). But, unexpectedly, evidence piled up that he was right, and it came not from research on epinephrine and its relatives, but from studies on drugs that *blocked* some of the actions of epinephrine.

First, in 1910, Dale had discovered the phenomenon of "ergotoxin reversal" of epinephrine action. He found that epinephrine injected intravenously into a dog increased blood pressure in a characteristic fashion. However, if a dose of ergotoxin (a chemical derived from ergot —a fungus that grows on rye) was first given and then followed a little later by the initial dose of epinephrine, epinephrine *lowered* blood pressure instead of increasing it. If the second dose of epinephrine had done nothing, Dale could have explained it easily as drug antagonism; ergot had simply blocked epinephrine action. But a *reversal* was harder to explain. Almost forty years later, thanks to Ahlquist, we know that this reversal occurs because tissues responsive to epinephrine have several types of adrenoceptors, his alpha (α) and beta (β) receptors. Ergot blocks only alpha receptors, leaving the beta receptors still responsive to epinephrine. Therefore Dale's first injection of epinephrine activated alpha receptors and triggered constriction of arterioles that increased blood pressure; the epinephrine also stimulated beta receptors, but not so powerfully as alpha receptors. The second injection of epinephrine could activate only beta receptors, and so caused blood pressure to fall.

Then in the 1940s, Mark Nickerson in Utah found that a chemical called dibenamine produced precisely the same effect (Fig. 6.20). Neither ergot nor dibenamine is used clinically, but their action provided proof that an *alpha*-blocking drug could blot out some of epinephrine's widespread actions without affecting others.

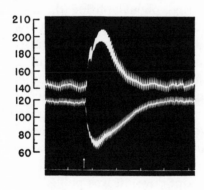

Figure 6.20.   The upper tracing shows the rise in arterial blood pressure after an intravenous injection of epinephrine. When blood pressure has returned to its initial level, an injection was given of a drug (dibenamine) that blocks alpha receptors. Repetition of the initial dose of epinephrine caused blood pressure to *fall*. The block of alpha receptors prevented epinephrine from raising blood pressure, but epinephrine could still activate beta receptors, dilate arterioles, and cause a fall in blood pressure.

Then came the discovery of *beta* blockers. The first two never got beyond laboratory tests—one was too toxic and the other was suspected of causing cancer—but the third, propranolol, is still widely used in a number of clinical disorders. It doesn't block any *alpha* receptors, but blocks all *beta* receptors, for example, those in the heart (where it blocks epinephrine- and norepinephrine-induced increases in heart rate and force of contraction) and those in bronchi (where it prevents bronchodilation produced by epinephrine and Isuprel).

One discovery led to another. Beta blockers are now known to exist as two types, β_1 and β_2, which block either β_1 or β_2 receptors, respectively. How does this discovery help you if you have high blood pressure? If your physician has been treating you with a drug that blocks *all* beta receptors in an attempt to slow your heart and decrease its force of contraction, it will also block beta receptors in your bronchi and constrict the fine air tubes; if you are an asthmatic, you will not appreciate this. But if he can treat you with a drug that specifically blocks β_1 receptors in the heart but *not* β_2 receptors in the bronchi, you will definitely welcome the advent of the more specific drug.

In essence, pharmaceutical research chemists are now chemically subdividing the sites of action of norepinephrine into smaller and smaller chunks—as far as cell function is concerned—so that the physician now has drugs that can suppress a single function of your bodywide sympathetic nervous system and provide you with a highly specific beneficial effect with less and less chance of undesired drug actions.

The receptor concept, developed first and most convincingly for the autonomic nervous system, has now become an exceedingly important aspect of cell, tissue, and organ biology. Modern techniques, using radioactive activators and blockers of receptors, have made it possible to separate receptors from cells, determine the density of receptors per cell, work with receptors as relatively pure chemicals, learn whether damaged receptors can act as foreign substances that might be the cause of some autoimmune diseases (in which body cells attack their own tissues), and explore the concept that the number and activity of receptors may provide clues to prognosis in certain types of cancer. It has greatly extended our basic knowledge of insulin action, brain function, and communication among a wide variety of cells. The concept that several slightly different receptors can bind the same transmitter has also spread to explain curious actions of other drugs, for example, why a well-known antihistamine drug can block only some of the actions of histamine (production of hives) but not others (secretion of gastric hydrochloric acid). Today a new histamine blocker (cimetidine) can specifically attach itself to histamine receptors in the stomach and greatly reduce hydrochloric acid formation there, another spin-off from basic research on cell receptors that has revolutionized the treatment of gastric and duodenal ulcers.

The concept also extends to several types of acetylcholine receptors. To take the simplest example, the effect of acetylcholine released at autonomic ganglion cells is blocked by nicotine, TEA, or C-6, but the effect of acetylcholine released at parasympathetic *post*ganglionic fibers is not; instead it is blocked by *atropine*. Therefore there must be at least two types of acetylcholine receptors, one that binds to nicotine and another which binds to muscarine (which activates it) and atropine (which blocks it). This discovery of "nicotine" cholinoceptors in voluntary muscle has at last shed light on a previously mysterious disease, myasthenia gravis, now believed to be a disease of "nicotinic" cholinoreceptors, possibly due to destruction of some receptors by antibodies (autoimmune disease).

Now we can answer the *seventh* question: Are there ways of preventing or intensifying one or more of these chemical events, the events that we call chemical transmission of the nerve impulse from postganglionic fiber to cell receptor? Yes, a large number of drugs, acting in a variety of ways, can profoundly modify chemical transmission; they can do the following:

Interfere with the synthesis of norepinephrine at any point from the initial building block in the nerve fiber to the final product, norepinephrine (for example, xylocholine).

Block the release of NE from its storage vesicles (for example, bretylium).

Deplete the storage sites of their NE so that little or none is available for release (for example, reserpine and guanethidine).

Be a "look-alike" for NE and fill or partially fill the storage granules and so decrease the amount of storage room available for NE (for example, alpha-methyldopa).

Be a "look-alike" for NE and occupy NE receptors and effectively prevent NE from triggering cell functions. Thus they can block β_1 receptors in the heart and decrease heart rate and blood pressure without interfering with functions of the sympathetic nervous system mediated through α or β_2 receptors, or they can block α receptors or both α and β receptors.

In addition to finding drugs that act on the peripheral parts of the sympathetic nervous system, industrial chemists have also produced new drugs that lower blood pressure by acting on the central nervous system or by directly dilating arterioles (such as hydralazine and prazosin).

Let us also remember that in the race to find drugs that stimulate or block parts of the sympathetic nervous system, there have been many "spillovers" into other areas of medical science: the whole concept of specific drug receptors (including opiate and endorphin receptors) and the challenging hypothesis that some diseases may be due to disorders of receptors (diabetes and myasthenia gravis); the discovery of other chemical transmitters (such as dopamine); the use of dopa as the first effective treatment for Parkinson's disease; new drugs for the treatment of glaucoma (to replace those that narrow the pupil); discovery of specific histamine receptors (H-2) and drugs, such as cimetidine, that block them and suppress formation of hydrochloric acid in the stomach, making them invaluable in the treatment of peptic ulcers; a new drug (dopamine) that dilates blood vessels in kidneys when these are intensely narrowed, as in traumatic shock; the role of monoamine oxidase (MAO) inhibitors in body and especially brain functions; and the design of new drugs to treat asthma by stimulating β_1 receptors (isoproterenol, metaproterenol, and bethanecol).

You would think that with such a wide variety of drugs that block or modulate the activity of sympathetic nerves somewhere between the brain and fingers and toes, there should be more than enough antihypertension drugs. This is true, if you are convinced that hypertension is caused by an overactive sympathetic nervous system or that enough drugs have been designed to have precisely the specific corrective action for each patient with hypertension (mild, moderate, or severe), and no other effects. In fact, each of the drugs mentioned above has a drawback; even the most specific of all—the β_1 blockers—can cause too slow a heartbeat or, in patients with heart disease, too weak a contraction. The sympathetic blocking agents would be easier on the patient if they could be used in lower dosage as "add-on" drugs to permit some regulation of automatic functions to continue. But this means using two or more drugs whose beneficial effects would be additive and would not introduce new undesirable effects. To what could the potent drugs be added? Obviously, it must be to a drug that in itself lowers blood pressure safely, and by a mechanism that does not interfere with the normal nervous regulation of our bodies. These drugs came along in 1957 and soon became the basic treatment for all hypertensive patients; they did not lower blood pressure in patients with normal blood pressure, but they did in patients with hypertension. They were not powerful enough to use in patients with severe, malignant hypertension, but, acting in concert with the sympathetic blockers, they provided an effective system of treatment that used lower doses of each and caused fewer undesirable actions. These were the oral diuretics—drugs that caused an increased flow of urine *and* an increased loss of sodium and chloride as well as water.

7

The Kidney Revisited

At the beginning of the twentieth century, when hypertension had been established as a disorder quite separate from Bright's disease and when physicians at last had ways of measuring blood pressure in man, some began to wonder what *caused* hypertension. The discovery of the anatomy, physiology, and pharmacology of the sympathetic nervous system led some to believe that overactivity of this system might be involved, but there was no way to decrease its activity until the 1930s and 1940s. Around the end of the nineteenth century, a few believed that hypertension was due to too much salt in the diet, and by 1904 Leo Ambard and Eugene Beaujard, two French interns, advocated treating hypertensive patients with a salt-free diet. Common table salt is sodium chloride. Initially the culprit in salt was believed to be chloride; however, seven years later, Emil Pfeiffer of Wiesbad identified the *sodium* ion as the villain. His recommendation for treatment was also a sodium chloride-free diet but, in addition, eliminating all other sodium-containing foods, drinks, and drugs. In 1920 Frederick Allen of New York rediscovered the salt-free diet and in 1944 Walter Kempner at Durham re-rediscovered it, this time in the form of a rice, fruit, and fruit juice diet. In 1976 Edward Freis in Washington, D.C., stated firmly that "the evidence is very good if not conclusive that reduction of salt in the diet to below 2 gm / day would result in prevention of essential hypertension and its disappearance as a major public health problem."

All of these convictions should have launched periodic all-out antisalt campaigns; however, neither patients nor their physicians shared these convictions. Patients resisted them because a salt-free or low-salt diet is unpalatable, at least to Americans and Europeans. The average American diet consists of 5–15 grams of salt daily; a "salt-free" diet contains less than 1 gram. Patients with hypertension, most of whom are free from symptoms, preferred no treatment at all to treatment with a salt-free diet. Their physicians resisted the diet because no one was quite sure of the mechanism involved, and no properly controlled study had ever been done that would serve as ammunition to "convince" their patients.

In the 1950s scientists began to work on how a "salt-free" diet might lower blood pressure. In 1952 William Raab in Vermont proposed one mechanism by demonstrating that his hypertensive patients on a salt-poor diet responded less vigorously to injections of epinephrine. Louis Tobian at Ann Arbor proposed another in 1960, that a high-salt diet (or inadequate excretion of salt by the kidney) led to accumulation of sodium and water in the walls of blood vessels; this would thicken the walls and narrow the channels for blood flow and require a higher pressure to overcome increased resistance to flow. In 1968 Axelrod's group at Bethesda reported a third mechanism, that sodium retention led to decreased ability to store norepinephrine in the fine terminal sympathetic nerve fibers, thereby making more norepinephrine available to stimulate the heart and narrow the smallest arterial branches.

All of these findings did persuade some physicians and some of their patients to give the salt-free diet another trial, but most patients refused to continue with salt-poor food and drink, and so a well-controlled study has not yet been done. Sir George Pickering, on the subject of low-salt diets, quoted the king in *Alice Through the Looking Glass*, who says, "There is nothing like eating hay when you're faint . . . I didn't say there was nothing better. I just said there is nothing like it."

However, if what was needed was fewer sodium ions in the body, one could accomplish this in two ways: One was to decrease the intake of sodium in the diet, and the other was to increase the output of sodium from the body. The latter could be accomplished either by enforced sweating or by eliminating more sodium in urine. The first way—increased sweating—was unacceptable to populations raised on body deodorants; the second might be practical if one knew precisely how the kidneys worked, in health, and had a rational basis for modifying normal renal function.

The Structure and Function of the Kidney

Except for knowing the size, shape, and color of the kidney and that it produced liquid urine and occasionally extremely painful solid stones or gravel, physicians knew nothing of the structure and function of the kidney until 1662. In that year Lorenzo Bellini, a 19-year-old student of physics at Pisa, cut open a kidney and deduced that what appeared to be streaks on the cut surface were in fact extremely fine tubes (Fig. 7.1). Two years later Marcello Malpighi, who in 1661 had turned his relatively crude microscope onto the lungs to discover pulmonary capillaries, examined the kidney and, with the aid of his micro-

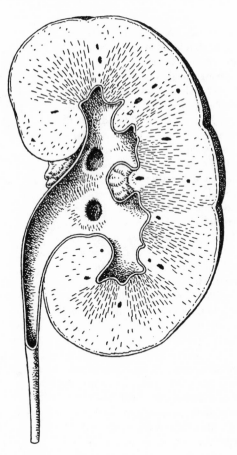

Figure 7.1. What Bellini saw when he sliced a kidney in two lengthwise. What formerly were believed to be lines, he deduced to be extremely fine tubes. Bellini wrote, "If you compress these filaments, you will find water welling up everywhere. If you are not afraid to present this to your tongue, you will discover a certain saltiness and in some the taste of urine. If you apply a glass lens to your eye, urine is very clearly seen welling out as if gushing forth from so many little water pipes." The next year, Bellini the medical student became Professor Bellini at Pisa. (From "The Kidney" by Homer W. Smith. © 1953 by Scientific American, Inc. All rights reserved.)

scope and amazing perception, proposed what we now know to be the correct structure of the nephron, the functional unit of the kidney.

One hundred and eighty years went by before Carl Ludwig, the same person who devised the recording mercury manometer (p. 223), proposed a brilliant hypothesis to explain the process of urine formation. Ludwig, then only 26 years old, conceived that as blood flows through each ball or tuft of specialized capillaries in the kidney, the capillary walls act as a fine sieve or filter that allows extremely small molecules such as salts, urea, and water to pass through its pores and enter the capsule enclosing the capillary tuft. (This tuft was originally named the Malpighian corpuscle, but is now called a glomerulus.) Ludwig reasoned that the blood pressure in the capillaries acts as the driving or

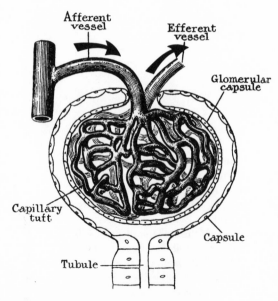

Figure 7.2.   A glomerulus. At the top left is a large arteriole (afferent vessel)—a branch of an artery—entering the glomerulus (see arrow); the arteriole divides into numerous capillaries that look like a mass of wriggling worms. Fluid and salts filter across the walls of the capillaries into the capsule that encloses the ball of capillaries. The capillaries then come together again to form a second, smaller arteriole, which leaves the glomerulus as an efferent arteriole (see the arrow, top right). The mean blood pressure (approximately the average of the systolic and diastolic pressures) in the main renal artery is about 100 mmHg. The blood pressure in the glomerular capillaries is much higher than in capillaries elsewhere in the body—about 70 mmHg instead of 25 or 30 mmHg. This is because the inlet to the glomerular tuft is much wider than the outlet, and, as a result, the main resistance to blood flow is through the second (efferent) arteriole. This high blood pressure provides the force to overcome the osmotic pressure of plasma proteins (which would tend to draw fluid *into* the capillaries) and so filters large amounts of protein-free fluid into the glomerular capsule. The resistance to flow through the efferent arteriole into the second capillary bed decreases blood pressure beyond the glomerular capillaries to a level too low to filter more water and salts from the blood.

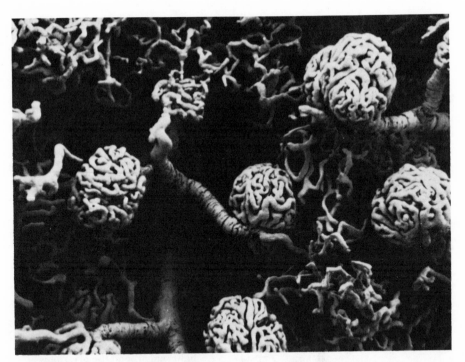

Figure 7.3.　Glomeruli at high magnification. The coils of blood vessels seen here are glomeruli in the kidney, magnified 260 times. A glomerulus is unique because it is composed of capillaries interposed between two arterioles. (From *Tissues and Organs: A Text-Atlas of Scanning Electron Microscopy*, R. G. Kessel and R. H. Kardon. © 1979 by W. H. Freeman and Company.)

filtering force. Cells (red and white blood cells and platelets), large protein molecules (such as plasma albumin and globulin), and blood lipids are unable to pass through the sieve; they remain in the capillary blood. The filtered fluid then takes a devious route into a winding, tortuous tubule that leads to the ureter and bladder, but along the way much of the tubular fluid is reabsorbed.

Figures 7.2 and 7.3 show two arterioles for each glomerulus: The larger brings blood to the glomerulus and the smaller carries it away. The smaller one is not a vein, as you might expect, but is still an arteriole; it soon divides and subdivides into a second capillary bed that surrounds each tubule (Fig. 7.4). This secondary capillary net supplies conduits for reabsorbed fluid to reenter blood and flow back into the general circulation; it also provides a mechanism for secreting additional substances in blood directly into the tubule and then into the urine.

What provides the force for reabsorption of tubular fluid into blood?

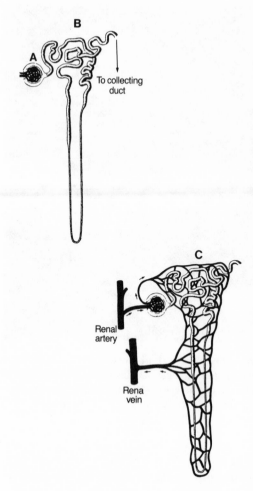

Figure 7.4. The nephron. The nephron, the functional unit of the kidney, consists of three parts: (A) the glomerulus, described earlier, (B) a long, twisted, tortuous convoluted tubule, and (C) a network of fine blood vessels surrounding the tubule. The glomerular capsule leads to a twisting, coiled tube (B) (the proximal convoluted tubule), followed by a straight segment that first runs toward the center of the kidney and then makes a 180° turn back to the glomerulus, where it becomes a second coiled tube (distal convoluted tube) that then leads to a collecting duct. All of this is surrounded by a capillary network, shown in (C) that arises from the arteriole leaving the glomerulus. The tubular capillaries then merge into a vein that empties into the renal vein. The capsule forms a tight seal around the arterioles at their entrance and exit.

There are approximately 2 million nephrons in the human kidneys. The total surface area of their capillaries is about 30,000 square centimeters. The tubules stretched end to end would go on for about 70 miles. Obviously vast surfaces are available for filtering, reabsorbing, and secreting fluids.

In 1899 Ernest Starling, British physiologist, proposed this explanation: Because blood leaving the glomerular capillaries had lost much of its water, the retained proteins were concentrated. Thus the concentration of water in the secondary capillary network (surrounding the tubules) was greatly decreased and water in the tubules returned to the blood by osmosis.

To understand osmosis, one first needs to know about diffusion of molecules and semipermeable membranes. Molecules in solution are constantly in random motion, just as O_2 and CO_2 are. If the concentration of molecules of one particular type is greater in one region than in another, there are more collisions and more motion. The net effect is that molecules move, by a process called diffusion, from a region of higher concentration to a region of lower concentration, and the concentrations in the two regions tend to become equal (Fig. 7.5). Living tissues are composed of semipermeable membranes. What semipermeable really means is that a membrane may be freely permeable to one substance and impermeable to another. In the renal tubule the membrane is freely permeable to water molecules, but impermeable to large protein molecules. Consider in Fig. 7.5 the left side of the membrane to contain tubular fluid and right side to contain fluid in the tubular capillaries. Tubular fluid will have a high concentration of water molecules but no protein molecules, while capillary fluid will have a high concentration of protein molecules and a low concentration of water molecules. Water molecules are more concentrated in pure water; they are less concentrated in a mixture of protein molecules and water; therefore they tend to move across the membrane until the water concentration is the same on both sides; by the process of osmosis, water returns from the tubular fluid to enter the blood in the capillaries surrounding the tubules.

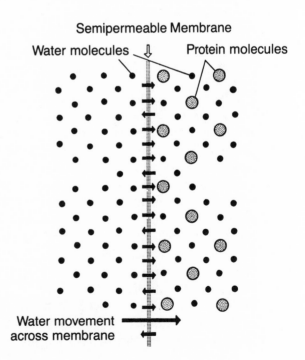

Figure 7.5.   One of the ways in which water that has left the blood by glomerular filtration returns to the circulation is by osmosis (see text).

Osmosis is one mechanism by which much of the water that had been filtered returns to the blood circulation; another is by countercurrent distribution of water between the two long, thin parallel loops of tubule whose thin walls are in intimate contact with each other.

So far speculation on how the kidney functioned was just that, though it was carefully reasoned and logical. However, it was time for direct proof. In the early 1920s a professor of pharmacology at the University of Pennsylvania, A. N. Richards, was unhappy about his inability to explain to several medical students the mechanism for the diuretic action of caffeine (a diuretic is a drug that increases the flow of urine). He and his colleague Joseph Wearn set out to correct this, one of thousands of gaps in basic knowledge that have through the years turned teachers into teacher–researchers. Richards, later to become President of the National Academy of Sciences, was a compulsive believer in obtaining direct evidence, and Wearn took up his challenge. He reasoned that if a capsule enclosed each tuft of glomerular capillaries and fluid from capillary blood entered this capsule, there must be a space between the wall of the capsule and its capillary loops, and he should be able, somehow or other, to gain access to that space. If he could then remove a sample of fluid from it and analyze it, he should know for sure what passed across the walls of the glomerular capillaries and what stayed behind. Furthermore, because the tubules conducting this filtrate were hollow, he could collect samples of fluid at different points along these tubes and determine changes in chemical composition of filtered fluid as it passed on its way to the ureter.

Easy? Richards and Wearn had the idea and the determination. What they needed now were three things. First they needed a sharply pointed, hollow needle or micropipette fine enough and controllable enough to pierce a glomerular capsule (a glomerulus is about 0.2 millimeter in diameter) or a tubule (about 0. 02 millimeter wide) without ripping the capsule or damaging the capillaries; the needle had to be advanced by a delicate mechanical device and guided by direct visual control obtained by using a special microscope. At the 1921 meeting of the American Association of Anatomists, Richards watched Dr. Robert Chambers of Cornell demonstrate his micromanipulator capable of making injections into single cells; here was the apparatus to solve the first problem (Fig. 7.6). However, there still remained the difficult problem of drawing out quartz tubing to a very fine diameter (still hollow) and then managing to put a sharp cutting bevel at the top. Richards was

Figure 7.6.   A.N. Richards in 1937.
Richards's apparatus. The beam
of an arc lamp (A) was directed
downward at a mirror (B) and then
upward through a hole in a board
holding a frog (C) to a microscope
(D). A vertical stand (E) holds the
micropipette; the system is adjusta-
ble in three dimensions. An adjusta-
ble bulb (F) holding mercury is connected through tubing to the micropipette (G).

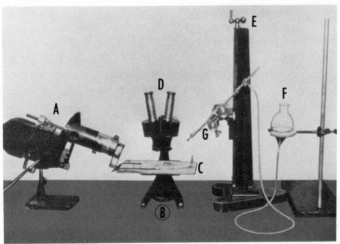

blessed by having access to a superb glassblower, James Graham, who
came from a long line of glassblowers in Glassboro, New Jersey. Graham
tells the story of his first meeting with Richards in 1922:

New to the University, I had said that their method of making the needle for
injection into the glomerulus was crazy. Dr. Hayman said to come up to Dr.

Figure 7.7.   James Graham, A. N. Richards' glassblower, "pulled" all of Richards' micropipettes. Fine scientific glass blowing is now almost a lost art.

Richards' laboratory and tell the story. So I plunged into the inner sanctum, picked up the needle holder and promptly knocked off the tip that they had spent all morning preparing. Dr. Richards turned, saw what happened, and gave me a real blistering, winding up by saying, "I want to kill you, but I can't think of the way that will give me the most pleasure."

I went back to my shop and was packing up to leave for good, real sore. In about 15 minutes Dr. Richards came in to say he was sorry. Still lippy, I told him to forget it. It was my dumb trick, but I couldn't take another blast such as I just had. His answer was typically Dr. Richards, "You are God damn right it was a dumb trick; you broke up an experiment that six people had worked all day to prepare. Now get your gear back on the tables, and come up tomorrow morning and show me this wonderful method that has been the cause of a totally lost day."

From that time on Graham pulled out all of Richards' pipettes and instructed staff in his technique of fracturing the tip to get a proper bevel.

Second, they needed to be able to see and puncture individual glomeruli in living animals; they learned from the science of comparative biology that two species—the frog and the mud puppy (*Necturus*)— had very thin kidneys, so thin that one could shine a light through them. The kidneys were so placed that one could immobilize the very thin edge sufficiently to make a clean puncture of a capsule or a tubule; thus one could both collect fluid from it and inject materials into it.

Third, they needed microchemical techniques to measure, in extremely small amounts of fluid, as small as 0.1 cubic millimeter, the chemical components of plasma filtered and reabsorbed in the normal process of urine formation; Richards, Wearn, and associates had to develop these from scratch.

When all this was done and the fluid analyzed by techniques not available to Ludwig sixty years before, the fluid in the glomerular capsule and in the bladder was found indeed to be free of protein, as predicted by Ludwig. Furthermore, fluid filtered into capsules contained substances (such as sugar) that were not present in urine in the bladder. Obviously there had been both filtration and reabsorption. Tubular reabsorption was a necessary component of this elaborate system, because filtration removes most nutrients, such as glucose, amino acids, and vitamins from glomerular capillary blood, and the body's circulating blood would soon be depleted of these if not recaptured from tubular urine. By this mechanism, substances essential to life are conserved and recycled and waste products are eliminated. The kidney obviously does more than eliminate urine; it really regulates the amount of fluid in the body and the composition of body fluids.

But Richards and Wearn were not satisfied with learning only the overall plan of filtration–absorption. They also wanted to know the details: *where* each substance was reabsorbed. Using an ingenious technique (Fig. 7.8) and infinite patience, they learned that different segments of the tubule reabsorbed different salts (Fig. 7.9) and so exercised specific, fine control over the chemical composition of circulating blood to maintain "the constancy of the internal environment of the body," as propounded by Claude Bernard seventy-five years earlier. After the frog and mud puppy experiments were completed, Richards' colleague,

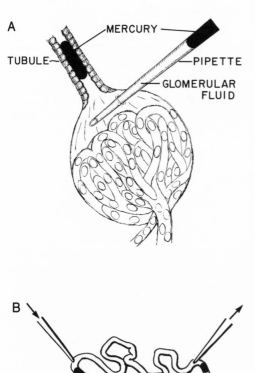

Figure 7.8. (A) Diagram of a pipette inserted into the capsule surrounding a tuft of glomerular capillaries. Lowering pressure in the pipette draws fluid into it; the composition of the fluid can then be analyzed by microtechniques. Richards and Wearn developed an ingenious technique of first blocking the tubule, that conducts glomerular fluid toward the ureter, with a small drop of mercury so that there could be no backflow and only newly formed glomerular fluid could be drawn into the pipette. (B) Using two droplets of mercury injected into a tubule to block two ends of one segment, Richards and Wearn isolated a portion of a tubule, inserted a micropipette into each end of the segment, and perfused it (see arrows) with a solution of known composition. By determining the change in composition of fluid that had passed through the segment, they knew what had been reabsorbed. They then analyzed samples from all accessible segments of tubules and mapped the individual chemical factories along the entire tubular "assembly line."

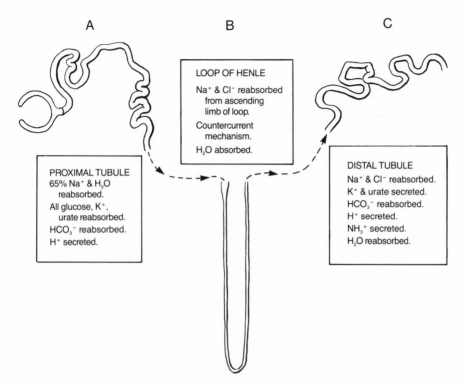

Figure 7.9. Locations of the various "out" (reabsorption), "in" (secretion), and "in and out" (exchange) processes along the tubule: (A) proximal convoluted tubule, (B) loop, and (C) distal convoluted tubule. One can almost visualize hundreds of highly intelligent chemists and physicists stationed along the tubules who continuously receive information from the rest of the body about its chemical composition and continuously remove or add specific ions, molecules, and even hormones to keep the body's chemicals at optimal concentration and the body's fluids at optimal volume (Cl^-, chloride ion; H^+, hydrogen ion; HCO_3^-, bicarbonate ion; H_2O, water; K^+, potassium ion; Na^+, sodium ion; NH_3^+, ammonia).

Arthur Walker, repeated the work in three species of mammals (rats, guinea pigs, and opossums) to satisfy critics who justifiably questioned whether the mud puppy was really a representative model for man.

We now also know from tests devised by Homer Smith and others the approximate volumes of fluid involved in man. The human glomeruli collectively filter about 180 liters of fluid into the tubules every day. Of this about 99% of the water is reabsorbed, leaving only 1%, or less than 2 liters a day, as urine. Of the filtered salts, 99.6% of the sodium is reabsorbed in the tubules, along with 99.5% of the chloride, over 99.9% of the bicarbonate, and 92.6% of the potassium.

Homer Smith paid tribute to the elegance of the techniques and the dedication of Richards and his colleagues:

The micropuncture technique not only established the filtration hypothesis beyond any doubt, but also laid the foundations for our knowledge of segmental function in the nephron. For twenty years a man and his pupils studied frogs and mudpuppies! It seems unlikely that the immediate future will see a comparable series of investigations, concentrating on one objective, sustained for so long a period, and involving as many technical difficulties, as is represented in this work. Richards has remarked that the major credit should not come to him, but rather it should go to the many investigators who carried out the bulk of the actual work. True enough, perhaps, but through these twenty years someone had to maintain continuity, esprit de corps, high standards of performance, perspective, critical acuity, and courage when the going was particularly rough; and, probably in many instances, to reduce complicated series of data to a comprehensible paper. Richards' name [must be visualized] on every paper in the small type that reads From the Laboratory of Pharmacology of the University of Pennsylvania.

And so the micropipette work established that urine was formed largely by a filtration–reabsorption process. But this didn't settle the question of whether tubules might also secrete substances directly into the tubular fluid flowing through them.* Indeed, a lively controversy developed over this now important matter. Richards and Wearn were convinced that filtration and reabsorption were the main or only mechanisms involved in urine formation. Homer Smith in New York and Eli Kennerly ("E. K.") Marshall in Baltimore were convinced that segments of the tubules had the ability to secrete materials in the tubular fluid that did not get there by pure filtration. Much of their conviction came from their studies of comparative anatomy and physiology of the kidney. They, together and separately, investigated the mud puppy, frog, toadfish, birds, fish, snakes, turtles, chickens, rabbits, and man. They reasoned that during the millennia as man evolved, migration of creatures from salt water to fresh water brought one kind of adaptation, and return of fresh water creatures to the sea brought another kind (Fig. 7.10).

Some marine animals swallow salt water and absorb a large amount of it from the intestines; they excrete far more of this salt and water

---

*Reabsorption and secretion are terms used here to define the direction of movement of chemical substances, without any implication of the biological mechanism involved. Reabsorption is movement from inside the tubule, through its walls into tubular capillary blood; secretion is movement from tubular capillaries through the tubular wall to the fluid in the tubule.

through their gills than through their kidneys. On the other hand, fresh water fish probably absorb water through their gills and excrete most of this through their kidneys. In fact, there was great variation in the size of glomeruli and the length of the different segments of their tubules; total tubular length ranged from 2 to 58 millimeters. But, most important, Smith and Marshall also found some species, for example, the goosefish, readily available at the Bar Harbor fish market, that had essentially no glomeruli at all (aglomerular fish). Although the goosefish could not *filter* water and salts, it still formed urine. Clearly, the urine had to come from active secretion by renal tubules—there was no other

Figure 7.10.   Some of the different types of nephrons in different species of land and sea animals. Some have no glomerulus, some only a glomerulus and a proximal tubule, and some have a complete nephron (glomerulus and proximal and distal tubules with a connecting thin segment or loop) (see text).

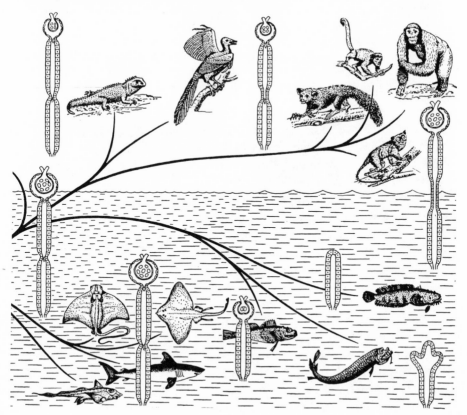

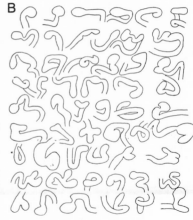

Figure 7.11. The goosefish (*Lophius piscatorius*).

(A) The goosefish has a ratio of 2,000 nephrons without glomeruli to 1 nephron that has a "pseudo-glomerulus." Nevertheless, it still forms urine. (B) Tubules dissected from the kidney of the goosefish. In this sample of 54, each has one blind ending where one would expect to find a glomerulus.

explanation (Fig. 7.11). Richards dismissed this observation with the comment, "At last Marshall has found an animal that agrees with his theory." But then Marshall showed that mammals (dogs) could excrete in their urine a red dye he injected into their blood, even when he carefully decreased blood pressure in their glomerular capillaries so that it was too low to filter *any* fluid, but high enough that some blood continued to flow through tubular capillaries. Richards at last had to concede that tubules, even in mammals, had the ability to secrete materials from blood into urine. (One of these substances later turned out to be penicillin!).

As we shall see, agreement on a triple mechanism (filtration–reabsorption–secretion) was essential for understanding the action of diuretics and designing new and better ones. Research over the next few decades by a new generation of renal physiologists—Berliner, Gilman, Wirz, Giebisch, Gottschalk, Mudge, Davenport, and Beyer, a few of the dozens in laboratories in the United States and abroad—identified substances filtered and mostly reabsorbed and others mostly secreted by tubular cells into the tubule. Even more important, they completed the task of pinpointing the precise segments of the tubule responsible for reabsorption and for secretion of various components of plasma, and they learned the mechanisms involved.

We now think of the kidney as a master chemical laboratory that tries to maintain the constancy of the salt and water environment in which our body cells and tissues function. It does this by continuous surveillance and overhauling of blood. Each minute the two kidneys, less than 0.5% of the weight of the body, receive about 20% of the blood pumped by the heart. This means that about 1,700 quarts of blood, or 900 quarts of plasma, flow through the renal artery each day; of these 900 quarts, about 180 are filtered across the glomerular capillaries into tubules. The tubules then reabsorb about 178–179 quarts a day, and 1–2 quarts flow out as urine. A complicated, mind-boggling process? Yes, but also a more efficient, precise, and delicate one than any artificial kidney built by human medical engineers, for it is an organ capable of making decisions that maintain the proper composition of body cells.

Diuretics

By 1950 physiologists had provided a sound scientific base on which they, pharmacologists, and chemists could plan a logical synthesis of powerful diuretics to eliminate salts and water from the body. Up until then, many centuries had yielded only three drugs* that increased the flow of urine: caffeine, a mild diuretic; digitalis, powerful, but only in patients with heart failure who had accumulations of fluid under their skin and in abdominal and chest cavities; and mercury.

Caffeine came first. Shrubs and berries containing caffeine and similar compounds were discovered independently by many ancient civilizations and used in coffee and tea mainly for its stimulating effect, though its diuretic action did not go unnoticed. (Remember that it was ignorance of *why* caffeine acted as a diuretic that prompted Richards' work of the 1920s and 1930s.) Its mechanism of action is now believed to be

---

*Irving Page believed that there was a fourth old-time diuretic. He wrote, "You will recall that Dr. Sylvius at the University of Leyden in 1679 knew of the diuretic properties of oil of juniper. He believed he could improve the extracts by putting the berries in pure alcohol and distilling the mixture. The result [gin] was success beyond his dreams. Within a few years, all Holland found itself suffering from ills that could be cured only by Dr. Sylvius' medicine."

complex; by an action on the heart and circulation (which probably includes narrowing the arterioles leaving the glomeruli), it increases blood pressure in and blood flow through glomerular capillaries and so increases the amount of filtered fluid; it probably also has a selective action on tubules that increases elimination of salt from the body. Today caffeine is rarely prescribed medically as a diuretic.

Digitalis was the second diuretic to be found (1785). William Withering's discovery of digitalis (Fig. 7.12) illustrates beautifully the contribution of a broadly trained, perceptive physician. He was an English physician by vocation, but a superb botanist by avocation. His first book, published in 1776, was *A Botanical Arrangement of All the Vegetables Growing in Great Britain*. His second book tells how he discovered the diuretic properties of digitalis (foxglove):

Figure 7.12.   The foxglove (*Digitalis purpurea*). The plant was described in 1542 by Fuchsius, who gave it its botanical name, *Digitalis*, because of its resemblance of the blossom to a tip of a finger. In 1785 William Withering described its medicinal use in *An Account of the Foxglove*. He wrote, "It has a power over the motion of the heart to a degree yet unobserved in any other medicine." His book contained only one illustration—a color plate of the foxglove flower and leaf. He did this because in the 1700s physicians collected their own drugs and he wanted to be sure they picked the proper plant. Digitalis, as prescribed 200 years later, is still the powdered leaf of the foxglove plant. (*Foxglove* is probably derived from *folk's glove*.)

In the year 1775, my opinion was asked concerning a family receipt for the cure of the dropsy. I was told that it had long been kept a secret by an old woman in Shropshire, who had sometimes made cures after the more regular practitioners had failed. I was informed also, that the effects produced were violent vomiting and purging; for then diuretic effects seemed to have been overlooked. This medicine was composed of twenty or more different herbs; *but it was not very difficult for one conversant in these subjects, to perceive, that the active herb could be no other than the Foxglove.* [Italics added].

My worthy predecessor in this place, the very humane and ingenious Dr. Small, had made it a practice to give his advice to the poor during one hour in a day. This practice, which I continued until we had an Hospital opened for the reception of the sick poor, gave me an opportunity of putting my ideas into execution in a variety of cases; for the number of poor who thus applied for advice, amounted to between two and three thousand annually. I soon found the Foxglove to be a very powerful diuretic.

The early diuretics were used largely to decrease or eliminate abnormal fluid collections in the body caused by a failing heart; Withering lived in the days before hypertension was recognized as a disease.

Digitalis is still a very important drug and universally used in patients with heart failure. It has no selective action on the kidney, but, by improving the performance of the cardiac muscle as a pump, it increases blood flow through the kidney and increases glomerular filtration and the formation of urine. Digitalis is not a satisfactory drug for daily use to increase the excretion of sodium in urine of patients with high blood pressure, most of whom have no heart failure.

The third diuretic was mercury. Mercury had several uses in medicine over many centuries, depending on the mercury compound the physician prescribed. As calomel (mercurous chloride), it was a cathartic; as bichloride of mercury, it was an antiseptic; as a mercuric compound, it was, from 1495 to 1909, the only antisyphilis drug and, indeed, mercuric salicylate was still in use even after Paul Ehrlich's 1909 discovery of his "magic bullets" arsphenamine and neoarsphenamine. Today pharmacology textbooks no longer list mercury as a chemotherapeutic agent, and some have dropped it from their chapter on diuretics. However, from 1919 (when the diuretic action of mercury was discovered by Alfred Vogl, then a third-year medical student in Vienna and obviously a very keen observer at the bedside) until the 1960s it remained the most potent diuretic known. How did Vogl find his new diuretic?

On October 7, 1919, in postwar Vienna, Johanna M. was admitted to the First Medical University Clinic in Vienna under the care of Dr. Paul Saxl for treatment of congenital syphilis and complications. The diagnosis was evident, and treatment impossible. During rounds Dr. Saxl asked Vogl, a third-year medical student, to inject salicylate of mercury into the patient every other day; he thought it too late for it to be of any good, but at least it was active treatment and would do no harm. The drug was not available on the ward and Vogl phoned the pharmacy. While on the phone, Vogl was approached by a former army surgeon who had been discharged when the huge Austro-Hungarian army disintegrated and who was now trying to establish a private practice. Producing a small box from his pocket, the surgeon said, "I received this sample in the mail this morning; it's a new mercurial antisyphilitic, Novasurol. Maybe you can use it instead." And with a sad smile he added, "I have no patients, anyway."

At that time a new generation of hospital nurses was evolving, well educated and well trained. Making precise and beautiful charts was their pride, with everything recorded in various colors. They collected urine from each patient and measured its volume daily. Blue columns of varying height indicated the 24-hour production. On the day of the first injection, a tall, blue column on Johanna's chart indicated that her urine output had markedly increased. This appeared again after the second and third injections. Vogl excitedly mentioned it at rounds; his report was greeted with a benevolent smile and a lengthy discussion of biological rhythms.

When after a lapse of 4 days he started the injections again, the tall blue columns promptly reappeared. Vogl then injected Novasurol into a patient with advanced congestive heart failure in whom other drugs had no effect. Within 24 hours the patient had urinated more than 10 liters! Vogl was convinced that they had just witnessed "the greatest man-made diuresis in history." As Vogl later said, "we repeatedly reproduced these miraculous results, causing deluges at will, to the mutual delight of the patients and ourselves." It was evident now that the new antisyphilis drug was also a powerful diuretic. And so it was that mercurial diuretics (of which Novasurol was the first) were discovered. Vogl moved on to Berlin for a while to continue his studies and Dr. Saxl and Robert Heilig, Vogl's student successor on the ward, began to work with mercurials. You will not find the name of Vogl the medical student in

Saxl's 1920 paper or in Saxl and Heilig's 1920 article, but that is how a weak antisyphilis drug became a powerful diuretic.

Knowledge of how the kidney functioned was then so meager that little more than an apparent cause–effect relation between injection of mercury and increased urine flow could be established. But the organomercurials, as they came to be called, were the first of the modern diuretics. We know today that they interfere with the reabsorption of both sodium and chloride ions by the tubules, an ideal mechanism for a diuretic. Unfortunately, they acted best when given by intramuscular injection (unpleasant when diuretic action is needed for months or years), and when improperly used have toxic effects, including damage to the kidneys themselves.

Oral Diuretics

All of the new knowledge and hypotheses that I have just related to you—observing a relation between the amount of salt in patients' diets and their blood pressure, learning the structure and function of the kidney, and measuring the capacity of this organ to filter, reabsorb, and secrete (by different mechanisms at different points along the nephron)—made the oral diuretics possible. But several other important discoveries, some initially unrelated to urinary excretion of salt or to hypertension, were also needed.

The first of these was a biochemical discovery that had to do with the elimination of a waste product, carbon dioxide (CO_2), by the lungs. One of the main functions of the lungs is adding O_2 to venous blood; equally important is removing excess CO_2 from it. It has long been common knowledge that CO_2 and H_2O react to produce carbonic acid (H_2CO_3). However, in 1924 a Copenhagen chemist, Carl Faurholt, determined the *speed* of the reaction; it turned out that it was not very fast. Faurholt was not primarily interested in biological applications, but his fellow townsman O. M. Henriques was, and Henriques began to wonder how carbonic acid could give up its CO_2 during the short time— less than 1 second—during which each red blood cell was in transit through pulmonary capillaries. He calculated that if only simple chemical reactions were involved, such as the formation of carbonic acid (H_2CO_3) from CO_2 and H_2O and the reverse reaction, formation of carbon dioxide and water from carbonic acid, and if these were as slow as reported, only a small fraction of CO_2 evolved by tissues could be excreted by the lungs.

To solve this paradox (because 100% of CO_2 tagged for excretion *is* excreted by healthy lungs), in 1928 Henriques measured the effect of plasma on the release of CO_2 and then the effect of a mash made from the insides of red blood cells. Plasma had no effect, but the red cell mash accelerated the reaction to far greater activity than would ever be needed. Obviously an enzyme (a special protein that speeds a chemical reaction without being chemically changed itself) was involved. It remained for a Cambridge physiologist, F. J. W. (Jack) Roughton, to discover a new enzyme in 1930; he named it carbonic anhydrase. It was present in red blood cells (not in plasma) and tremendously speeded up the otherwise slow reaction of $CO_2 + H_2O$ to form H_2CO_3, and the reverse. Roughton calculated how long it took red blood cells in man to move through capillaries in the lung, and how long it would take, without his enzyme, for the lungs to eliminate 90% of the CO_2 normally evolved during this passage. Red cells, he figured, took $\frac{3}{4}$ of a second for the trip in a resting man, and only $\frac{1}{3}$ of a second when he exercised, but it would take about 250 seconds to evolve 90% of the CO_2. Obviously something had to make the reaction proceed at least 340–700 times faster. He then calculated that the amount of carbonic anhydrase in human red blood cells could speed the change from carbonic acid to CO_2 and H_2O by about 13,000 times! Nature doesn't skimp by supplying barely adequate resources to do a job!

Roughton was particularly pleased by his discovery, because he had also discovered that he was the most direct living descendent of William Harvey. Harvey had no children, but his brother did, and Roughton had traced his lineage directly to him; in fact, when I visited Roughton's personal library, it contained more books on lineage than on physiology! Roughton was intrigued by the fact that his ancestor, Harvey, had discovered the circulation of the blood and that he, his direct descendant, had discovered the enzyme that made it possible for blood to accept CO_2 from tissues and release it in lungs, so making uptake of O_2, and life, possible.

It was a very important discovery, even if carbonic anhydrase was present only in red blood cells. But as often happens, Roughton's discovery stimulated other scientists to look for carbonic anhydrase elsewhere in the body. Horace Davenport, an American physiologist, found it in the lining of the stomach in 1939. Davenport then thought along the following lines: If it is present in the cells of an organ (the stomach) primarily concerned with secretion of ions (secretion of hydrogen ions as hydrochloric acid) and one of the chief functions of the kidney is transfer of ions (sodium, potassium, chloride, bicarbonate, and hydrogen, to list a few), perhaps the same enzyme exists in the kidneys to speed their reactions. In 1941 Davenport and Alfred Wilhelmi washed animal kidneys to remove any blood in them and so get rid of the enzyme in the organ's red blood cells, ground up the blood-free organ in a glass mortar, dissolved the mash in water, and by chemical analysis identified carbonic anhydrase.

So carbonic anhydrase was present in red cells and had an indispensable function in getting rid of CO_2. And it was also present in kidneys. But what was its function there? Another discovery was needed. It was made by a renal physiologist, Robert Pitts, though he did not connect it at the time to diuretics. Body fluids, on the whole, are normally slightly alkaline, but urine is usually acid. Pitts and his associate Robert Alexander announced in 1945 that the normal process of acidifying urine took place in the tubules with the help of carbonic anhydrase. There CO_2 and H_2O could readily form carbonic acid that could then disassociate into hydrogen ions (H^+) and bicarbonate (HCO_3^-) ions. The hydrogen ion, H^+, could then be exchanged for a sodium ion, Na^+; the H^+ crossed the tubular cell into tubular fluid and Na^+ was reabsorbed from tubular fluid into blood. This process both saved sodium for the body and eliminated excess H^+, acidifying the urine as it passed down the tubules to the bladder.

Sulfanilamide and Diuresis

We will return to the kidney and its carbonic anhydrase, but let us first recall a clinical observation made in 1937 on patients receiving the then-new miracle drug, sulfanilamide, for treatment of serious bacterial infections. Hamilton Southworth at the Johns Hopkins Hospital noted that two of fifty patients treated with sulfanilamide began to breathe deeply; this can be a sign of excess acid (hydrogen ions) in the blood. As a result, he studied fifteen consecutive patients treated with sulfanilamide; the blood of each showed evidence of excess acid, or acidosis. This could be due to excessive loss of basic ions from the body; the sodium ion (Na^+) is one of these. Pharmacologist E. K. Marshall at Hopkins then showed that a large single dose of sulfanilamide administered to dogs produced acidosis, and Strauss and Southworth demonstrated that in three normal human subjects sulfanilamide led to acidosis, diuresis, and an increase in the renal excretion of sodium and potassium (Fig. 7.13).

In 1940, two Cambridge biochemists, David Keilin and Tadeusz Mann, found that the miracle drug sulfanilamide had, among its other actions, the property of blocking the action of carbonic anhydrase. Two years later Rudolph Hober found that sulfanilamide caused urine of frogs to become more alkaline, indicating that the kidneys were excreting an excessive amount of sodium.

Now let us return to the kidney and carbonic anhydrase. The clincher for Pitts' ideas on the formation of acid urine was this effect of sulfanilamide, which had now proved to be an enzyme inhibitor as well as an antibacterial drug. For if Pitts was correct, sulfanilamide should interfere with the normal process of the formation of hydrogen ions and the exchange of sodium ions for hydrogen ions. When carbonic anhydrase activity was decreased, this exchange would be reduced and more sodium ions would be excreted in the urine.

In 1949 William Schwartz, then at Boston's Peter Bent Brigham

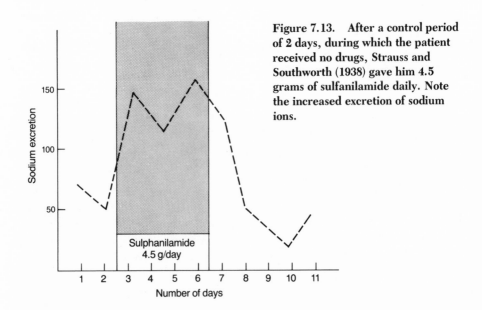

Figure 7.13. After a control period of 2 days, during which the patient received no drugs, Strauss and Southworth (1938) gave him 4.5 grams of sulfanilamide daily. Note the increased excretion of sodium ions.

Hospital, learned of Pitts' work on the role of carbonic anhydrase in acidifying urine and gave sulfanilamide to three patients in an attempt to block the activity of renal carbonic anhydrase and to see if it would decrease the formation of hydrogen ions in renal tubular fluid and increase sodium and water excretion. It did act as a diuretic, but he had to give large, nearly toxic doses, and decided that sulfanilamide was not suitable for routine use to eliminate sodium ions.

Schwartz became interested in other problems, but realized that a good chemist might profitably play around with the sulfanilamide molecule and modify it to make a diuretic that was both potent and safe. He urged Dr. Richard Roblin, a chemist at American Cyanamid Company (now Lederle Laboratories) to attempt the synthesis of other carbonic anhydrase inhibitors.

The story now shifts to two large drug companies. Roblin at American Cyanamid did synthesize a number of sulfanilamide-like compounds, including, in 1950, acetazolamide (Diamox). This was a very potent inhibitor of carbonic anhydrase and in 1953–1954 was heralded as a new oral diuretic for eliminating edema in patients with congestive heart failure. It did indeed carry out more sodium in urine; however, it eliminated basic sodium bicarbonate along with neutral sodium chloride, and, as a result, the blood of some patients became more acid, as it had with sulfanilamide. And it didn't always work well upon repeated use; some sort of resistance to its action developed. Finally, it occasionally caused undesirable central nervous system symptoms. So it had a short life as a spectacular new diuretic. But as often happens with potent chemicals, a new and quite unexpected development led to its use in treating another disorder, glaucoma, in which the fluid pressure within the eye is too high. In 1951 a Swedish first-year medical student, Per Wistrand, found carbonic anhydrase inside the eye. In 1954, a young ophthalmologist, Bernard Becker, treated patients with glaucoma with Diamox and produced what he hoped for, a decrease in pressure within the eye. Thus when Diamox reached the market in 1954, there was a new use for it, entirely unsuspected by any of those who developed it.

Our story now moves to the other pharmaceutical company, Sharp & Dohme, near Philadelphia. In 1943 the company inaugurated a "renal program" within its research organization. This renal program was also initiated because of a new miracle drug—penicillin. It was wartime, penicillin had just been discovered, and there was an overwhelming demand for it, both abroad and at home. Large-scale production methods had not yet been devised, the drug was scarce and costly, and, to make matters worse, as much as 80% of the penicillin administered ran out of the body in the patients' urine. Penicillin turned out to be a substance of the type that E. K. Marshall had found to be readily secreted by the kidney's tubules into the urine. This made it difficult to maintain high levels of penicillin in blood and tissues and, of course, it reduced the effectiveness of penicillin against infection. Building upon the vast new knowledge of renal function, the company hoped that the staff of the new renal program might find a safe substance that would block tubular secretion of penicillin and keep it in the body. Sharp & Dohme had an additional interest in financing renal research: Some of the sulfa drugs had been found to cause kidney damage and the company wanted to find the cause and see if damage could be prevented. (Parenthetically, it should be added here that no pharmaceutical company would have financed a renal program in 1943 if it had not been for the spectacular advances in renal physiology between 1923 and 1943.)

The company already had on its staff James Sprague, who would head the chemical side of the renal program. He had joined Sharp & Dohme six years earlier and was director of organic chemistry. One of the company's products in 1937 was an antiseptic, 30% of which was glycerin. World War II cut off the supply of glycerin and Sprague was asked to find a substitute for it or develop a better antiseptic. Sprague turned first to mercury compounds, knowing that these were both antiseptic and diuretic. Company management vetoed the idea of a new mercurial antiseptic, so, between 1937 and 1943, he concentrated on the diuretic aspect. At that time one theory was that mercury produced diuresis by reacting with sulfur-containing enzymes in the kidney to interfere with a specific tubular function. A compound that was nontoxic but which still had this action of mercury seemed worth developing. One of today's most powerful diuretics, ethacrynic acid, which was synthesized by Sprague in 1951, did have this type of action and was almost ready for use in 1954, but it was set aside for a higher priority: work on the thiazide diuretics. The debut of ethacrynic acid was delayed for almost a decade.

A young Ph.D.–M.D. just out of the University of Wisconsin was chosen as pharmacologist for the renal program. His name was Karl Beyer, and he, together with chemists Sprague and Frederick Novello, was destined to discover chlorothiazide (Diuril) an instant best seller oral diuretic when it came on the market fifteen years later.

As a young boy Beyer knew that his future lay in medicine. His father, a veterinarian, was understandably sympathetic, and when the boy's bedroom became too small for his afterschool chemistry experiments, he provided him with an additional room on the second floor of their home. Beyer not only made it to and through medical school, but anticipated a current trend by getting a Ph.D. degree as well. He had an early interest in comparing the chemical structures of compounds with their biological activity; he displayed this interest and the advantages of his combined training as chemist, pharmacologist, and physician while still a student at Wisconsin. There he single-handedly designed, synthesized, and tested, in animals and humans, metaraminol, a blood pressure-raising drug still of importance today.

After graduation, Beyer wanted to continue exploring the relation between the chemical structure of a compound and its action on the body. This required collaboration with a competent and imaginative chemist. The National Institutes of Health had not yet begun their support of research and universities had only modest research budgets, so he chose a drug industry with a commitment to research and with chemists eager to create. He found an ideal colleague in Sprague at Sharp & Dohme. In 1943 Beyer wasn't a renal physiologist, but he had good credentials and Sharp & Dohme immediately sent him off to New York City to work for a short period with Dr. James Shannon, then a leader in renal research and later to become director of the National Institutes of Health.

Back at Sharp & Dohme, their renal program's first scientific success (though a financial failure) came from a well-planned attempt to conserve penicillin by preventing its rapid loss in urine. The group used a substance, *para*-aminohippuric acid (PAH), known to be safe because it had been used by physiologists to test kidney function. It was also secreted by tubules into urine, as was penicillin. Could PAH compete with penicillin for this tubular excretory mechanism and block the loss of penicillin in the urine? It could and did, but to be effective it took a great deal of the substance, almost half a pound a day! But the financial failure of PAH had its bright spots: First, it showed that the idea that two chemicals could compete for the same secretory mechanism was sound, and second, it showed that a laboratory in a commercial drug company could make a basic contribution to renal physiology—discovering that a single chemical compound (PAH) could block the excretion by renal tubules of another (penicillin) without at the same time blocking the excretion of anything else of importance.

Three years later, Sprague synthesized a second compound to block penicillin, Carinamide. It required less drug per day, 20 grams, but this was still too much to swallow. For stockholders, this second product was a second financial flop, but it added a second basic contribution to renal physiology and pharmacology. It showed that the kidney could do three things to a single compound. It could filter it, it could secrete it through the tubules, and, finally, it could reverse this action and reabsorb it into the bloodstream.

But progress was again slow; it was not until 1951 that Sharp & Dohme had synthesized their third product, probenicid (Benemid), also designed to keep penicillin in the body. It was the most potent conserver of penicillin of all their compounds (it required only 2 grams a day), but, ironically, by then penicillin was being mass produced so cheaply that decreasing loss through the kidney was no longer of any practical consequence. There was simply no market for Benemid and it was another money loser.

Good scientists learn not to throw away "useless" things. A little later, Benemid did prove to be useful (and commercially profitable) in promoting the excretion of uric acid and treating patients with gout, a disorder characterized by excessive amounts of uric acid in blood. In 1950 Robert Berliner and his associates had found the renal tubular mechanism for excreting urates in man and, during the next year, Bishop, Rand, and Talbott noted that Benemid greatly increased uric acid excretion in normal man and in a patient with gout. Here is another case (like that of mercury and of Diamox) in which a potent drug had several uses. This time a drug designed to keep penicillin in the body turned out to be valuable in getting uric acid out of the body and was an effective treatment for human gout. But that took a few years; by 1953 Merck had purchased Sharp & Dohme and Beyer and Sprague were told that the renal program might have to be abandoned.

Who came to their rescue? Unknowingly, it was Roblin and American Cyanamid's renal program. In 1950–1951, they produced Diamox and in 1954–1955, it was a financial success as a diuretic. Merck, Sharp & Dohme (MS&D) got the message and the renal program got a reprieve and a new idea. Cyanamid's Diamox was a sulfonamide. So Beyer and Sprague thought, why not look here among MS&D's collection of similar compounds for a better diuretic?

Beyer had always believed that the substance worth developing was one that would eliminate sodium, chloride, and of course water, but not bicarbonate. His chemist colleagues created a number of substances similar to sulfanilamide (Fig. 7.14), each of which had to be tested in animals for their diuretic effect. They began to find substances that did eliminate Na^+, Cl^-, and water; the most promising structure looked like compounds B and C in Fig. 7.14. On a hunch, Novello, Sprague's colleague, decided to swing one end of compound C around, close the ring, and compound D, chlorothiazide (Diuril), was born.

This was at least the third time that sulfanilamide was the starting point. The second time was in the 1940s, when it led to a series of valuable antibacterial drugs. The first time was less fortunate: Jacobs and Heidelberger at the Rockefeller Institute for Medical Research in New York hoped to find a drug that was nontoxic and effective against pneumococcal and streptococcal infections. In a systematic search in 1915, they prepared sulfanilamide but, in line with then current dogma, they thought that in order to fight infection, a substance had to be directly lethal to bacteria, and they did not think that a substance as chemically simple as sulfanilamide could kill bacteria directly!

Much later, Heidelberger wrote, "The possibility that any substance as simple as sulfanilamide could cure bacterial infections never entered our heads, nor did our microbiologist even ask to test it. As slaves to an idea, we missed the boat in 1915, losing the chance to save many thousands of lives, and the development of the sulfonamides was delayed twenty years."

Now let us return to chlorothiazide. For hundreds of years, physicians thought of diuretics as drugs useful in eliminating abnormal collec-

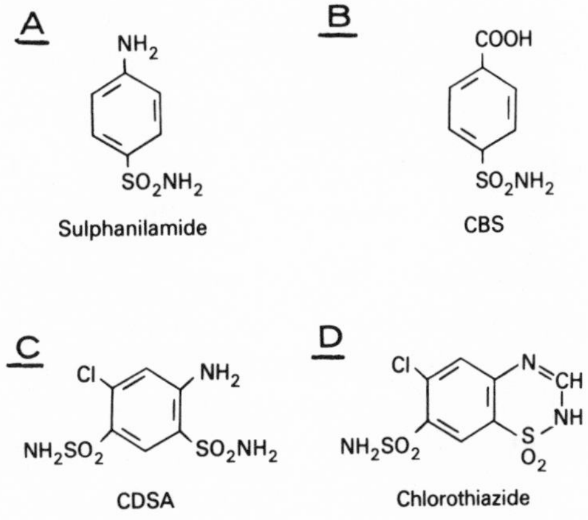

Figure 7.14.   Beyer, Sprague, and Novello decided to make a series of chemical compounds based on the sulfanilamide (sulphanilamide) molecule, compound A (a weak diuretic). Compound B was better, compound C more so, and it led directly to compound D, chlorothiazide (Diuril), and then to hydrochlorothiazide (Hydrodiuril).

tions of fluid in the body (especially in patients with congestive heart failure), but not as drugs to lower abnormally high blood pressure; possibly this is because physicians have been more interested in treating the outward manifestations of congestive heart failure than in preventing heart failure. So it came as a surprise that the first two clinical papers introducing chlorothiazide to physicians proposed it for the treatment of hypertension, rather than for relieving congestive heart failure.

In September 1957 Edward Freis and Ilse Wilson in Washington and William Hollander and Robert Wilkins in Boston independently reported that the thiazide diuretics were effective in lowering blood pressure in patients with essential hypertension. Because they have a twin action of decreasing edema in patients with congestive heart failure and of lowering high blood pressure, and are remarkably safe drugs, thiazides immediately ranked with antibiotics as the most important pharmacological discoveries of the last four decades.

Who thought of using an oral diuretic for the treatment of high blood pressure? Horace Smirk came close to being the first. In 1948, when he was a pioneer in the use of hexamethonium, he reported this experience with two patients:

At an early stage of this investigation, one or two patients who had been taken off hexamethonium bromide because of a temporary shortage were placed on a Kempner salt-free diet. When supplies of the drug became available, dosage at about the original level was resumed. One of our patients who had taken earlier doses without notable symptoms became unconscious, and another had an excessive fall of blood pressure to 95 systolic while lying flat and with the foot of the bed raised. This last patient experienced at rest a strong precordial pain which appeared to be anginal. Subsequent investigation showed that the Kempner diet and also a salt-poor diet (0.2 g. of sodium in 24 hours) enhanced the response to hexamethonium bromide.

There is therefore a definite indication that the blood-pressure-lowering effect of hexamethonium salts is enhanced by salt deprivation, an observation which is of clinical importance in the treatment of hypertensives, particularly those with congestive heart failure.

Smirk, however, never made the logical switch from a salt-free diet to mercurial diuretics (the only potent diuretic then available) as an adjunct to hexamethonium treatment of hypertension.

Beyer's scientific articles on the kidney published in the 1940s and 1950s give no hint of a search for an antihypertension drug; he was working largely on ways of keeping penicillin in the body. There was one exception. In a 1954 paper on renal mechanisms, he mentioned that he had supplied a promising diuretic (compound B in Fig. 7.14) to a medical group in Wisconsin, his alma mater, for use on hypertensive patients; Beyer referred only to their "unpublished experiments" and gave no measurements of blood pressure. Perhaps the important business of patent rights had to be taken care of before he could be openly enthusiastic about diuretic treatment of hypertension.

In 1977 (twenty years after the first publication of diuretic treatment of hypertension) Beyer wrote,

Even before the probenecid work had been brought to a practical conclusion, we turned to the renal modulation of electrolyte balance. Incidentally, any third-year medical student can recognize gross edema [abnormal collections of fluid]. If he remembers his physiology, the various causes of edema and the forms it takes are comprehensible to him. It was clear that a good orally active, safe diuretic agent suitable for day-to-day usage would be a godsend. Moreover, if a low salt diet (salt restriction) was useful in the management of hypertension, then what we proposed to call a saluretic [saline diuretic] agent should be doubly important. It should get rid of excess extravascular fluid, edema. It should lower hypertensive blood pressure also, or so we thought. All this was set forth in a memorandum* to management of the company (Sharp & Dohme) when the program was initiated. Actually at the time of introduction of chlorothiazide, a delicate aspect of the clinical trials was to get our friends in the management of hypertension to recognize that a diuretic, actually a saluretic agent, could be basic antihypertensive therapy.† We did not assess the activity of chlorothiazide in hypertensive animals prior to clinical trial. At the time, that methodology seemed even less convincing than the literature on clinical response to dietary salt restriction.

In other words, Beyer was convinced all along that too much sodium chloride in the body was a cause of hypertension, or at least an important factor in preventing effective treatment by antihypertension drugs. He was so convinced that he did not even test the drug on experimentally produced hypertension in his laboratory.

Chlorothiazide (Diuril) was a landmark discovery because it is an effective diuretic, practically nontoxic, and has now become very inexpensive (a tablet costs less than an aspirin or vitamin pill). It and its successor, hydrochlorothiazide (Hydrodiuril) became the basic, first-line

---

* Lost or tossed out long, long ago.

† But Freis wrote in *1971*, "Because of our prior experience with low sodium diets and mercurial diuretics *we were most eager* to assess these new diuretics for the treatment of hypertension."

treatment recommended by physicians for literally millions of patients with hypertension. This is because treatment with Diuril was not "worse than the disease" and millions who began treatment continued it faithfully for years. When necessary, other drugs are added to achieve the desired result. If the ultimate goal of medicine is to prevent disease, or the serious complications of disease, this may now be possible for hypertension.

I have often been asked, once a miracle drug such as sulfanilamide, penicillin, or hydrochlorothiazide is discovered, marketed, and readily available, why the search goes on, or is even intensified, for new related compounds. Of course, there is a profit motive, the financial gain that comes from building a slightly better mousetrap. But there are other more important reasons. The first axiom of pharmacology is "No drug has only one action in the body." Some of these other actions (treatment of glaucoma by Diamox, designed to be a diuretic; treatment of gout by Benemid, a drug designed to retain penicillin in the body) are useful; some are annoying, unpleasant, or downright toxic. Sometimes a miracle drug requires backup by a drug with an entirely different mode of action. Sometimes some patients don't respond well; sometimes they overrespond; and sometimes a patient develops his own resistance to a drug's action. Of great importance to the success of hydrochlorothiazide (Hydrodiuril) was that elimination of excess sodium in the urine greatly increased the effectiveness of many other antihypertension drugs; this permitted the latter to be used (with Hydrodiuril) in doses that produced the desired effect but which were low enough not to produce undesired ones. And then (to be discussed later) hypertension is not a simple disease with one cause, and different drugs must be designed for treating different types of hypertension.

Hydrochlorothiazide was no exception to the axiom that all drugs have more than one action in the body. In addition to its primary job of eliminating more sodium and chloride ions, used over long periods it often caused excessive excretion of potassium ions and increased reabsorption of uric acid. Excess potassium loss can be countered by increasing potassium intake either by gulping down a solution of potassium chloride or by eating foods (such as bananas and apricots) that are rich in potassium. It can also be prevented by using new and different kinds of diuretics. One of these is triamterene, the first of the oral diuretics that increased the elimination of sodium and water, but not of potassium; it has now become a useful clinical therapeutic agent for correcting or preventing a deficiency in potassium caused by the thiazides.

As mentioned earlier, in 1951 chemists at MS&D undertook a search for substances with the beneficial diuretic characteristics of the mercurial diuretics, but without their toxicity. Upon discovery of the thiazides, work on the top candidate, ethacrynic acid, stopped until 1962, when Everett Schultz at MS&D announced that it had been synthesized and tested. It turned out to be a saluretic–diuretic agent far more potent than Diuril. It acts almost immediately, acts briefly, and causes a degree of sodium loss four to five times that of the thiazides. An important part of the sodium loss produced by ethacrynic acid seems to result from interference with reabsorption of sodium in a region of the tubule unaffected by chlorothiazide (see Fig. 7.15).

In 1964 chemists in the Hoechst laboratories in Frankfurt, Ger-

Figure 7.15.   Approximate site of the major effects of diuretics. The finding that diuretics could produce their main effects by acting on different parts of the tubule provided physicians with drugs that could add to the useful effects of other diuretics or correct their undesirable consequences.

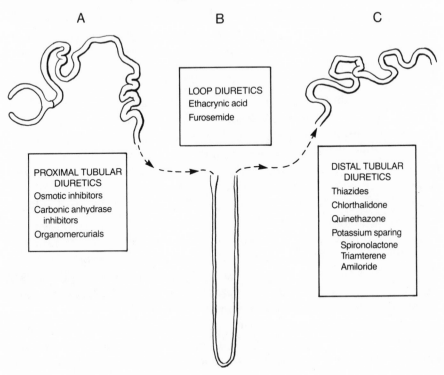

many, also got involved in this fascinating business of molecular modification or manipulation and introduced a new sulfonamide derivative,
furosemide, again distinguished from the thiazides by its more intense
and shorter action. In both respects furosemide resembles ethacrynic
acid: It inhibits reabsorption of sodium at a specific point in the tubule
(see Fig. 7.15) and its potency could result in excessive loss of water,
sodium, and potassium. And so the search goes on for diuretics with the
ideal desired action and little else.

What have we learned from research on diuretics about the process
of discovery? First of all, once the physiological basis of renal function
was clearly understood, research on diuretics moved ahead more quickly
and productively than in all recorded history. Second, the golden period
of basic research on the kidney, 1920–1950, involved the interaction of
physiologists, biochemists, anatomists, pharmacologists, marine biologists, comparative physiologists, and clinicians; these included scientists
working in universities, physicians working in hospitals, and scientists
working in research laboratories of the drug industry. Third, scientific
discovery here, as it often does, took a tortuous path: Hypotheses were
not always correct, theories often needed revision, apparent failure often
turned into success, and carefully planned research on a specific cell or
organ often paid off most handsomely in unexpected ways or in unrelated parts of the body.

Let us go from generalities to specifics. Basic research on kidney
function led to the realization that three main processes were involved
in the formation of urine: filtration (largely a function of the heart and
circulation), tubular reabsorption, and tubular secretion. It also demonstrated that these processes operated at specific sites along the
nephron, used different biochemical mechanisms, and that these were
subject to separate regulation and manipulation. The discovery of sulfanilamide, not intended to be a diuretic, led to a careful bedside observation (sulfanilamide can cause both acidosis and diuresis). The discovery
of carbonic anhydrase in red blood cells led to a basic understanding of
the acidification of urine. The enzyme is present in the tubule and promotes an exchange of sodium ions for hydrogen ions and sulfa drugs can
inhibit this action of carbonic anhydrase. This led to the beliefs that any
chemical that inhibited carbonic anhydrase was a diuretic (correct) and
that any chemical that didn't, was not (incorrect). Some powerful new
carbonic anhydrase inhibitors were found to be poor diuretics, but valuable in treating patients with glaucoma or gout. Some new compounds

that had no effect on carbonic anhydrase were found to be almost too potent as diuretics! We might add that the discovery of penicillin and its rapid excretion in urine led to financing an important renal program in industry that eventually produced Diuril and Hydrodiuril.

Most remarkable of all was that the goal in research on diuretics had always been to find a substance to remove excess fluid in the tissues of patients with congestive heart failure. In this case it also led to an effective treatment for hypertension. It is difficult indeed to predict precisely where basic research will lead. Also, we should not forget that basic and applied research work together to advance each other: The practical search for an oral diuretic led, all along the line, to a better understanding of many basic biological processes, especially in renal function, and basic research on the kidney inspired applied research on diuretics.

Hypertension Revisited

Let's retrace the story of hypertension. In its first phase (most of the nineteenth century), physicians recognized high blood pressure only as an accompaniment of Bright's disease (a serious, usually fatal disease of the kidney). In the second phase hypertension was accorded independent status as a disorder and severed its obligatory connection with Bright's disease. In the third phase, the present, hypertension has become one of the most common of all medical disorders and Bright's disease quite uncommon. But memory is short: We once celebrated the acumen of physicians that separated Bright's disease into two diseases— Bright's disease and "essential" hypertension—but we are now paying too little attention to separating "essential" hypertension into one, two, three, or more diseases.

Yet some patients with high blood pressure do have a specific type of high blood pressure with a recognizable cause. Ernest Labbé in France found in 1922 that high blood pressure may be due to a tumor of the adrenal medulla (the tumor has the impressive name of pheochromocytoma) that periodically secretes epinephrine into the general circulation. This type of hypertension can be relieved by surgical removal of the tumor. In 1934 Harry Goldblatt and his associates in Cleveland found that deliberate narrowing of renal arteries by small clamps caused high blood pressure in experimental animals (this will be discussed later). In

1938 David Rytand at Stanford and Murray Steele and Alfred Cohn in New York identified another specific type of high blood pressure due to congenital constriction of the aorta within the thorax (coarctation of the aorta; see p. 196), easy to diagnose because blood pressure is high in the arms, above the constriction, and low in the legs, below the narrowed segment: It too can be corrected by modern vascular surgeons. In 1955 Jerome Conn at Ann Arbor identified a fourth type of hypertension due to increased secretion of aldosterone, a hormone of the adrenal cortex that regulates tubular reabsorption of sodium ions; quite logically he named the disease "primary aldosteronism." It too can be treated by surgical removal of the tumor, if present, or by administration of a drug, spironolactone, that specifically blocks the effect of aldosterone. And then there is a fifth type of hypertension, high blood pressure associated with coma, convulsions, and renal failure that may occur as "toxemia" (or "eclampsia") late in pregnancy; a sixth type due to a disorder of the pituitary gland; and, in the rat, a seventh type, an inherited type of spontaneous high blood pressure. An eighth type is caused by increased fluid pressure within the cranium, and a ninth is associated with the use of some oral contraceptives. It is quite possible that with continued basic research on the circulation we will find more and more sharply defined types of hypertension with specific causes, and fewer and fewer patients with "essential hypertension" (a name that simply expresses ignorance of the cause of high blood pressure).

One of these nine types deserves special attention because in recent years we have learned a great deal from it. Interestingly enough, it's the one discovered by Goldblatt that is caused by restriction of arterial blood flow to the kidneys. So, after telling you earlier in Chapter 6 to forget about the kidneys as a cause of high blood pressure, we are returning to them and their modern role in hypertension.

Hypertension and the Kidney

In 1898 Robert Tigerstedt and Per Bergman in Stockholm minced rabbit kidneys, injected an extract of the tissue into another rabbit, and found that it increased the animal's blood pressure. They believed that they had demonstrated clearly that a chemical component of the kidney—they named it "renin"—could cause hypertension. Others tried to duplicate their experiment but couldn't, and the observation was pretty much forgotten until 1934, when Harry Goldblatt did his now classic experiment.

Goldblatt knew, of course, that many previous workers had tried to connect damage to the kidneys, caused in a variety of ways, to development of high blood pressure, and he wondered if a common factor might be at work. If so, the logical candidate would be renal ischemia. (*Ischemia* comes from two Greek words, *ischo*, to keep back, and *haima*, blood; in English, it means a local decrease in blood flow due to mechanical obstruction of the artery to a part.) Goldblatt's hypothesis was that renal ischemia, whether produced mechanically or by disease, should be followed by an increase in blood pressure. He chose the simplest way to produce renal ischemia—mechanical constriction of one or both of the main renal arteries immediately after they branched off the abdominal aorta. He devised a simple clamp that fit snugly around a renal artery of a dog and that permitted him to vary and control the degree of narrowing over months without any further surgical procedures or discomfort to the dog. Figure 7.16 shows the result of severe narrowing of both renal arteries.

It was obvious that if man behaved like the dog, ischemic kidneys produced something or released something that got into the general circulation and resulted in a pretty good imitation of naturally occurring hypertension. Even though blood pressure was normal in every artery except those to the kidney, the clamps on the two renal arteries had

Figure 7.16. Fourteen days of severe narrowing of the main artery to the left kidney of a dog did not lead to an increase in blood pressure. Then Goldblatt constricted the artery to the right kidney as well. Blood pressure gradually increased over 1 month until it reached a high level (between 280 and 300 mmHg); with some variation it remained high for 11 months and then tended to decrease slightly.

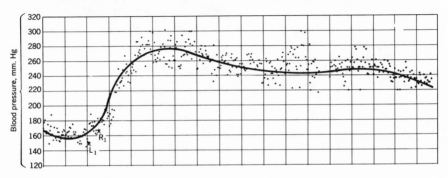

tricked specific cells deep within the kidney into believing that the animal was suffering from *low* blood pressure and its cells were obliged to secrete something into the general circulation to restore blood pressure to normal and protect kidney tissue. Since arterial pressure was already normal, the kidney's effort at self-preservation produced *hyper*tension. The specific cells that produce and release this substance are pictured in Fig. 7.17. Was the substance Tigerstedt's *renin?* Little was heard of renin after the early 1900s, until 1938, when three groups—George Pickering's in Oxford, Eugene Landis' in Philadelphia, and G. Hessel's in Germany—did confirm Tigerstedt's work, including the presence of renin in venous blood from the kidney.

Surgeons knew that local narrowing occasionally occurred in one or more arteries (coronary, cerebral, renal, femoral) and, using X-ray techniques, they screened patients with hypertension to see whether their renal arteries were narrowed; some were. Vascular surgeons repaired or replaced obstructed arteries and the hypertension faded away. So it was now clear that not all hypertension was "essential hypertension," and that the cause of at least a small segment of a huge problem could be identified and eliminated.

But Goldblatt's experiment was just the beginning. The real question was, What was renin? The answer came in 1940, when two chemists working in Indianapolis found that renin by itself didn't raise blood pres-

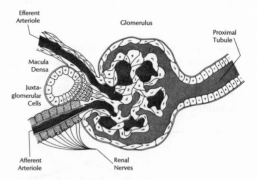

Figure 7.17.   How the kidneys help to regulate their own function. We have incompletely pictured the arterioles entering and leaving the kidney as ordinary small arteries. In actuality, the afferent arteriole (entering the glomerulus) is lined with special cells ("juxtaglomerular" cells, simply meaning "near the glomerulus") that secrete renin directly into the bloodstream. These cells are influenced by sympathetic nerves (blocked by beta-blocking drugs) that change the caliber of the arteriole; these special cells appear to be activated by a change in tension within their walls and are tension or pressure receptors. A second regulatory mechanism is the macula densa, whose cells respond to a change in the concentration of sodium and chloride by influencing the release of renin. So the kidneys, like many other organs in the body, have some control over their own performance.

sure at all. They dissolved purified renin in physiologic salt solution and perfused it through an artery; it did not constrict the artery or its finer branches. However, if they dissolved it in plasma, renin demonstrated definite constrictor properties. It didn't take long then to demonstrate that renin was an enzyme that acted on a globulin normally present in blood plasma. The product of the interaction was a powerful blood pressure-raising substance, forty times as potent as norephinephrine. They called the active substance angiotonin (now called angiotensin). The name of one chemist was Oscar Helmer. The other was a perceptive, clairvoyant young physician—perceptive because he realized early in life that chemistry was going to be of great importance to medicine, and clairvoyant because, after finishing medical school and a two-year internship, he accepted a position as director of the chemical division of the Kaiser Wilhelm Institute in Munich for three years (1928–1931), with major responsibility for the study of brain chemistry. Back in the United States, in 1931, he worked for some years at the Rockefeller Institute. You know his name, Irvine Page, the same who was the first to prove that "essential" hypertension was not "essential" and who began the drive in 1935 to treat hypertension instead of ignoring it (see p. 236).

In 1939, now at the Lilly Laboratory for Clinical Research, Page and Helmer found the nature of the substance that actually produced "renal hypertension" and named it angiotonin. Very shortly thereafter, Eduardo Braun-Menéndez and associates in Buenos Aires independently discovered the same substance, but they named it hypertensin. In 1958, in one of the rare displays of statesmanship in science, each team, reinforced by a few martinis, agreed to give up half of their baby's name, and angiotonin–hypertensin became angiotensin. When Bumpus and Schwyzer each synthesized it in 1957, angiotensin really went center stage. Once thought to be important only in a limited number of patients with hypertension due to renal artery obstruction or renal disease, it is now known to be one of the most potent physiological substances known.

Before going further, we need to say more about the formation of active angiotensin (Fig. 7.18). We have already mentioned that renin—released from the kidney—is an enzyme that acts on a globulin normally present in blood plasma to form a third compound, angiotensin I. Neither renin, plasma globulin, nor their chemical product (angiotensin I) by itself raises blood pressure. However, when venous blood passes through pulmonary capillaries, a special enzyme in the cells of lung cap-

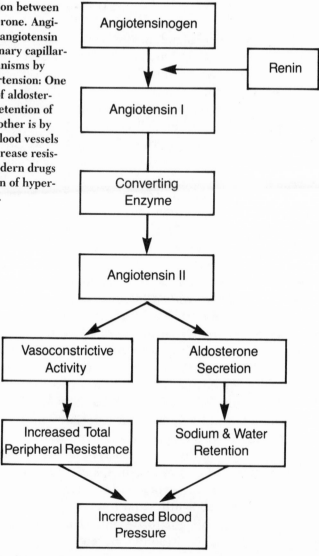

Figure 7.18. Interaction between angiotensin and aldosterone. Angiotensin I, converted to angiotensin II by cells lining pulmonary capillaries, now has two mechanisms by which to produce hypertension: One is through the release of aldosterone, which favors the retention of sodium and water; the other is by direct action on small blood vessels to narrow them and increase resistance to blood flow. Modern drugs can block the production of hypertension at several steps.

illaries converts angiotensin I into angiotensin II, and it is *angiotensin II* that raises blood pressure. This second enzyme (appropriately named *angiotensin converting enzyme*, and of course immediately known as ACE) is of interest because it demonstrates again that organs are apt to have two or three functions instead of one (the lung is no longer only a gas exchange system), and because it provides another point of attack against angiotensin II and the hypertension it causes. The first way would be to decrease the formation of renin in the kidney (by beta blockers), a second would be to interfere with the formation of angiotensin I in blood, the third to block the conversion of angiotensin I to II by ACE (by the use of a new drug, captopril), and the fourth to block by another new drug (saralasin) receptors on blood vessels and prevent a local response to angiotensin II.

I have just mentioned some blocking agents—one with which you're already familiar (beta blockers) and two new ones: captopril and saralasin. Because all beta blockers interfere with the release of renin, this suggests that the sympathetic nervous system has some control over renal hypertension. Captopril, by blocking ACE, decreases or blocks the formation of angiotensin II by the body without interfering with the clinical use of angiotensin, which, given intravenously, can raise low blood pressure in emergencies. Saralasin, by occupying angiotensin II receptors on arterioles, blots out that part of "essential hypertension" that is not "essential" but due to the renin–angiotensin system; it therefore has both a diagnostic role and a therapeutic use.

This is not all that angiotensin II does. In 1958 F. Gross at Ciba Pharmaceutical Company proposed that angiotensin II stimulated release of aldosterone by the adrenal cortex and to a large extent regulated it; in 1960 Jacques Genest in Montreal and John Laragh in New York found that angiotensin definitely regulated release of aldosterone in man. Aldosterone, you will recall, is a hormone that regulates body sodium by promoting sodium reabsorption in renal tubules. Rare aldosterone-forming tumors of the adrenal cortex release enough of the sodium-retaining hormone to cause a specific type of hypertension.

So the kidney controls the kidney! Secretion of the kidney's renin leads to angiotensin II, which acts on the adrenal cortex to release aldosterone that controls sodium reabsorption.

We still don't know the full spectrum of activity of angiotensin. It probably has an action on that part of the brain that regulates thirst by influencing water intake; it probably has some control over a pituitary hormone (the *anti*diuretic hormone) whose main function is to increase reabsorption of water by the kidney. So angiotensin is involved in several mechanisms: one that regulates blood pressure to ensure adequate blood flow to the kidney, one that regulates sodium reabsorption in the kidney, and one that regulates both water intake and water excretion. It is obvious that a competent physician today must have a pretty good understanding of the complexities of the human body, how disorders come about, how best to correct these, and the actual mechanisms by which drugs help his patients.

This is not the end of the hypertension story. Even though we have fifty new drugs that can lower high blood pressure in appropriate patients and even though we know how each of these drugs acts on its target cells, each (singly or in combination) must, as far as we now know, be taken for a lifetime to maintain blood pressure within normal limits. This creates problems with compliance, expense, and undesired effects. The ideal solution to a medical problem is to *prevent* the disease, not treat it for a lifetime once it has begun. Prevention of high blood pressure, however, usually requires knowledge that we do not yet have (with the exception of very special and uncommon types of hypertension)—we don't know what *causes* it (as we do with diseases such as smallpox and poliomyelitis), and so it is difficult to prevent it.

But, you will say, we do know the cause: It's secretion of renin, or malfunction of salt-excreting mechanisms, or overactivity of the sympathetic nervous system. But we don't know the "cause of these causes." For example, even if there were agreement that hypertension is due to inadequate elimination of salt—that leads to accumulation of fluid in the walls of arterioles, thickening them, narrowing the blood channel, and increasing resistance to blood flow—we still have not answered the basic question, What causes the inadequate elimination of salt *in the first place?* Or if there were agreement that hypertension is due to excessive activity of the sympathetic nervous system, of renin-producing cells in the kidney, or of the adrenal gland in producing aldosterone, we again have not answered the basic question, What caused this increased activity in the first place? Some wise man (I. F. Stone) remarked, "If you expect to see the final results of your work, you haven't asked a big enough question." We haven't yet asked the big enough question because we are too busy controlling the disease that 37 million Americans already have.

So at the moment, lacking this basic knowledge, we cannot prevent hypertension in one swift motion (as in vaccination against smallpox or swallowing a few drops of polio vaccine). We probably *can* prevent full-blown, severe hypertension if we diagnose it early enough (which means mass-screening 150 million adults in the United States alone), treat it early enough (which means that about 37 million "patients" begin treatment even before they have any signs or symptoms of the disease, except for a set of numbers), and treat it continuously for a lifetime (which means strict adherence to regular use of present or improved drugs, even though these may cause more discomfort and annoyance than mild hypertension itself).

The task is not an easy one. It's easier to obtain full and continuous and even compulsive cooperation when there is a threat of a truly dread disease (smallpox or poliomyelitis) than with hypertension. This is because for many years patients with bad numbers may have had no symptoms, and because every physician knows of patients with severe hypertension who have lived a full and happy life without any antihypertension treatment at all. It's hard to get enthusiastic cooperation of a physician and his patients under such circumstances. We tried to stop the consumption of alcohol with an amendment to the constitution and failed; we tried to stop smoking with explicit warnings from the Surgeon General, the American Heart Association and the American Lung Association and essentially failed; we've tried to stop the use of cocaine and heroin by strict laws and failed.

The first step in preventing hypertension (without having the basic facts regarding its cause) must be to present honestly the risks associated with having mild hypertension. This has not always been done; for example, one prominent advocate of drug treatment of hypertension recently wrote, "There was a 2600% reduction in combined morbidity–mortality associated with treatment [as compared to the control group that received no active drug]." My mind can grasp a 100% reduction in morbidity–mortality, but 2600% reduction is beyond my comprehension.

The best study of these risk factors was the Framingham study, which began in 1949. The investigators were William Kannel and a team supported by the National Heart and Lung Institute of the National Institutes of Health. They decided to do a fourteen-year follow-up of almost an entire community with a fairly stable population; they selected Framingham, Massachusetts, and signed up 5,209 men and women between the ages of 30 and 62 years, none of whom initially had any symptoms or illnesses related to hypertension. Some did have hypertension that met the number definitions of 165 / 95 or higher; some had normal blood pressure (140 / 90 or lower). The remainder (less than 165 / 95 and more than 140 / 90) had borderline hypertension.

The medical team made measurements and observations on these 5,209 persons over a 14-year period. In a series of reports beginning in 1951, they showed statistically that patients who had high blood pressure had strokes four times as often and developed heart failure about four to five times as often as those who maintained normal blood pressure. They also had a shorter life expectancy. This does *not* mean that high blood pressure by itself *caused* these diseases and shortened life-span, but it was a risk factor—it contributed to the likelihood of a subject's suffering or dying from these diseases of the heart and blood vessels. There were, of course, other risk factors, including smoking, a high-cholesterol diet, and obesity. Having one increased risk factor (high blood pressure) does *not* mean that everyone with it will have a stroke, heart attack, or short life-span; but it does mean that if you have hypertension and want the odds for your health and long life to be in your favor, you should try to keep your blood pressure within normal limits. Some cardiologists believe that "essential" hypertension itself is the result of many different factors, no one or two of which can produce hypertension by itself.

Considering that there are not enough physicians in the United States to diagnose and regulate treatment for 37 million men and women with high or borderline blood pressure, some have suggested that we consider a different kind of management. One is to try to identify those most likely to move from borderline to severe hypertension and to make a determined campaign there. Another is to have special hypertension clinics manned with physician assistants who are trained to deal with the recognition and treatment of hypertension and who are carefully supervised by a cardiologist. A third came from Colin Dollery in England (with tongue in cheek) who proposed the following:

My vision of the hypertension clinic in 30 years time is of a row of consulting rooms. The patient will arrive and go into one, there will be a radiantly beautiful nurse sitting there and she will take the blood pressure and make a few comments to the patient and then issue some pills off the counter and the patient will go away. The next time the patient comes, he will go into a different door, but there will be the same radiantly beautiful nurse to receive him, and this will be the entire regulation of the pressure. But the radiantly beautiful nurse will not be a human, it will be an automated electronic humanoid so it will always be the same and the patient will therefore always identify with exactly the same person delivering care. The robot will be wired up to a computer that will be programmed by [an expert cardiologist] which will just issue the pills strictly on what the blood pressure readings are.

We have come a long way in learning the natural history of hypertension, in learning how to control pressure that is already too high or in keeping it from rising. We still have unsolved problems in addition to those just mentioned. One question is, Will drug treatment of hypertension prevent or reverse atherosclerosis? A second is, Will blood pressure once at a normal level for some time stay there if drugs are stopped? And another is, will drug therapy that is effective in reducing "the numbers" also reduce the thickness of arterial and arteriolar walls and decrease the thickness of the left ventricular wall? There is reason to believe it could, because the walls of the pulmonary artery and right ventricle of a newborn baby are thick, but within a few weeks, because of a marked decrease in pressure in the pulmonary artery and in the work of the right ventricle, they become considerably thinner than the walls of the left ventricle and aorta. Another question is, What will be the overall effect on other body systems of antihypertension drugs taken faithfully for 20, 30, or 40 years; will patients live longer but enjoy life less?

8

What Have You Done for Me Lately?

Thomas Jefferson wrote that he had no concerns for the new America as long as it had a well-informed, enlightened citizenry. I wrote this book to provide our citizenry with more information and enlightenment on the origins of important discoveries in medicine and surgery.

At the end of my introductory chapter, I mentioned briefly the study that Robert Dripps and I began in 1971, but I noted only a few conclusions that we drew from it. This was deliberate, because it was my hope that each of you, while reading Chapters 2–7, would form some opinions, conclusions, and convictions of your own about the process of discovery and how to encourage and accelerate it, and that you, as an enlightened citizenry, would develop a strong interest in molding national biomedical science policy. However, because our rather massive collection of data rests in the Government Printing Office, and because studies of similar magnitude may not be carried out by other scientists, I should tell you in this final chapter some of the conclusions that we and our many consultants formed from our pretty thorough and, I believe, objective analysis of more than 6,000 published scientific articles or books.

First let me remind you that the 1940s, 1950s, and 1960s produced an unusually large number of genuine "breakthroughs" in biomedical science that directly improved human health. Examples are learning to control most infectious diseases by sulfa drugs, penicillin, streptomycin, and other antibiotic drugs; preventing polio by an oral vaccine; correcting cardiac defects by open heart surgery; replacing obstructed arteries in heart muscle, brain, and limbs; transplanting organs such as the kidney; and treating high blood pressure with new drugs.

But in the late 1960s, despite the continuing achievements in the science of medicine, some people were impatient about the lack of daily or weekly "breakthroughs" with immediate application to man, and about the continued existence of many diseases. President Lyndon Johnson in 1966 expressed this concern when he said:

Presidents need to show more interest in what the specific results of research are in their lifetime, and in their administration. A great deal of *basic* research has been done . . . but I think the time has come to zero in on the targets by trying to get our knowledge fully applied. . . . *We must make sure that no life saving discovery is locked up in the laboratory* [italics added].

President Johnson's words popularized a new set of terms: research in the service of man (implying that there are *two* types of biomedical research, one in the service of man and another that is *not*), strategy for the cure of disease, targeted research, mission-oriented research, programmatic research, commission-directed research, contract supported research, and payoff research. And the President's remarks have been summarized as "research is fine, but results are better."

Lyndon Johnson tilted support of research toward immediate application to patient care of what was already known and away from encouraging discovery to roll back ignorance. There was no real basis for the President's view, except for a study by the Department of Defense on the development of military weapons. No one at that time (1966) in or out of government had done broad, objective "research on medical research"—research to find out how discoveries really have come about, what speeded them, and what held them back. Robert Dripps and I believed it mandatory to undertake such a study.* After all, it was unreasonable that decisions on how best to spend billions on biomedical research should be based on personal opinions or prejudices, gut reactions, pressure from special interest groups, and a few fascinating, convincingly spun anecdotes.

So we plunged into the task of "research on research." With the help of many consultants, we read and evaluated more than 6,000 scientific articles that might qualify as important stepping stones for advances in ten fields: open heart surgery, vascular surgery, coronary

---

*Our study, that began in the summer of 1971 and ended in 1977; Dr. Dripps died suddenly of coronary occlusion on October 30, 1973.

insufficiency (heart attacks), drug treatment of hypertension, management of abnormal cardiac rhythms by pacemakers and cardiac resuscitation, use of oral diuretics, new diagnostic methods, antibiotic and chemotherapeutic drugs, intensive care units, and prevention of poliomyelitis. We devoted much time and careful thought to selecting and analyzing 663 "key articles." We defined a key article as one that did one of the following:

1.   Had an important effect on the direction of subsequent research and development that, in turn, proved to be important for *clinical* advance in one or more of the clinical advances under study.

2.   Reported new data, new ways of looking at old data, a new concept or hypothesis, a new method, a new drug, a new apparatus, or a new technique that either was essential for full development of one or more of the clinical advances or greatly accelerated it. The key article might report basic laboratory investigation, clinical investigation, development of an apparatus or its essential components, synthesis of data and ideas of others, or wholly theoretical work.

3.   Described the final step in a clinical advance, even though it was an inevitable step requiring no unusual imagination, creativity, or special competence. Some of our consultants were reluctant to designate some of these final, applied steps as key articles because they were fully predictable; however, we decided to include them because our study disclosed a number of instances in which the final step was "inevitable" but no one took it for many years (e.g., the final step in vascular surgery appeared inevitable in 1910, but no one took it until 1940!).

A study was *not* labeled a key study, even if it won the Nobel Prize for its author, if it had not yet served directly or indirectly as a step toward solving one of the ten clinical advances under study.

What did we learn from this study of key articles?

Basic Versus Applied Research

We wanted to know how many key articles reported "basic" research and how many reported applications of it ("getting the knowledge fully applied," to quote President Johnson). To do this we needed a definition of basic research. I thought it best to use the definition employed by the Federal Government, because each of its agencies annually reports the percentage of appropriations that each has spent on basic and on applied research. I assumed that to do this they must have a uniform definition of basic science. I wrote to the President's Science Advisor. He was most cooperative and soon I had a 12-inch-high stack of articles and reports from various federal agencies that either conduct research or support it; all dealt with their definition of basic research. Unfortunately, each defined it differently! I had no choice but to produce my own working definition: Research is *basic* when the investigator, in addition to observing, describing, and measuring, attempts to determine the *mechanisms* responsible for the observed effects. My definition means that basic research can be on healthy or sick man, or on animals, tissues, cells, or subcellular or molecular components. This definition differs from the concept of some laymen and scientists who believe that research is more and more basic when the unit investigated is smaller and smaller, the most basic being submolecular; our definition does not label work on small units, such as cells, as "basic" if it is purely descriptive and the investigators are not concerned with determining *mechanisms*. This definition of basic research thus steers clear of whether the research was "investigator initiated" or "commission initiated," whether "undirected" or "directed," whether supported by grant or by contract, because who initiated, directed, or supported the research has nothing to do with whether it is basic.

Briefly, this is what we found: Almost 62% of the "key articles" were clearly "basic" research; the other 38% fell into other categories of applied research and development, critical analysis and reviews of published work, or synthesis of new concepts.

Abraham Flexner, without specifically defining basic research, described exceptionally well the difference between basic, undirected science and applied science. A noted medical educator and architect of the restructuring of American medical schools in the early 1900s, he spelled it out when he recalled a conversation he had some years earlier with George Eastman, founder of Eastman-Kodak:

Mr. Eastman, a wise and gentle, far-seeing man, gifted with exquisite taste in music and art, had been saying to me that he meant to devote his vast fortune to the promotion of education in useful subjects. I ventured to ask him whom he regarded as the most useful worker in science in the world. He replied instantaneously, "Marconi." I surprised him by saying, "Whatever pleasure we derive from the radio or however wireless and the radio may have added to human life, Marconi's share was practically negligible." I shall not forget his astonishment on this occasion. He asked me to explain. I replied to him: "Mr.

Eastman, Marconi was inevitable. The real credit for everything that has been done in the field of wireless belongs, as far as such fundamental credit can be definitely assigned to anyone, to Professor Clerk Maxwell, who in 1865, carried out certain abstruse and remote calculations in the field of magnetism and electricity. Maxwell reproduced his abstract equations in a treatise published in 1873. Other discoveries supplemented Maxwell's theoretical work during the next fifteen years. Finally in 1877 and 1888 the scientific problem still remaining—the detection and demonstration of the electromagnetic waves which are the carriers of wireless signals—was solved by Heinrich Hertz, a worker in Helmholtz's laboratory in Berlin. Neither Maxwell nor Hertz had any concern about the utility of their work; no such thought ever entered their minds. They had no practical objective. The inventor in the legal sense was of course Marconi, but what did Marconi invent? Merely the last technical detail, the now obsolete receiving device called a coherer, almost universally discarded. . . . Hertz and Maxwell invented nothing, but it was their apparently useless theoretical work which was seized upon by a clever technician and which has created new means of communication, utility, and amusement by which men whose merits are relatively slight have obtained fame and earned millions. Who were the fundamentally useful men? Not Marconi, but Clerk Maxwell and Heinrich Hertz. Hertz and Maxwell were geniuses without thought of use. Marconi was a clever inventor with no thought but use." One thing I said he could be sure of [was] that . . . throughout the whole history of science most of the really great discoveries which had ultimately proved to be beneficial to mankind had been made by men and women who were driven, not by the desire to be useful, but merely by the desire to satisfy their curiosity.

"Curiosity?" asked Mr. Eastman. "Yes," I replied, "curiosity, which may or may not eventuate in something useful, is probably the outstanding characteristic of modern thinking. It is not new. It goes back to Galileo, Bacon, Sir Isaac Newton, and to the Greeks, and it must be absolutely unhampered. Institutions of learning and institutions of research should be devoted to the cultivation of curiosity and the less they are deflected by considerations of immediacy of application, the more likely they are not only to contribute to human welfare, but to the equally important satisfaction of intellectual interest which may indeed be said to have become the ruling passion of intellectual life in modern times."

Dr. Dripps and I also wanted to know how many of the key articles in our study reported research that at the time it was done was unrelated to the solution (or partial solution) of a clinical problem; in other words, in how many did the scientist seek knowledge for the sake of knowledge. Considering our broad definition of a key article, the number was unexpectedly large—42% of all key articles. Such research was usually done in sciences unrelated to medicine (such as physics, chem-

istry, veterinary medicine, botany, and agriculture); it was also unpredictable and usually accelerated advance in more than one field of science
and industry. A classic example in this group was Wilhelm Roentgen,
who, while studying a basic problem in the physics of rays emitted from
a Crookes' tube, discovered X rays which immediately became vital for
the precise diagnosis of many diseases and later for the treatment of
some; they also had many industrial uses.

Another example was Landsteiner's discovery of human blood
groups in 1900 when he was investigating a basic problem in immunology and had no thought of the importance of his discovery to the transfusion of blood; indeed, he made no mention of its possible relation to
transfusion reactions. On the other hand, the same Landsteiner, in 1909,
found that a nonbacterial material (a virus) caused poliomyelitis in monkeys; this again was basic research, but this time clearly related to a
clinical problem.

We also wanted to know whether President Johnson was correct
when he implied in 1966 that we then knew all we needed to know and
that all we had to do was apply it. Actually, there was some basis for his
belief, because medical science had come a long way in the immediately
preceding forty years. Let us take a look at medicine in 1776:

When Herman Boerhaave, the most accomplished and celebrated physician of
the 18th century, died, he left behind him an elegant volume, the title-page of
which declared that it contained all the secrets of medicine. Every page of that
volume, except one, was blank. On that one was written, "keep the head cool,
the feet warm, and the bowels open." This legacy of Boerhaave to suffering
humanity typified, not inaptly or unjustly, the acquirements, not of medical
science, but of medical art at the close of the 18th century. Empiricism, authority, and theory ruled the medical practice of the world at that time. The result
of therapeutical experience from Hippocrates to Boerhaave was fairly summed
up by the latter in the eleven words we have just quoted. To quiet the nervous
system, to equalize the circulation, to provide for the normal action of the
intestinal canal, and to leave all the rest to the healing power of nature was
sound medical treatment, and it was as far as a sound therapeutics had gone a
hundred years ago.

So began a 366-page volume published in 1876, *A Century of American
Medicine 1776–1876*, celebrating 100 years of American independence.

Even in the twentieth century, Lawrence J. Henderson wrote,
"Somewhere between 1910 and 1912 in this country [the United States],
a random patient, with a random disease, consulting a doctor chosen at

random had, for the first time in the history of mankind, a better than fifty–fifty chance of profiting from the encounter."

Johnson was right in being impressed by the rapid-fire rate of discoveries in medicine between 1922 (when insulin was discovered) and 1966, but he underestimated the vast amount of ignorance that still existed in the field of health and disease.

Let us consider knowledge and ignorance in some of the disorders of the heart and circulation discussed in Chapters 2–7.

In the last three decades, we have learned to use new drugs to lower blood pressure in patients with hypertension and so lessen the risk of atherosclerosis, stroke, coronary occlusion, and heart attacks. But we still do not know the cause of high blood pressure in most patients, and the number of patients with hypertension has not decreased. We do not know how to motivate 100% of the population to be screened for high blood pressure or how to initiate and maintain effective therapy in all those who are found to have high blood pressure.

We have learned how to place catheters in the hearts of small babies and identify congenital heart lesions, and we have learned how to do palliative open heart operations on some and corrective procedures on others. But we do not know how many cardiac defects in newborn babies are true genetic defects and how many are due wholly or partly to the environment of the fetus; and, except for some defects known to be due to rubella virus, we do not know the causes of congenital heart disease and are not yet able to replace defective genes.

We know how, by surgical procedures, to correct or bypass obstructions in the aorta, coronary, femoral, carotid, vertebral, and renal arteries; in 1980 surgeons in the United States alone performed 135,000 coronary "bypass" operations. But we do not know how to prevent the atherosclerosis that causes the obstruction, or how to diagnose and treat early atherosclerosis and make expensive surgical procedures unnecessary.

We know how to place electrodes on a patient's thorax and, by appropriate electric shocks, convert serious or fatal cardiac arrhythmias to normal rhythm, but we do not know how to prevent the coronary obstruction that leads to heart attacks (death of part of the heart muscle) and initiates the abnormal rhythms that sometimes lead to sudden death.

We know how, by closed chest cardiac compression and mouth-to-mouth resuscitation, to maintain circulation and respiration in a patient whose heart has stopped. But for a patient whose heart is still beating but is failing, we do not know what basic biochemical mechanisms have been impaired nor how to restore full cardiovascular function.

We know how to insert an artificial pacemaker into a heart beating too slowly to maintain life and we can even power it with nuclear energy. But we do not know how to prevent the block in the conducting system of the heart that made the artificial pacemaker necessary.

We have sophisticated physiological tests that tell us precisely what function of the lungs is damaged by disease and how badly. And we know that smoking contributes to pulmonary disease. But we do not know the cause of the damage to the lung in pulmonary emphysema, how to stop its progress even if detected early, and how to prevent pulmonary heart disease caused by emphysema.

How will we ever solve these and thousands of other problems? In my opinion, by the public developing as deep a concern for *discovery of new knowledge* as it now has for *"health maintenance," delivery,* and *cost.* Lewis Thomas has said,

We tend to obscure our ignorance by making it seem that the problem has been solved—that blood lipids are the answer to atherosclerosis and that coronary bypass surgery is the final answer to coronary artery disease. We must face up to our present state of ignorance and recognize that an entirely different type of knowledge than we now have will be necessary to solve problems such as atherosclerosis. We must also realize that when the actual cause of atherosclerosis is found, in all likelihood it will be a very simple one, and, when the treatment or prevention is discovered, it is likely to be inexpensive and simple.

The discovery of polio vaccine supports Thomas' views. In the 1950s, the National Foundation for Infantile Paralysis had to decide whether to put very large sums of money into the design and development of body respirators for patients whose respiratory muscles were paralyzed, into research on elaborate, expensive, electronically controlled artificial limbs, into evaluation of treatment by hot fomentations as proposed by the Sister Kenney Foundation, or into basic research on viruses, their culture, and their identification. It opted for all-out support of basic research on the life and death of *viruses in general,* hoping that something would be learned that would help in the war against polio virus. This decision paid off. Within a few years, Enders, whose primary scientific interest was in viruses, but in mumps and not polio viruses, learned how to grow polio virus in quantity outside of the human body (at a time when it was believed that this virus could survive in the laboratory only in the brains of monkeys), and shortly thereafter polio vaccines were ready for clinical trials. Paraphrasing Flexner, after Enders learned how to grow polio virus in quantity, polio vaccine was inevitable. And the cost of preventing polio became almost negligible.

Either–Or Versus *Both*

Intelligent national policy on support of medical research requires that the public and those who work full-time for the public (Congress and the voluntary health agencies) understand the necessity of long-term, stable support for basic, undirected research as the means of gaining the new knowledge and understanding of basic biological processes that are essential for the prevention and control of disease.

This does not mean choosing between support of basic research and support of applied research. It's not an either–or matter. We can do both and *must* do both. We do not tell a patient with a badly damaged heart valve that we are concerned only with learning enough to prevent such damage and that he should wait until we learn enough; we proceed promptly to replace the damaged valve with the best possible man-made valve (made through applied research and development). But our long-term goal must be *understanding enough about body functions* to be able to *prevent* all diseases or to provide early diagnosis and effective treatment for those that so far have resisted prevention. We cannot have all basic research and no applied research, nor can we have all applied research and no basic. We also cannot have a back-and-forth policy of doubling funds for basic research and turning off applied research for five years, and then doubling funds for applied research and turning off basic research for the next five years.

The slogan of the American Heart Association is "Research is the starting point for all medical advance." When research succeeds, it is also the *ending* point—for disease and for the tremendous national financial burden of health care.

Epilogue

In 1872–1873 a distinguished English scientist, John Tyndall (see page 138) toured American cities giving lectures on science to general audiences. This was in an era when Americans had to be a practical people, still concerned with pushing westward, still fighting Indians, and just recovering from a civil war. In addition to donating all royalties from his book *Lectures in America* to the advancement of scientific research in America, Tyndall also gave Americans some free advice:

You have scientific genius amongst you, scattered here and there. Take all unnecessary impediments out of its way. Keep your sympathetic eye upon the originator of knowledge. Give him the freedom necessary for his researches, not overloading him, either with the duties of tuition or of administration, not demanding from him so-called practical results—above all things, avoiding that question which ignorance so often addresses to genius, "What is the use of your work?" Let him make truth his object, however unpractical for the time being it may appear.

Sources of Illustrations

Fig. 1.1   Cordano, A., CVRI.*

Fig. 1.2   Cordano, A., CVRI.

Fig. 2.1   Briscoe, M. H., CVRI.

Fig. 2.2   Wright, Robert, Dept. Pathology & CVRI.

Fig. 2.3   Briscoe, M. H., CVRI.

Fig. 2.4   Briscoe, M. H., CVRI.

Fig. 2.5   Briscoe, M. H., CVRI.

Fig. 2.6   Briscoe, M. H., CVRI.

Fig. 2.7A   Gibbon, John (1937). "Artificial maintenance of circulation during experimental occlusion of pulmonary artery," p. 1109. *Arch Surg* **34**, 1105–1131 (© Am Med Assoc).

Fig. 2.7B   Gibbon, John (1954). "Application of a mechanical heart and lung apparatus to cardiac surgery," p. 173. *Minn Med* **37**, 171–180.

Fig. 2.8   Singer, Charles (1925). *The Evolution of Anatomy* (p. 61). Alfred Knopf, New York.

Fig. 2.9   Rokitansky, Carl (1875). *Handbuch der Pathologishen Anatomie*, 3 vol. Braumüller u. Seidel, Wien.

Fig. 2.10   (1957). *Med J Aust* **2**, 331.

Fig. 2.11   Malpighi, Marcello (1661). "De Pulmonibus observationes anatomicae." B. Ferronius, Bologna.

Fig. 2.12   Briscoe, M. H., CVRI. (Based on William Harvey's 1851 letter to Paul Schlegel; see Opera Omnia, William Harvey, Bowyer, London, 1766.)

*CVRI = Staff member, Cardiovascular Research Institute, University of California, San Francisco.

Fig. 2.13A   Fabricius, Hieronymus (1603). *De Venarum Ostiolis*. (Reprinted in Opera Anatomica, Meglietti, Padua, 1625.)

Fig. 2.13B   Harvey, William (1628). *Exercitatio Anatomica De Motu Cordis et Sanguinis in Animalibus*. Fitzer, Frankfurt.

Fig. 2.14A, B Folkow, Björn and Neil, Eric (1971). *Circulation* (p. 157, Fig. 11-6-A). Oxford University Press, London.

Fig. 2.15A   Porter, R. and Bradley, J. D. (1855). U.S. Patent Office #12753.

Fig. 2.15B   DeBakey, Michael (1935). U.S. Patent Office #2,018,999.

Fig. 2.16   Hasse, Oscar (1874). *Die Lammblut Transfusion beim Menschen*. Edward Hopper, St. Petersburg.

Fig. 2.17   Fujita, Tsunes, Tokunaga, Junichi and Inoue, Hajime (1971). *Atlas of Scanning Electron Microscopy in Medicine* (p. 84, Fig. 118). Elsevier Biomedical Press, Amsterdam.

Fig. 2.18   Briscoe, M. H., CVRI.

Fig. 2.19   Zucker, Marjorie B. (1980). "The functioning of blood platelets," p. 87. *Scientific American* June 1980. Originally published in: Baumgartner, H. R.: Platelet interaction with vascular structures. In: "Thrombosis: Risk factors and haemorrh. (Stuttg.) *Suppl. 51*, 161–176 (1972).

Fig. 2.20   Comroe, J. H. (1974). *Physiology of Respiration*, 2nd Ed., p. 184. Year Book Medical Publishers, Chicago.

Fig. 2.21A   Leeuwenhoek, Antonii van (1722). *Anatomia et Contemplatio, Opera Omnia*.

Fig. 2.21B   Zucker-Franklin, D., Greaves, M. F., Giossi, C. E. and Marmont, A. M. (1981). *Atlas of Blood Cells: Function and Pathology*, Vol. 1. Edi Ermes, Milan. Electron micrograph courtesy of H. Kayden.

Fig. 2.22   Krogh, August (1941). *The Comparative Physiology of Respiratory Mechanisms* (pp. 62 & 63). University of Pennsylvania Press, Philadelphia.

Fig. 2.23   Phalen, Robert F., Yeh, Hsu-Chi, Raabe, Otto G. and Velasquez, David J. (1973). "Casting the lungs *in situ*," p. 262. *Anat Rec 77*, 255–263.

Fig. 2.24   Bastacky, Jacob. Donner Laboratory, Lawrence Berkeley Laboratory, University of California.

Fig. 2.25   Weibel, Ewald (1979). *Stereologic Methods. Vol. 1. Practical Methods for Biological Morphometry* (p. 323, Fig. 8-10-1). Copyright: Academic Press Inc. (London) Ltd.

Fig. 2.26   Netter, Frank (1969). *CIBA Collection of Medical Illustrations: Vol. 5, Heart*. Section II, Plates 60 & 61. CIBA, Summit, N.J.

Fig. 2.27   Abel, J. J., Rowntree, L. G. and Turner, B. B. (1914). "On the removal of diffusible substances from the circulating blood of living animals by dialysis," pp. 285 & 291. *J Pharmacol Exp Ther 5*, 275–316.

Fig. 3.13   Netter, Frank (1969). CIBA Collection of Medical Illustrations. Vol. 5. Heart. Section II, Plate 12. CIBA, Summit, N.J.

Fig. 3.14A   Einthoven, W. (1901). "Un nouveau galvanomètre". Arch N Sc Ex Nat 6, p. 625. Photograph of this original apparatus in museum of the University of Leiden, June, 1960.

Fig. 3.14B   2-Channel Holter Recorder, Model 7200. Courtesy of Instruments for Cardiac Research, Inc., Liverpool, N.Y.

Fig. 3.15   Wiggers, Carl J., "The Heart." Copyright © May, 1957 by Scientific American, Inc. All rights reserved.

Fig. 3.16   Forssmann, Werner Theodore Otto (1929). "Die Sondierung des rechten Herzens." Klin Wochenschr 8, 2086–2087 and 2287.

Fig. 3.17   Comroe, J. H. (1982). "The nature of scientific discovery." Encyclopaedia Britannica Medical and Health Annual, pp. 64–85, Chicago, 1982.

Fig. 3.18   Taffel, Alexander (1943). Visualized Physics, p. 174. Oxford Book Co., New York.

Fig. 3.19   Hertz, Helmuth (1977). In Echocardiography with Doppler Applications and Real Time Imaging. (N. Bom, Editor). Martinus Nijhoff, Publisher, The Hague.

Fig. 3.20   Sokolow, M. and McIlroy, M. (1981). Clinical Cardiology, 3rd edition, p. 89. Courtesy of N. B. Schiller. Lange Medical Publishing, Los Altos, California

Fig. 4.1   Courtesy of University of Pennsylvania School of Medicine.

Fig. 4.2   Tyndall, John (1869). "On the blue color of the sky and on the polarization of light by cloudy matter generally." Philosophical Magazine 37, 384–394.

Figs. 4.3   Courtesy of James Eckenhoff, Northwestern University School of Med-
& 4.4   icine (published on pp. 19 & 21 of Anesthesia Since Colonial Times.) Lippincott, Montreal and Philadelphia.

Fig. 4.5   Courtesy of Robert Byck, Editor (1975). Cocaine Papers by Sigmund Freud. Stonehill Publishing, New York.

Fig. 4.6   Bernard, Claude (1857). Des Substances Toxiques (p. 321). J. B. Baillière et Fils, Paris.

Fig. 4.7   Courtesy of Norman Staub, CVRI, University of California, San Francisco. In Comroe, J. H., Physiology of Respiration, 2nd ed., 1974, p. 16. Year Book Medical Publishers, Chicago.

Fig. 4.8   Beaconsfield, P., Birdwood G., and Beaconsfield, R., "The Placenta." Copyright © August 1980, Scientific American, Inc. All rights reserved.

Fig. 4.9   Comroe, J. H. (1974). Physiology of Respiration, 2nd edition, p. 241. Year Book Medical Publishers, Chicago.

Fig. 4.10   Briscoe, M. H., CVRI.

Fig. 4.11A   Briscoe, M. H., CVRI.

Fig. 4.11B   Williams (1858). U.S. Patent #19323.

Fig. 4.12   Morris, D. C., King, S. B., Douglas, J. S., Wickliffe, C. W. and Jones, E. L. (1977). "Hemodynamic results of aortic valve replacement with the porcine xenograft valve." *Circulation* **56**, 841–844. By permission of the American Heart Association ©.

Fig. 5.1   Stewart, G. N. (1910). "A clamp for isolating a portion of the lumen of a blood vessel without stopping the circulation through the vessel" (p. 648). *JAMA* **55**, 647–649.

Fig. 5.2   Malinin, Theodore I. (1979). *Surgery and Life. The Extraordinary Career of Alexis Carrel*. Harcourt, Brace, Jovanovich, New York.

Fig. 5.3A   Carrel, A. and Guthrie, C. C. (1906). "Uniterminal and biterminal venous transplantations" (p. 268). By permission of *Surgery, Gynecology & Obstetrics* **2**, 266–286.

Fig. 5.3B   Carrel, A. (1912). "Results of the permanent intubation of the thoracic aorta" (p. 247). By permission of *Surgery, Gynecology & Obstetrics* **15**, 245–248.

Fig. 5.3C   Carrel, A. and Guthrie, C. C. (1906). "Uniterminal and biterminal venous transplantations" (p. 272). By permission of *Surgery, Gynecology & Obstetrics* **2**, 266–286.

Fig. 5.4   Carrel, A. and Lindbergh, C. A. (1938). *The Culture of Organs*. Chapter II, Plate III. Paul Hoeber, New York.

Fig. 5.5   Carrel, A. (1902). "La technique operatoire des anastomoses vasculaires et la transplantation des viscères." *Lyon Med* **98**, 862–863.

Fig. 5.6   Coronary bypass techniques. Source unknown.

Fig. 5.7   Conti, C. R. (1977). "Coronary Arteriography" (p. 229). *Circulation* **55**, 227–237. By permission of the American Heart Association ©.

Fig. 5.8   Courtesy of Dr. Alexander Margulis, Dept. Radiology, University of California, San Francisco.

Fig. 5.9   Briscoe, M. H., CVRI.

Fig. 5.10   Briscoe, M. H., CVRI.

Fig. 5.11   Edwards, Jesse E., Claget, O. T., Drake, R. L. and Christensen, N. A. (1948). "The collateral circulation in coarctation of the aorta," p. 334. *Proc Staff Meet Mayo Clin* **23**, 333–339.

Fig. 5.12   Edman, Thomas (1959). "Knitting spare parts for human bodies." *Textile Industries*, Dec. 1959.

Fig. 5.13   Courtesy of Dr. Julius Jacobson II, Director, Vascular Surgical Service, Mt. Sinai School of Medicine, New York City.

Fig. 5.14   Benditt, E. P. (1977). "The origin of atherosclerosis." *Sci Am* **236**, 74–85.

Fig. 5.15   Netter, Frank (1969). "Types and degrees of coronary atherosclerotic narrowing or occlusion." In *CIBA Collection of Medical Illustrations: Vol. 5, Heart.* Plate 49, p. 214. CIBA. Summit, N.J.

Fig. 5.16   Vogel, J. (1847). *The Pathological Anatomy of the Human Body.* Translated from the German by George E. Day. Lea & Blanchard, Philadelphia.

Fig. 5.17   Pletscher, A. and DaPrada, M. (1975). In *Biochemistry and Pharmacology of Platelets.* CIBA Foundation Symposium 35 (new series). Electron micrograph by Tranzer, J. P. Elsevier, Amsterdam.

Fig. 6.1   Photograph of Franklin D. Roosevelt courtesy of Wide World Photos, New York.

Fig. 6.2   Courtesy of Elizabeth Cuzzort (Mrs. Edward Singer), Stillwater, New Jersey. Originally published in *Med Times,* Manhasset, 1941 and 1944.

Fig. 6.3   Hales, Stephen (1727). *Vegetable Staticks* (Fig. 19). W. & J. Innys and T. Woodward, London.

Fig. 6.4   Ludwig, Carl (1847). "Beitrage zur Kenntniss des Einflusses der Respirations bewegungen auf der Blutlauf in Aorten systeme." *Müller's Arch Anat* 4, 242–302.

Fig. 6.5   Segall, Harold N. (1976). "N. C. Korotkoff 1874–1920—Pioneer Vascular Surgeon," p. 817. *Am Heart J* 91, 816–818.

Fig. 6.6   Rushmer, Robert F. (1955). *Cardiac Diagnosis* (p. 166). Saunders, Philadelphia.

Fig. 6.7   Briscoe, M. H., CVRI.

Fig. 6.8   Kessel, R. G. and Kardon, R. H. (1979). *Tissues and Organs: A Text-Atlas of Scanning Electron Microscopy.* W. H. Freeman, San Francisco © 1979.

Fig. 6.9   James, D. Geraint, Editor (1978). *Circulation of the Blood,* in Chapter 7. Gawel, M. J. and Rose, F. C., p. 121. By permission of Pitman Medical Publishing Co., England.

Fig. 6.10   Oliver, George and Schäfer, E. A. (1895). "The physiological effects of extracts of the suprarenal capsules" (Fig. 1). *Physiol* 18, 230–276.

Fig. 6.11   Cordano, A., CVRI. Based on experiment of Otto Loewi published in *Pflueger's Arch* 189, 239–242, 1921.

Fig. 6.12   Briscoe, M. H., CVRI. Modified from Comroe, J. H. (1963). *Physiology for Physicians* 1, 5–8.

Fig. 6.13   Thomson, William A. R. (1978). *Medicines from the Earth* (p. 86). McGraw-Hill, Maidenhead, England.

Figs. 6.14   Briscoe, M. H., CVRI. Modified from Comroe, J. H. (1963) *Physiology*
& 6.15   *for Physicians* 1, 5–8.

Fig. 6.16   Briscoe, M. H., CVRI.

Fig. 6.17   Falck, Bengt (1962). "Observations on the possibilities of the cellular localization of monoamines by a fluorescent method." *Acta Physiol Scand* **56,** Suppl. 197.

Fig. 6.18   Gilman, A., Goodman, L. and Gilman, A. (1980). *The Pharmacologic Basis of Therapeutics*, sixth ed. Chapter 4, Mayer, S. E., p. 72. Macmillan Publishing Co., New York City.

Fig. 6.19   Micrograph produced by Dr. John E. Heuser, Washington University School of Medicine, St. Louis, MD.

Fig. 6.20   Nickerson, Mark and Goodman, Louis (1947). "Pharmacological properties of a new adrenergic blocking agent, dibenamine," p. 169. *J Pharmacol Exp Ther* **89,** 167–185.

Fig. 7.1   Smith, Homer W. (1953). *The Kidney*, p. 42. *Sci Am*, Jan. 1953. All rights reserved.

Fig. 7.2   Cushny, Arthur R. (1917). *The Secretion of the Urine*. Longman, Green & Co., London.

Fig. 7.3   Kessel, R. G. and Kardon, R. H. (1979). *Tissues and Organs: A Text Atlas of Scanning Electron Microscopy*, p. 225. W. H. Freeman, San Francisco © 1979.

Fig. 7.4   Smith, Homer W. (1953). *From Fish to Philosopher*, p. 141. Little, Brown and Company, Boston. © Renewed 1980 by F. R. VanVechten.

Fig. 7.5   Simpson, G. G., Pittendrigh, C.S. and Tiffany, L. H. (1957). *Life. An Introduction to Biology*, p. 83. Harcourt, Brace Co., New York City.

Fig. 7.6   Starr, Isaac (Editor) (1969). *Alfred Newton Richards. Scientist and Man. Ann Int Med*, Suppl. to vol. 71 (Nov.).

Fig. 7.8A   Reproduced with permission from Pitts, Robert F. *Physiology of Kidney and Body Fluids*, 3rd ed., p. 40. Copyright © 1974. Year Book Medical Publishers, Inc., Chicago.

Fig. 7.8B   Cordano, A., CVRI.

Fig. 7.9   Briscoe, M. H., CVRI. Modified from numerous drawings.

Fig. 7.10   Smith, Homer W. (1943). *Lectures on the Kidney*. University of Kansas Press, Lawrence. (In 1953 this illustration was published in slightly modified form in "From Fish to Philosopher" by Little, Brown and Company, Boston).

Fig. 7.11A   Tyson, Edward. Manuscript in Library, Royal College of Physicians, London.

Fig. 7.11B   Marshall, E. K. and Grafflin, A. L. (1928). "The structure and function of the kidney of Lophius Piscatorius." *Bull Johns Hopkins Hosp* **43,** 205–230.

Fig. 7.12   Withering, William (1785). *An Account of the Foxglove and Some of Its Medical Uses*. Robinson, G. G. J. and J., Birmingham.

Fig. 7.13   Strauss, M. B. and Southworth, H. (1938). *"Urinary changes due to sul-fanilamide administration,"* p. 42. *Bull Johns Hopkins Hosp* **63**, 41–45.

Fig. 7.14   Beyer, Karl H. (1982). "Chlorothiazide," p. 15. *Br J Clin Pharmacol* **13**, 15–24.

Fig. 7.15   Briscoe, M. H., CVRI. Modified from numerous drawings.

Fig. 7.16   Goldblatt, Harry, Lynch, J., Hanzel, R. F. and Summerville, W. W. "Studies on experimental hypertension, I. The production of persistent elevation of systolic blood pressure by means of renal ischemia," p. 358. Reproduced from the *Journal of Experimental Medicine*, 1934, **59**, 347–379. © Permission of The Rockefeller University Press.

Fig. 7.17   Davis, James O. "Control of renin release." In: Davis, J. O., Laragh, John and Selwyn, Amy: *Hypertension: Mechanisms, Diagnosis and Management* (1977). Allan Iselin, Illustrator. H-P Publishing Co., New York City.

Fig. 7.18   Modified from diagram showing action of captopril on angiotensin I. Courtesy of Squibb & Co.

Index